TOWARD A FRAMEWORK FOR

VIETNAMESE AMERICAN STUDIES

EDITED BY

LINDA HO PECHÉ, ALEX-THAI DINH VO,
AND TUONG VU

TOWARD A FRAMEWORK FOR VIETNAMESE AMERICAN STUDIES

History, Community, and Memory

TEMPLE UNIVERSITY PRESS

Philadelphia • *Rome* • *Tokyo*

TEMPLE UNIVERSITY PRESS
Philadelphia, Pennsylvania 19122
tupress.temple.edu

Library of Congress Cataloging-in-Publication Data

Names: Peché, Linda Ho, 1979– editor. | Vo, Alex-Thai Dinh, 1983– editor.
| Vu, Tuong, 1965– editor.
Title: Toward a framework for Vietnamese American studies : history,
community, and memory / edited by Linda Ho Peché, Alex-Thai Dinh Vo,
and Tuong Vu.
Description: Philadelphia : Temple University Press, 2023. | Includes
bibliographical references and index. | Summary: "This collection is the
first work of its kind to synthesize the current state of Vietnamese
American studies. Offering cutting edge analysis from social sciences
and humanities perspectives, this volume serves as a foundational
resource and a site for interrogating underexplored facets of the
field"— Provided by publisher.
Identifiers: LCCN 2022029451 (print) | LCCN 2022029452 (ebook) | ISBN
9781439922880 (cloth) | ISBN 9781439922897 (paperback) | ISBN
9781439922903 (pdf)
Subjects: LCSH: Vietnamese Americans—Study and teaching. | Vietnamese
Americans—Social conditions. | Vietnamese diaspora. |
Vietnamese—United States. | Vietnam (Republic)—Intellectual life.
Classification: LCC E184.V53 T67 2023 (print) | LCC E184.V53 (ebook) |
DDC 305.8959/22073—dc23/eng/20221011
LC record available at https://lccn.loc.gov/2022029451
LC ebook record available at https://lccn.loc.gov/2022029452

Printed in the United States of America

9 8 7 6 5 4 3 2 1

CONTENTS

    1981–2020 / CHRISTIAN COLLET   133

8   Diversity in Identities, Industries, and Business Strategies:
    Female Vietnamese American Entrepreneurs
    / JENNIFER A. HUYNH   154

9   Trapped within the White Frame: Vietnamese Americans
    in Post-Katrina New Orleans / NGUYEN VU HOANG   178

PART III PARADIGMS OF DIASPORIC KNOWLEDGE

10 The Unreconciled: Phan Nhiên Hạo's Poetry of Diasporic
    Testimony / HAI-DANG PHAN   199

11 Diasporic Nationalism: Continuity and Changes / DUYEN BUI   222

12 Remembering War and Migration: Mapping the Contours
    of Diasporic Vietnamese Memoryscapes / QUAN TUE TRAN   240

13 Devotion in Diaspora: Invoking Holy Mothers
    among Vietnamese American Faith Communities
    / THIEN-HUONG NINH   257

14 The Preservation and Production of Diasporic Knowledge:
    Oral History and Archival Contributions / THUY VO DANG   273

    Timeline of Key Events and Selected Milestones in
    Vietnamese and Vietnamese American History, 1900–2021   287

    Notes   305

    References   325

    Contributors   353

    Index   357

ACKNOWLEDGMENTS

The idea for this book came from Nancy Bui, the founder and director of the Vietnamese American Heritage Foundation (VAHF), based in Austin, Texas. Like many of us, she was once a refugee. Losing our country and feeling marginalized in America as a people without history are pains that many of us share, deep inside our hearts.

The VAHF deserves recognition for its contributions to the development of this volume, the preservation of community histories, humanitarian efforts, and numerous other projects, including support for Linda Ho Peché's efforts to develop the Vietnamese in the Diaspora Digital Archive (ViDDA). We are indebted to Nancy Bui and all her colleagues at the VAHF for their dedication to the resilience of Vietnamese communities in the United States, in Vietnam, and across the diaspora.

The book was inspired by a workshop on Vietnamese Republicanism organized in October 2019 by the U.S.-Vietnam Research Center at the University of Oregon in Eugene. The contributions by many scholars at the workshop made it possible to firmly situate the history of Vietnamese Americans within the long arc of modern Vietnamese history—a history defined in no small part by the shared struggle for the realization of many republican values and ideals.

This volume also benefited from the generous support of many individuals and organizations, especially the Republic of Vietnam Legacies Fund, which supported a postdoctoral fellowship for Alex-Thai Dinh Vo with the U.S.-Vietnam Research Center during 2019–2020 and a course buyout for

Tuong Vu to work on this and other books. An edited volume involves an enormous amount of work, and this book would not have been possible in such a short time frame without their generous support.

The University of Oregon, in particular the Global Studies Institute, provides a home for the U.S.-Vietnam Research Center, which was founded in 2019 to promote research and education about Vietnam, U.S.-Vietnam relations, and the Vietnamese American community. The university offers not only funding but also facilities where conversations took place and work was accomplished. We are extremely grateful for the enthusiastic help offered by Dennis Galvan, Lori O'Hollaren, Cindy Nelson, and Holly Lakey. We can never hope for a better team than those who stood beside us despite the severe budget cuts due to the pandemic.

The book must stand on its intellectual value, and we cannot express enough thanks to our collaborators, who have brought to the project so much knowledge, data, and skills. We are tremendously privileged to have had the opportunity to work with such a diverse range of scholars, both junior and senior, both Vietnamese Americans and those outside of the community, and in many disciplines in both the social sciences and the humanities. If this book is successful, it is primarily because of the authors of the substantive chapters in the book—and to you all, we thank you for such an enriching experience!

Shaun Vigil from Temple University Press has patiently and kindly guided us through the submission and review process. Shaun saw value in this project early on and wisely advised us to reconceptualize this volume in order to strengthen the quality and the appeal of the book. He made the oftentimes difficult experience with publishing a pleasant one, for which we are grateful.

We dedicate this book to the Vietnamese American community, including our children.

TOWARD A FRAMEWORK FOR
VIETNAMESE AMERICAN STUDIES

INTRODUCTION

Linda Ho Peché

Alex-Thai Dinh Vo

Tuong Vu

The year 2020 marked forty-five years since the end of the Vietnamese civil war and the arrival of the first large group of Vietnamese refugees in the United States. Among Asian Americans, the Vietnamese are one of the newest groups to resettle in the United States and the fourth largest, behind Chinese, Asian Indian, and Filipino populations.[1] They make up part of an estimated 22.6 million Asian Americans, overall 6 percent of the 328 million Americans—the fastest-growing group compared to White, Black, and Latinx populations.[2] Indeed, Vietnamese Americans are an active part of diversifying the face of a nation.

This book builds on decades of existing scholarship on Vietnamese Americans but offers an alternate chronological origin. It traces a set of nationalist and republican ideologies, civic and social networks, literary and intellectual proclivities, and cultural and artistic sensibilities that came to influence life in America to the now-defunct nation of the Republic of Vietnam (1955–1975), years before the bulk of the population arrived in the United States (Goscha 2017; Tran N.-A. and Vu T. 2022). As editors of this volume, we hope that this historiographical resituating creates an epistemological space for the interdisciplinary dialogue between subfields that often don't cross-pollinate but would benefit in doing so.[3] According to Y Thien Nguyen in this volume, the issues of *nation building* have more often been the purview of historians of modern Vietnam, while questions of *community formation* are an inquiry mostly taken up by scholars in Ethnic studies and Asian American studies. We posit that a deeper dive into the dynamic, vibrant, and sometimes fractious civic life and culture that emerged in postcolonial South Vietnam allows for a deeper understanding of the diversity of Vietnamese American cultural, civic, and political engagements in the present.[4] As such, this volume is not a comprehensive history of Vietnamese America but a working framework with which to approach Vietnamese American studies.

This approach takes advantage of cutting-edge research in Vietnamese history and the Vietnam War that has substantially pushed the frontiers of our knowledge beyond long-standing U.S.-centric scholarship. As the authors in this volume elucidate, the discursive circulation of ideologies such as Vietnamese nationalism, republicanism, and anticommunism sprang from local roots and experiences long before the United States became involved in Vietnam. It is no longer prudent to dismiss those ideological roots as inauthentic copies of foreign ideas, nor is it appropriate to characterize the adherents to those ideologies as opportunistic foreign collaborators. Those ideologies may have later been codified and formalized into an official doctrine through the coercive capabilities of the South Vietnamese nation-state, but they were at times contested or appropriated, buried at one point only to be exhumed later, deployed under certain circumstances, reproduced, and transported across the Pacific to be (re)presented in the social, cultural, political, and everyday lives of ordinary people. In sum, to understand Vietnamese America, we should begin, figuratively and literally, in South Vietnam.

By connecting Vietnamese Americans to their roots in South Vietnam, the chapters in this volume at the same time center them as agents of their own narrated histories and sometimes conflicting ideas of identity and community. While not assuming an undifferentiated collective agency, we are centering actors and the ways they negotiate and navigate the civic, economic, gendered, and racial landscapes of American life. This collection of chapters works against representing Vietnamese Americans as a model minority to justify conservative policies but also criticizes scholarship that focuses too deeply on refugee subjectivity merely as a site for the critique of American empire. Thus, our authors posit that Vietnamese Americans are not victims of or accomplices to American imperialism but are full agentive subjects aware of and acting on ideologies and values that partly originated and developed during the emergence of the Republic of Vietnam (RVN).

In this introduction, we first outline some of the formative scholarship and theoretical paradigms that have been employed in the study of Vietnamese Americans; continue with a historical overview that sets our origin point chronologically closer to 1954, cartographically below the seventeenth parallel, and conceptually to the sociohistorical constructs of South Vietnam and Vietnamese America; and conclude with an overview of the structure of this volume and its contribution to framing a fresh approach for understanding, researching, teaching, and learning about Vietnamese Americans.

Contending Paradigms and Perspectives on Vietnamese Americans

While Vietnamese presence in the United States dates as far back as the 1920s, the scholarship about Vietnamese Americans began in earnest following the collapse of the RVN in 1975 (Keith 2019). As the largest group of resettled asylum seekers in American history, Vietnamese Americans first attracted interest from politicians, government officials, journalists, health professionals, and legal specialists. Their involvement resulted in policy- or service-oriented reports that met the practical needs of various government and service agencies as they assisted newly resettled Vietnamese Americans, most of whom arrived with neither financial assets nor linguistic skills. Often, this work on the "new" immigrants primarily focused on the psychological traumas of war and displacement, unfortunately cementing an association with pathology, mental health issues, and maladjustment that applied to any new Vietnamese newcomer (e.g., Starr and Roberts 1982).

The first social history and social science scholarship was overwhelmingly concerned with questions relating to the process of immigrant acculturation into American society. Historically, this approach directed the thinking about Asians (and other ethnic minorities in the United States between the 1920s and the 1960s) as foreigners on a successive path toward assimilation (Yu 2002). These studies were generally motivated by well-intended concerns for the welfare of Vietnamese refugees and their ability to adapt to broader American society.[5] Perhaps in a reaction to the growing refugee fatigue from an American public, some of this work often relied heavily on essentialist notions of cultural authenticity to make the case that the Vietnamese were worthy of acceptance because of their seemingly superior resiliency and adaptability. Paul Rutledge referred to a "Vietnamese philosophical outlook on life that differs little from that of many middle-class Americans," which he offered as a "model of cultural integrity and adaptation" (Rutledge 1992: 46; 146–147). With similar good intentions, the anthropologist James Freeman's collection of oral histories cast Vietnamese Americans as model minorities in the attempt to correct misconstrued characterizations of them as welfare abusers that take away jobs (Freeman 1989:13–15). This allowed for Vietnamese Americans to be cast as "good subjects," but, as some have argued, at the expense of promoting racialized notions that pitted them against other communities of color (Nguyen V. T. 2002). By the 1990s, 79 percent of Vietnamese American children were classified as second generation, and in the subsequent decade formative studies were published that allowed insights into family dynamics, gender roles, identity, and the second generation.[6]

For their part, Vietnamese American communities and individuals have been prolific contributors and commentators of their own experiences. As early as the 1950s, transnational Vietnamese students and professionals created Vietnamese- and English-language publications and participated in public discourses to offer their sometimes-conflicting political views on the evolving situation in Southeast Asia, advocated for policies in their homeland, and educated the American public about their community by organizing cultural events (Pham V. 2003). Post-exodus, Vietnamese Americans found platforms for self-expression through popular music, memoirs, arts, and literature.[7] Only rarely did these early works break into the English-language mainstream, nor were they taken seriously by academia, save for a few notable exceptions (Nguyen N. N. 1982; Truong N. T. 1985; Tran T. V. 1988; Hayslip 1989). The nascent genre of English-language Vietnamese American nonfiction literary production in the 1980s had to compete with what has become the canonical Vietnam War literature, which prioritized a myth-making, first-person, American-centric perspective (Christopher 1995).[8] Additionally, it was given little serious academic attention from Asian American studies, except perhaps solely as celebratory escape narrative testimonials crafted for an American audience to correct misconstrued biases about the community. Monique Truong framed this genre as a counter to mainstream literary and discursive representations of Vietnamese refugees (Truong M. 1993: 27). Elaine Kim, in acknowledging the absence of Vietnamese American writers for a 1987 volume for *Cultural Critique*, posited that it was likely because of the delineations of the field, which mostly engaged with "American-born, American-educated Asians whose first language is English" (Kim 1989: 88). Fortunately, the subsequent decades have seen an increase in literary (fiction and nonfiction) publications, mainly by 1.5- and second-generation Vietnamese American novelists.[9]

In academia, a subsequent wave of scholars emerged from Ethnic studies and other humanities fields, trained in ethnographic and cultural studies methods, and were often community insiders themselves. While earlier studies focused primarily on acculturation, this scholarship challenged celebratory narratives and the model minority myth and began to contest the cultural biases of assimilationist frameworks, foregrounding issues of economic exploitation, institutional and structural racial discrimination, and other systems of power in American society (Nguyễn-Võ T. H. 2005). Their work emphasized the commonalities in the experiences of the Chinese, Japanese, Korean, Asian Indian, and Filipino immigrants, who have been in this country since the nineteenth century, as well as of the relatively recent refugees from Vietnam, Laos, and Cambodia (Chan S. 1991; 2006). This new work analyzed the social constructs of identity and community, problematized the interworkings of cultural politics and cultural production, and worked against a unified essentialist notion of what constitutes being Vietnamese across class, generation, gender, and cultural politics (Vo Dang T. 2005; Võ

L. T. 2008; Aguilar-San Juan 2009; Peché 2012; VanLandingham 2017; Truitt 2021).

Responding to a call for a transnational framework for studying migration, scholars also turned to analyzing an increasingly translocal, heterolocal, diasporic, and global world (Schiller, Basch, and Blanc 1992). The 2000s was also the time when Vietnam became more fully integrated into the global economy, with its enactment of an enterprise law in 2000 and its accession to the World Trade Organization in 2007. As agents of transnational forces that neither the United States nor the communist regime in Vietnam is capable of fully controlling, Vietnamese Americans in these studies appear to enjoy much greater agency in their roles as business, political, social, and cultural entrepreneurs on the global stage. Their sense of identity is much less burdened by past traumas, even though it is still full of ambiguities and contradictions. By tracing Vietnamese Americans' close links to the homeland and other diasporic communities around the world, this approach opened up new directions for research on the complexities and ambiguities of identity, on changing international politics and global economy, and on the complicated politics of this community as it continues to evolve. This approach continues to capture the real and perceived power of Vietnamese Americans as intermediaries between their host country and their homeland, and between Vietnamese in Vietnam and various transnational forces (Thai H. C. 2008; Collet and Furuya 2010; Lieu N. 2011; Eckstein and Nguyen 2011; Valverde 2012; Tran Q. T. 2012; Hoskins 2015; Hoang K. K. 2015; Tran Q. T. 2016a; Nguyen-Akbar 2016; Peché 2016; Ninh T.-H. 2017; I. Small 2019).

Critical refugee studies have also emerged as an influential strand of theoretical thought. This framework emerges from postmodernist paradigms that are concerned with challenging claims to objectivity and universalism in the prevailing academic power structure, employing a postcolonial critique to unmask American imperialism, and using queer and feminist critiques to untangle heteronormative assumptions (Yanagisako and Delaney 1994). The formative scholarship in this vein is best characterized by the work of Yen Le Espiritu, who aimed to identify, deconstruct, and analyze the "hidden and disguised violence behind the term 'refugee'" (Espiritu 2006; 2014). Moving beyond the experiences of refugees, this work seeks to challenge narratives that implicitly or explicitly justify racial and gender hierarchies and U.S. militarism and intervention in Vietnam and elsewhere. By tracing the military bases from the Philippines to Guam, where Vietnamese refugees of the first wave passed through en route to the United States, Espiritu coins the concept of "militarized refugees" to demonstrate how these Vietnamese refugees "emerged out of and in turn bolster U.S. militarism." (Espiritu 2014: chap. 2). Similarly, Mimi Thi Nguyen recasts the figure of the Vietnamese refugee as "the twice-over target of the gift of freedom—first through war, second through refuge—suggesting that the imposition of debt and obligation to express gratitude precludes the subjects of freedom from escaping those colonial histories that deemed them unfree" (Nguyen M. T. 2012). By asserting that the "gift of freedom" from the United States has a violent origin in American intervention, Nguyen joins Espiritu in challenging the claims of U.S. rescue and liberation and the humanitarian rhetoric of American officials.[10]

The critical refugee studies approach offers a powerful critique of American militarism and imperial pretensions. This approach inspires and intersects with a new wave of postcolonial, critical scholarship focused on diasporic literature and culture that seeks to not only document but to interrogate the refugee/immigrant experience.[11] It is perhaps not a coincidence that this paradigm emerged in the mid-2000s amid the American invasion of Afghanistan and Iraq. Yet, for some, the approach is U.S.-centric in that it is a critique overwhelmingly directed at U.S. policy, framing Vietnamese refugees merely as passive subjects of the American empire (Nguyen Phuong Tran 2017: 10). Vietnamese refugees after the first wave in fact had less to do with U.S. policies than with those of the communist government from which they fled. Although the critique of American militarism is justified, researchers in Vietnamese studies contend that the power of the United States vis-à-vis local Vietnamese actors is exaggerated (e.g., R. B. Smith 1983; Miller and Vu 2009; Nguyen L.-H. 2012). Furthermore, they point out that the exclusion of other actors (namely Vietnamese communists, their Soviet and Chinese patrons, and their Laotian and Cambodian Khmer Rouge comrades) from the broader analysis not only oversimplifies the deeply fractious and multivalent nature of the Vietnamese civil war and Indochinese wars but also underestimates the agency of South Vietnamese actors.[12] Within the communist bloc, the intense Sino-Soviet, Sino-Vietnamese, and Vietnamese-Cambodian animosities and rivalries for domination were the primary cause of the Third Indochinese War and the massive exodus of Indochinese refugees after 1975.

Although it is unfeasible to inventory every publication about Vietnamese Americans, we hope to have provided a broad overview of the major theoretical frameworks that have influenced and informed current scholarship. The chapters in this volume are forging new historiographies and paradigms in Vietnamese American studies, expanding on and sometimes contesting past frameworks, and building on the rich and varied scholarship that situates Vietnamese Americans front and center as agents of their own histories. While most Vietnamese Americans arrived in the United States as refugees after American involvement ended on April 30, 1975, with the evacuation of Saigon, this volume locates the birthplace of the Vietnamese diaspora within the ideologies of modernization and republicanism that developed before and during the Republic of Vietnam eras. This is where we propose to begin.

Modern Vietnamese History and Vietnamese Americans

The Republic of Vietnam, whose collapse in 1975 created the Vietnamese diaspora, traced its lineage to the nationalist revolutionary movement that emerged in early twentieth-century colonial Indochina, when young activists influenced by republican thoughts from European, Chinese, and Japanese thinkers began to agitate for cultural reform and political independence. While attempts at revolts such as the one led by the Vietnam Nationalist Party were brutally suppressed by the colonial government, groups that promoted cultural and political reform but did not directly challenge colonial rule flourished and exerted significant social influence (Nguyen M. T. 2020). By the 1930s, communism, or more accurately Stalinism, began to attract followers in Vietnam, who contended with other groups in the nationalist movement for popular support (Vu T. 2017). When the Stalinists under Hồ Chí Minh seized power in late 1945 at the end of World War II, a civil war broke out between them and their enemies just as both were fighting the French.

Following the defeat of French forces at the Battle of Điện Biên Phủ, the 1954 Geneva Accords divided Vietnam into two geopolitical entities along the seventeenth parallel: the Democratic Republic of Vietnam (DRV) in northern Vietnam and the Republic of Vietnam (RVN) in southern Vietnam. The accords stipulated a three-hundred-day free-movement period allowing people to relocate to the zone they preferred. Consequently, approximately one million people migrated south. Conversely, about 130,000 moved north; the majority were soldiers and officials associated with the northern government.

The DRV, backed by the Soviet Union and China, were led by Stalinists and adhered to the communist ideology, while the RVN, backed by the West, aspired to a democratic republic.[13] These ideological and geopolitical alignments are significant for understanding the exodus of so many Vietnamese after the end of the Vietnam War. As a communist regime, North Vietnam (and later unified Vietnam) was a class-based political order under the dictatorship of the Communist Party rather than the popular sovereignty institutionalized in constitutional rights and laws. The RVN, despite its many problems as a newly established political entity during wartime, was fostering a degree of freedom and popular sovereignty wherein power resided in the people. Here, popular sovereignty was enshrined in a constitution and legal order to constrain the arbitrary power of the government and hold it accountable to the people.

Consequently, many who were living under the southern regime and would eventually become Vietnamese refugees in America came to identify with republican values and ideas (giá trị cộng hoà) of popular sovereignty, democracy, and liberty. For many, the divide between the north and the south and the subsequent war (1954–1975) was an ideological affair concerning these contrasting sociopolitical values, ideas, and identities (Vu T. and Fear 2019). Although the RVN was ruled for many years under President Ngô Đình Diệm's autocracy and subsequently under several military governments, popular and elite adherence to republican values remained strong and resulted in the creation of a relatively liberal constitutional regime after 1967. Under this regime, a dynamic political culture and vibrant civil society emerged that was vocal in defending civil liberties and vigorous in keeping the power of the government in check (Luu T. and Vu T., 2023). While many southerners opposed foreign intervention into Vietnam, many considered the war to be fundamentally a struggle of self-defense to protect the RVN and republican values from the communist threat to subdue them.

As the conflict gradually escalated between North and South Vietnam, all of Indochina became embroiled in war. Laotians, Cambodians, and Vietnamese with opposing ideological beliefs engaged in violent conflict, armed with American, Soviet, and Chinese weapons. On March 8, 1965, the first U.S. troops landed in Vietnam, followed by forces from South Korea, Thailand, the Philippines, Australia, and New Zealand. With the Soviet Union, China, North Korea, and other communist states sending militaries and supplies to aid North Vietnam, the war became a stalemate. Under heavy domestic pressure from the U.S. public to end America's involvement in the war, President Richard M. Nixon reached an agreement with North Vietnam at the 1973 Paris Conference to withdraw American combat troops. Without American military support and with declining financial aid amid a continuous military onslaught by communist forces, Saigon, the capital of the RVN, fell on April 30, 1975. Abetted by communist Vietnam, Cambodian and Laotian communist forces also conquered Cambodia and Laos at about the same time.

The fall of Indochina in 1975 saw a massive exodus of people fleeing communist rule.[14] We focus on Vietnamese here, but large numbers of Cambodians and Laotians also left their countries. The first wave of Vietnamese fleeing Vietnam began in early April 1975 with the evacuation of 2,600 children under Operation Babylift. Thousands of Vietnamese associated with the South Vietnamese regime or the American military and embassy soon followed. Operation New Life (April 23 to November 1, 1975), aided by the 1975 Indochina Migration and Refugee Assistance Act, processed 111,919 Vietnamese refugees through Guam. In total, the first wave saw over 130,000 Vietnamese refugees evacuated by air and by sea to U.S. military processing stations in Guam, Wake Island, and the Philippines before being transported to four mainland bases—Camp Pendleton in California, Fort Chaffee in Arkansas, Eglin Air Force Base in Florida, and Fort Indiantown Gap in Pennsylvania—and matched up with sponsor families. Unlike later waves, most people who left in this one were members of the social and political privileged elite. Most were ethnic Vietnamese from wealthier socioeconomic backgrounds, well educated, English speaking, and westernized, with political connections. They included ranking politicians, officials, soldiers, professionals, civil service workers, employees of American agencies or companies, and relatives of U.S. citizens.

However, war did not end in 1975 with the fall of Saigon, Phnom Penh, and Vientiane; or more accurately, one war ended but others emerged. Class and cultural warfare soon followed across the region as communist regimes dispossessed, persecuted, imprisoned, and (especially in Cambodia) massacred their class enemies, religious leaders, and "bourgeois" intellectuals. In South Vietnam, many associates of the southern regime, including elected officials, civil servants, military officers, police officers, teachers, writers, artists, and religious leaders, were sent to "reeducation" camps (trại cải tạo, euphemism for prisons with forced labor), while their families were among the hundreds of thousands forcibly relocated to uninhabited mountain forests commonly referred to as New Economic Zones (or Khu Kinh Tế Mới; Nguyen V. C. 1983; Nguyen H. 2011). Cambodian and Laotian communist governments pursued many similar policies, with higher degrees of brutality (Cambodia) and irrationality (Laos) (Kiernan 1996; Evans 1990). A mere three years after 1975, war erupted between Cambodia, in an alliance with China, on the one hand, and Vietnam, backed by the Soviet Union, on the other.

All three countries in late 1977 witnessed the mass exodus of refugees marking the beginning of the second wave, which dwarfed the first. This wave, which lasted into much of the 1980s, was intertwined with the war among the communist "brothers" (Chanda 1986). Distrusting the loyalty of its ethnic Chinese population and wanting to seize their property, the Vietnamese government sought to expel them from the country. Nearly a quarter million ethnic Chinese left Vietnam for China or Hong Kong. They were joined by an even larger number of Vietnamese, Cambodians, and Laotians fleeing from communist rule, either overland to Thailand or by sea to Southeast Asian countries. The hundreds of thousands of Vietnamese who left on small and overcrowded fishing boats came to be known as "boat people" (thuyền nhân). Pressured by the number of asylum seekers, the United States responded with legislation to ease entry restrictions and admit more refugees, to allow them to change their status from "parolee" to "permanent resident," and to facilitate their domestic resettlement.[15] Hence, between 1978 and 1982, the United States admitted 280,500 Vietnamese refugees, twice the number of the first wave. In this war among the former communist allies, each of whom harbored their own imperialist pretensions, the United States, among other sympathetic nations, played the role of the outside rescuer after having been expelled in 1975.

Tens of thousands of refugees lost their lives at sea, many were attacked by pirates, and reports emerged of women and girls who were raped, abducted, and sold to brothels in Thailand. Their tragedies prompted an international effort not only by the United States but by many European and Asian nations, many of whom had been reluctant to get involved. Under the auspices of the United Nations High Commission for Refugees (UNHCR), the Orderly Departure Program (ODP) was established in 1979 to reduce the number of Vietnamese refugees making dangerous passages by boat or across land borders by enabling a safe and orderly avenue to resettle in the United States and other countries from Norway to Israel and Brazil. Over time, the ODP allowed several routes for resettlement in the United States. The family reunification program enabled a large number of Vietnamese Americans who arrived in the first and second waves to sponsor immediate family members who were still in Vietnam. The 1987 Amerasian Homecoming Act gave preferential immigration status to Vietnamese children of U.S. fathers. Under this act, approximately 23,000 Amerasians and 67,000 of their immediate relatives were allowed to enter the United States and receive refugee status and benefits.[16] Another avenue permitted the admission of Vietnamese who were former U.S. government or company employees. The last was the Humanitarian Operation Program, which allowed for the resettlement of 34,300 former associates of the RVN government who had been imprisoned by the communist regime for as long as two decades after the war, making them and their dependents the largest category of Vietnamese refugees to the United States (Dizon 1997).[17] Under the ODP, from 1980 and 1997, the number of Vietnamese resettled in the United States was 458,367 (J. X. H. Lee 2015: 128).

The history of Vietnamese Americans is compelling, not only in the context of modern Vietnamese history but also in the seemingly irreconcilable paradoxes and contradictions in their relationship with America. They arrived as exiles from the RVN, an ally of the United States, but American public sentiment in 1975 was generally against resettling the South Vietnamese in the United States. During the war, many public intellectuals, such as Noam Chomsky, admired communist North Vietnam, while Congress voted to slash military aid to South Vietnam in the last year of the war (Willbanks 2004: 215–216). Most Vietnamese Americans are generally grateful to the United States for rescuing them from political persecution under communism and giving them opportunities to rebuild and resettle. Yet many resent the U.S. government for abandoning the RVN, which led them to become refugees in the first place. Many distrust American democratic institutions such as Congress, the universities, and the media, which they blame for the demise of the RVN.

The contradictions mounted after they were reluctantly and hastily accepted into the United States. By deliberate policy of the American government, Vietnamese refugees were scattered around the mainland United States, but over time and through second migrations they established large and vibrant ethnic enclaves in California, Texas, Louisiana, and Virginia, among other areas.[18] Decades after the war, Vietnamese Americans remain deeply attached to their abandoned homeland even while they have long accepted the United States as their home and have worked to build a future for their children and grandchildren. Many Vietnamese Americans are profoundly anticommunist and have no love for the regime in Hanoi, but their annual remittance to the tune of billions of dollars has helped fuel economic growth under that regime since the 1990s.[19] Vietnamese Americans have suffered from both overt and latent racial and ethnic discrimination, yet some hold racist attitudes toward other people of color. They are often touted in the media and by politicians for their unexpected success in assimilating into American society. Yet such a "model minority" image obscures the mixed socioeconomic experiences of their communities.

The numerous paradoxes and contradictions about Vietnamese Americans reflect the complex history of modern Vietnam, the diversity of South Vietnamese society where they came from, the politics of the Vietnam War, racial and ethnic relations in the United States, intergenerational conflicts within the community, and the evolving relationship between the United States and communist Vietnam.

Demographic Overview and Sources of Diversity

Between 1975 and 2000, 988,000 Vietnamese refugees and immigrants resettled in the United States.[20] Many arrived in one of three waves and were dispersed throughout the country, including areas that were climatically and culturally different from Vietnam. Unlike those in the first wave, who benefited from more generous aid from the U.S. government in the 1970s, many in the second and third waves were farmers, fishermen, merchants, or former military-civil servants and military officials from small provinces and rural areas. They arrived at a severe economic disadvantage in terms of English proficiency and marketable job skills. Many had sustained physical and mental wounds from their perilous journey, years of physical and psychological torment in reeducation camps, and the pain of losing or being separated from loved ones (E. Lee 2015: 327).

Aside from the linguistic and cultural barriers that made integration difficult, most Vietnamese refugees, including those arriving in the first wave, faced resentment as well as racial and ethnic discrimination from Americans. The difficulties inherent in adjusting to a new life, along with economic instability and social conflict, prompted some young Vietnamese to join youth gangs and engage in violent and criminal activities. Some Vietnamese remained in place while many remigrated to warmer climates, places with better living conditions and more job opportunities, or sites closer to relatives, friends, or other Vietnamese. Most Vietnamese are now concentrated in California (40 percent), Texas (12 percent), Washington State (4 percent), and Florida (4 percent). The ten U.S. cities with the largest Vietnamese populations are the greater Los Angeles area; San Jose; Houston; Dallas; San Francisco; Washington, DC; Seattle; San Diego; Atlanta; and New York (Alperin and Batalova 2018).

According to the Census Bureau, in 2018 the Vietnamese population in the United States was estimated to be 2,162,610. Comparatively, it has grown significantly faster than the U.S. average over the last twenty years.[21] Demographically, 40 percent of the Vietnamese population is below thirty years of age, 50 percent are between thirty and sixty-five, and 9 percent are sixty-five and older. Vietnamese are much more likely to be first-generation immigrants than the U.S. average; approximately 68 percent of the 2.1 million are foreign-born immigrants, 75 percent of whom have lived in the United States for more than ten years, while the remaining 25 percent have been in the United States for less than ten years. Although Vietnamese Americans have a higher percentage of foreign-born immigrants than most other Asian American groups, 82 percent of the population are U.S. citizens, 7 percent higher than the Asian American average.[22] However, only 51 percent of the total population is English proficient, which is much lower than the average among all other Asian groups and the overall U.S. foreign-born population. The low percentage of English proficiency may be related to the recency of migration given that the majority of those with limited English proficiency are adults and foreign-born Vietnamese. Approximately one million people five years of age and older speak Vietnamese at home, thus making it the fifth-most-spoken language in the United States.[23]

Lower English proficiency could also explain why Vietnamese generally have a lower educational attainment level than other Asian Americans and the national averages. For example, 29 percent of the Vietnamese population has less than a high school diploma, compared to the 13.4 percent national average. Only 26 percent have a bachelor's degree or higher, compared to the 49 percent among the Asian American average. With an annual median household income of $60,000 in 2015, Vietnamese have a lower median than most Asians in the United States by $13,000, despite having a higher employment rate. As a result, more Vietnamese are living in poverty than other Asian groups. Despite that, Vietnamese Americans' economic status has improved substantially in recent years, with the median household income increasing to $65,643 in 2017, higher than the $61,372 for the general U.S. population.[24] About 65 percent of Vietnamese are homeowners, a rate that is much higher than that of other Asian groups.[25]

Vietnamese earn their income from various lines of work. According to the 2017 American Community Survey, over one million Vietnamese sixteen years and older are employed. Of these, 34.5 percent are employed in management, business, science, and the arts; 29.3 percent in service industries; 16.8 percent in sales and office positions; and 14.6 percent in production, transportation, and material moving. Many Vietnamese have established businesses in heavily concentrated Vietnamese and Asian communities, such as Little Saigons and Chinatowns. They are usually small businesses that provide services and goods, like supermarkets, restaurants, bakeries, auto repair shops, or beauty/nail salons. These jobs, however, are mostly held by recent immigrants and those with limited educational backgrounds and job skills. Younger Vietnamese and those who arrived in earlier waves are often more educated and provide professional and technical services in the computer and networking industries.

Many Vietnamese have the financial resources to send remittances to support family members and to invest in businesses and real estate in Vietnam. In 2020, Vietnamese living abroad sent $17.2 billion in remittances to Vietnam through formal channels, accounting for 5.0 percent of the country's GDP.[26] In 2019, of the $16.8 billion, remittances from the United States account for about 60 percent of all remittances sent to Vietnam. Remittances continue to be an important asset for Vietnam, especially for financial aid for families and relatives and investment in production, business, and real estate.[27]

Vietnamese Americans have demonstrated a robust commitment to civic engagement, particularly in local and state government. With the highest rate of naturalization among all immigration groups, more than 80 percent of Vietnamese Americans are U.S. citizens, thus making them eligible to vote and run for elected office. Using this advantage, many 1.5-generation Vietnamese have attained public office in states such as California and Texas. They include Van Tran, Andrew Do, Janet Nguyen, Ta Duc Tri, Bao Nguyen, and Hubert Vo. Two Vietnamese have been elected to the U.S. Congress: Joseph Cao (R-LA) in 2008 and Stephanie Murphy (D-FL) in 2016.

Most first-generation Vietnamese identify with and support the Republican Party, believing that it was more supportive of the RVN during the Vietnam War and has a tougher stance against communism and China. Vietnamese, especially the first generation, have used their voting power to push for laws and regulations that help preserve their ideals, values, and identities, such as adopting the flag of South Vietnam as the symbol of the Vietnamese community in the United States. A central focus among first-generation Vietnamese is Vietnam, their homeland. Staunchly anticommunist because of the effect of the war and its aftermath, this generation often stages political protests against the Vietnamese government and its representatives, exposes current human rights violations and suppression of religious freedom and the press, and lobbies U.S. politicians to demand specific changes and reform in Vietnam.

In contrast to those of the older generation, the issues that are central to younger and second-generation Vietnamese are not solely limited to Vietnam but rather include social, economic, and political issues directly affecting them and their generation. Subsequent generations of Vietnamese Americans lean more toward the Democratic Party and support progressive change on issues such as health and social welfare; equal rights based on sex, gender, and race; student-loan forgiveness; immigration reform; global warming; gun violence; and police brutality. These political differences with the first generation illuminate intergenerational rifts, but they are also a testament to the diverse ways in which Vietnamese Americans have navigated the complex and multivalent state, civic, economic, gendered, and racialized landscapes of American life.

Indeed, these intergenerational political contrasts reflect the profound differences in life experiences, even between different waves of refugees. The 130,000 refugees of the first wave in 1975 suffered from a profound shock caused by the sudden loss of their homeland together with their jobs, careers, property, families and friends. For those who left in the 1980s as "boat people," the sources of trauma included additional hardships under the communist regime and the sufferings during their terrifying journeys out of Vietnam. Many experienced imprisonment and starvation after the communists took over South Vietnam. Many encountered pirates and witnessed deaths and rapes while fleeing the country. Few in the first wave could have imagined what life was like in post-1975 Vietnam or how horrifying the escape from Vietnam was for second-wave refugees. By the 1990s, many of the first wave had been well established as middle-class American citizens and were able to take advantage of Vietnam's economic liberalization and the ability to visit. The 1990s also saw the last large batch of refugees, who were political detainees and their families arriving through the ODP process. Members of this group avoided dangerous ocean voyages, but they had suffered the longest and most directly under communist rule. To the extent we can speak of a Vietnamese American community, the diversity of life experiences and the circumstances of immigration are just as important for understanding its demographic, historical, and political evolution.

The Chapters Ahead

The structure of this volume forges a new framework for Vietnamese American studies, situating Vietnamese Americans front and center as agents of their own histories. We hope to move beyond existing paradigms and perspectives to better understand this complex community. In the three major sections outlined below, the authors delineate a new discursive Vietnamese American historiography; conduct deep-dive explorations into social, political, and entrepreneurial endeavors; and offer new concepts and epistemological approaches to how memory is nurtured, produced, and circulated in the Vietnamese diaspora.

Part I, "New Directions in Historiographies," centers on the decolonizing, civic organizing, activism, and literary and intellectual work in Vietnam, going back to the colonial period, that carried over a set of ideals and identities to its diasporic communities. In Chapter 1, "Legacies and Diasporic Connectivity: Dialogues and Future Directions of Vietnamese and Vietnamese American Studies," Y Thien Nguyen critically reviews the historiography of the Vietnam War and the Republic of Vietnam and advances a perspective that reconceptualizes Vietnamese America as the political, cultural, and institutional legacy of Republican Vietnam. In doing so, the chapter highlights how the study of Vietnamese America can guide questions and problematics in the study of the Republic and, vice versa, the ways in which the historical exploration of the Republic can shed light on contemporary dynamics within Vietnamese America.

The next two chapters highlight the vibrant intellectual culture and wide-ranging civic efforts in South Vietnam that have left enduring legacies in Vietnamese America. In Chapter 2, "Voluntarism and Social Activism in Wartime South Vietnam," Van Nguyen-Marshall examines the public life in South Vietnam going back to the colonial period. Her focus is on voluntary activities in the Republic of Vietnam, which were numerous and wide-ranging. They included mutual-aid societies, school clubs, professional societies, and philanthropic and civic organizations. By exploring the nature and meaning of people's voluntary activities and political activism, this chapter argues that civil society in the Republic was alive and robust despite wartime constraints and sometimes state repression.

In Chapter 3, "Universities and Intellectual Culture in the Republic of Vietnam," Wynn Gadkar-Wilcox traces the process through which intellectuals in the Republic of Vietnam created a unique environment through their participation in the development of new universities, academic fields, journals, and religious and secular organizations. By examining journals and the writers who influenced them, this chapter shows how this intellectual culture served to support the modernization of the RVN through its commitment to cosmopolitan, modernist, and republican values and ideas, while rarely being explicitly anticommunist.

Chapter 4, the final chapter in this section, bridges life in Vietnam with civic participation efforts and activism in the United States while challenging the conventional understanding of Vietnamese Americans' anticommunism in scholarship. In "The August Revolution, the Fall of Saigon, and Postwar Reeducation Camps: Understanding Vietnamese Diasporic Anticommunism," Tuan Hoang traces Vietnamese anticommunist beliefs over nearly a century from Vietnam to the diaspora. These intense beliefs emerged among Vietnamese nationalists in the late colonial period and were powerfully shaped by their experiences during the subsequent decades amid revolution, civil war, and postwar persecution by the communist regime.

Part II, "Explorations of Vietnamese America," explores the extensive transnational social networks and civic engagement experiences that developed in Vietnam and shaped the cultural, economic, and political life of the diaspora through the generations, whether in navigation of the resettlement process, in business operation, or in political participation and activism. This part outlines the challenges facing Vietnamese Americans and their strategies to build community, organize for political power, and take advantage of economic opportunities. They have achieved significant success, although in some cases they have also internalized and reproduced the racist structures of American society.

Chapter 5 by Elwing Suong Gonzalez, titled "Building a Place in the Space of Los Angeles: Vietnamese Refugee Community Creation, 1975–1990," examines the efforts and goals of, and the challenges and conflicts surrounding, early Vietnamese refugee community development in Los Angeles, which housed the largest concentration of Vietnamese refugees in the United States in the first decade of resettlement. This chapter explores the efforts of community leaders in meeting their community's needs and creating a place in the crowded and rapidly changing space of Los Angeles while balancing and addressing the demands and expectations of both government policy and various factions within the community.

In Chapter 6, "Vietnamese Americans and Their Homeland: Transnational Advocacy Efforts and Diasporic Ties," Ivan Small expands our scope to include the contacts and relationships between Vietnamese Americans and other diasporic Vietnamese political, humanitarian, and religious organizations across the globe—namely, those in Canada, Europe, and Australia. This chapter explores the influence of these humanitarian efforts, both in and beyond Vietnam and based in secular, religious, or pan-Asian organizations, that reconnect the diaspora to the homeland and bring to the fore issues of inequality, democracy, globalization, and human rights.

Chapter 7 turns to Vietnamese American political mobilization. In this chapter, Christian Collet traces the forty-year evolution of Vietnamese American politics in civil and electoral realms, emphasizing the strategies undertaken by activists to gain support for an ambitious agenda: the incorporation of Vietnamese Americans and the democratization of Vietnam. The author examines various strategies, from demonstrations and transnational activism at the grassroots level to efforts to gain access to U.S. institutions primarily through voting and candidacy.

In Chapter 8, titled "Diversity in Identities, Industries, and Business Strategies: Female Vietnamese American Entrepreneurs," Jennifer Huynh draws on data from the U.S. Census, the National Survey of Business Owners, and interviews with Vietnamese entrepreneurs across the United States. Focused on the experiences of Vietnamese women-owned businesses, including their diverse industries, identities, and business strategies, Huynh's chapter highlights how Vietnamese American women are changing the entrepreneurial landscape of the United States.

Chapter 9 is a reminder that Vietnamese diasporic communities do not live in isolation and that their everyday lives are in fact intertwined with other communities, often communities of color. In "Trapped within the White Frame: Vietnamese Americans in Post-Katrina New Orleans," Nguyen Vu Hoang investigates how Vietnamese communities often reified and participated in racist acts even while experiencing discrimination themselves. Based on fieldwork in a Vietnamese community in New Orleans East, this chapter examines a number of racist practices in an in-depth analysis of the racialized views of Vietnamese Americans in New Orleans.

Part III, "Paradigms of Diasporic Knowledge," offers innovative approaches to the study of collective memorialization and diasporic knowledge that challenge official and institutional narratives and suggest new and exciting avenues for future analyses. The authors in this section challenge collective memory by highlighting individualized histories: they explore diasporic nationalism in the hashtag age, examine ideas of motherhood and nation in popular religion, catalog the "memoryscapes" of war and migration, and document the challenges, cultural politics, and labor involved in institutionalizing community archives.

In Chapter 10, "The Unreconciled: Phan Nhiên Hạo's Poetry of Diasporic Testimony," Hai-Dang Phan reflects on his engagement as a literary scholar and translator with the work of the contemporary poet Phan Nhiên Hạo (b. 1967). Contextualized within and against the landscape of Vietnamese American literature since the early 1990s, Phan Nhiên Hạo's work as a Vietnamese-language poet living in the United States is an especially illuminating case study of (Vietnamese) poetry as a resilient mode for literary acts of witness and testimony in the diaspora, as well as a resistant form driven by ways of poetic knowing, of writing and reading lyrically, that seek to individualize history, reject the idea of a dominant collective memory, and challenge postwar narratives of reconciliation.

In Chapter 11, "Diasporic Nationalism: Continuity and Changes," Duyen Bui explores how nationalism manifests in the Vietnamese diaspora. Under a movement-oriented lens, diasporic nationalism becomes a factor in mobi-

lizing people into collective action. In a case study of a Vietnamese transnational organization, symbols of history and the past stored in memory are
incorporated with new forms of representation to encourage community
organizing for effecting change in the homeland. This research on diasporic nationalism reveals how nonstate actors can develop an idea of a nation
outside of state control and use it as a tactic to contest state power.

In Chapter 12, "Remembering War and Migration: Mapping the Contours of Diasporic Vietnamese Memoryscapes," Quan Tue Tran provides an
overview of how and why Vietnamese Americans and their counterparts in
the diaspora remember two definitive events in contemporary Vietnamese
history: war and migration. It historicizes and catalogs the different "memoryscapes" that have emerged from these events and animate the diaspora,
including memorials, archives, commemoration events, and cultural productions. The chapter reveals the diversity and complexity of refugee memory work, as well as its implications.

Titled "Devotion in Diaspora: Invoking Holy Mothers among Vietnamese American Faith Communities," Chapter 13 by Thien-Huong Ninh explores how, for both the Vietnamese Catholic and Caodai groups, holy mothers have emerged as emblems of their deterritorialized nation in the diaspora.
On the basis of ethnographic data collected in California, the author argues
that Vietnamese refugees and their U.S.-reared descendants have been able
to recentralize their fragmented communities through the innovative adaptation of holy mother worship. Through their shared devotion to holy mothers, these Vietnamese American faithfuls have also rebuilt relations with coethnic coreligionists living throughout the world.

In Chapter 14, "The Preservation and Production of Diasporic Knowledge: Oral History and Archival Contributions," Thuy Vo Dang focuses on
the different kinds of Vietnamese American grassroots and community-fund-
ed archival and oral history projects that have been established to vie for a
documented place in history. These preservation efforts are significant to the
diasporic Vietnamese community in that they provide a platform for alternate narratives about the Vietnam War and its aftermath. This chapter offers
an overview of current community efforts and the challenges and successes
they have faced in working with archival institutions, universities, and libraries.

Taken together, this section analyzes how the Vietnamese diasporic community represents, sometimes reifies, and often challenges definitions and
narratives about the refugee experience and nationhood in exile through
personal testimony and literature, memorialization events, popular religious
practices, and preservation efforts. Vietnamese Americans remember, preserve, connect, and embody collective and individual experiences in the con-

text of their relationship with their former homeland, broader diasporic Vietnamese communities, and future generations of Vietnamese Americans.

Conclusion

This volume seeks to engage with fresh research in Vietnamese studies to better understand the rapidly changing landscape of Vietnamese America. We take Vietnamese agency seriously to fully appreciate the complexities forged during the processes of nation building in postcolonial South Vietnam during the Cold War and community building after their resettlement in the United States. Vietnamese Americans' civic engagement and political activism, in fact, date back before the time of immigrant arrival and even before U.S. intervention in Vietnam. Individuals, religious communities, and civic organizations have actively grappled with constraints imposed by historical circumstances. Today Vietnamese Americans are playing transformative roles across national borders: first, by redefining and shaping America, and second, by effectively influencing social, political, and economic developments in Vietnam through their advocacy, memorialization and preservation efforts, and participation in the global economy.

The last decade has witnessed the proliferation of source materials (both in Vietnamese and English) from which the field of Vietnamese American studies has emerged. Such materials include novels, memoirs in various forms, documentaries and feature movies, collections of poems and short stories, and oral history archives.[28] The immense diversity of these materials gives us hope that the field can push against disciplinary boundaries in the study of Vietnamese Americans. Furthermore, we developed this volume with college instructors in mind and hope this provides a useful pedagogical framework for teaching about this complex community. At the end of the book, readers will find a Timeline of Key Events and Milestones in Vietnamese and Vietnamese American History (1900–2021) that highlights historical events instrumental to understanding who Vietnamese Americans are and how they have been connected to their homeland and have established a community in the United States.

The study of the Vietnamese diaspora presents an important intervention in our understanding of the complex nature of this globally interconnected contemporary moment, revealing the lingering effects of Cold War politics and the dialectical relationship between grassroots and state-sponsored ideologies (such as republicanism, democracy, communism, and anticommunism). What is at stake here is not only the emergent delineation of the budding field of Vietnamese American studies but also a broader epistemological concern with the ways in which knowledge and history have been produced and reified about subjects who are non-Western and mostly non-English speaking. The last few years of a global pandemic have laid bare just how interconnected our world is and how the legacies of colonialism, war, and economic exploitation continue to replicate quality-of-life disparities in developing countries and even within the borders of the richest economies of the world, resulting in the mass migrations of refugees and both voluntary and involuntary immigrants.

Our framework—a revamped historiography, a deep-dive exploration of civic participation, and an analysis of collective memory—has the potential to apply much more broadly to the study of other emerging diasporic groups from all over the world: from Syrian to Sudanese, from Rohingya to Afghan communities, to name a few. This volume's historiographical reorientation is a reminder that understanding immigrant communities does not start with their arrival in the United States; our deep concern for exploring the rich history of civic, social, religious, and entrepreneurial engagement is a strong argument for characterizing our subjects as active, agentive participants on a global stage; and last, this volume pushes the boundaries of where we might find emerging and alternative diasporic knowledges. We have found them in the intimate writings of a displaced poet, the artistic renderings of a holy mother figure, the geopolitics involved in constructing local war memorials, in the global hashtag activisms demanding government accountability, and in the struggles for inclusion into the seemingly impenetrable halls of institutional archives.

We hope that readers will find the Vietnamese American community and its complexities just as fascinating as we have and will perhaps be inspired by this framework to expand and continue our understandings of the community and of other communities who have enriched and will continue to enrich American life.

PART I

NEW DIRECTIONS IN HISTORIOGRAPHIES

LEGACIES AND DIASPORIC CONNECTIVITY

*Dialogues and Future Directions of Vietnamese
and Vietnamese American Studies*

Y Thien Nguyen

Introduction

In October 2020, Vietnamese Americans in support of the reelection of President Donald J. Trump organized "Trump Journey MAGA 2020" to travel from Southern California to Washington, DC. During this October "caravan," Vietnamese Americans came out en masse. Arriving on October 14, some 1,500 Vietnamese American Trump supporters marched alongside the Capitol's greens, bearing "Trump 2020" signs and slogans supporting conservative causes. As the caravan of Vietnamese American Trump supporters made its way across the country, meet-and-greet rallies were held at key Vietnamese American centers along the way. At these rallies, consistent were chants that rang: "Who defeated the Chinese communists?" "Who defeated socialism?"—"Donald Trump!" It was as if the political mantle once bequeathed upon revered Vietnamese anticommunist leaders had been transferred to an orange-tanned white man with blond hair. While these rallies entailed the flag-waving and sloganeering of a typical Trump rally, activities that traditionally characterize a Vietnamese American communal gathering were also evident (e.g., the singing of the South Vietnamese national anthem, salute to the South Vietnamese flag, and karaoke of popular South Vietnamese songs). The flurries of flags mixed American, South Vietnamese, and Trump symbols into a sea of red and yellow, blue and white upon which divergent histories converged.[1]

While such an event undoubtedly demonstrated the broad and organized Vietnamese American support for Trumpian politics and the Republican Party, Vietnamese American mobilization surrounding the 2020 presidential election also highlighted how the community's wartime and refugee past have been reconfigured within the contemporary American social landscape. Since flight from the homeland in 1975, Vietnamese refugees in the United States have consistently reutilized the symbols of their fallen nation to mobilize, organize, and represent an anticommunist Vietnamese community overseas. Most indicative of this reproduction is the widespread recognition of former Republic of Vietnam flag by Vietnamese Americans as the official symbol of their community. Similarly, the former South Vietnamese anthem, "*Tiếng Gọi Công Dân*" (Call to the Citizens), is regularly sung in Vietnamese American social and political gatherings; men dressed in full military garb bearing South Vietnamese military insignia are often seen standing in attendance at Vietnamese American cultural and political events (Nguyen V. T. 2012: 911–942; Hoang T. 2021);[2] and political narratives and terminologies originating from South Vietnam are found replicated in contemporary Vietnamese American community discourse (Nguyen Y. T. 2021: 397–457). As these examples demonstrate, Vietnamese America was formed through the reconstituting of political ideas and practices that derive from the South Vietnamese past.

While the formation of a Vietnamese American community is historically complex and experiences can differ greatly from one locale to the next, in this essay I hope to highlight an important relationship thus far underexplored in the contemporary scholarship on Vietnamese Americans: the connectivity between South Vietnam and Vietnamese America. Here, I mean not only the historical influences of the South Vietnamese past on the Vietnamese present but also the theoretical relationship between processes of *national formation* in South Vietnam and *community formation* of the Vietnamese diaspora overseas. Scholastically, the former has been under the purview of historians of modern Vietnam, while the latter is an inquiry taken up by scholars in Ethnic studies and Asian American studies. In part because of disciplinary divisions in contemporary academia, scholars of these two fields rarely engage with one another, are inspired by different sets of questions, and are informed by different perspectives. Yet the temporal, cultural, and political entwinements between South Vietnam and Vietnamese America (and consequently between processes of national formation and community formation) provide ample grounds for interdisciplinary dialogues that may contribute to the theoretical and empirical expansion of both fields of study.

While much of this essay is theoretical, I draw on my own research into Republican anticommunism to empirically illustrate the relationship between national formation and community formation as it pertains to the study of South Vietnam and Vietnamese America. For the purposes of this essay, I define *Republican anticommunism* as a hegemonic and dynamic nationalist ideology that has been shaped and reshaped by South Vietnamese and Vietnamese American actors across history. It is a sociopolitical construct that was produced and promulgated by the Republican state; became "consolidated" through efforts by state and nonstate actors; existed as the predominant form of politics and framework of interpretation for actors in South Vietnam; and was eventually transported along with the Vietnamese refugees to construct their communities abroad. Far from an automatic or natural consequence of collective or personal trauma due to war and refugee flight, anticommunism became socially prevalent through the activities of South Vietnamese and Vietnamese American political actors to build, promote, and institutionalize the anticommunist ideas and practices. I use the descriptor *Republican* to highlight both the original historical context under which this particular ideology was conceived and actualized and also the ideal to which the ideology hearkens—that is, the establishment of a modern republic.

As Tuan Hoang (Chapter 4 in this volume) argues, anticommunism in Vietnam predates the formation of the Republic of Vietnam. However, in this essay, I place emphasis on the state-derived anticommunism of the Republican era because it was during this period that existing social forms of anticommunist beliefs were codified and formalized into an official doctrine reinforced by the coercive capability of a nation-state. States, as Itzigsohn and vom Hau argue, are important for the creation and dissemination of ideas and identities (Itzigsohn and vom Hau 2006: 193–212). During the Republican era, previous forms of anticommunist beliefs and activities became centralized in the Republican state. The state appropriated the existing "free-floating" forms of anticommunism within the Vietnamese society and deployed those ideas for its own use and legitimacy (Mann 1984: 185–213).[3] However, in doing so, the Republican state also popularized these ideas, transforming anticommunism into something standard, familiar, and hegemonic.[4]

In this essay, I propose a theoretical scaffold on which the relationship between South Vietnam and Vietnamese America can be examined and studied. The following sections first briefly review the scholarship on the historical representation of the Vietnam War and the Republic of Vietnam. The essay argues that, despite advances in the field to take seriously the Republic of Vietnam as a historical actor and its role in the war and national formation in South Vietnam, the field lacks a diasporic perspective and fails to examine the lasting effects of the war and nation-building efforts on the communities of refugees in the wake of Saigon's collapse. Second, while historical scholarship on South Vietnam fails to consider the legacies of this fallen nation, the scholarship on Vietnamese America (despite its concerns with memory and the wartime past) lacks retrospective examination of how aspects of contemporary Vietnamese America constitute reconfigurations of

ideas, institutions, and discourse originating from the nation-building process in South Vietnam. The essay concludes with comments on possible future research agendas that take seriously historical connectivity between
South Vietnam and Vietnamese America.

Republican Vietnam and National Formation

In large part, historical scholarship on the Vietnam War has focused on questions related to American interventionism and the rise (and ultimate success) of the communist movement in Vietnam. Depicted as a war in which
a peasant guerrilla force managed to defeat the most powerful and modernized armed force in the world, the Vietnam War has captured the imagination of peace activists, political and military historians, and scholars of empire alike. For many Americans, the Vietnam War signifies a period of deep
national division, the emergence of an antiwar movement, and growing public mistrust of the government due to the military's deliberate deceptions
about the conduct of the war. As depicted through many historical works
on the Vietnam War, the victory of the communist guerrillas not only spelled
American imperialist follies abroad but also probed questions of morality
and justice, problematizing the American claim to be champions of democracy and freedom (McMahon 2002: 159–184; Nguyen V. T. 2013: 144–163;
Herring 1991: 104–119; Ryan and Fitzgerald 2009: 621–653; M. Small 2010:
543–553; Campbell 2007; Langguth 2012).[5] Within this literature, the communist side represents those who championed the cause of Vietnam nationalism, fighting for Vietnamese self-determination and independence from
French colonial and American imperial rule. Their victory in 1975 not only
reinforces the notion that the communists were on the "right side" of history but also narrates the indomitable capability of an indigenous people to
stand against an imperialist force (Duiker 1990: 2; Harrison 1989).

Compelling as this historiography may be, the historical narrative generally deployed by historians of the war omits any serious discussion of the
anticommunist Vietnamese nation that had come into being south of the
seventeenth parallel. In the general historiography of the conflict, South Vietnam and its anticommunist ambitions are often treated as "aberrant," uncomfortable historical anomalies that are best avoided, ignored, or explained
away (Tran N.-A. 2013: 3–9; Miller and Vu 2009: 1–16).[6] When the Republic
does have a role in the historiographic retelling, it is treated as a corrupt
entity or an American puppet to be juxtaposed against the nationalist credentials of the Vietnamese communist movement (Kolko 2001; Tran N.-A.
2013: 1–15).[7] The treatment of the Republic as a historical anomaly—rather
than a competing nationalist force—has allowed much of the existing scholarship to disregard its political history, its role in the Vietnam War, and its

idealistic strivings for an independent, modernized, and prosperous nation—an idealism that was similar to that of many of the emerging nations within the postcolonial world. Ironically, while the literature tends to equate *national liberation* with the communist movement in Vietnam, it was the Saigon government rather than the communist insurgency that really deployed nationalism in the battle over the "hearts and minds" (Race 1972: 179–81; Vu T. 2007: 175–230).

The omission of the Republic of Vietnam in historical scholarship on the Vietnam War has spurred a wave of new studies examining the intellectual, diplomatic, political, and social dimensions of South Vietnam. Focusing on the nation building during the First Republic, Phillip Catton demonstrates that Ngô Đình Diệm's efforts, although flawed, constituted a well-intentioned endeavor toward a particular vision of Vietnamese modernity (Catton 2003). Edward Miller contests earlier portrayals of Diệm as an American puppet by highlighting the unique personalist philosophy of the First Republican president, his broad—at least initially—base of political support, and the conflicts between American foreign policy and South Vietnamese nation-building efforts (Miller 2013). Similarly, Geoffrey Stewart's study of the "Special Commissariat for Civic Action" recasts the national project of the Republic through the eyes of its state agents and state builders. His work centers on the First Republic's endeavor for modernization through the cultivation of a new citizenry and establishment of a unique framework for a nation (Stewart 2017). Aside from these political histories of the Republic, Olga Dror examines the production of youths in South Vietnam through a social history of schoolbooks and pedagogical texts (Dror 2018).

Despite the growth of studies on the Republic of Vietnam and the much-appreciated turn toward historical agency, a systematic and comprehensive understanding of the national project in South Vietnam is lacking. These recent studies have prioritized the First Republican period at the cost of forgoing comprehensive examination of how South Vietnam politically and socially changed during its existence. While the Diệm administration was consequential in establishing the political and ideological foundations of the Republic, the period that followed is significant in transforming, contesting, and redefining certain values laid out under Diệm. The defining works of the field, thus, have been limited by their periodization, often focusing on the early temporal slice of Republican history rather than examining the entirety of the era (Goscha 2016; K. Taylor 2013).[8] This limitation has prevented the scholarship from systematically examining the continuities of ideas, institutions, and forms of politics and has precluded exploration of how such continuity was possible within a context of coups, regime changes, political instability, and civil war.

Certain nation-building initiatives of the First Republic, for example, were continued (albeit significantly reconfigured) by subsequent regimes despite the fall of the Diệm regime in 1963. The Strategic Hamlet program stands as a case in point. Originally conceived as a personalist project for Vietnamese modernization under the Diệm administration, the program officially was supposed to have ended with the death of Diệm in 1963.[9] However, concepts central to the Strategic Hamlet initiative, such as the modernization of the countryside through the erection of fortified communities, continued to be applied in the counterinsurgency and nation-building projects of subsequent administrations. Rural modernization and the reconfiguration of the fortified village concept for counterinsurgency are evident in the New Life Hamlet (*Ấp Đời Mới/Ấp Tân Sinh*) program during the Directorate and the Self-Defending—Self-Developing Communities (*Cộng Đồng Tự Vệ—Cộng Đồng Phát Triển*) initiative of the Second Republic.[10]

In my own research, I demonstrate how an ideological education program initially enacted under the First Republic (1955–1963) persisted despite the regime changes and political turmoil which characterized much of the Republican era. I point to how certain goals, practices, and norms became associated with ideological work during the Republican era, how these ideational aspects became institutionalized, and how later regimes drew on, mimicked, and expanded on the experiences of those that predate them to reconfigure and revamp preexisting ideological activities (Nguyen Y. T. 2021).

I emphasize viewing the Republican era in its entirety because of what a comprehensive vantage signifies for the examination of national formation in South Vietnam. Far from something exclusive to the First Republic, nation building was a perpetual, systematic, and state-directed effort across the twenty-odd years of South Vietnam's existence. Although these efforts varied significantly across the Republican era, the project to create a viable, anticommunist, and independent Vietnamese Republic endured and was taken up by not only the Diệm administration but also the regimes that followed it. Subsequently, through their efforts to construct and develop an anticommunist nation, Vietnamese refugees (who were essentially former citizens of the Republic) would carry the ideas, practices, and politics of the Republican era to new communities overseas.

In my view, the Republican national project laid legacies on the people it affected. States, as other scholars have shown, are important for the construction, promotion, and perpetuation of ideas, institutions, and norms (Evans, Dietrich, and Skocpol 1985: 3–38; Weber 1976; Fagen 1969). On the one hand, states are necessary for the creation and maintenance of discourses, laws, and structures of governance within a polity (Huntington 1968). On the other hand, while states are important for the "institutionalization" of a polity, they are also important for creating space for citizens' civic engagement and political participation. Here, how citizens respond to the values, programs, and agendas imposed by a state matter. The discourses and norms deriving from the state can become "consolidated," variable in how they are received and engaged with by society as a whole. Citizens' participation in state projects can provide opportunities through which the goals and aims of the state are contested, evaluated, and modified by the populace. Through this political participation, ordinary people can also encounter state ideas and institutions, acquiring and becoming familiarized with state discourses and ideas (Selbin 1999: 19–29, 32–33).[11]

For South Vietnam, national formation was inextricably tied to the project of creating an anticommunist society. As oft-repeated across the Republican era, the task to "build the nation" (*dựng nước*) must go hand in hand with the mission to "save the nation" (*cứu nước*) from communism.[12] The various regimes across the Republican era instituted anticommunist laws directed at suppressing communist ideologies and organizations.[13] Individuals engaging in communist or communist-sympathetic activities could face lengthy prison sentences or, at times, execution. Republican administrations also instituted holidays and commemorations to generate a broad anticommunist political culture. The "Day of National Resentment" (*Ngày Quốc Hận*) (instituted under the premiership of Nguyễn Khánh in 1964), for example, entailed annual state-directed activities, including military marches, public speeches by government officials, and government-sponsored exhibits documenting "communist atrocities." Citizens, however, were encouraged to enthusiastically participate in these state-sponsored events, by such means as attending rallies and demonstrations, engaging in "political study" of state-produced texts, contributing arts and poems for state-sponsored cultural productions, and engaging in collective commemoration.[14] Similar encouragement of societal participation occurred during the Communist Denunciation Campaign of the First Republic or the drive to form fortified villages during the Second Republic. Thus, while the creation of an anticommunist nation in South Vietnam entailed state-led institutionalization, this process of national formation also necessarily included the political integration of nonstate actors in the national affairs of the Republic.

Across the Republican period, efforts to form an anticommunist nation transformed anticommunism from a state doctrine into a hegemonic "cultural script" widely deployed by state and nonstate actors alike. Republican anticommunist ideas, terminologies, and narratives are found reflected in newspapers, novels, poetry, music, and theater. As others have argued, while the Republican state did not compel writers to produce anticommunist texts, it did encourage and, at times, sponsor anticommunist cultural production (Tran N.-A. 2013: 16–17; Hoang T. 2013: 99–167).[15] Coercive efforts of the Republican states to eliminate communist influences reinforced the anticommunist discursive production. Republican regimes enacted laws and decrees to criminalize communist literature, organizations, activities, and even thoughts. The Republican state, furthermore, implemented comprehensive, systematic, and violent counterinsurgent campaigns, seeking to "exterminate" not only guerrillas in the jungles but also those "communist sympathizers" within the civilian population.[16] Thus, state projects and programs promoting anticommunist nationalism existed in tandem with laws and coercive methods meant to eliminate communist and communist-sympathetic activities in South Vietnam. This dual aspect of Republican ideological work allowed a national, anticommunist political culture to flourish and become consolidated across the Republican society.

Given this history of persistent and, at times, intense nation building in South Vietnam, one cannot assume that the social, ideological, and cultural effects of these efforts simply ceased following the collapse of the Republic. While the Republican state proper no longer existed after 1975, the narratives, ideas, and practices that had become familiar, hegemonic, and widespread throughout the Republican era continued. These are the products of the twenty-odd years of Republican national formation during which citizens acquired anticommunist political, ideological, and culture repertoires that had informed their lives in South Vietnam. In their flight from the homeland, these refugees brought with them the ideals, loyalties, and discourses of their former nation. Rather than disappearing into the historical abyss, Republican anticommunism was drawn on by Vietnamese refugees to construct their diasporic communities overseas. As those in South Vietnam used existing anticommunist repertoires to interpret their experiences during war, those who fled the country after 1975 drew on the narratives transported over to frame their experiences as refugees. Succinctly, the social, political, and cultural byproducts of what was *national formation* in South Vietnam laid the foundation for *community formation* in Vietnamese America. In this light, scholars who study South Vietnam and the Vietnam War can valuably contribute to the examination of how past institutions, culture, politics, and discourses inform the creation of a Vietnamese refugee community in the United States.

This is not to say that reproduction from South Vietnam to Vietnamese America was "natural" or automatic. Rather, this reproduction (as with any other social process in history) is shaped through conflicts, struggles, and contestations. Debates over how an aspect of South Vietnam should be reproduced (or even whether this aspect should be reproduced) are to be expected. Even the reusage of the South Vietnamese flag—a symbol so evidently central to Vietnamese American identity—was at one point questioned and challenged.[17] The history of how and why certain aspects are retained while others are erased remains to be written. Furthermore, certain ideas, practices, and institutions may become marginalized at one point in history, only to reappear and become dominant at a later point. Here, the reputation and memory of Ngô Đình Diệm stands as a quintessential case. Demonized after his death in 1963, Diệm was eventually rehabilitated by his supporters during the Second Republic (Nguyen Y. T. 2021: 242–310).[18] This rehabilitation process continued into the post-1975 era within Vietnamese refugee communities, where Diệm is now remembered as a patriot whose death was an avoidable but catastrophic tragedy for the Republic. Fruitful deductions can emerge from examining the historical continuities, as well as the discontinuities, between the South Vietnamese past and the Vietnamese American present.

In these regards, historians of the Republican era must play the important role of examining the origins and historical transformation of cultural, social, and political aspects that have been reproduced from South Vietnam. They can fruitfully answer questions about why certain aspects of South Vietnam are reproduced and others are not. Reproduction, furthermore, does not necessarily mean linear or static continuity from the Republican era and into Vietnamese America. The nuances that historians of Vietnam can provide will move contemporary scholarship toward a rich, complex, and empirically grounded understanding of both communities and speak to the historical and diasporic connectiveness between South Vietnam and Vietnamese America.

Vietnamese Americans and Community Formation

If Republican anticommunism was an important aspect of politics in the South Vietnamese past, its importance continues into the Vietnamese American present. While early studies of Vietnamese refugees almost exclusively focused on their cultural and economic adjustment to American life, recent examination of the community has charted an interdisciplinary agenda that brings together diverse disciplines. Of particular importance, this scholarship has recently turned toward collective memory to explore how the community negotiates with its anticommunist, war-ridden, and refugee past. Thuy Vo Dang highlights how anticommunism operates as a "cultural praxis—a mode for engaging in memory and meaning-making practices" (Vo Dang 2008: xii). For Vo Dang, Vietnamese American anticommunism and its usage in commemoration and collective memory allow Vietnamese refugees to "discuss the complexity of post-war grappling with death, loss, exile, survival for those on the ground" (Vo Dang 2008: xii). Similarly, Karin Aguilar-San Juan discusses how Vietnamese Americans engage in "strategic memory projects," mobilizing symbols and representations of their history of war and refugeeism to build the cultural, economic, and political infrastructure of the community (Aguilar-San Juan 2009). Phuong Tran Nguyen's recent *Becoming Refugee Americans* highlights how nostalgia, "pain of exile," and the political desire to differentiate the overseas community from communist Vietnam were melded into the formation of Vietnamese America. He argues that "although thinking about the past rekindled traumas of war and exile, most emigres did not have the luxury of forgetting about Vietnam" (Nguyen P. T. 2017: 61). Indeed, shaped by traumas of war and refugee flight, Vietnamese American music, arts, and literature reflected a nostalgic longing for the South Vietnamese homeland while vilifying the communist regime that had taken power.

Despite these scholars' intellectual concern toward the refugees' South Vietnamese past, exploration of that past relies less on actual examination of South Vietnamese history and society than on the postwar renditions of that society captured in cultural productions, oral histories, and commemorative practices of refugee Vietnamese Americans. In part, the problem of how South Vietnam factors into the study of Vietnamese Americans is a consequence of how this emerging scholarship approaches the Vietnam War and the postwar refugee migration. For one, when it comes to the historical bearings that South Vietnam has on Vietnamese America, this scholarship relies on the orthodox historical narrative of the Vietnam War literature, which views the conflict as primarily an imperialist intervention by the United States. Here too, the political, ideological, social, and institutional dimensions of the Republic are ignored and, when provided a historical role, treated as corrupt, "aberrant," or puppetlike, taking on America's imperial mission. The anticommunist political culture of the southern Republic, as conceptualized in these studies, is less a product of ideological work or indigenous nation building by the Republican state than it is an imitation of American foreign policy or a psychological response to the horrors of communist violence and forced migration (Le C. N. 2009; Valverde 2012; Vo N. M. 2004; Nguyen Y. T. 2018: 65–103).[19]

To arrive at a more nuanced and historically grounded understanding of how South Vietnam and Vietnamese America are related, the scholarship must first reconfigure its understanding of Vietnamese America's past, its perception of the Vietnam War, and the historical implications of that war. In the recent literature reviewed above, the treatment of the Vietnam War and its relationship to Vietnamese America largely conform to the "critical refugee studies" approach outlined by Yen Le Espiritu in 2006. Her call for a redirection of the study of Vietnamese refugees (and refugees at large) rests on a critique of how the Vietnamese refugees have been historically represented and subjectified in American discourse. For Espiritu, traditional scholarship has represented the Vietnamese as the "good refugee," conjoining depictions of refugees as passive and pathetic victims in dire need of American "rescue" with caricatures of Vietnamese Americans as part of the successful and assimilated Asian American "model minority." Such a depiction, on the one hand, reinforces orientalizing narratives that "naturalizes Vietnam's neediness and America's riches." On the other, it shifts the conversation away from the imperialistic dimensions of American foreign policy and allows the United States to retrieve international legitimacy after its defeat in the Vietnam War. Writing in the context of another American war unfolding in Iraq and Afghanistan, Espiritu argues that the field must take the Vietnamese refugees as a site of critique, understanding their history and formation as "subjects of US war and imperialism" (Espiritu 2006: 410–433).

Although Espiritu provides an eloquent, critical, and important redirecting from the assimilation-centered frameworks of earlier studies, critical refugee studies is an inadequate framework for addressing the full ideological, historical, and political scope of the Vietnamese refugee experience. There are two main issues with such a framing. First, the treatment of "Vietnamese subjectivity" is primarily a product of American involvement in Vietnam. Anticommunism, as such, is understood not as the result of the South Vietnamese history of national formation but as a seemingly strategic response to the racial, political, and social landscape of the United States. While one can agree that postwar American memory work has sought to repaint the Vietnam War as a "good war" and that these efforts have led to the excision of the South Vietnamese side of the story, Vietnamese American subjectivities cannot be reduced to something simply "asserted" by Vietnamese Americans because their history is excluded from American discourse. Nor are Vietnamese American political beliefs and ideologies merely "adopted" by Vietnamese Americans to make themselves visible and understood (Espiritu 2006: 410–433). Such a depiction implies the primacy of the United States in the making of political subjectivities in the South Vietnamese and Vietnamese American context. It avoids discussions of the primary responsibility of the Vietnamese themselves for the historical crafting, development, dissemination, and, ultimately, transplantation of anticommunist beliefs and practices.

Espiritu is correct to note that Vietnamese American subjectivity "cannot be exclusively defined within the US context." However, it is further the case that these subjectivities did not solely emerge from the "US war in and occupation of Southeast Asia." Republican anticommunism, as it existed in South Vietnam, was not some ideological import that came with "US 'counterinsurgency' actions, anticommunist insurgency, terrorism counteraction, and peacekeeping operations" (Espiritu 2006: 410–433). It is a product of the activities of state builders in South Vietnam who actively sought to institute anticommunism as their own state ideology—at times, through programs scorned, unratified, or contested by their American advisers. The conceptualization provided by Espiritu, ultimately, lends too-great explanatory power to American hegemony and conflates the anticommunism of South Vietnam and Vietnamese America with the anticommunism that exists in American foreign policy.[20]

Second, while Espiritu acknowledges that "Vietnam is a country and not a war," she is primarily concerned with the production of "American identities and for the shoring up of US militarism" and thus leaves little room for excavating how Vietnamese subjectivities are historically forged, apart from those explicitly linked to American-related processes (Espiritu 2006, 410–433). She does not provide a way to understand Vietnam as that "country" but recasts Vietnam—as traditionally done in the historiography of the war—as little more than a background for exploring and critiquing American actions and subjectivities. Here, I am not calling for the examination of some premigration, orientalized Vietnamese/Asian "culture" or the (re)discovery of some primordial essence of Vietnamese ethnicity. Rather, my critique lies in the need for proper engagement with processes of national formation in this geographical space we call Vietnam.

A similar approach to South Vietnam is found in Phuong Tran Nguyen's (2017) recent book. While Nguyen acknowledges the importance of premigration social notables, symbols, music, and culture in the creation of Vietnamese America, his section on the history of South Vietnam stretches little more than 7 pages within the 220-page book (Nguyen P. T. 2017: 23–30). In the narration, he dwelled more so on American "imperialist" intents in Southeast Asia than on the activities, goals, and ideals of South Vietnamese political actors. When the South Vietnamese were mentioned, the focus was on the "hand-picked" and "mediocre" leaders and elites who "lacked either the desire or the authorization to share power" (Nguyen P. T. 2017: 27, 28). South Vietnam, as argued by Nguyen, constituted of "little more than a diverse collection of religious, political, economic, and geographic interest groups"—an argument that reflects the orientalist impressions of at least one writer of *The Guardian* during the mid-1960s (Nguyen P. T. 2017: 27; *The Guardian* 1966). In Nguyen's view and that of others, the "anticommunist republic" (Nguyen 2017: 27) was little more than an American political creation. As that "aberrant" historical anomaly, the Republic of Vietnam is deprived of its political legitimacy, nationalist authenticity, and historical agency through these depictions.

Nguyen's work, furthermore, is not oblivious to the rampant anticommunist ideology within Vietnamese America. His book tackles the issue in depth, interweaving how anticommunism was melded into the identity, collective memory, and cultural politics of Vietnamese exile communities overseas (Nguyen P. T. 2017: 77–96). However, he fails to connect that Vietnamese American anticommunism with the ideological and nation-building activities that have transpired in South Vietnam. Nguyen is correct in pointing out how Vietnamese American anticommunism has been shaped by the experiences of refugees and their interactions with the American (Cold War) political landscape. However, Nguyen fails to historically examine the anticommunism that was animated in South Vietnam, opting to caricaturize this ideology as primarily a product of American interventionism. In doing so, he presents the post-1975 manifestation of the anticommunist ideology as comprehensible and explainable while depicting the anticommunism that existed prior as artificial, anomalous, and negligible for understanding Vietnamese America. He fails to conceive the anticommunism of Vietnamese Americans as an extension or a recalibration of ideas, rhetoric, and narratives once developed in South Vietnam. He, like others in the field, fails to connect South Vietnam and Vietnamese America.

As suggested in the previous section, the complexities of anticommunist politics so eloquently articulated in the recent literature on Vietnamese America have deep historical moorings. These moorings have consistently borne themselves (and continue to bear themselves) in Vietnamese America. The diverse "praxis" of anticommunism that Vo Dang identified is not solely founded in the United States (Vo Dang 2008). Rather, it has existed in national commemorative practices, celebrations, and cultural productions from South Vietnam. Citizens of the Republic of Vietnam once mourned soldiers who died for the "just cause" (*chính nghĩa*) of anticommunism, celebrated mythological heroes and heroines, and annually observed state-instituted holidays.[21] "Black April"—the annual commemorative holiday that marks the fall of Saigon in 1975—is otherwise known as "Ngày Quốc Hận" (Day of National Resentment; Vo Dang 2008: 105).[22] While Vietnamese Americans annually date this commemoration to April 30, the holiday was originally dated July 20 to signify the signing of the Geneva Accords; and, similar to its transmogrification into the Vietnamese American context, South Vietnamese commemoration of the Day of National Resentment involved anticommunist mass demonstrations, public speeches, and social remembrance.[23]

We find in early Vietnamese America political movements that drew on the anticommunist discourse, norms, and politics of the former Republic. These movements were not only important for the articulation of a Vietnamese refugee identity; they were also crucial for the formation of community, belonging, and solidarity among the exiles overseas. Early Vietnamese refugees were enmeshed in what I have elsewhere called the "Homeland Restoration" movement. Essentially a paramilitary movement, the goal was to "restore" the lost nation of South Vietnam—through either the specific reconstruction of the Republic of Vietnam or, at the very broadest, the construction of a noncommunist Vietnamese state. The conceived reconstruction of the homeland was violent in nature, entailing the forcible overthrow of Vietnamese communism through popular insurrection and guerrilla war. In mobilizing for this movement, Vietnamese refugees drew on familiar Republican anticommunist terminologies, rhetoric, and discourse to articulate their vision for the possibility of successful communist overthrow. The movement also aided in reviving anticommunist political violence against suspected communists and communist sympathizers, reconstituted political legitimacy for former South Vietnamese military officers and service members, and reinstituted political forms and discourses that glorify anticommunist nationalism and the Republic of Vietnam (Nguyen Y. T. 2018; Nguyen Y. T. 2021: 414–423).

Emerging in concert with this movement to "restore" the homeland were efforts by Vietnamese exiles to increase protections for refugees fleeing the homeland and to demand human rights in Vietnam. These efforts similarly drew on existing anticommunist discourses, particularly those narratives emphasizing the brutality of communist rule, religious persecution, cultural destructions, and "crimes" and "atrocities" committed by communists across Vietnamese history. Former Republican anticommunist narratives, on the one hand, aided in generating an image of a struggling, repressive, miserable postwar Vietnam within which compatriots, family, friends, and relatives were desperate to escape or radically change. On the other hand, mobilizers deployed familiar politicized language and discourses to popularize a vision of communist overthrow through guerrilla uprising while simultaneously providing the moral rationale for human rights advocacy. Because these movements were framed through familiar and existing bodies of beliefs, mobilization for human rights and homeland restoration brought together diverse coalitions of social activists, clergy members, intellectuals, former politicians, cultural producers, and military veterans (Nguyen Y. T. 2021: 410–412, 423–426).

Resultantly, an increasingly vocal, organized, and politicized community was formed through this mobilization—a community whose identity is premised on the refugees' status as victims of communism. Mobilization around common causes placed the disparate Vietnamese communities in dialogue with one another, promoted cultural activities, established shared holidays, (re)instituted nationalist symbols, and generated an "imagined community" of an anticommunist diaspora overseas. Thus, redeployment of Republican anticommunism to address the contemporary challenges and concerns of Vietnamese refugees aided in the formation of Vietnamese America (Nguyen Y. T. 2021: 398–405). Here, the legacies of nation building (the past discourses and politics of the Republican era) significantly factor into how the Vietnamese American community was formed and what shape this community ultimately took.

Charting a Research Agenda

In this essay, I have argued for a historical framework that approaches Vietnamese American anticommunism from its roots in the nation-building process that transpired in South Vietnam. This approach does not obfuscate the attention to Vietnam as a "war" (as Espiritu fears), nor does it treat Vietnam as just a "country." Rather, it takes South Vietnam as a site to explore the construction of Vietnamese subjectivity, institutions, and practices. In the context of a geopolitically divided world, this process of national formation left lasting legacies that can be found in the identities, beliefs, and politics of contemporary Vietnamese America. This approach does not necessarily discount the interventionist role of the United States in shaping the historical happenings in Vietnam. However, rather than viewing the United States as a hegemonic force that unilaterally determined the beliefs and activities of the South Vietnamese (and subsequently Vietnamese Americans), this approach treats US foreign policy and military activities as the background on which Vietnamese actors navigated, both in conformity and opposition. This Vietnam-centered approach, thus, diverges sharply from approaches that call for the centering of American subjectivity and actions in Vietnam. Rather than utilizing the conflict in Vietnam and Vietnamese subjects to address the "shaping and articulation of US nationhood" (Espiritu 2006), it addresses the role of the United States only when it factors into how Vietnamese actors shaped and articulated their own Vietnamese nationalism and belonging.

To correct any misconceptions, I do not here call for a scholarship that prioritizes the "South Vietnamese side" of the story but rather an approach that views South Vietnam and Vietnamese America as dynamic, social constructs, intimately linked through history and people (Anderson 2006; Hobsbawn and Ranger 1983: 1–14; Giddens 1987, 1990; Gellner 1983). The South Vietnamese voices and perspectives this paper has highlighted represents not some "correct" or "authentic" portrayal of the historical past but rather something political and biased and, thus, should be treated as such. No more "real" than "North Vietnam" or this territorial space we today refer to as "Vietnam," "South Vietnam," like any other nation, is a consequence of political conflicts and the efforts by state and nonstate actors to construct and develop an "imagined community" of compatriots. This essay, thus, advocates for a broad and comprehensive research agenda that examines the sociohistorical *construction*, *development*, and *movement* of ideas, practices, and institutions that originated through efforts to build a nation in South Vietnam and have (re)manifested in Vietnamese refugee communities abroad. To engage in such an enterprise, the first step is to examine South Vietnam as a socially constructed national society—in terms of not only that "imagined community" but all the social and political activities that contribute to the reification of the nation. From there, the task is to trace how and why beliefs and practices that were formed and developed in South Vietnam migrated, how these beliefs and practices are reconfigured abroad, and how they contribute to the formation of a Vietnamese diaspora.

While this essay has been focused on the reconstitution of Republican anticommunism, this state-derived ideology constitutes but a slice of the South Vietnamese and Vietnamese American history. We find in early Vietnamese America the emergence of charitable and social service organizations seeking to provide refugees a voice in the relocation process, advocate for community funding, and expand social and economic opportunities for those within the community (Tran 2007). However, little in the scholarship points to how South Vietnamese civil society may have shaped associational organizations in Vietnamese America. Van Nguyen-Marshall (Chapter 2 in this volume) details the pluralistic civil society that emerged in South Vietnam. As with the transmogrification of Republican anticommunism into the diasporic context, one cannot assume that the diverse organizations, associations, and relationships that once constituted civil society in South Vietnam simply disappeared with the collapse of the Republic in 1975. Her work lays the foundations for possible exploration of how and whether contemporary "mutual assistance associations," volunteer agencies, charities, social service organizations, or advocacy groups in Vietnamese America had any roots in, or drew inspiration from, the "associational life" of the South Vietnamese past.

Thien-Huong Ninh (Chapter 13 in this volume) explores the reconstitution of "holy mothers" in Vietnamese diasporic communities since the fall of Saigon. For Ninh, the remaking of religious practices and beliefs by Vietnamese refugees "not only recentralized their fragmented communities . . . but have also played a pivotal role in popularizing these female religious figures." Indeed, as Vietnamese refugees carried with them their political ideas and practices during their flight abroad, they similarly "carried their holy mothers . . . and transplanted their faith on new soil." Ninh's work is the stepping-stone for a broad sociohistorical examination of how diverse religious organization, beliefs, and practices stemming from the Republican era were transplanted abroad to shape the religious engagement of Vietnamese Americans today.

Similarly, in the realm of music, theater, and the arts, *nhạc vàng* and certain cultural and theatrical forms from the Republican era have influenced contemporary Vietnamese American productions (Lieu 2011: 79–91; Nguyen Y. T. 2018; Reyes 1999). Scholars of musicology and the theatrical arts can fruitfully examine the transformation of this musical form as it enters new digital spaces and media platforms and reaches a diasporic audience in the post-1975 era. Vinh Phu Pham has begun this discussion, pointing to how songs like "Chiều Tây Đô" are a "legacy of the [Republic of Vietnam]" and how the reusage of the Republican past is a source of "livelihood" for this musical genre (Pham V. P. 2019).[24] In the realm of intellectual culture, Wynn Gadkar-Wilcox, in Chapter 3, demonstrates the cosmopolitan and modernist nature of South Vietnamese intellectuals. Although his piece focuses on the Republican era, he calls for greater consideration of the "antecedent history" of Vietnamese Americans, particularly with respect to the social, cultural, and intellectual dimensions of South Vietnam. His work is a starting point for examining continuities in political thought and philosophical tenors that migrated from South Vietnam to Vietnamese America. South Vietnam also boasted a comprehensive and robust educational system influenced by both French and American curricula (Trần V. C. 2014: 4–25; Nguyễn T. L., Trần H. T., Nguyễn V. T., Trần N. N., and Lê Q. T. 2006). Whether and how pedagogical philosophies and practices from South Vietnam are replicated in the educational programs (such as Vietnamese-language classes and textbooks for Vietnamese American children) operating in contemporary Vietnamese America may also be a fruitful site for research.

The scope for new research excavating the historical and transnational relationships between South Vietnam and Vietnamese America is vast. As scholars of these communities, we must begin viewing South Vietnam and Vietnamese America through a lens of historical continuity and connectiveness and understand how past efforts to construct a South Vietnamese national society lent themselves to the construction of a Vietnamese diaspora overseas. In doing so, scholars of both Vietnam and Vietnamese America can come into closer dialogue and build on one another's research. In my view, such dialogue is necessary for the expansion of both fields and can generate diverse agendas that are both diasporic and historical.

2

VOLUNTARISM AND SOCIAL ACTIVISM
IN WARTIME SOUTH VIETNAM

Van Nguyen-Marshall

Introduction

At a major academic conference in the United States, an audience member asked me why scholars needed to know about South Vietnamese civil society, my presentation topic. This exchange took place in 2016, a quarter of a century after George Herring (1990) wrote a mea culpa on behalf of American historians for having ignored, and therefore remained uninformed about, America's Vietnamese allies. While the historiography on the Vietnam War has made substantial progress in the last few decades, there is still lingering resistance in scholarship and popular history to acknowledge that people in South Vietnam had agency and history.[1]

This chapter redirects attention to South Vietnamese society in an effort to understand how some residents of the Republic of Vietnam (RVN), particularly those living in towns and cities, experienced and responded to the upheavals that accompanied the creation of their country and the war that eventually led to its demise. By focusing on people's voluntary activities, which are essential components of civil society, this chapter illustrates that South Vietnamese people were actively engaged with their communities and society. The evidence shows that civil society not only existed but was also significant, dynamic, and robust. South Vietnamese people's public activities were consequential, particularly in the lives of the participants. In many cases, however, associated activities also had an impact on the wider communities, state-society relationship, and nation building.

In much of the literature about the Vietnam War, nation building is characterized as the purview of American agencies, technocrats, and academics.

With few exceptions (Catton 2002; Miller 2013; Stewart 2017), Vietnamese people rarely appear as leaders or actors in discussions about nation building and social development. Like the conventional narrow depictions of Vietnamese Americans as either beneficiaries of American generosity or victims of U.S. imperialism, people of South Vietnam are cast in limited roles in the historiography of their country. They are either mute objects of U.S. social engineering or obscurantists who rejected and abused American development aid. This chapter highlights South Vietnamese people's activism in the public realm, some of which contributed to the public good and to nation building. Their activities demonstrate that despite the many disruptions and challenges associated with decolonization, national division, war, authoritarian rule, and external intervention, people in South Vietnam still managed to claim space for meaningful civic activities and engagement. In this way, the research on South Vietnamese associational life also offers insight into the social and civic activism of the Vietnamese diaspora in the United States. Many Vietnamese refugees continue to be engaged in philanthropic and community activities in their new host country, a tradition that was well honed in South Vietnam.

While many contemporary scholars, activists, and policy makers consider civil society as an independent arena of social activities and a panacea against state tyranny, others take a more pessimistic view (Bratton 1989; Wiktorowicz 2000). The latter recognize that state-society interpenetration was more often the case than the exception throughout history and that civil society can support the status quo as well as subvert it (Gramsci 1971: 12–13, 261–263; Bourdieu 1986). Furthermore, historians of colonized and non-Western societies have found evidence of robust civil societies in circumstances where democratic and human rights have been withheld from the people (Berry 1998; McHale 2004; Peycam 2012). These findings suggest that the nature and potential of civil society are varied and often do not correspond to any idealized model or follow a prescribed trajectory.

As with many historical case studies (Wiktorowicz 2000; Landau 2008), South Vietnam's civil society was plural, exhibiting potential to support as well as challenge state-elite dominance. Residents of South Vietnam voluntarily established and participated in a wide range of organizations and social activities in the realm of mutual aid, philanthropy, social service, religion, culture, and leisure. They engaged in these public activities for diverse reasons, ranging from advancing personal interests to contributing to the common good. Their participation did not start in 1954, however; as the next section shows, the history of collective social engagement dates back to the premodern period. Moreover, as demonstrated by Ivan Small in this collection, their associational life did not end in 1975. Many Vietnamese living overseas after the end of the war continue to be active in society. One can trace the Vietnamese diaspora's activism to a long tradition of community self-help, charity, and civic engagement rooted in Vietnam's history.

The Historical Roots of Associational Life

Associational life has deep roots in Vietnam. Alexander Woodside (1976) observed this over five decades ago and has argued that modern Vietnam was shaped by the Vietnamese intelligentsia's quest for a political community on a national scale. My research shows that collective life was important on all levels of society and was pursued for social and personal purposes as well as political ones. Moreover, the history of associational life predates the French colonial era. Historical evidence suggests that since at least the fifteenth century, voluntary mutual-aid and social organizations had existed in villages and towns, particularly in the Red River Delta of northern Vietnam. Regulations and encouragement for associational life were enshrined in village covenants (hương ước), which set out the laws and procedures for village governance (Bùi X. Đ. 1985: 45). By the Nguyễn Dynasty (1801–1945), many types of societies existed in villages. There were groups (phe) for elite members of society as well as associations (hội) for ordinary folks. The latter were diverse and included rotation-credit organizations, trade guilds, martial arts clubs, chèo musical theater associations, and societies for celebrating weddings, funerals, and the Lunar New Year (Nguyễn T. C. 1993).

In addition to mutual-help organizations, people were also encouraged to participate in philanthropy. Informed by Confucian ethics of benevolence and the Buddhist practice of compassion, Vietnamese society had philosophical and religious support for charitable activities. The imperial state was keen to encourage private charity, as it provided society with cohesion and could help mitigate severe inequity that might lead to rebellions. By the nineteenth century, the Nguyễn monarchs had a system of granaries that were used to regulate grain price and supply (Nguyen-Marshall 2008: 23–26). In times of famine, granary rice could be used as low-interest loans or donations for the needy. Under the rule of Emperor Tự Đức (1847–1883), the local elite in the villages were tasked with building, supplying, and maintaining granaries. During French rule, colonial authorities dismantled this system. Nevertheless, some villages still maintained their granaries well into the 1920s (Nguyen-Marshall 2007: 164).

Vietnamese people continued to participate in public life during the French colonial period. While there were restrictions such as the requirement to register with the government and to avoid politics, Vietnamese were permitted to form self-help, social, cultural, and philanthropic associations. Since Vietnamese men and women were barred from political life, especially in Tonkin and Annam,[2] joining social and civic organizations offered entrée into public life.

Both secular and religious organizations existed and were popular. In the early twentieth century, both the Roman Catholic and Buddhist communities in Vietnam experienced a surge in the number of voluntary lay associations. This increase stemmed from global trends that influenced both religious traditions—namely, the Catholic Action and Buddhist Revival Movements. The Catholic Action Movement originated in the late nineteenth century, but its resurgence in the 1930s led to the creation of many lay Catholic organizations in colonial Vietnam. The Catholic hierarchy encouraged such development in order to assert more influence on the lay population. Participation in Catholic associational life allowed believers to engage with their faith and other coreligionists. Associational life also encouraged Catholics to carry out charitable and civic work in service of the broader society. As a result, many Catholic associations were founded. For example, the Society of Saint Vincent de Paul was established in 1933 to carry out charitable work throughout Tonkin (Keith 2012: 154). Catholic children and youths could join age-appropriate Catholic groups, such as the Catholic Boy and Girl Scouts, Catholic Youth Association, and Young Catholic Workers (Keith 2012: 156–160; Phan P. H. [1965] 2004). Many of these Catholic organizations continued to operate with vigor in the RVN.

Similarly, Vietnamese Buddhists saw a proliferation of many philanthropic and social organizations in the late colonial period as the result of the Buddhist Revival Movement. This transnational movement emerged from the perception that Buddhism needed modernization and reform. One of the many goals of the Revival Movement was to make Buddhism more relevant in society (DeVido 2009). To this end, Buddhists were encouraged to establish associations, engage with the wider society, and participate in social service. In the 1930s and 1940s, there was a proliferation of Buddhist organizations, including Buddhist associations for each of the regions of Tonkin, Annam, and Cochinchina. One particularly popular mass organization was the Buddhist Youth Family Movement (later known as Gia Đình Phật Giáo) (Nguyen T. V. 2006: 103). Founded in 1940, this organization provided ordinary Buddhists, including women, youth, and children, with a social network and a way to engage with one another and society. This organization would play an important role in South Vietnam's society and politics. In addition, many Buddhist women became active in founding associations, volunteering at pagoda schools and orphanages, fundraising to repair temples, and taking part in relief activities (DeVido 2014).

Secular voluntary organizations also existed during the French colonial period. In addition to forming cultural, social, and professional clubs, secular organizations founded charitable institutions and carried out social improvement projects. Among the earliest efforts were the Eastward Movement (Đông Du) and the Eastern Capital Free School (Đông Kinh Nghĩa Thục). Both were spearheaded by anticolonial scholars who aspired to make modern education more accessible (Marr 1971: Chaps. 6, 7). The former, established by Phan Bội Châu in 1907, was a program that sent youth to study in Japan, the center of modernity for East Asian reformers and revolutionaries at the turn of the twentieth century. The Eastern Capital Free School, associated with another prominent nationalist, Phan Châu Trinh, offered free classes to students on modern subjects in mathematics, languages, and science. Both endeavors were shut down by the colonial authorities, who discerned the nationalist agenda undergirding the undertakings. The supporters of these projects were indeed nationalists who believed that access to modern education was a prerequisite for any attempt to dislodge the French from Indochina.

Both of the above movements were short lived, but they had significant impacts on subsequent nationalist activities, such as the Quốc Ngữ (Vietnamese alphabet) movement. Determined to spread literacy in Quốc Ngữ among the masses, a group of fifteen intellectuals formed the Association for the Dissemination of Quốc Ngữ Study (Hội truyền bá học Quốc ngữ) in 1937. In its first year, 400 students of all ages enrolled, and this number jumped to 1,300 in 1939. By 1944 the association had forty-nine branches throughout Vietnam. The program depended on private donations and volunteer instructors. In 1944 the program had 1,971 volunteer teachers for its 59,827 students (Marr 1981: 180–181).

In addition to education and literacy, Vietnamese also established charities to care for orphans, support poor students, and provide disaster relief. By the 1920s, Vietnamese in urban areas were regularly entreated to contribute to civic and charitable projects. Newspapers such as *Women's News* (*Phụ nữ tân văn*), *French Asia* (*Báo đông pháp*), and *Women's Herald* (*Phụ nữ thời đàm*) took part in promoting various causes and in urging readers to contribute. The Great Depression (1929–1930) made many of these charities and fundraising events even more urgent. Among the first charitable childcare institutions founded and administered by Vietnamese people was the Dục Anh (Nurturing of Children) Society. Established in 1931 by a group of upper-middle-class women, this society ran two charitable daycare centers for children of laboring families (Nguyễn Ngọc Linh 1961: 371; Đào T. K. D. 1973). The society raised funds by canvassing for donations, holding charity fairs, operating a lottery, and running various businesses such as a bakery and a hair salon. This female-dominated charity continued operating until 1975, making it one of the longest-lasting charitable endeavors in South Vietnam.[3]

Another example of Vietnamese-led philanthropic activity was the League of Light (Đoàn Ánh Sáng), which was founded in 1936 by the influential literary group Tự Lực Văn Đoàn (Self-Strengthening Literary League). The League of Light sought to improve housing conditions for the rural poor. Inspired by a transnational modern reform movement, the League of Light was "arguably the largest philanthropic grassroots organization founded by Vietnamese" in the French period (Nguyen Martina Thucnhi 2016: 19).

The above discussion illustrates that during the colonial era Vietnamese activists accessed the public realm through their participation in charity and social work. Although out of necessity their voluntary endeavors were relatively conservative, these activities still held potential for subversion. Their associated participation provided opportunities to spread anticolonial messages, increase social cohesion, and demonstrate Vietnamese people's capability for administrative and governing duties.

Voluntarism in South Vietnam

With the long history of voluntary charitable and civic activities, it is not surprising that this tradition continued into the postcolonial period. After the signing of the Geneva Accords in 1954, the country was divided and people were allowed to move to the region of their choice. In the upheaval of decolonization and national division, people continued to participate in voluntary work.

Many colonial-era philanthropic activities continued to operate. The Dục Anh Society, for example, not only remained open but also expanded. In 1955 it ran an orphanage with 160 children and two daycare centers for 210 children. The society also held workshops to teach women embroidery, sewing, and cooking.[4] Even though the society employed paid workers, it still relied heavily on volunteers. By 1973, the society had thirty paid staff and twenty volunteers working at their various centers (Đào T. K. D. 1973: 25).

Some northern charities also relocated south after the division. Among those organizations was the An Lạc orphanage. A wealthy widow, Vũ Thị Ngãi, established this orphanage in Thanh Hóa province at the beginning of the First Indochina War (1946–1954). The orphanage began informally with Vũ Thị Ngãi taking in children who had been displaced or orphaned by the war. As the fighting spread to her hometown, she moved the orphanage first to Nam Định and then to Hải Phòng in 1949. By the time the orphanage relocated to the south, it was caring for over a thousand children. Weeks before the war ended on April 30, 1975, Vũ Thị Ngãi moved her orphanage once again—this time to the United States.[5]

Betty Tisdale, an American and a longtime supporter of the orphanage, was instrumental in helping evacuate Vũ Thị Ngãi and about two hundred children of An Lạc from South Vietnam. Known as the "Angel of Saigon," Tisdale has been celebrated in American society for her effort.[6] Like other stories about the "rescue and liberation" of Vietnamese refugees, as discussed in the Introduction, the narrative of Tisdale's work elides the U.S. contribution to the escalation of war. Also missing from this social memory are the many Vietnamese, specifically Vũ Thị Ngãi and other Vietnamese female volunteers who kept An Lạc running for decades. Consequently, in the narratives about the fall of Saigon, South Vietnamese people's agency was eclipsed by American humanitarian endeavors.

In addition to the many orphanages and charity daycare centers, South Vietnamese also founded other philanthropic institutions, such as care facilities for people with disabilities, leprosy, or mental illness (*Bản Thông Tin* [1971?]: 24–25). Both Catholic and Buddhist charitable organizations proliferated in the RVN. Christian aid organizations such as Caritas International, Catholic Relief Service, and the Mennonite Christian Service became involved in South Vietnam and founded many social service institutions, which were staffed by Vietnamese nuns and volunteers. The Daughters of Charity of Saint Vincent de Paul (Bác Ái Vinh Sơn), for example, were in charge of four Caritas facilities: a daycare, orphanage, social center, and nutrition center (Lê T. S. 1970: 20). Buddhist charitable facilities also increased. In 1959, the Vietnam Buddhist Charitable Association (Hội Từ Thiện Phật Giáo Việt Nam) was founded in Chợ Lớn, offering free primary schooling, sewing classes, and a Western and Eastern medical clinic (*Bản Thông Tin* [1971?]: 44). By 1965, the Vĩnh Nghiêm Buddhist pagoda in Saigon operated a charity clinic where patients paid a token fee for medical care. The clinic consisted of twelve rooms, including a laboratory and an X-ray facility (Lê T. S. 1970: Appendix; Nguyễn H. Q. 1973: 55).[7]

In addition to building care institutions and medical clinics, individuals and organizations also participated in relief activities for victims of war and natural disasters. People's response to the disaster caused by the 1964 typhoon season, considered at that time to be the worst in many decades, illustrated their readiness to work for the common good. The consecutive typhoons and subsequent floods destroyed 90 percent of homes in Quảng Tín province. These storms also flooded five million acres of land and killed seven thousand lives in the central provinces.[8] The government set up an interministerial committee to coordinate and oversee the relief effort, which lasted several months. Joining forces with the government were a wide range of organizations, including social clubs, religious groups, unions, youth associations, and women's organizations. Youths and students also participated by setting up their own youth committees, involving groups such as university student unions, Boy and Girl Scouts, the Catholic and Buddhist youth associations, Vietnam National Youth Voluntary Service (Đoàn Thanh Niên

Chí Nguyện Việt Nam), and the Youth Voluntary Association (Hội Thanh Niên Thiện Chí).[9] Volunteers helped mobilize support and collected material and monetary donations. Hundreds of student volunteers also went to the affected provinces to help set up temporary shelters, distribute aid, rebuild homes and roads, bury human and animal corpses, and provide basic medical care.

Volunteers also were needed in war-relief activities, particularly for refugee support. Along with the immense destruction to whole communities and the environment, the war caused massive numbers of internal refugees. Population displacement became more problematic when the war intensified in 1965, after the United States deployed combat troops and North Vietnam started mounting major offensives in the south. The fighting created nearly twelve million internal civilian refugees, who fled or were relocated because of the fighting (Wiesner 1988: xviii). During the two major communist offensives in 1968 and 1972 (the Tết and Easter Offensives, respectively), individuals and organizations played an important role in helping wounded and displaced individuals. In the aftermath of the Tết Offensive, for example, students volunteered to build shelters, distribute aid, and provide first aid. Some even volunteered with the Red Cross to collect the corpses from the streets (Chan Khong 2007: 107).

Similarly, following the Easter Offensive of 1972, many civilians participated in relief efforts. According to a U.S. embassy report, the attack created eight hundred thousand refugees in the first six weeks.[10] Because of the ongoing fighting, the "brunt of the [relief] effort had to be carried out largely by local officials and voluntary workers," such as the Vietnam Confederation of Labor and the Ấn Quang Buddhist Welfare Organization, and private groups.[11] People from all sectors of society contributed in a variety of ways. The faculty of Saigon University, for example, spearheaded a campaign in which members donated one day's pay to a refugee fund. Saigon University students put on a fundraising variety show, while Vạn Hạnh University students canvassed 500,000 đồng in donations.[12] The daily newspaper Sống Thần initiated a massive project to collect and bury close to two thousand corpses along Highway One between Quảng Trị and Huế, where fleeing civilians and military personnel had been attacked (Nguyen-Marshall 2018). People ranging from wealthy merchants to illiterate market women donated funds for this project.

Disaster- and war-relief efforts like those discussed above brought together people and groups with diverse sociopolitical standings and views. Outside of these cooperative occasions, some groups' relationships with the state, and indeed with other groups, were at times antagonistic. Student unions of Saigon and Huế Universities, for example, often staged demonstrations to voice their opposition to various government policies that affected students, such as the expansion of the draft and imposition of military training for high school students. As Wynn Gadkar-Wilcox's chapter in this volume reveals, academics in South Vietnam were relatively free to express their views. There were, however, some limitations, and when restrictions proved unbearable or unreasonable, academics, along with writers and publishers, countered by organizing protests. Students and academics would use their publications and associations to speak out against censorship as well as other issues, such as the war, corruption, American intervention, and poverty. Indeed, South Vietnam's civil society was an arena where groups with diverse views and goals coexisted, competed, and sometimes collaborated.

Another group of actors in South Vietnam's civil society comprised agents of the U.S. government and foreign aid agencies. These foreign entities attempted to influence society by providing funds and advice to select groups and projects. In addition to the international Christian organizations mentioned above, many nonprofit humanitarian and development organizations operated in South Vietnam. These included the International Rescue Committee (IRC), the American Red Cross, and Asia Foundation. By 1971 there were thirty-three American nongovernmental organizations (NGOs) working in South Vietnam. Their combined budget for 1970 was $12.6 million.[13] In addition to these NGOs, the U.S. government was also prolific in funding social aid. From 1955 to 1975, the United States spent $87.7 million on relief and rehabilitation and another $267.4 million on social development (i.e., health, sanitation, and education; Dacy 1986: 206–208). Some Vietnamese philanthropic organizations and humanitarian projects received funds, material aid, and technical support from these NGOs and the U.S. government.

While some Vietnamese endeavors benefited from foreign funding, foreign support sometimes came with negative consequences. One was the growing dependence on foreign aid, and another was the development of a "psychology of abundance" (Carter 2008: 227). According to American officials who investigated corruption, this mindset discouraged spendthrift and contributed to the lack of oversight. As a result, aid was often wasted and misused. This in turn contributed to a more general and pervasive problem of corruption in South Vietnam, which became worse as the war dragged on. Historians have cited many instances of corruption, such as aid not reaching the intended target but instead ending up in the black market. It is important to note that Vietnamese were not the only ones implicated in corruption. Americans also took part in theft of aid, along with other corrupt activities (Herring 2002: 198; Carter 2008: 227).

Vietnamese themselves were cognizant of the problem of corruption in humanitarian work and were highly critical of it. Vietnamese journalists, writers, and scholars were keen to denounce the issue of corruption in general, and with regard to aid in particular. Newspapers often carried reports of corruption, particularly when it involved government officials. Even student newspapers did not shy away from exposing such abuses. During the 1964 flood-relief effort, for example, the Huế student union newspaper published a scathing article denouncing government mismanagement and misuse of aid.[14] One daily newspaper, *Sóng Thần*, was actually founded for the sole purpose of uncovering corruption. In other words, while corruption did exist, there were also many in the RVN who condemned it and tried to stem this problem. Some organizations, such as the School of Youth for Social Service (discussed below), were discriminating when it came to aid; the school's leadership had a policy of not accepting support from agencies with political agendas or links to a government.

Nation-Building Endeavors

In addition to supporting the vulnerable population, such as orphans and refugees, many residents of South Vietnam also tried to contribute to social development. This section focuses on two among many development endeavors that were spearheaded by Vietnamese: the Popular Polytechnic Institute and the Buddhist School for Social Service. The former focused on education and the latter on community development.[15]

The Popular Polytechnic Institute

The Popular Polytechnic Institute (Trường Bách Khoa Bình Dân, hereafter PPI) was a nonprofit voluntary project that offered free night classes to adults on a variety of academic subjects and basic literacy. This institute was one of the many undertakings of the Popular Culture Association (Hôi Bách Khoa Bình Dân), which also published a respected journal, *Bách Khoa*. As Gadkar-Wilcox notes in this collection, *Bách Khoa* journal aimed to contribute to nation building by offering a pluralistic and tolerant forum for social, intellectual, and cultural discussion. The Popular Culture Association also built cultural centers and libraries throughout Vietnam. Founded in October 1954, the PPI (and its parent organization, the Popular Culture Association) was an initiative of a group of young, university-educated men. Many of the founders had foreign graduate degrees and promising career prospects.[16] Some had heeded the call of the new prime minister, Ngô Đình Diệm, to return to Vietnam to help build the new nation (Huỳnh V. L. 2008). The creation of this free school, which occurred within three months of the signing of the Geneva Accords, was one response to this call.

In their desire to contribute to nation building, the PPI founders identified education as an underdeveloped sector needing attention. In this approach, they reflected the thinking of those scholar patriots of the late nineteenth and early twentieth century. According to one founding member, Huỳnh Văn Lang, he and his colleagues were inspired by Vietnam's many modernizers and educators, such as Nguyễn Trường Tộ (1830–1871), Trương Vĩnh Ký (1837–1898), and Phan Châu Trinh (1872–1926) (Huỳnh V. L. 2008). These were important Vietnamese nationalist figures who contributed to modernizing education in Vietnam. Although both Nguyễn Trường Tộ and Trương Vĩnh Ký worked with the colonial government in various capacities, their writings, translations, and publishing efforts helped to modernize, educate, and inform Vietnamese society. Phan Châu Trinh, as mentioned above, played a major role in the founding of the Eastern Capital Free School, an obvious model for the PPI. In evoking these nationalist educators, Lang was suggesting that he and his colleagues were following in their steps.

In contrast to the Eastern Capital Free School, the PPI had a longer life. The PPI operated from 1954 to 1975, while the Eastern Capital Free School was closed within a year. Because of its longevity, the PPI taught hundreds of thousands of students. When it first opened, the PPI organizers were expecting several hundred people to enroll, but instead, 8,000 students applied. The institute quickly expanded its capacity and was able to accept 1,500 students in the first session.[17] In the second session, which started in May 1955, the institute was able to accommodate 1,869 students. The high demand prompted the Popular Culture Association to open more teaching centers in the Saigon-Cholon area. In the following years, sixteen association chapters along with the associated PPI were established in other cities and towns throughout South Vietnam.[18]

The popularity of the PPI attested to the South Vietnamese population's desire for education but also to the inadequacy of the Franco-indigenous education of the previous era. By 1943, only 8 percent of school-age children attended school, while a large majority were illiterate (Nguyen Phuong Thuy 2014: 28). Moreover, the education available for local children was anachronistic and parochial. Rather than preparing students for the modern world, the Franco-indigenous schools emphasized outdated and conservative notions of Vietnamese culture and values (Kelly 2000: 11–19). It is therefore not surprising that the PPI attracted many Vietnamese to its offerings of free classes on modern subjects such as literature and grammar, economics and business, politics and society, science and technology, languages, and physical education.

In the early days of the PPI, three-quarters of the students were male and one-third were employees at private and public enterprises.[19] The introduction of the adult literacy program in August 1955 no doubt changed the demography of the student population. One could expect a higher number of unskilled and underemployed students enrolled in the literacy program. In fact, this program was very popular, attracting close to two thousand students in the first session. The PPI became even more popular in 1961, when it started offering Ministry of Education–approved primary and secondary school equivalency diplomas and national exam preparatory courses (Hội Văn Hóa Bình Dân 1967: 40).

The association's accomplishments over the next thirteen years were remarkable. By 1967 courses were offered at six different centers throughout the Saigon-Cholon area alone and involved over one hundred volunteer instructors during any academic session, many of whom were teachers, professionals, or technical experts. From 1954 until 1967, the PPI in Saigon taught twenty-five sessions to 43,329 students. In addition, the adult-education program graduated 84,065 students from 1955 until 1967 (Hội Văn Hóa Bình Dân 1967: 10). These figures do not include the number of students who graduated from the association's sixteen regional chapters or data for the period 1967–1975.[20]

Given its achievements, it is astonishing that the institute and the association have received little attention in the historiography. With the exception of the association's influential *Bách Khoa* journal, little mention has been made of the association's work in mass education. One possible reason is that the association's close connection to the RVN and U.S. authorities might have tainted it, making its work appear to be an American-led project or a U.S. propaganda stunt rather than a genuine effort by Vietnamese to effect improvement.

Indeed, there were strong links between the association's leadership and the RVN and U.S. governments. As mentioned earlier, the founding members were highly educated and privileged. Huỳnh Văn Lang, for example, worked in the Ministry of Finance and later was the director of the Foreign Exchange. More importantly, Lang was a high-ranking member of the Cần Lao Party, the secret and powerful party of Ngô Đình Diệm's brother, Ngô Đình Nhu.[21] Another leading member, Đỗ Trọng Chu, served in the Office of the General Commissioner for Refugees and then in 1960 joined the Foreign Service (Nguyễn N. N. 2014). Chu's wife, Trần Thị Mẫu, who was the director of a PPI in Gia Định, was an elected member of South Vietnam's first Constituent Assembly. While the leadership had strong connections with the government, the army of volunteers who sustained the program were ordinary people, albeit of the educated class.

The close connection with the RVN government certainly facilitated the establishment of the PPI. It also helped the Popular Culture Association mobilize financial and material aid. The association received substantial aid from both the government and foreign aid agencies. In 1954, the institute received approximately 43,000 *đồng*[22] from the government and another 30,000 *đồng* from the IRC. By 1956, the Asia Foundation became a supporter of the PPI as well, providing more financial aid to the association.[23]

As the PPI expanded, the government and foreign aid agencies provided more financial help.

In their politics, both the IRC and the Asia Foundation were closely aligned with the U.S. government. Both organizations shared the U.S. government's aspiration of keeping South Vietnam noncommunist and within the U.S. sphere of influence. Founded in 1933 to provide relief to refugees worldwide, the IRC actively supported the Ngô Đình Diệm government when the country was divided. One of the IRC's founding members, Joseph Buttinger, was especially instrumental in helping Diệm gain American support (Chester 1995: 160–162). In a similar manner, the Asia Foundation had a "parallel agenda" with the U.S. government in wanting to keep Asia free from communism (Chou 2010: 23). In fact, the U.S. government, specifically the National Security Council, selected and approved the slate of founding members when the Asia Foundation was first established. These organizations' intimate relationships with the U.S. government were brought to light in 1967 when it was uncovered that both the Asia Foundation and American Friends of Vietnam were receiving indirect CIA funding (Chou 2010: 23; Chester 1995: 165–178; McGarr 2004: 1046–1047).

The IRC and Asia Foundation saw in the Popular Culture Association an ally, whose work would raise the level of education of the masses while taking the initiative away from communists, who had "been allowed to initiate and control popular education movements."[24] The IRC therefore argued strongly that the U.S. Operations Mission (USOM) in Saigon should support the expansion of the association's activities. IRC officials averred that the PPI was carrying out useful nation-building activities.[25] In the IRC's reports and retrospective publications, it is clear that the organization saw the PPI as an IRC achievement. The success of the PPI and other activities of the Popular Culture Association were invariably highlighted in these publications. In the IRC's thirty-nine-page report on its global accomplishments over a period of thirty years (1933–1963), two entire paragraphs were devoted to the PPI. This was significant coverage considering that only two pages were devoted to all of Asia.[26]

Despite the synchronicity between the Popular Culture Association and U.S. state-building objectives in the RVN, this was a Vietnamese initiative, motivated not only by leaders' perceptions about education and its role in society but also by examples rooted in Vietnamese history. The PPI leaders found inspiration in late nineteenth-century scholar-patriots who promoted education as a way to make Vietnam strong and capable of challenging French colonial rule. Moreover, when considering the other participants in the PPI— namely, the thousands of volunteer instructors, support staff, and students— it is clear that this endeavor was propelled by ordinary Vietnamese, who were responding to a genuine need in society. The PPI operated for over two decades, serving people who wanted to improve their education, skills, and prospects.

Buddhist School of Youth for Social Service

A decade after the PPI was established, Zen monk Thích Nhất Hạnh founded the Buddhist School of Youth for Social Service (SYSS). Like the PPI, the SYSS sought to contribute to nation building, but in a more comprehensive way. The school trained young Buddhist volunteers to carry out development work in villages. Student volunteers received two years of in-class instruction and field training before being sent to various villages, where they were committed to work for at least three years. The SYSS was strongly committed to the community development approach, emphasizing the importance of grassroots initiatives, local participation, and sustainable, small-scale projects.[27]

The SYSS was an emblematic manifestation of Thích Nhất Hạnh's philosophy of engaged Buddhism, which in turn was rooted in the Buddhist Revival Movement discussed above. Under the First Republic, the Buddhist Revival Movement—which aimed to make the religion more relevant and central in society and in national politics—gained urgency. Some Buddhist leaders feared that President Ngô Đình Diệm, whose family had strong connections to the Catholic hierarchy, was favoring Catholics and transforming Vietnam into a Catholic nation (Pham V. M. 2001: 14). Buddhist anxieties were intensified when nearly six hundred thousand Catholics migrated south in 1954 after the signing of the Geneva Accords. The RVN government's attempt to settle migrants deepened suspicion about Diệm's bias toward Catholics. The underlying tension between Diệm and the Buddhist community exploded in 1963 when his government's restrictions on the display of religious flags provoked mass Buddhist protests, which in turn led to harsh state crackdowns.

President Diệm's poor handling of the Buddhist Protest Movement damaged his credibility and authority and undoubtedly contributed to the coup against him on November 2, 1963. Following his overthrow, the Revival Movement continued to be important in guiding many Buddhist groups. The Unified Buddhist Congregation was formed in 1964, fulfilling one Revival goal of unifying Buddhists and strengthening their position in society. Thích Nhất Hạnh was a strong advocate in the Revival Movement since the 1950s, using his position as editor of the *Vietnamese Buddhism* (Phật Giáo Việt Nam) journal to promote reform and the concept of engaged Buddhism (Nguyen, T. V. 2006, 123–4). Thích Nhất Hạnh played an important role in the founding of Vạn Hạnh, the first Buddhist University in Vietnam in 1964. The SYSS, which officially opened in 1965, reflected the aspirations and goals of Thích

Nhất Hạnh and the larger endeavor to reform the religion and strengthen its influence.

The SYSS curriculum integrated rural development and Buddhist studies. Students were taught about education, economics, public health, and organization. The curriculum also emphasized the importance of self-reliance, empowerment, and social justice. Students learned that their roles were not only to improve people's living conditions but also to stimulate consciousness, which would lead to a social revolution that was based on Buddhist beliefs of "love, wisdom, cooperation, and communication."[28] In line with the philosophy of community development, local participation and volunteerism were critical to the work of development. With regard to village participation, SYSS cadres were not there to "do" development but to help villagers articulate their needs and help them plan and execute the work. The villagers were not the objects but the agents of development. Before SYSS cadres could hope to carry out their work, they needed to spend long periods in the village—to be like fish in water—in order to gain trust and acceptance.[29]

Volunteerism was an important component of the SYSS, with regard to not only the villagers but also the students. SYSS workers were not paid wages but were expected to subsist with support from the local community. In fact, like the PPI, the school operated by volunteers. Besides the four full-time employees, the rest of the administrative, support, and teaching staff were volunteers. The school also relied on volunteers to raise funds to build and maintain the school and to provide modest scholarships for students. Since the school had a policy against accepting aid from governments or political organizations, fundraising was an important source of revenue for the school. According to Sister Chân Không (Cao Ngọc Phượng), the school was once offered funding from the Asia Foundation, but to get the money, the school had to distance itself from its own founder (Chan Khong 2007: 90–92). By 1966, Thích Nhất Hạnh had become a prominent advocate for a peaceful resolution to the war. While this might appear to be a moderate stance, particularly for a religious leader, at the height of the Cold War, his call for peace was controversial. For the RVN authorities, Thích Nhất Hạnh's political views were treasonous. As a result, his passport was revoked when he was visiting the United States, and he was essentially exiled. The SYSS director, Thích Thanh Văn, did not disavow the school founder, and so the Asia Foundation withdrew its funding offer.

The two development projects examined in this section were clearly different from each other. They differed in their political outlooks, approaches to development, and respective relationships to the state and foreign donors. More politically conservative and supportive of the status quo, the Popular Culture Association was mainly concerned with raising people's level of education and culture. The association leaders were happy to accept funding from the government, the United States, and international aid agencies, since these entities shared the association's goal of building a noncommunist South Vietnam. In contrast, the SYSS leaders aspired to transform society through a combination of Buddhist and community development philosophies. For the SYSS founder, achieving peace was central to addressing issues of poverty and development, and therefore the SYSS rejected aid from political entities that supported the war. Despite their differences, both projects lasted until 1975 and attracted thousands of volunteers and supporters, who were the backbone of these endeavors. The longevity of the two projects indicates that there were many who supported their goals and aspirations; supporters' volunteerism also showed that they were strongly committed to the respective endeavor's vision of nation building.

Conclusion

The many voluntary projects that Vietnamese people established and maintained in the RVN illustrate that South Vietnamese were active in the public realm. People voluntarily engaged in a diverse range of public and associated activities that reflected individuals' political, religious, and social views. Participants had many choices for public engagement. First of all, they had the choice of whether or not to participate. Secondly, participants could decide on both the content and scope of their involvement. In other words, people generally made conscious choices with regard to their associational activities. Thus, people's choices provide some insight into their priorities, commitments, and aspirations. Whether they volunteered at an orphanage, free school, refugee camp, or community development project is suggestive of their views regarding the needs of society, obligations of citizens, and nation building.

Participants' motivations were undoubtedly also diverse. Some participants were driven by personal needs, such as to protect their livelihoods in times of upheaval. Some became involved to forge social connections in order to improve their personal socioeconomic standing. Still others were probably motivated by altruistic sentiments, religious beliefs, or patriotic desires. These motivations were not exclusive and more than likely overlapped in many cases.

As the practice of self-support and community activism has a long history in Vietnam, it is not surprising that these practices were continued when South Vietnamese resettled in disparate lands after 1975. In the United States, Vietnamese Americans quickly established old and new social networks to provide mutual aid, charity, and development assistance, as Ivan Small and Elwing Suong Gonzalez's chapters in this volume show. Vietnamese American religious lay organizations, service groups (such as the scouts), business associations, alumni groups, literary societies, and cultural groups were founded wherever there were large Vietnamese populations. As in the case of South Vietnam, Vietnamese associational life in the United States is diverse, reflecting the plurality of views and concerns of the Vietnamese diaspora. In their activism and rich associational life, Vietnamese Americans, like those in the RVN, defied the narrow stereotypes often imposed on them. They are a diverse group of people, many of whom actively sought ways to shape their lives, to help each other, and to aid the wider community.

Archives

National Archives II (Trung Tâm Lưu Trữ Quốc Gia), Ho Chi Minh City, Vietnam

- Presidential Office Document, First Republic, 1955–1963
- Presidential Office Document, Second Republic, 1967–1975
- Prime Minister's Office Document, 1954–1975, Vietnam National Archive, II

General Sciences Library, Ho Chi Minh City, Vietnam

- Restricted collection on the Republic of Vietnam

Vietnam Center and Sam Johnson Vietnam Archive, Virtual Vietnam Archive, Texas Tech University

3

UNIVERSITIES AND INTELLECTUAL CULTURE
IN THE REPUBLIC OF VIETNAM

Wynn Gadkar-Wilcox

Introduction

Among the more than two hundred thousand people who escaped by boat from Vietnam in the late 1970s were a disproportionate number of Vietnamese intellectuals and their families (Vo N. M. 2004/2015: 167). Because many intellectuals were subject to particularly brutal treatment in reeducation camps after the fall of Saigon in 1975, they were more likely to flee (Huynh J. Q. and Cargill 2015: 3). Many of these intellectuals found that language barriers, discrimination, and a skeptical view of their Vietnamese qualifications made it difficult to continue their academic careers in a formal way on reaching their destinations, including the United States. However, they kept their careers alive by founding publishing houses, writing in newspapers and journals, and establishing literary societies or keeping those formed in Vietnam alive in their new home.[1]

Understanding the experiences of Vietnamese Americans requires a clear and thorough comprehension of the milieu of the Republic of Vietnam from which they emerged. This chapter examines this environment from the perspective of the intellectual culture of the newly founded universities in the South. The journals, literary societies, and cultural groups that were associated with this new university culture were very different. Some were affiliated with particular religions, such as Catholicism, Buddhism, or the millenarian Buddhist Hòa Hảo religion, with its origins in the Mekong Delta. Some were politically radical, while others were more conservative, and still others hardly touched on politics at all.

Despite these differences, South Vietnam's intellectual culture had four prominent features. First, it was cosmopolitan. Universities, and the journals they spawned, sought out faculty, ideas, and opinions from around the world. The Republic of Vietnam's intellectuals were obsessed with novel foreign ideas and sought to understand Vietnamese culture and history through new and innovative lenses. Second, it was modernist. Intellectuals strove to have a vision of the future and argued about what policies would lead to a path of economic and cultural growth for their country. Third, it was influenced by French cultural and intellectual trends in the 1950s and early 1960s, and then more prominently by American trends from the mid-1960s to 1975. Fourth, it was noncommunist and republican in orientation, while rarely being explicitly anticommunist.[2] As Tuan Hoang's chapter in this volume indicates, this noncommunism, rather than virulent anticommunism, distinguishes intellectuals at universities from some religious groups, such as Catholics, Hòa Hảo, and Cao Đài, and some political parties, such as the Đại Việt Party, which adopted anticommunist postures much earlier.[3] Even for intellectuals, the noncommunism of the intellectuals in the Republic of Vietnam often developed into a more full-throated anticommunism among Vietnamese who fled to the United States after 1975. Nevertheless, the other aspects of intellectual culture—cosmopolitanism, modernism, and an appreciation for cultural borrowing from French and American cultures—remained a legacy on which future generations of Vietnamese Americans built, creating a bridge between the history of the Republic of Vietnam and the history of Vietnamese Americans. Appreciating this legacy is another way to understand the vibrancy and pluralism of Vietnamese civil society in the RVN period and to appreciate the agency of the Vietnamese who worked to construct this society in the Republic, as Van Nguyen-Marshall notes.[4]

To elucidate these themes, this chapter examines the conditions under which universities were established (or reestablished) in the Republic of Vietnam between 1954 and 1975; examines the influence of the major journals, particularly those focusing on the humanities and social sciences, that emerged from those universities; and then reflects on particularly influential figures.

The Development of the University of Saigon after the Geneva Accords (1954–1963)

The original university of the Republic of Vietnam was the National University of Vietnam, which became the University of Saigon in 1957. This university had its origins in the *Université Indochinoise*, a university in French Colonial Indochina that was designed to replace the imperial civil service examination system. The *Université Indochinoise* was originally founded in

1906, but political disruptions in 1907–1908 left it stillborn. It was recreated in 1917. In 1949, a joint agreement between the French government and the new, noncommunist State of Vietnam, led by the ex-emperor Bảo Đại, created a new University of Hanoi out of the old *Université Indochinoise,* co-run by a joint French and Vietnamese faculty, with a smaller branch in Saigon.

The signing of the Geneva Accords in July 1954 left the main campus of the University of Hanoi under the jurisdiction of the communist government. For that reason, most of the faculty and about 85 percent of the students moved to the Saigon branch campus of the university. They joined more than eight hundred thousand other emigrants from the north who took advantage of Article 14(d) of the accords, which provided for the free movement between the northern and southern regions of Vietnam for the first three hundred days after the accords commenced (Hansen 2009: 178–179).

This period of travel and transition left the university in some disarray. On May 11, 1955, however, the French officially turned over the Ministry of Education of the Vietnamese government in Saigon, at which point it ceased to be a joint Franco-Vietnamese institution and became the National University of Vietnam. After the establishment of the University of Huế as the second "national university" in March 1957, the name of the National University was changed to the University of Saigon. The new university was in the capable hands of its new rector, Nguyễn Quang Trình, who was a professor of physics on the faculty.

Nguyễn Quang Trình had acquired a Ph.D. in physics at the Sorbonne in 1943. Returning to Vietnam by 1953, he joined the faculty of the University of Hanoi and was elected dean of the Faculty of Science in 1954 before being named its first Vietnamese rector in 1955. Nguyễn Quang Trình took over an educational institution that was rapidly changing. Though French faculty continued to be a major part of the University of Saigon through the 1950s and early 1960s and the first-year course in French literature was retained, most instruction rapidly transitioned from French to Vietnamese, and more Vietnamese faculty were recruited as they returned from studying in Europe. This was a period of rapid growth for the University of Saigon. From 1954 to 1962, its enrollment went from around two thousand to nearly thirteen thousand students (Jones 1962).

The new professors at the University of Saigon were generally free from excessive interference from the Ngô Đình Diệm regime. This freedom was not total. During the height of the Buddhist crisis in 1963, for example, the Diệm regime took decisive action against student and Buddhist protests. They arrested students involved in the protests, beat the protesters, and temporarily shut down the universities (Jacobs 2006: 153–154). In 1965, the Phan Huy Quát government removed philosophy and literature professor Nguyễn Đăng Thục (1909–1999) from his post at the University of Saigon for signing

a petition calling on the Republic of Vietnam government to negotiate with
the pro-communist National Liberation Front (NLF), but he was able to obtain a similar position as a professor at Vạn Hạnh University less than two
years later (Đỗ Đ. H. et al. 2004: 1149). Researchers could also occasionally
run afoul of government censors, but in comparison to the censors in the
Democratic Republic in the North, this was a relatively rare occurrence.[5]

In 1961, the Diệm administration—using Diệm's older brother Ngô Đình
Thục, the archbishop of Huế, as an intermediary—pressured the University
of Huế to transfer philosophy professor Nguyễn Văn Trung to the University of Saigon, possibly because he was part of a group of professors with academic degrees from the University of Louvain in Belgium whom the Diệm
regime considered too sympathetic to Marxism (Hoang T. 2013: 475–476). A
similar circumstance occasioned the transfer of Cao Văn Luận, the rector of
the University of Huế, to a faculty position at the University of Saigon in 1963.

In general, however, professors were free to write and think as they wished.
The relative autonomy afforded the university resulted in the proliferation
of academic journals both formally and informally associated with universities. In the case of the University of Saigon, the Faculty of Medicine, Faculty of Science, and Faculty of Law each eventually put out their own formal
journal publications (University of Saigon 1967: 240). But perhaps the most
significant of these formally affiliated journals was *Đại Học Văn Khoa*, the
Annals of the Faculty of Letters at the university, which was published by the
university and the Ministry of Education starting with the 1957–1958 issue.

The pages of *Đại Học Văn Khoa* give a glimpse of the cosmopolitan nature of both the faculty and the ideas circulating among the Faculty of Letters at the University of Saigon at the time. The faculty featured a number of
luminaries among Vietnamese intellectuals. Nguyễn Đình Hòa (1924–2000),
who was freshly returning to Vietnam after completing a Ph.D. at New York
University and who would later become a teacher of Vietnamese language
and literature at Southern Illinois University in the United States, taught
many of the classes in linguistics ("Ban Giảng-Huấn, 1957–8" 1958). Nguyễn
Đăng Thục joined him in teaching Vietnamese language and literature, as
well as teaching classes in philosophy and directing the administration.

Trương Bửu Lâm (b. 1933) returned to Vietnam in 1957 after completing
a Ph.D. dissertation on the nineteenth-century relations between Belgium
and Japan at the University of Louvain, which was at the time a major conduit for Vietnamese intellectuals. He taught historiography and Vietnamese
history (Truong-buu-lam 1955; 1957). He was joined in teaching history by
the Renaissance man Bùi Quang Tung (1912–2001), who had by that time
already enjoyed illustrious careers as an attorney and as a Sinologist for the
Ecole Française d'Extrême-Orient, in addition to being a historian of Vietnam. (In the early 1960s, Bùi Quang Tung would leave Saigon to become a

professor of public administration, attorney, and diplomat in Gabon and Zaire. He would eventually retire to Paris [Thai V. K. 2001].)

These new Vietnamese faculty members were joined by a host of French and American instructors, many of whom were also new. The French instructors who continued from the University of Hanoi included Alexandre Mavrocordato, a professor of literature and philosophy of Greek, Hungarian, and French origin whose mother was a direct descendant of Louis XVI. Mavrocordato (who used only his last name in many of his writings) had come to Saigon from a career in Morocco, was fluent in many languages, and frequently served as a translator for articles in *Đại học văn khoa* and other journals.

The Americans on the faculty of the University of Saigon were primarily those sponsored by the Michigan State University Advisory Group and the United States Agency for International Development (USAID). Organized by a chance meeting between Michigan State University professor Wesley Fishel (1919–1977) and future president of the Republic of Vietnam Ngô Đình Diệm in 1951, the advisory group became a major supplier of technical assistance to the Republic of Vietnam, as a conduit for USAID funding. One of the Michigan State group's primary functions in these early years was to provide professors on a visiting basis for the University of Saigon and to bring professors from the university back to Michigan State for training (Ernst 1998: 8–9).

Michigan State professors sent to the University of Saigon included the rather extraordinary Father Robert Crawford, a Vincentian priest from Philadelphia who had a Ph.D. in theology and taught philosophy and English at the university starting in 1955. When not teaching, Crawford ran an orphanage for Vietnamese youths with polio. In 1975, about a week before the fall of Saigon and the unification of Vietnam, he bribed the guards at Tân Sơn Nhất airport and flew the orphans out on an unauthorized World Airways plane, which eventually landed in Oakland. After that, he whisked the orphans to Oregon, where he designed a new orphanage out of an abandoned beer hall.

The Michigan State Advisory Group also assisted the US Office of Education's Division for International Education in bringing University of Saigon professors to the United States for training. In June 1956, Rector Nguyễn Quang Trình traveled to Michigan State to investigate U.S. university operations. Michigan State president John Hannah hosted him and facilitated his visits with the university's students and faculty.[6] This visit prompted Nguyễn Quang Trình to request the U.S. Department of State's assistance in funding visiting professors to come to teach American literature, microbiology, political science, and modern architecture.[7]

The Michigan State group was intimately connected to another significant nongovernmental organization: the American Friends of Vietnam, which featured Wesley Fishel as "one of its most active officers" (Morgan 1997: 83). The American Friends of Vietnam was founded in 1955 by a group of prominent individuals in the United States, including Cardinal Francis Spellman, Justice William O. Douglas, and Senators Mike Mansfield and John F. Kennedy. Many of these luminaries had met Diệm during his trip to the United States in the early 1950s. They were favorably impressed by him and were convinced of the need to help him build a noncommunist Vietnam (Morgan 1997: viii–ix). In 1957, thanks to the American Friends of Vietnam and the Division of International Education of the U.S. Office of Education, eight faculty members from Saigon came to the United States to observe students and training.[8]

The writings of the professors at the University of Saigon—at least those from the Faculty of Letters—reveal the same global, cosmopolitan spirit that these exchanges would suggest. The first pages of *Đại học văn khoa* featured a French-language article by the dean of the Faculty of Letters, Nguyễn Huy Bảo, a graduate in international law from the old Faculty of Law at the Sorbonne. The article, which was also offered in an English translation by Professor Alexandre Mavrocordato, is entitled "Eastern Values, Western Values, and Human Values." In an essay larded with references to luminaries of European thought, including Rudyard Kipling, Paul Valéry, George W. M. Reynolds, André Siegfried, Paul Claudel, Hippolyte Taine, and Jean-Jacques Rousseau, Nguyễn Huy Bảo claims that Western and Eastern values sharply contrast but that civilizations around the world should embrace the best parts of both.

Articles like this from the new university in Saigon contributed to an already-dynamic intellectual milieu. In his memoir, Nguyễn Đình Hòa recalls that the "increase in vernacular publishing" in this "exciting cultural atmosphere" resulted in the popularity of such journals as *Văn-hoá ngày nay* (Culture Today), *Phổ Thông* (Popularity), *Văn hữu* (Literature and Friendship), *Bách Khoa* (Polytechnic), *Sáng Tạo* (Creativity), *Trẻ* (Youth), and *Thế kỷ 20* (Twentieth Century). These journals covered an astounding array of new and stimulating topics (Nguyen D. H. 1999: 159–160). The inaugural January 1957 issue of *Bách Khoa*, which established that the journal was intended to contribute to the development of the nation by offering a variety of perspectives, both highbrow and lowbrow, from religions and cultures from across the world.[9] *Bách Khoa* would feature a dizzying array of topics, from jazz music in American culture to the poetry of Saint-Exupéry, along with discussions of minority cultures, including Islam, in Vietnam (Nguyễn Văn Trung 1958; Dohamide 1965).

Additionally, personalism exercised considerable influence on the Republic of Vietnam in the 1950s. Personalism is best known as the official ideology of the Ngô Đình Diệm regime, mostly articulated and developed by Diệm's brother Ngô Đình Nhu (1910–1963), on the basis of the ideas of French Catholic philosopher Emmanuel Mounier (1905–1950). It has been described as "a form of communitarianism that aimed to split the ideological differences between liberal individualism and Marxist collectivism" (Miller 2013: 138). But personalism is also more than that description implies. It encompasses ideas from other (predominantly French) thinkers who were also read in Vietnam in this period, including Gabriel Marcel, Jean Lacroix, and Maurice Nédoncelle. Moreover, these thinkers continued to be read and commented on after the end of the Diệm regime. Duy Lap Nguyen (2020: 51–84) has recently helpfully reframed personalism as a kind of anticolonial Marxist humanism. In fact, Mounier cautioned that anticommunism is a "sufficient crystallizing force for a return to fascism" (Judt 2006: 215). His philosophy was a critique of Stalinism and capitalism from within the Marxist tradition, as a means to cure Marxism of its Stalinist error and reshape it in humanist form so that capitalism could be defeated. That ideology is at the heart of the personalism of the Diệm regime, and its influence can be clearly seen in the writing of leftist intellectuals in the Republic of Vietnam up until 1975.

The Formation of Huế University and the University of Dalat, 1957–1963

In view of the success of the new national university in Saigon, pressure began to build on the Diệm government to found an institution of higher education to serve the people of central Vietnam. In 1956, Diệm sent representatives from the Ministry of Education along with Rector Nguyễn Quang Trình to investigate conditions in Huế. They found that central Vietnam did not have sufficient capacity at that time to support an autonomous university, and they suggested that a Huế branch of the national university be founded. This Huế branch would be under the supervision of Nguyễn Quang Trình as rector, but the day-to-day operations would be run by the famed priest and educator Father Paul Cao Văn Luận (1908–1986).

Cao Văn Luận, who likely did not care for that arrangement, lobbied against it. He argued that the flaws in communication systems between Huế and Saigon would produce unnecessary delays and complications. After two months, Diệm's administration relented. On March 1, 1957, a fully independent university, a "second national university" with equivalent status to the University of Saigon, was established in Huế by Ngô Đình Diệm's presidential decree, with Father Cao Văn Luận to serve as rector (Cao V. L. 1972: 280–281; Trương T. D. 2020: 205–206). At that point, the University of Saigon, which had formally been called the "National University of Viet Nam," took on its informal name, and Huế University was born.

Cao Văn Luận was born in Hương Sơn district in Hà Tĩnh province to a prominent Catholic family of north-central Vietnam in 1907, though his files incorrectly record his birth date as 1908 (Vũ L. T. 1997: 23). He was initially educated at the Pellerin School in Huế. Then in 1933, he traveled to Hanoi to study at the Saint-Sulpice (Xuân Bích) seminary, where he received his baccalaureate degree in 1939. Almost immediately, he went to Paris to study at the Catholic Institute of the Sorbonne, where he graduated with a degree in literature and philosophy in 1942. In 1945, he earned a degree in Chinese from the School of Oriental Languages in Paris. The young priest returned to Vietnam in 1947 and ministered to the Catholics of Tuyên Hóa district of Quảng Bình province in north-central Vietnam. Then in 1949, he became a teacher at the famed Quốc Học School in Huế—a school that counted both Hồ Chí Minh and Ngô Đình Diệm as alumni.

In 1957, when Ngô Đình Diệm approached Cao Văn Luận with a proposal for him to become rector, Diệm emphasized both the cultural and strategic importance of Huế as reasons to found a university there. Culturally, as the former capital with long-standing academic roots, and as the former location of the Quốc Tử Giám (National School) and of the imperial Confucian examinations, it was important for cultural reasons and for pride in central Vietnam for Huế to have an independent university. Strategically, Diệm felt that he needed to demonstrate to Huế people that his government was going to protect them from communism and not let the city, which was relatively close to the seventeenth parallel that demarcated the North and the South, be overrun by communist infiltrators. He explained that "setting up a great university is no different than challenging the communists" (Cao V. L. 1972: 121). He repeated these sentiments in a speech inaugurating the university in 1957, in which he stressed that forming new universities was part and parcel of the "national revolution" started by anticolonialists nearly a century before and that these universities could revise "traditional knowledge" by "acquiring foreign values" to move the country forward.[10]

Rather than promoting anticommunist ideas, Cao Văn Luận emphasized free inquiry by hiring highly trained professors with a wide variety of opinions and backgrounds for his four original faculties: education, letters, law, and science. Shortly thereafter, an Institute of Sinology—appropriate for the location of the university in the former imperial capital—was established, and a Faculty of Medicine began to function in 1960 (Jones 1962: 554).

Cao Văn Luận did hire at least one avowed anticommunist: the historian and political scientist Father Nguyễn Phương (1921–1993), who came to Huế University shortly after completing a BA and an MA in history at the University of San Francisco. Nguyễn Phương would go on to write Ánh sáng dân chủ (Light of Democracy), which suggests that the Leninist view of democracy was misguided because the Communist Party in a one-party state would always be able to determine who counted as "the people" (Nguyễn P. 1957: 26–27; also Lenin 1974: 406–409). But he also hired the distinguished continental philosopher Nguyễn Văn Trung (b. 1930), who had recently completed a Ph.D. at the University of Louvain. Though he criticized state-sponsored communism like that of the DRV for foreclosing freedom of thought, Nguyễn Văn Trung was also unapologetically a leftist who approved of the possibility of a genuine future revolution of workers and who excoriated the United States for fighting an imperialist war in Vietnam (Nguyễn Văn Trung 1965).

Cao Văn Luận used his connections to hire the best faculty from various places but also insisted from the start that all classroom instruction would be in Vietnamese, with the exception of courses in foreign languages and a few courses in medicine (Nguyen D. H. 1960: 9). Because of this requirement, Huế University featured fewer foreign professors than the University of Saigon in the late 1950s, but the ones Cao Văn Luận did hire were notable. Chen Ching-ho (in Vietnamese Trần Kính Hòa) was a distinguished Sinologist from Hong Kong whom he hired to head up the Institute of Sinology, which was founded in 1959 (Cao V. L. 1972: 189).

Adding to the international flavor of Huế University were a handful of German professors from the University of Freiburg. Cao Văn Luận recruited them as part of an agreement with the West German government that began in 1961.[11] The first German to arrive was Dr. Horst Gunther Krainick (1908–1968), a well-known pediatrician who was hired to coordinate the supply of laboratory equipment for Huế's medical school. He was joined by 1962 by Dr. Ruprecht Zwirner (1929–2010), an anatomist who studied the structure of nerves in the larynx; Dr. Erich Wulff (1926–2010), a psychiatrist; and Rudolf Weil, a physiologist (Lê Đ. T. 2010). They were later joined by others, such as Wulff's good friend Dr. Raimund Kauffman, who in addition to teaching physiology was also a professional photographer and writer; Dr. Raimund Discher, a specialist in internal medicine; and Dr. Alois Altekoester, an assistant clinician (Lê Đ. T. 2010; Hoàng P. N. P. 2012).

The new Huế University also featured a prominent journal publication. Đại học (University, or Great Learning), first published by the university in 1958, was under the editorship of Nguyễn Văn Trung until he left in 1963. Consistent with the mission of the university that was articulated by both Cao Văn Luận and Ngô Đình Diệm at its founding, Đại học sought to establish the Republic of Vietnam's "role in the world of nations" by both rooting itself in Vietnamese culture and seeking new ideas from around the world. Above all, it stressed that it would be a bastion of "independent thinking" where free ideas would be exchanged (Nguyễn Văn Trung 1958: 1). Given that its editor was a continental philosopher, it should not be surprising that issues of *Đại học* in this period featured discussions of Marx, Bergson, Camus, Heidegger, and the Christian philosophical anthropologist Maurice Nédoncelle. But it also featured articles on Vietnamese history, including articles on the Gia Long Emperor, founder of the Nguyễn dynasty, on literature, on rituals, and on political theory (Phan T. A. 2017: 10–12).

One final university was founded in this period: the University of Dalat opened its doors in 1958. Unlike the other two universities, however, the University of Dalat was a private, Catholic university. Its founding was possible because of its very close ties to the Ngô Đình Diệm administration. It was in large part the brainchild of Archbishop Ngô Đình Thục, the president's elder brother. It was funded with moneys from the Vietnamese Catholic Church and placed a special emphasis on training clergy in the positive climate, "which allows the students to maintain good physical condition and to grant them the best conditions for cultivating their spirit" (Trần Văn Thiện 1961: 9). Despite these Catholic origins, by 1962, less than one-quarter of the faculty and less than one-third of the students were Catholic. Many students from around the Republic of Vietnam flocked to Dalat to take advantage of the wonderful climate and free tuition offered there (Jones 1962: 554–555).

In its initial years, the university featured three faculties: education, letters, and science. The Faculty of Letters was mostly resident in Dalat, in houses provided on the university campus. But to attract enough faculty in mathematics and science, the college had to borrow professors from the University of Saigon and transport them to Dalat via chauffeured car, enticing them with free transportation, board, and lodging. The University of Dalat also differed from the universities in Saigon and Huế in its attitude toward the languages of instruction. Because of its status as a Catholic school and its interest in training students to be teachers in parochial schools, French and Latin were much more common, and comparably fewer courses were offered in Vietnamese. Since both the bishops that oversaw the university and the teachers of humanities subjects were frequently European Catholic priests, the University of Dalat did not have the same national feel as the public universities. Nevertheless, Dalat's university thrived in this favorable environment and grew rapidly, as did its counterparts in Huế and Saigon, until the political events of the early 1960s temporarily halted their progress.

The Crisis of 1963

On May 8, 1963, more than three thousand people celebrating *Vesak* (marking the birthday of Siddhartha Gautama Buddha) in Huế marched to the local radio station to protest the fact that government forces had ripped down their red, blue, and yellow Buddhist flags. To them, this action demonstrated Ngô Đình Diệm's clear favoritism toward Huế's Catholics—led by Diệm's elder brother Ngô Đình Thục, archbishop of Huế—and against the Buddhists. The Catholics had been allowed to fly a Catholic flag just weeks before. These protesters were met by the army, which used tear gas and grenades and fired on demonstrators, killing eight people (Joiner 1964: 915–916). Though Ngô Đình Diệm agreed to meet with students and other protesters and explained that he would hold all groups, including Catholics, to the same standard on the flag-flying issue, protests continued throughout the summer.

Students at Huế University were active in these protests, and many of them were arrested. They complained to their rector, Cao Văn Luận, that in addition to subjecting them to arrest, the government was also subjecting them to torture and threatening them. The students claimed they would set themselves on fire, as would monks, if their fellow students were not released. Alarmed, Cao Văn Luận called for the immediate release of students from jail and spoke to Ngô Đình Diệm's younger brother Ngô Đình Cẩn (1911–1964), unsuccessfully encouraging him to intervene and stop the crisis. These actions resulted in half measures by those elements close to Diệm, including Cẩn, who were sympathetic, but they were constrained and could do little. The person really influencing the actions in Huế was the far less sympathetic archbishop, Diệm's older brother Ngô Đình Thục (Cao V. L. 1972: 147–148).

Then on June 11, 1963, the monk Thích Quảng Đức famously burned himself to death in the middle of a major intersection in Saigon, turning the protests into literal conflagrations. As Cao Văn Luận and other faculty continued to plead for leniency for students involved in the process, they increasingly became targets of the state. On August 15, 1963, Nguyễn Quang Trình, who had been promoted to minister of education several years before, traveled to Huế to tell Cao Văn Luận that Ngô Đình Diệm had ordered him to be replaced (Cao V. L. 1972: 155; Vũ L. T. 1997: 29–30). The protest, however, did not abate. A few short months later, in November 1963, a group of dissident generals captured and killed Diệm and his brother Ngô Đình Nhu with the assent of the United States. Those events made it more difficult for universities and journals, who had to tack in the midst of these strong political winds. Over the next several years, however, intellectuals would prove to be resilient in the face of multiple changes in government.

Universities in the Interregnum Period (1963–1967)

The assassination of Ngô Đình Diệm inaugurated a period of coups and countercoups sometimes known as the "interregnum period" between the two organized Republics of Vietnam: the First Republic under Ngô Đình Diệm (1955–1963) and the Second Republic under the presidency of Nguyễn Văn

Thiệu (1967–1975). This period produced substantial instability for universities and temporarily disrupted the vibrant intellectual climate in the Republic of Vietnam.

Huế University provides a good case in point for these disruptions. Subsequent to the November 1963 coup, the new government, led by General Dương Văn Minh (1916–2001), reinstated Cao Văn Luận as rector of the university. Then General Dương Văn Minh and his coconspirators were deposed by the coup of Nguyễn Khánh in January 1964. By the summer of 1964, in the context of renewed Buddhist-movement agitation at universities and elsewhere in the country, Cao Văn Luận became one of a number of prominent Catholics accused of pushing for a countercoup against Nguyễn Khánh (1927–2013). So the rector, whom Ngô Đình Diệm had dismissed for being too sympathetic to Buddhist student protesters, was now dismissed by the Nguyễn Khánh government for being anti-Buddhist and for supposedly being sympathetic to the same Diemist parties that had ordered his removal in the first place. He was replaced by Bùi Tường Huân, who was seen as a figure friendly to the Buddhist movement (Cao V. L. 1972: 188–190).[12]

During the Buddhist movement, Huế University Medical School faculty Drs. Wulff and Kauffman staffed the medical tent at Từ Đàm pagoda, which had been set up to treat protesters, and they used their expertise to show them how to use masks, wet towels, and fresh lemon to counteract tear gas attacks from government forces. Wulff in particular appealed to the United States, the Vatican, and the United Nations to end the violence, and as a confidential informant to the U.S. Embassy and Department of State, he appears to have had the ear of influential figures, including U.S. Senator Frank Church of Idaho (1924–1984). In retribution for their criticisms and their assistance to protesters, Wulff and Kauffman were forced to leave the country (Hoàng P. N. P. 2012).[13]

In this contentious time of political strife, both on campus and off, the university's flagship journal, Đại học, was discontinued, and enrollment stagnated while the number of degrees awarded became very low.[14] The University of Huế was not alone in experiencing disruptions from the Buddhist crisis of 1963 and the subsequent political unrest of the interregnum period. At the University of Saigon, in the mid-1960s, protests and counterprotests ensued between students supporting the Unified Buddhist Sangha of Vietnam and groups such as the Saigon University Catholic Students Association (Topmiller 2002: 60–61). Some faculty and students who disliked Diệm's response quit or dropped out in protest.[15]

Furthermore, even before the coup against Diệm, universities were losing some of their support from U.S.-based nongovernmental organizations, particularly the Michigan State Advisory Group and the American Friends of Vietnam. Both groups existed because of substantial personal ties between

Diệm and key Americans. In the case of Michigan State, this person was most notably political science professor Wesley Fishel (and later also school president John Hannah). But the relationship began to fray when professors associated with the group wrote articles criticizing Diệm's administration. Michigan State professor Robert Scigliano observed in 1960 that there was no meaningful, "competitive political party system" in the Republic of Vietnam but rather a succession of parties, each functionally controlled by "the new national government" (Scigliano 1960: 345). Then in 1961, Adrian Jaffe, who taught at the University of Saigon in 1957–1958, joined with fellow Michigan State faculty member Milton C. Taylor to write a scathing indictment of Diệm's police state, pointing to the nepotism of Ngô Đình Diệm's family, criticizing restrictions on professors and banned books, and calling the Republic an "oligarchy" (Jaff and Taylor 1961: 20). This enraged Diệm, and Michigan State's contract was not renewed.

In the case of the American Friends of Vietnam, the organization owed much of its influence in Vietnam to the relationship between the Austrian-born former revolutionary socialist and International Rescue Committee member Joseph Buttinger (1906–1992) and Ngô Đình Diệm. In fact, the organization was essentially born to cultivate American public support for Diệm's regime in 1954 and 1955 (Morgan 1997: 20–22). But by 1960, Buttinger began to express reservations over the Diệm administration's heavy-handedness, and in September 1961, he submitted his resignation as chairman of the organization (Morgan 1997: 79). This led to a dispute between those who advocated continued support for Diệm, including the new chairman Lieutenant General John O'Daniel (1894–1975), and Buttinger and others who increasingly believed that the United States should support Diệm's removal. Though the American Friends of Vietnam would continue operating until 1975, the disputes involving Diệm and their aftermath undercut their ability to raise funds, leaving them with almost no money to continue supporting universities and educational exchanges (Morgan 1997: 103–104). The absence of this funding deprived the University of Saigon and Huế University of one of their major sources of technical coordination, a sponsor of the travel of their faculty and staff to the United States, and a major source of textbooks for their libraries.

Still, the interregnum period did see the continued development of new universities in the Republic of Vietnam. Two new universities were founded during this period. One was Vạn Hạnh University, a private university in Saigon supported through the United Buddhist Sangha and founded in 1964. The other was a public university for the Mekong Delta, Cần Thơ University, founded in 1967.

In the aftermath of the coalescence of the Buddhist movement in 1963, the United Buddhist Sangha sought to create an Institute for Higher Buddhist

Studies (also known at that time as the Saigon Buddhist Studies College) associated with Ấn Quang pagoda in Saigon. This institution was developed by the famed monk Thích Nhất Hạnh (b. 1924), as Van Nguyen-Marshall discusses in the previous chapter, and SYSS played an integral role in the early years of that institution (John Chapman 2007: 301). Its deputy rectors included Hồ Hữu Tường (1910–1980), the famed intellectual who had been a leader of Trotskyist thought in the 1930s, was a prominent leftist, and had been a vocal opponent of Ngô Đình Diệm and an advocate of neutralism in the Cold War.[16] He was joined by the more moderate Thích Minh Châu (1918–2012), an expert on Pali Buddhist texts who had just received his Ph.D. from the New Nalanda Mahavihara of the University of Bihar after many years studying in India. By the fall of 1964, with Thích Nhất Hạnh immersed in lecturing and political work, Thích Minh Châu became the rector.

Vạn Hạnh University could boast of an exciting and formidable intellectual environment, sustained by Thích Minh Châu's vision of creating a new university modeled on the vision of the great Buddhist Nalanda University of ancient times, fortified with the insights of modern ideas from around the world. The exchange of ideas was catalyzed by Vạn Hạnh University's journal *Tư Tưởng* (Thought), inaugurated in 1967.

The second university founded in the interregnum period was the public university in Cần Thơ, founded in the fall of 1966. Designed to serve the people of the Mekong Delta, this new university also reflected the increasing influence of the United States. The faculty and administration of the new university were frequently under forty years of age, and many of them came with newly minted American degrees. The university was led by its thirty-seven-year-old rector, the already-famed botanist Phạm Hoàng Hộ (1929–2017). In 1962, he was appointed dean of the Faculty of Pedagogy at the University of Saigon, but he quit in 1963 in protest of Ngô Đình Diệm's actions against the Buddhist movement. After a brief foray into politics at the end of 1963, he found himself back as a regular faculty member at the University of Saigon, and from there as the founding rector of Cần Thơ.

Though Phạm Hoàng Hộ and Nguyễn Ngọc Huy (1924–1990), Cần Thơ's Law Faculty dean, were both educated in France, the new university featured many prominent faculty members educated in the United States. By the mid-1960s, the United States was rapidly escalating its military involvement in Vietnam, and its investment in civil society was increasing, especially through USAID, which established a Higher Education Office in Saigon in 1967 (Hoshall 1971: 19). Cần Thơ University was thus on the front lines of a shift in cultural and intellectual emphasis away from France and toward the United States that gained momentum in the late 1960s. The dean of the Faculty of Letters, Lê Văn Diệm (1923–1999), for example, had earned his Ph.D. from the University of Minnesota, writing a thesis on the influence of Puritans on the transcendentalists, who came eager to introduce students at a brand-new university to Ralph Waldo Emerson and Nathaniel Hawthorne (Le V.-D. 1960).[17] Even the mission of the university moved it more in line with American models than French ones. These trends—using USAID grants and other available American funds to build university capacity along American lines—would characterize efforts to organize teaching and research from the beginning of the Second Republic period in 1967 to the end of the Republic of Vietnam in 1975, and an increasing emphasis on American culture would contribute to the cosmopolitan environment there.

Universities and Intellectuals in the Second Republic (1967–1975)

By 1967, the Republic of Vietnam was once again entering a period of stability and was regaining functioning democratic institutions. In 1965, a military regime led by Nguyễn Cao Kỳ as prime minister and Nguyễn Văn Thiệu had come to power and acceded to pressure from Buddhist protesters, civil society groups, and the United States for democratic reforms. The result was the election of a Constituent Assembly in 1966, which led to a draft of a new constitution in April 1967 and an election in 1967, in which a slate of Nguyễn Văn Thiệu (as president) and Nguyễn Cao Kỳ (as vice president) defeated a wide variety of alternative candidates. The political stability that this afforded, along with firm institutional and financial support from U.S. institutions (at least until 1974), created the conditions for universities to thrive.

This era was not without major difficulties. The Tết Offensive, early in 1968, disrupted the functioning of universities and journals to varying degrees, depending on the location and circumstances of the institutions involved. In the case of Huế University, this disruption was profound, as communist forces established control over the city by February 1 of that year and held the city for nearly a month. During phase 2 of the communist occupation of Huế, intellectuals, foreigners, and others deemed a threat to the communists were rounded up and imprisoned or killed. This group including four people associated with the collaboration between the University of Freiburg and the Medical School at Huế University. In February 1968, Dr. Horst Gunther Krainick; his wife, Elizabeth; Dr. Raimund Discher; and Dr. Alois Altekoester were rounded up by communist soldiers, taken away in a Volkswagen bus, shot in the head, and buried in a shallow grave (Dror 2014: xxviii–xxix; Trương T. D. 2020: 312).

Not only did the university lose faculty members but it could not operate while the entire city of Huế was a war zone, as was the case for most of February 1968. The infrastructure of the university, along with the city itself, took considerable time to be reconstructed after the disastrous events of February 1968. Adding to the difficulty, the communist occupation of Huế split the student body and faculty.

During this time, Huế University ethnology professor Lê Văn Hảo (1936–2015) was not only revealed to be an NLF member but also named the chair of the Revolutionary Committee—effectively, he was the mayor of communist-occupied Huế in February 1968. Lê Văn Hảo had completed a doctorate with an ethnosociological study of the structure of a French village and had become one of the foremost authorities on Huế culture during the Nguyễn Dynasty (1802–1945) (Le-Van-Hao 1961; Lê V. H. 1966). Former Huế University philosophy student Hoàng Phủ Ngọc Tường (b. 1937), who graduated from the university in 1964 with a philosophy degree and taught at the Quốc Học school in Huế, was responsible for setting up the makeshift tribunal at a small Catholic seminary, through which students were sentenced to death under his direction (Dror 2014: xxviii).

The eminent Vietnamese historian Nguyễn Thế Anh (b. 1936), who served as the rector of Huế University from 1966 to 1969, remembers this as the most difficult time in his life. He spent the initial years of his tenure trying to maintain the academic autonomy of the university and "keep the University out of the reach of political designs" amid the pressure of changing political environments, American escalation, and continuing protests. After the events of February 1968, he had to physically rebuild the university but more importantly heal the "deep wounds" left on the students by the actions of their colleagues and also by the deaths of their professors.[18] Resigning in 1969, Nguyễn Thế Anh became dean of the Faculty of Letters at Saigon University and helped build the history department there. Even after the Tết Offensive, assassinations (such as that of Minister of Education Lê Minh Trí in 1970) and protests (such as those that closed several universities for months in 1969 and 1970) would prove challenging (Hoshall 1971: 16–17).

Despite these events, the same basic characteristics of intellectual culture in the Republic of Vietnam persisted after the Tết Offensive: it remained cosmopolitan, continued to be largely noncommunist while lacking a substantial focus on anticommunism, and continued to expand. New universities continued to be founded, such as the Catholic Minh Đức University in Saigon, which opened in 1970, with a mission as a "Roman Catholic University in which other religions will participate."[19] The year 1970 also saw the doors open on Hòa Hảo University in the Mekong Delta, which featured an interesting collaboration between the Hòa Hảo Buddhist Sect and Brigham Young University, which was owned by the Church of Jesus Christ of Latter-Day Saints.[20] Starting in 1971, the Republic of Vietnam also began to open its doors to a number of community colleges and polytechnic universities (Nguyễn H. P. 2019: 97–99).

At Vạn Hạnh University, where enrollment was growing, the journal *Tư Tưởng* became a formidable force in debating philosophy and religion. As the 1970s dawned, the articles in the journal, which reflected divergent opinions from a number of different professors, nevertheless shared a similar trajectory, which coincided with Rector Thích Minh Châu's vision of establishing a Buddhist university that could incorporate the best elements of Western culture and philosophy while basing itself on Asian models. The rector wanted to avoid the crisis Western universities were experiencing because the three pillars on which European Universities of the age of enlightenment had been founded—"God, Man, and Science"—had all been called into question by the events and ideas of the twentieth century (Thich M. C. 1969: 8–9).

Articles in *Tư Tưởng* in the Second Republic period sharpened and rearticulated this theme by pointing out the shortcomings of enlightenment culture and suggesting that Buddhist values could supplement the areas in which Western culture fell short. The philosopher and priest Lê Tôn Nghiêm (1926–1993) developed an analysis, based on a reading of Martin Heidegger's *Being and Time*, that argued that Western philosophy overly relied on a vague and overused notion of being that tended to conflate ideas of being and existence with a transcendent idea related to a higher power. For this reason, he argues, Western metaphysics are vulnerable to nihilism, because the abstraction of being allows us to assume our own separateness from the ultimate questions of existence and thus our own responsibility for our actions (Lê T. N. 1969: 42–43). In contrast, Buddhist conceptions such as karma foreground the interrelationship between humans and their environment and the cause of one's "bound physical existence" in a larger community (Lê T. N. 1969: 94–96). Similarly, essays by the monk Thích Chơn Hạnh (fl. 2019) and Professor Ngô Trọng Anh (b. 1926) sought to develop the same critique of Western culture and positing of a Buddhist alternative through essays discussing the Buddhist influence on the thought of Friedrich Nietzsche (Chơn Hạnh 1970: 11–13; Ngô T. A. 1970: 29–31). Ngô Thanh Nhàn, who attended Vạn Hạnh officially from 1967 to 1968, remembers that although students found *Tư Tưởng* "not easy to read," they were inspired by their professors to seek out and read Nietzsche, Heidegger, and Sartre in the original.[21]

The most significant shift in the intellectual agenda of the Republic of Vietnam during the 1967–1975 period was the increasing interest in American culture, literature, and history. Throughout urban South Vietnam, countercultures of "hippies" and "cowboys" indulged in American fashion, drugs, and rock and roll. They were also interested in the ideological basis of hippie culture and advocated for an end to the war (Dror 2018: 252–267). This led to scholarly commentary on hippies, which criticized hippie sartorial choices and drug use but found hippie commitment to working for peace and "having a voice" laudable (Nguyễn T. V. 1968: 130). Urban intellectuals in the Republic of Vietnam were also interested in the American Civil Rights Movement. In "Martin Luther King: The Black Child of Saint Gandhi," Nguyễn Ngọc Lan compares the lives of King and Gandhi and discusses what he sees as the similar circumstances of their assassination. He concludes that the major difference was that King died at just thirty-nine years of age, before his words could have their full impact. Nonetheless, as people from across the globe were embracing King's message, Lan held out hope that "the time for the teaching of Martin Luther King's principles is just beginning" (Nguyễn Ngọc Lan 1968: 64–72). And in 1967 and 1968, the journal *Đất Nước* (The Country), which began in 1967 under the editorship of Nguyễn Văn Trung, featured translations of Malcolm X's "Ballot or the Bullet" speech and an article on the nature of anti-Black racism (X 1968: 103–140; Lý C. T. 1967: 117–128).

In the 1970s, this exciting cosmopolitan environment extended out beyond Saigon. Moreover, it continued—along with the publication of major journals such as *Sử Địa, Bách Khoa*, and *Tư Tưởng*—almost to the fall of Saigon in 1975. Trần Hoài Bắc (b. 1954), who was an English major at the University of Dalat from 1972 to 1975, explains the frenetic pace of intellectual innovation in that environment:

> As far as I remember, Southerners read everything and every author, dead or alive. Whenever I think back on those years, it still amazes me how people of the Republic of Vietnam could find time to read and translate and to write so much in such a short time (just about twenty-one years) while a deadly war was raging on all around them. They read and translated Pasternak, Solzhenitsyn, Sholokhov, Tolstoi, Dostoyevsky, Chekov, Turgenev, Andre Gide, Albert Camus, Jean-Paul Sartre, Victor Hugo, Francois Sagan, Stendhal, Goethe, Arthur Koestler, Kawabata, Mishima, Hemingway, John Steinbeck, Margaret Mitchell, Tagore, Krishnamurti, to name but a few. They penned furiously too, as if there were no tomorrow, producing both prose and verse in all different genres. Book upon book got published in every city or town on any given day.[22]

Conclusion

The fate of the intellectuals of the Republic of Vietnam after the fall of Saigon varied widely. Some took the opportunity to leave Vietnam during earlier times of political crisis. Many other intellectuals who received degrees from France or Belgium escaped to France or Canada (most often Quebec) after 1975. Many of those trained in the United States who left after 1975 returned to the United States.

Despite these differing experiences, in various publications in Garden Grove or San Jose, California; Montréal, Quebec; or Paris, the spirit that these intellectuals had cultivated in universities and in publications in the Republic of Vietnam continued. That spirit was cosmopolitan, modernist, and influenced by cultural ideas coming from France and the United States, and it was not initially particularly anticommunist—though anticommunism grew among intellectuals as a result of their experiences, particularly for those who were detained in reeducation camps after the fall of Saigon, as explained by Tuan Hoang in the next chapter. Despite these experiences, the intellectual culture they had nurtured in the South continued to flourish in a healthy array of Vietnamese American newspapers, magazines, journals, and publication houses, as Vietnamese American intellectuals sought to continue the interdisciplinary and sophisticated scholarship they had carried on in the Republic of Vietnam.

It is notable how much the description of the cosmopolitan, heterogeneous, and not particularly anticommunist university students, faculty, and intellectual milieu contrasts with scholarship depicting first-generation Vietnamese immigrants in the United States as highly insular (Reed-Danahay 2018: 606).[23] This is ironic because they are, in many cases, the very same people. First-generation Vietnamese Americans are described as culturally solidly tied to their homeland rather than their new nation, cautious about interacting outside of their own, and nostalgic about a rebirth of their former country, the Republic of Vietnam. These culturally preservationist attitudes are described as anti-cosmopolitan because they place "obstacles in the path of a cosmopolitanism that can be 'open to others'" (Reed-Danahay 2018: 612).

Yet the Republic of Vietnam's culture, for which these first-generation immigrants were longing, was *always already* a cosmopolitan culture. Longing for a return of the Republic of Vietnam is not a desire to return to an ossified, feudal Vietnamese tradition but a nostalgia for a dynamic culture in which Confucian ideas might compete with those of Nagarjuna and Krishnamurti one day and with Sartre, Heidegger, or Nietzsche the next. In considerations of the antecedent history and influences of first-generation Vietnamese Americans, greater links need to be made between the emergence of a Vietnamese American community and the social, cultural, and intellectual environment of the Republic of Vietnam, out of which much of that community originally emerged.

4

THE AUGUST REVOLUTION, THE FALL OF

SAIGON, AND POSTWAR REEDUCATION CAMPS

Understanding Vietnamese Diasporic Anticommunism

TUAN HOANG

Introduction

Vietnamese diasporic anticommunism has been prominent in the scholarship about Asian refugees and immigrants in the United States.[1] The
subject merits, for example, one of eight entries about Vietnamese in
an encyclopedia about Asian Americans (Vo Dang 2013).[2] Appearing in a
collected volume about anticommunism among ethnic refugees in the United States, its chapter is entitled "Better Dead Than Red" to suggest that it has
been a form of extremism (Le C. N. 2009). Both of these works note a series
of protests in Orange County, California, in 1999 against the Hi Tek TV and
VCR store, whose owner displayed a flag of Vietnam and a poster showing
Hồ Chí Minh. The Hi Tek episode receives its own entry in another encyclopedia about Asian Americans, and others have viewed it as a climax of anticommunism in Orange County and other Little Saigon communities (Le
L. S. 2011b; Nguyen K. 2020; Duong and Pelaud 2012).

Attention notwithstanding, Asian American studies scholarship has
largely treated the subject as an ahistorical phenomenon and, therefore, has
not offered a clear explanation. Diasporic anticommunism has been carica-
tured as unyielding and unchanging and criticized as detrimental to Vietnamese communities. Linda Võ, for example, has asserted that "those most
vocal and [who] garner the most media attention do not necessarily represent the needs or voice" of the community (Võ L. 2003: xv, xvi). Kieu-Linh
Caroline Valverde has likewise suggested that fear "of retaliation forces Vietnamese Americans into a silent majority" (Valverde 2012: 146). Less critical
in tone, Kim Nguyen nonetheless ascribes "the visibility" and "rhetorical

positioning of the protesters" to a "narrow anti-communist understanding of the Vietnam War onto the Vietnamese American body." She further points to the Vietnamese American support of the wars in Afghanistan and Iraq and argues that the "hyper-conservatism that distinguishes Vietnamese Americans from all other ethnic groups serves certainly the purposes of reinvigorating allegiance to past imperialist endeavors" of the United States (Nguyen K. 2020: 134–150). Diasporic anticommunism and pro-war sentiment are lumped together and interpreted in the context of American history and politics. Yen Le Espiritu is similarly critical of diasporic anticommunism by linking at least some of it to American imperialism. Allowing that "the refugees' public denouncement of the current government of Vietnam is understandable, even expected," Espiritu interprets anticommunism through the lens of American politics and imperialism. The "'anticommunist' stance," she argues, "is also a narrative, adopted in part because it is the primary language with which Vietnamese refugees, as objects of US rescue fantasies, could tell their history and be understood from within the US social and political landscape" (Espiritu Y. L. 2014: 96). In this view, Vietnamese refugees became anticommunist model minorities helping to justify, perhaps unwittingly, imperialism by attacking communism while praising American freedom.

Categorized broadly under "critical refugee studies," these views and related ones are hardly uniform.[3] The focus on imperialism, however, generally situates diasporic anticommunism against the background of U.S. history and the foreground of U.S. politics, leaving out its complex historical background (Le L. S. 2011a: 1–25).[4] As a consequence, much of this scholarship has viewed diasporic anticommunism as ideologically extreme, intellectually incoherent, psychologically irrational, politically at a standstill, and culturally damaging to the community. Commenting, for example, on the South Vietnamese flag, a long-standing symbol of diasporic anticommunism, at the Capitol riot in Washington, DC, on January 6, 2021, Viet Thanh Nguyen contends that the flag still represents nostalgia for the extinct Republic of Vietnam (RVN) in ways similar to the nostalgia for the Confederacy among some American southerners. Not only does this approach conflate Vietnamese particularism with American particularism but it also leaves out postwar developments related to the meanings of the flag in the diaspora (Nguyen V. T. 2021; Hoang T. 2021).[5]

This is not to say that scholarship is not attentive to Vietnamese particularism. On the basis of fieldwork in San Diego, Thuy Vo Dang concludes that "anticommunism is not only a political ideology for Vietnamese Americans but a 'cultural discourse' that underlies most of the community practices of first-generation-dominated organizations" (Vo Dang 2005: 66). In Orange County, Karin Aguilar-San Juan happened to conduct research during the Hi Tek protests and noted the presence of former political prisoners at the protest site. Aguilar-San Juan observed the effort of the protesters to "find common ground with Americans" through anticommunist exhibits and noted "infuriated refugees—many of whom spent years in Vietnamese reeducation camps before escaping to the United States—[who] made loud and clear in banners and rallies their opinion that 'freedom of speech is not free'" (Aguilar-San Juan 2009: 80).[6] Lan Duong and Isabelle Thuy Pelaud, while recognizing the active presence of former reeducation camp prisoners and the importance of their background, present a more critical view of protesters. These prisoners, the scholars note, had "encountered the violence of the communist state in Việt Nam, and thus their identities have been carved out of their experiences during and after the war" (Duong and Pelaud 2012: 261). In this respect, the carceral background of many protesters points to a crucial connection between their Vietnamese past and their American present. Elsewhere, political scientists have called attention to broader historical changes that affected Vietnamese politics in Little Saigon during the 1990s, and they have analyzed anticommunist protests as a part of a process of political incorporation (Collet and Furuya 2009; Collet and Furuya 2010: 13; Ong and Meyer 2008: 91–92).

Other scholars have been attentive to the historicity of this subject, if to different degrees and with different emphases. Studying the longer trajectory of politics in Orange County, Phuong Nguyen situates anticommunism under the umbrella of "refugee nationalism" (Nguyen Phuong Tran 2017).[7] More explicit on historical ties between the RVN and the postwar diaspora, Y Thien Nguyen argues that diasporic anticommunism has been a "remaking" of South Vietnamese anticommunism (Nguyen Y. T. 2018). Having conducted interviews with Vietnamese in Illinois, Hao Phan believes that there is "political diversity among Vietnamese Americans despite the fact that the whole community is anti-communist." He attributes this spectrum of opinions to two factors: life experiences in Vietnam before migration and the current political situation in Vietnam. In this view, anticommunism "is not a theoretical matter but the direct result of painful life experiences" in postwar Vietnam (Phan N. H. 2015: 84, 94). Such research gives more forceful analyses of the interactions between the past and present: a step in the right direction.

This chapter makes two arguments. First, diasporic anticommunism is not new; it is the latest manifestation of Vietnamese anticommunism. While diasporic anticommunism is not identical to earlier ideologies, their connections were more fluid and continuous: not perfectly linear but not broken either. In particular, intra-Vietnamese violence that began during the "August Revolution" was crucial to understanding this genealogy. This momentous event in August 1945 marked a shift from anticommunism mostly in theory to anticommunism in action for the next thirty years. Second, the chapter analyzes the impact of national loss and incarceration on the making of the diasporic variety of anticommunism. The abrupt fall of Saigon produced profound psychological effects on Vietnamese associated with the RVN, who experienced enormous economic deprivation and political oppression, including the incarceration in reeducation camps of military officers and government officials. This experience sharpened their anticommunist belief and contributed substantially to their activism later. It is not possible to understand diasporic anticommunism without exploring the experiences of these political prisoners, especially because tens of thousands of former political prisoners and their families came to the United States through the Humanitarian Operation Program during the 1990s. The mass migration of political prisoners renewed anticommunist activism in diasporic communities, including a marked rise in public demonstration that included the Hi Tek protests, where many former prisoners and their families kept a perpetual physical presence in front of the store.[8]

The Vietnamese Anticommunist Tradition

The anticommunist tradition has existed at least since late colonialism began with opposition to Marxism from colonial authorities and the Catholic Church. Colonialists and Catholics had different interests, methods, and reasons for opposing communism. Catholic anticommunism, in fact, had much to do with challenging French colonialism, as a number of Catholics were critical of the secularism of the French state and pointed to colonial oppression of Indochinese as a reason for the spread of communism (Keith 2012: 148–127, 177–207). Differences notwithstanding, both Catholics and colonialists considered communism a direct threat and, as a result, published many anticommunist materials. For colonial administrators, the communists were to be stopped and suppressed like any other organization that challenged colonial rule with real or perceived violence. On the other hand, the Catholic clergy viewed communism as synonymous with atheism and, therefore, as a grave threat to the church in Indochina. Anticommunist messages were integrated into Catholic moral instructions, and Catholic children were taught that communism attacked the church, the family, and the "moral order." Frequent were references to "the evil of Communism," and Catholic publications sometimes attacked positivism, utilitarianism, egalitarianism, and even "atheistic" Buddhism. Catholic anticommunist rhetoric was so effective that even the colonial authorities sometimes borrowed it for their own propaganda. One colonial leaflet included an illustration of communists burning books and beating a teacher. Another showed Vietnamese communists chopping down a Vietnamese tree at the order of a Russian Marxist (Marr 1981: 84–88).

These colorful if overwrought portrayals of communism were meant to strike terror into the hearts of ordinary Vietnamese. For many Catholics, however, anticommunism was not merely propaganda but a major issue with palpable implications. This point was well illustrated by the killing of a priest, Father Pierre Khang, at the hand of communist agitators during the Nghệ Tĩnh rebellion led by communists in 1930–1931. Contemporary Catholic accounts of the killing blamed the Indochinese Communist Party (ICP) for threatening the priest and other Catholics, killing him and several villagers, burning down the church, and forbidding parishioners from burying the dead. These stories were widely circulated among Catholics and became material for stronger denunciations of communism in the Catholic press. Publications such as the periodical *Vì Chúa* (For the Lord), whose priest-editor Nguyễn Văn Thích had written possibly the best-known anticommunist pamphlet of the 1920s, offered many philosophical and theological critiques of communism. In Saigon, the newspaper *La croix d'Indochine* (The Cross of Indochina) became perhaps the loudest anticommunist voice of its time among Catholic and non-Catholic publications. Supported by the Catholic property-owning bourgeoisie, it persistently attacked communist abolition of private property and targeted the opinions of the paper *La lutte* (The Struggle), run by Vietnamese Stalinists and Trotskyists in a rare collaboration (Nguyễn Văn Thích 1927).[9]

Although ecclesiastical and colonialist anticommunist rhetoric was vocal, the impact of anticommunism was limited at that time. Before 1945, revolutionary violence affected only a minority of Vietnamese, mostly Catholics. However, there was also growing tension between the communists and non-Christian religious groups: the Hòa Hảo, Cao Đài, and Buddhists. Those sects and the ICP strove for popular support during the 1930s, but their encounters did not lead to the level of conflict and bloodshed that was to occur in the 1940s (Woodside 1976: 182–200). Among members of the urban intelligentsia, opposition to communism remained in the realm of theoretical debate. The Hanoi-based Self-Strength Literary Group (Tự Lực Văn Đoàn), which exerted the most dominant literary and cultural influence on urban youth during the 1930s, was certainly opposed to class struggle. But it did not make anticommunism a major issue, focusing instead on advocacy for wholesale westernization on the one hand and severe criticism of the old Vietnamese order on the other. Some budding communist and noncommunist intellectuals went to the same schools or were friends. They tried to persuade one another but did not resort to violence (Jamieson 1993: 100–175).

The poet and publisher Nguyễn Vỹ, a prominent Buddhist noncommunist intellectual, provides an example. Living in Hanoi during the 1930s, he knew Võ Nguyên Giáp and Trường Chinh, adherents of Marxism and future members of the Politburo. Giáp loaned Vỹ dozens of French-language leftist magazines and books from Marxist authors such as Lenin, Bukharin, and Maurice Thorez. But the anticolonial and antifascist Vỹ was "disappointed" in communist theory and thought that Marxism, "if applied in Vietnam, would certainly destroy all moral foundations of the family, society, nation, the Vietnamese people, even the personal self." Giáp's attempts to persuade Nguyễn Vỹ did not cause him to change his mind, but they remained friendly and often bantered when running into each other on the street (Nguyễn Vỹ 1970: 381–394). Like Vỹ, most educated urbanites were neither Catholic nor supporters of colonialism. But they found Marxism wanting because, in the words of a scholar of Vietnamese communism, it would have "sacrificed traditional Vietnamese patriotism to proletarian internationalism" (Huỳnh K. K. 1982: 188). Or, as another scholar has put it, the communists "interpreted patriotism as outmoded tradition and internationalism as modern, a judgment with which most Vietnamese [at the time] disagreed" (Popkin 1985: 353). Even intense disagreements between Marxist and non-Marxist intellectuals were theoretical and not focused on specific programs. Violent outbreaks between communist and noncommunist Vietnamese were confined mostly to prison, where different anticolonial groups such as the ICP and the Vietnamese Nationalist Party (Việt Nam Quốc Dân Đảng; VNQDĐ), vied for control and conversion of one another (Zinoman 2001a: 200–239).

The Second World War and especially the August Revolution brought forth dramatic changes in the anticommunist outlook. This period was the beginning of decolonization and witnessed the growing influence of the ICP. Anti-ICP opposition also grew. Although not in a strong position as it had been, the VNQDĐ remained an important noncommunist player (Hoang V. D. 2008: 156–207). Moreover, several Đại Việt political parties emerged to present an alternative political and ideological challenge to the ICP. The Đại Việt parties opposed socialist internationalism, and at least a number of their leaders admired European fascist regimes. They reemphasized social Darwinism, a driving force among the previous generation, as the basis for an independent postcolonial Vietnam. The multiplicity of the Đại Việt parties demonstrates fragmentation that plagued noncommunist nationalists in subsequent years, yet their emergence demonstrated ideological alternatives to Vietnamese communism (Quang Minh 1996: 11–191). The stage was set for a new kind of contestation in revolutionary ideology and politics.

As the military situation turned very volatile in early 1945, the communist and noncommunist parties jockeyed for advantages in anticipation of the Allied victory. In northern Vietnam, the VNQDĐ and the Đại Việt created a new formal alliance while independently operating several military training schools. In the South, the Cao Đài and Hòa Hảo solidified power in their areas of influence while expressing support for Japan's "pan-Asianism." In Saigon, the Trotskyists reconstituted themselves into a new political party and reestablished contacts with the smaller Trotskyist groups in the north. Against them were ICP-associated Stalinists, who formed the Vanguard Youths (Thanh Niên Tiền Phong) and attracted hundreds of new members with a nationalistic rather than communist appeal. Using nationalistic rhetoric, the Vanguard Youths constantly attacked the Trotskyists and called for "the People's government to punish them" by assassination (Ngô V. 2000: 307).[10] Such threats and attacks fomented the revolutionary violence that soon engulfed Vietnamese anticolonial politics and helped to create new ideas and rationale for a broader anticommunist ideology.

Much of the anticommunist ideology was shaped by fighting among Vietnamese, especially ICP-directed violence against noncommunist groups. Even before Hồ Chí Minh's declaration of independence, most communist-led Việt Minh groups, to quote a historian of the August Revolution, "probably spent as much time selecting Vietnamese 'traitors' and 'reactionaries' for elimination as trying to kill Japanese" (Marr 1997: 234). Even though revolutionary violence varied from place to place, the overall cost was steep for non- and anticommunists. In the northern mountainous area, for example, the Việt Minh exercised considerable "red terror" on Vietnamese officials. In the Red River Delta, the Việt Minh preferred to "threaten or cajole government officials rather than to eliminate them" but still killed many lower-level officials. The situation worsened after Hồ Chí Minh's declaration of independence. Although communists were the victims of some attacks and killings, they were a lot more successful at eliminating their real and potential rivals than the other way around. One estimate puts the number of deaths of "alleged enemies of the Revolution" at several thousand from late August to September alone, and "tens of thousands" of others were detained for weeks and even months (Marr 1997: 235, 519).

As revealed by the official history of the People's Army of Vietnam (PAVN), Việt Minh teams of "national defense" and "self-defense" engaged in episodic fighting against three enemies in late 1945 and early 1946: the French, the Chinese, and noncommunist Vietnamese, including the VNQDĐ. Fighting the last category was especially "complicated" because it involved the police and "the people" in addition to the defense corps. Việt Minh teams relied on a variety of tactics depending on location and circumstance: "isolating" the noncommunist enemies from their comrades and supporters, "surrounding" them with revolutionary forces, "punishing" (i.e., assassinating) them even "in front of the Chiang troops," and "protecting" areas already controlled from possible invasion by "traitors" and "collaborators" (*Lịch Sử Quân Đội Nhân Dân Việt Nam* 1977: 213–217).[11] Access to the files at the Sûreté, the French police headquarters, allowed them to identify and arrest or liquidate colonial spies, agents, and potential foes in Hanoi, Huế, and Saigon. Many assassinations of real and potential rivals were carried out in Hanoi (Goscha 2007: 105; *Công An Thủ Đô* 1990: 18).

Although the Việt Minh took great care to keep this history out of circulation during the French War, it fueled greater anticommunism among many survivors. In southern Vietnam, assassinations and armed conflicts led to a "balkanization" of the region among the communists and the Hòa Hảo, Cao Đài, and Catholics (Biggs 2012: 127–151). In the northern and central regions, members of noncommunist political parties went into hiding. In his memoir, former South Vietnamese ambassador to the United States Bùi Diễm, a member of the largest Đại Việt Party, wrote about the "outright war between the Vietminh and the nationalists" in a chapter aptly called "The Terror" (Bui Diem 1987: 46). The Đại Việt Party was overwhelmed by Võ Nguyên Giáp's troops and secret police, and the party leader ordered members to withdraw and escape in the summer of 1946. Bùi Diễm was able to flee to a fortified Catholic area; not so lucky was his party's leader, who disappeared without a trace. The violence had triggered greater anticommunism among the Đại Việt and other opponents of the communists. "I watched the destruction of the nationalists," recalled Bùi Diễm decades later, "from a victim's perspective" (Bui Diem 1987: 49).

In important respects, *victim* became *the* operative word for anticommunists from the 1940s onward. After the August Revolution, anticommunists continued to formulate their critiques philosophically, but also increasingly with stories and eyewitness accounts designed to strike fear in the Vietnamese. Because of the ascent of the Việt Minh during the First Indochina War, an anticommunist ideology circulated in selected circles but did not blossom until after the Geneva Accords. Not long after the installment of Ngô Đình Diệm as prime minister, anticommunism found a venue for expression in South Vietnam. The first five years of Diệm's rule saw a flourishing of anticommunist publications from Saigon and other southern cities. Accompanied by the Denounce Communist (Tố Cộng) Campaign, the publications focused on communist brutality and spread anticommunist propaganda on an unprecedented scale. Many featured writings by fervent anticommunist émigrés from North Vietnam and criticized three aspects of communism: revolutionary violence and repression, class struggle, and thought control. The fact that most of these anticommunist authors were *not* Catholic highlighted a significant change from the leading role that Catholics had played in the 1920s and 1930s (Hoang T. 2009: 17–32; Tran N.-A. 2013).[12]

This state-sponsored anticommunism was part of the nation-building competition between Saigon and Hanoi. Each side claimed the mantle of nationalism and sought to portray the other side as illegitimate. From the 1950s, the imprisonment of anticommunists became a preponderant theme in South Vietnamese literature. An example is *Tù Ngục và Thoát Ly* (Prisons and Escapes), a popular book that employed a simple narrative style to reach less-educated readers (Thanh Thảo 1957). It opens with an introduction from an officer of the Commissioner of Refugees to the President (Phủ Tổng Ủy Di Cư Tị Nạn) and a preface by the president of the Association of Vietnamese Communist Victims (Hội Nạn Nhân Cộng Sản Việt Nam). The narrator recalls his experience in Việt Minh zones in central and northern Vietnam during the second half of the 1940s. Initially "invited" by the police to leave his village for his "own security," he and others were later accused of being "reactionaries" and held in prison camps. Each camp held between two hundred and two thousand inmates, placed in barracks divided according to gender and categories of political or "economic" prisoners. Even after release, former inmates were required to report regularly to cadres. For these and other reasons, inmates spent their time devising ways to escape from the camps and head to French- or Catholic-controlled zones (Thanh Thảo 1957; see also Hoang T. 2021: 22–23). This genre of wartime incarceration peaked under President Nguyễn Văn Thiệu in the Second Republic, exemplified by a serialized and fictionalized work called *Trại Đầm Đùn* (The Đầm Đùn Camp). Described as a "novel based on reportage" (*phóng sự tiểu thuyết*), a not-uncommon genre since late colonialism, its lengthy description of life in a large prison camp during the French War further essentialized the dangers of communists (Trần Văn Thái [n.d.] 1973). The Saigon regime also propagated news and fiction that highlighted attacks and assassinations by the PAVN and the National Liberation Front (Mặt Trận Dân Tộc Giải Phóng Miền Nam Việt Nam; NLF). It popularized an anticommunist saying from President Nguyễn Văn Thiệu: "Don't believe what the communists say but look closely at what they have done." In comparison to the postwar era, not many southern Vietnamese were incarcerated by the communists. Yet anticommunist South Vietnamese portrayed communist imprisonment to be hardly better, and sometimes worse, than death or destruction caused by armed attacks by the NLF or the PAVN. The themes of imprisonment and victimhood were consistent with the era of the August Revolution and proved intrinsic to the anticommunist propaganda in South Vietnam.

The Fall of Saigon and the Shock of National Loss

The overview above shows that Vietnamese anticommunism began early but exploded as a reaction to revolution, decolonization, and warfare. Likewise, scholars of diasporic anticommunism should benefit from studying the reaction to the fall of Saigon among anticommunists. The collapse shocked all anticommunist South Vietnamese. Its abruptness further left many South Vietnamese in disbelief, depression, and even denial. This state of mind could be discerned in a number of memoirs and reflections. "The loss of the country still stuns us," writes a refugee some thirty-five years later. "We did not know what to think about the sudden collapse of Vietnam; like drunkards we all seemed to be in denial" (Vo N. M. 2011: 23). Another recollects that on April 29, "the heaviest, most overwhelming feeling was that of total, incomprehensible failure: I had failed. I had failed my family. I had failed my colleagues. I had failed my country" (Nguyen Le Hieu, n.d.: 393). "I rubbed my eyes," recalls a former U.S. embassy employee who watched Soviet tanks on his street. "Am I dreaming or is it reality?" (Phạm G. Đ. 2011: 23). Most South Vietnamese were not prepared for the quickness of this conclusion.

Another example comes from the prominent South Vietnamese novelist Duyên Anh, who published a book-long memoir devoted to his memories of that fateful day. Even though this memoir was published twelve years after the event, the shock of losing South Vietnam remains palpable on the pages. He elaborates, as if assuming that the book speaks for the people on the losing side:

> *Saigon the Longest Day* is from Vietnamese writers, from authentic Vietnamese souls, not from American journalists getting their dough from the CIA and from the KGB. The world, especially the third world, and especially countries where their own people fight and kill one another over communist and capitalist ideologies, by American bombs and Russian rockets, should learn from the experiences in *Saigon the Longest Day*. The longest day resulted from twenty of the harshest years in the history of warfare. Then, after that day, [came] the longest months and years of poverty, stupidity, hatred, prisons, reeducation camps. And warfare still. (Duyên Anh 1988: 5)

This passage includes an articulation of noncommunist and anti-American nationalism. The last two sentences, however, shift the blame to the communists and link the demise of South Vietnam to postwar economic decline and political incarceration. "And warfare still" means that the communists had won the South yet continued to wage war against Vietnamese like himself. On that fateful day, Duyên Anh listened to the announcement of unconditional surrender and thought, "Why surrendering without a fight? I see the same tearful question behind the haggard looks of Saigonese around me" (Duyên Anh 1988: 125–126). The loss of Saigon was painful, but the *manner* of loss was worse for him and other anticommunists.

For the losing side, the profound collective loss tied together the fate of the South Vietnamese. National loss is often portrayed as spiritual death. "I lived like a body without a soul," writes a former prisoner, "at once anguished, pained, ashamed, and hopeless" (Bảo Thái 2002: 22). He continues, "I felt as if we were living a nightmare [after the fall]. Only two months before, my

family had a peaceful life in Đà Lạt. . . . In a short time, all good things disappeared [and] I had nothing left other than two empty hands" (Bảo Thái
2002: 23, 25). Such examples show the link between the fall of Saigon and
their subsequent suffering, including the reeducation camp experience. Some
did not accept the communist victory. For a small number, the abrupt loss
of South Vietnam motivated them to join or organize armed resistance in
the 1970s and 1980s. Nguyễn Thanh Nga, for example, recalls her participation in an anticommunist group not long after the fall of Saigon. The group
was led by a Catholic priest who had served as a military chaplain. Calling
itself National Restoration (Phục Quốc), the group was based in Hố Nai, a
post-1954 settlement of northern Catholics. Nga was assigned by the priest
to recruit more members, and "the number of young men joining the movement grew and enthused us" before the organization was infiltrated and
destroyed a few months later (Nguyễn T. N. 2001: 23–25). Another example
is Võ Đại Tôn, a former colonel who left for Australia in 1975 and then put
together a resistance political organization and attempted to infiltrate Vietnam in the early 1980s. Hiding in a Laotian jungle on April 30, 1981, he recol-
lected the humiliation of the fall of Saigon, especially the hour when the
South Vietnamese leader "Dương Văn Minh announced unconditional surrender to the Communists and ordered all of us soldiers to put down our
arms . . . leading Vietnam to absolute poverty and decline in the face of
progress" elsewhere (Võ Đ. T. 1992: 13).[13] Utterly disgraced by the surrender,
Tôn channeled the humiliation into a desire to return to Vietnam and agitate the people to resist the postwar regime. His experience suggests a link
between the fall of Saigon and diasporic support for the homeland liberation
movement of the 1980s (Nguyen Phuong Tran 2017: 77–96; Tran T. N. 2007).[14]
    Of course, only a very small minority of anticommunists engaged in active
resistance. Many others turned the initial shock to an emotive call to oppose
the Vietnamese Communist Party (VCP). For many, the victorious communists continued to oppress the Vietnamese people after the end of the war.
"April of 1975," states the preface of a collection of poetry by a former prisoner living in Canada, saw "a maddening storm that sank the country into
darkness, when countless families were broken up, when young men and talented people and officers of the Republican military were sent to prisons" (Lê
K. A. H. 2004: 5). Moreover, unconditional surrender was dishonorable and
unacceptable to nationalist Vietnamese, and many anticommunists emphasized that they opposed the decision to surrender. A former Marine notes that
"over 90 percent of Marine officers were imprisoned" and remembers fellow
officers who died in the camps where he was kept: after 1975, they "continued
to fight . . . because of honor, duty, and the nation" (Tô V. C. 2005: 147).
    In the minds of many, anticommunism did not stop after April 1975 just
because the military was ordered to surrender. Instead, they turned memo-

ries of the shameful fall into motivation for opposing the Communist Party. After the shock of national loss subsided, anticommunists interpreted the event by weaving together two lines of thought. First, the decision to surrender unconditionally was unacceptable because they viewed themselves, and not the Vietnamese communists, to be the legitimate claimants to the mantle of Vietnamese nationalism. Second, the decision to surrender came from one person and did not represent the decision of the South Vietnamese military. This military had fought the communists for over two decades, but because of Dương Văn Minh, it did not get a fair chance to fight and demonstrate its worth. It was very difficult for the anticommunists to accept defeat, but it was doubly difficult for them to accept defeat without having engaged in a battle for Saigon. The decision to surrender was shameful, and the manner of loss was dishonorable. Shame and dishonor, in turn, further motivated anticommunists to oppose the postwar government.

The Anticommunist Experience in Reeducation Camps

In addition to the shame of national loss, the incarceration of South Vietnamese military officers and governmental officials contributed significantly to the making of diasporic anticommunism. Incarceration was only one of the postwar policies—which included rapid collectivization of the economy, anti-bourgeois cultural campaigns, classification of southerners according to family background, and expulsion of ethnic Chinese—that led to the "boat people" exodus. Incarceration, however, affected the most politically prominent and influential groups of the Saigon regime. The shock of national loss and the suffering from incarceration provided a one-two punch that strengthened diasporic anticommunism and the determination to oppose the VCP. Thanks to memoirs, much is known about the experience of incarceration. Hà Thúc Sinh published the first major memoir, *Đại Học Máu* (Blood University), in the United States. He began writing it as soon as he landed in a Malaysian refugee camp in 1980, completed it four years later in San Diego, and saw its publication shortly thereafter. At more than eight hundred pages, this memoir details the daily life of detainees in three southern reeducation camps during the first three years after the Vietnam War (Hà T. S. 1985). More memoirs followed in the 1980s and especially the 1990s and 2000s, including many published online (Đỗ V. P. 2008).[15]

A survey of these memoirs shows that the prisoners emphasized the cruelty of camp personnel. They describe both systemic dehumanization and cruelty committed by individuals, using such words as "nightmare" (*ác mộng*), "darkness" (*đen tối*), and "hell" (*địa ngục*), and refer to camp wardens, officers, and guards variously as "animals" (*thú vật*), "devils" (*quỷ*), and "red devils" (*quỷ đỏ*). While some accounts show flashes of humor, the memoir-ists highlight dehumanization to demonstrate that Vietnamese communists were lacking in human decency, punitive and unjust in practice, and totalitarian on the whole. Dehumanization is most vividly portrayed in cases of corporeal deprivation, especially hunger and thirst; injuries and ailments; and poor medical care. Hunger was a constant preoccupation. "Hunger was horrific in Communist prisons," writes a former Marine, adding that a "prisoner's mind was always thinking about different ways to survive" (Đặng V. H., n.d.: 147). "We were never full during all of the time [kept] in the north," writes another Marine. He specifies that each prisoner was allowed two hundred grams of cooked flour for breakfast, 250 grams for lunch, and another 250 grams for dinner: a very small sum for men engaged in hard labor (Nguyễn N. M. 1977: 205). Prisoners ate any animal they could catch at camps and work sites, including insects and reptiles. One writer even witnessed a fellow inmate finding half a dozen newly born field rats and swallowing them raw. Surprisingly, he did not get sick (Đặng V. H., n.d.: 147). But others were not so lucky, and many memoirs note that inmates contracted dysentery, diarrhea, and other illnesses as a result of eating poisonous plants by mistake. Humiliation went hand in hand with physical deprivation. One writer remembers the trip taken to the north in a ship, during which prisoners were kept in the brig. It was very tightly packed, and they could not stretch out or lie down. At mealtime, ramen noodles and Chinese-made dried food were thrown from above. There was little space for urination and defecation, and the stench of body waste was unbearable. The experience was too brutal for at least one prisoner, a military physician, who killed himself before the ship landed (Mai V. T. 1980–1981: 277–280).

Torture was also widespread in reeducation camps, especially during the first few years after the war. Because escape was considered among the worst offenses, captured escapees were punished severely in several ways, usually starting with a beating. Vương Mộng Long graphically describes one such beating after his second attempt to escape. In 1978, he and three other prisoners escaped from a camp in Yên Bái Province, which ended with the death of one prisoner in the jungle. The rest were captured and kept in one camp unit for the first three days before they were transferred to another unit. On the first day, a "very young guard" found a "reactionary poem" on Long and struck his face with an AK-47, knocking out one of his teeth. The guard returned the next day and broke one of Long's ribs. After the transfer, Long endured daily beatings of "more or less two hours" by four young guards. He was left in a public room until the evening, and he looked so lifeless that rumors of his death made their way to other camps and even to his family in the south (Vương M. L. 2012). At a camp in Long Khánh, which had been used as an Army of the Republic of Vietnam (ARVN) base during the war, several prisoners tried to escape during the first six months in detention.

They were caught and hung upside down in Conex containers. These heavy and sturdy steel containers had been used by the U.S. Army to ship materials. Now converted to hold human beings, the containers were completely dark when shut and extremely hot during the dry season. Detainees in the Conex containers were also beaten nightly. Punishment was most severe and frequent during the first few years after the war as a way to deter prisoners from escaping from detention centers and reeducation camps. Prisoners could also be beaten for lesser offenses. In some cases, cadres even killed prisoners for the slightest provocation. One guard, for instance, shot and killed an inmate at a work site because the man did not respond quickly enough to his order (Đỗ V. P. 2008: 21).

Another punitive measure was detention in a cell, usually without food or water. In one form or another, all reeducation camps had a "discipline house" (*nhà kỷ luật*) for inmates who had committed violations. After his second escape, Vương Mộng Long was thrown into the discipline house. His hands and feet were shackled. At noon he was fed the only meal of the day: a bowl of cooked "thumb-size dried cassava," a starchy root, that was covered with dust (Vương M. L. 2012). Long did not specify the length of his punishment, but it was not uncommon for captured escapees to be held in a discipline house for months. Prisoners learned from experience that not seeing someone again after six months meant that he had died in the discipline house. In a rare case, a prisoner was taken out of an underground discipline room after a year; his "legs were paralyzed," and he had developed kidney stones. He was "skin covering bones" but still alive (Đặng L. 2004: 135–136). Besides holding captured escapees, Conex containers also served as a discipline house in some of the southern camps. "The Conex," describes a former prisoner, "was considered a kind of an improvised cell" (Nguyễn H. H., n.d.). Left in the open and without shade, the containers were very hot during the day and very cold at night. This memoirist recalls that a former ARVN captain was thrown into one such container and died several weeks later. Camp authorities announced that he had committed suicide, but the prisoners believed that torture and deprivation had led to his death. In some cases, Conex containers were used as temporary jail cells. One prisoner, a non-ARVN young man who had joined an anticommunist militant group, was held in one in 1977. On capture, he and sixteen other members of the militant group were transported to a detention area and thrown into two Conex containers. They were held inside these containers for forty-five days before being transferred to a larger camp (Trần V. L. 2015).

The brutal treatment strengthened the anticommunist belief among prisoners. Extensive corporal punishment convinced the inmates that "reeducation" was no more than a cover for exacting revenge on the losers. Very often, and especially during the first few years of incarceration, camp authorities berated prisoners for supporting the "imperialist Americans" and fighting against the revolution. The inmates were required to write "confessions" of "crimes" that they had committed against the revolution and, during political lectures and study sessions, to speak about those self-incriminating crimes. The experience of punishment reinforced the prisoners' belief that violence was inherent to the communist system. The fact that most camp cadres and guards had received no more than rudimentary schooling suggested to prisoners that the communist system placed violence over knowledge and blind obedience over justice. It fortified their conviction that it is morally righteous to oppose communism absolutely. Hà Thúc Sinh's memoir, for example, mentions the trial and execution of a fellow prisoner who spoke out against the reeducation policy during a public lecture. After confining the prisoner in a Conex container, the camp authorities staged a trial before all the inmates. They gave a long speech detailing the prisoner's "crimes," sentenced him to death, and executed him a few minutes later. Sinh ends the chapter by stating that "the dead are free of debt, but the living must remember [what happened] so they can avenge" those executed. The living are obligated to fight the injustice of the communist system; otherwise, the living "are worse than dogs" (Hà T. S. 1985: 501).

Though the war ended in 1975, communist violence in reeducation camps showed the prisoners that the war did not really end. A memoir by Tô Văn Cấp focuses on eight prisoners who died from beatings, torture, illnesses, and failed escape attempts. Commemorating the heroism of South Vietnamese officers who died in battle during the war and that of officers who died in postwar incarceration, Cấp writes:

> My comrade-in-arms and my superiors passed away in different ways. Some died bravely for the nation in battle and were buried in coffins decorated with flowers and the flag, with friends bidding them farewell and their families caring for their graves. [Others] had fulfilled their military duty but [after the war] were led into the jungle by the enemy to die, without their military units and their families, without a grave to help their children find their corpses, without a cigarette, a candle or incense. . . . However you departed, you honored the martial spirit of [the Marines]. (Tô V. C. 2005: 325)

In other words, those who died during the war and those who died in postwar reeducation camps were one and the same. Reeducation camps sought to change the prisoners' allegiance, but the opposite occurred. Prisoners strengthened their political identity and appropriated the deaths of other prisoners in their opposition to Vietnamese communists.

In addition to their ordeal in reeducation camps, prisoners were worried about the welfare of their family members back home. For the first few years, most prisoners kept in northern Vietnam did not have any contact with their families. Even after initial contact, mail was infrequent and letters from family were cautiously worded to avoid confiscation. During the first years after the war, family members of the prisoners had no news about their whereabouts. If the inmates were kept in the dark about their families, the families received vague answers, or none at all, from the authorities. In one case, a young wife found out where her husband was detained. In August 1975, she went to the camp with the wives of other prisoners, but the guards refused to let them visit. She returned two months later but was again turned away. Two guards called their husbands "reactionaries" and "counterrevolutionaries" and even threatened to shoot the women. On their third visit nine months later, the prisoners had been moved. It took another year before she received a letter from her husband from a reeducation camp in the North. Another five years passed before she made the first successful visit to a camp in Nam Hà (Bảo Trân 2005: 178–189).

For prisoners in the South, family visits could be more frequent because travel was easier. Yet they too encountered hostility from authorities as well as arbitrary regulations on visits. According to Nguyễn Kim Hoàn, her husband was a former ARVN officer who eluded arrest by moving his family to a Catholic village in the southern province of Sóc Trăng. Because of the lack of teachers in the area, they were given positions teaching math at a local high school. In 1976, a year later, the state security sent soldiers and police to arrest Hoàn's husband on November 20, the Charter Day of Teachers (Ngày Nhà Giáo Việt Nam). Although her husband was detained in the South, it took Hoàn a year and many petitions to track down the location of his detention in Cần Thơ. One year later, he was moved to Camp Cồn Cát, on an island of the province Hậu Giang. Although Hoàn could visit him monthly, each trip now took her three days, and she had to make arrangements with other teachers to substitute for her. After these exhausting journeys, she was only allowed to meet her husband for fifteen minutes. The guards glowered at visitors and prisoners and would heap verbal abuse on anyone straying from even the most minor regulations. Food and supplies were inspected carefully. Sweet potatoes, for example, were halved, and small containers of salt and sesame were stirred up to make sure that nothing was hidden in them (Nguyễn K. H., n.d.: 115–133). In some camps, authorities created more regulations after a visit, such as requiring prisoners to consume all food from families within a week or it would be thrown away (Jolie 2004: 169).

Association with the former regime worsened the already-dire economic situation of the prisoners' families. Just as northerners had been subjected to classification before 1975, southern Vietnamese were classified according to their family background. Families of communist revolutionaries could receive benefits from the state, including job preferences. Conversely, spouses and children of "counterrevolutionaries," including reeducation camp prisoners, were low in the new hierarchy and often faced discrimination. One woman, for example, was dismissed from her factory job when it was discovered that her incarcerated husband had worked in the RVN's Bureau of Psychological Warfare (Nha Chiến Tranh Tâm Lý; Bảo Trân 2005: 184). Many families were forced by the government to move to the countryside, where few economic resources were available to them. Memoirs by family members of the incarcerated also stressed the heavy psychological toll that they experienced in poverty. The prisoners understood that postwar policies such as collectivization, the creation of new economic zones, and the classification of families were blatantly discriminatory and gave rise to a host of intractable problems for the people. Some memoirs note the similarities between life inside and outside the camps, as if those experiences were two sides of the same coin. After a prisoner was granted a rare ten-day leave to see his family, he returned to tell his fellow inmates that "food has become the common topic of conversation" and "the main concern nowadays is how to obtain rice and other items" (Tran T. V. 1988: 288).[16] The shared suffering of the prisoners and their families showed them that the communist system oppressed not only prisoners but also other southerners and, ultimately, the entire country.

In addition, prisoners were subjected to constant humiliation about their nationalist identity. Cadres and guards frequently ridiculed their noncommunist nationalism, even calling prisoners "criminals" (kẻ có tội). More often they were called "reactionaries" (phản động) and "counterrevolutionaries" (chống cách mạng). Most offensive to the prisoners were "henchmen" (tay sai), "puppets" (ngụy), and "puppet soldier [and] puppet government" (ngụy quân ngụy quyền). "Hired soldiers for American imperialists" (lính đánh thuê cho đế quốc Mỹ) was another common phrase. Prisoners were expected to refer to themselves with these terms when writing confessions and discussing study materials (Đinh T. L. 2008: 137). South Vietnamese officers and officials were thus seen by the guards as imperialist rather than nationalist, "American" and foreign rather than Vietnamese. According to a political lecture, the South Vietnamese were "created and built up by imperialism, became effective instruments against our people, [and] were public enemies of the people" (Chánh Trung 1989: 29). The association with foreign powers directly disparaged their nationalism.

The brutal treatment of prisoners fueled their belief that the VCP was obsessed with the protection of its power at the expense of the rest of the country. Contact with the local people in the North generally reinforced this belief, and many prisoners felt sorry for northern Vietnamese. While a number of memoirs begin with a critique of the VCP as persecutors of former enemies and southerners, they end with a broader critique of communism as an oppressor of *all* Vietnamese: southerners and northerners, enemies and supporters of the socialist revolution alike. In their eyes, the VCP's failure to create a prosperous postcolonial Vietnam meant that its leadership was concerned with preserving its own power. For the prisoners, deception, as exemplified by the planned assaults of prisoners by northern civilians, characterized the modus operandi of the VCP.

Many memoirs also point out the lack of formal education among most cadres and guards as evidence that communist legitimacy was based on revolutionary violence rather than scientific knowledge. One memoirist recalls that his camp commander had a "sixth grade or seventh grade" education, which was decidedly "low" in the eyes of the prisoners, who, after all, had at least a high school diploma, with a significant number having been educated at a university, professional school, or military academy (Nguyễn V. D., n.d.: 512). One prisoner felt "frustrated and angry" not only because his side lost the war but also because the winners were uneducated: they were, he said in tears, "so weak, so stupid" (Tran T. V. 1988: 65). The belief that postwar Vietnam was controlled by the uneducated further depressed and angered the prisoners. In addition, the prisoners believed that Vietnamese communists were pseudo-nationalists. In Hà Thúc Sinh's words, prisoners saw that the communists "possessed a false pride and a superiority complex" while "communist soldiers and generals believed in their skill, power, and ability to instruct the puppets" (Hà T. S. 1985: 191). The prisoners believed that guards and cadres resorted to force, violence, and revolutionary credentials to mask their lack of education and technical knowledge: hence a feeling of "false pride" or false superiority. In some respects, this belief that they were the legitimate claimants of Vietnamese nationalism helped them endure carceral hardship. As South Vietnamese nationalism was routinely dismissed, their opinion of the camp authorities reinforced their moral righteousness and strengthened their noncommunist nationalism. The suffering and humiliation of incarceration worsened the experience of national loss, but it also gave prisoners newfound rationale and determination to oppose Vietnamese communism. As a writer points out, the carceral experience "showed that *[prisoners] could never accept Vietnamese communists and co-exist with them*" (Phạm V. C., n.d.: 11). Such anticommunist convictions did not stay in Vietnam but traveled with prisoners after they migrated to the United States and other parts of the world.

Conclusion

As is noted in the Introduction to this volume, Vietnamese refugees and immigrants came to the United States in several waves that bore different experiences in adaptation and integration. While diasporic anticommunism was not the same as adaptation, it too has moved at different paces and undergone different emphases in different periods. During the 1970s and 1980s, Vietnamese refugees were preoccupied with survival and adjustments. They might not have organized as many public protests and displayed South Vietnamese flags as often, but their anticommunism was consistent through activities such as the annual commemoration of Black April and support for homeland liberation organizations (Tran T. N. 2007: 101–145).[17] As a small number of prisoners escaped by boat after release from reeducation camps and resettled in North America, some joined refugees who had not been incarcerated to create informal networks for mutual support and activism. By the late 1980s, former political prisoners had established a number of regional and national organizations in the United States, and some worked to help political prisoners in Vietnam gain release and emigration (Demmer 2017). During the 1990s, the Humanitarian Operation Program led to a new critical mass of tens of thousands of former prisoners and their families, and many of the new arrivals quickly joined or created networks for support and activism (Đào V. B. 2000). As Vietnam shifted direction in the late 1980s and the Cold War came to an end in the early 1990s, the homeland liberation movement ceased to exist, and anticommunist Vietnamese shifted their hope to anti-VCP movements within Vietnam. The arrival of former prisoners reenergized anticommunist activism, especially in the form of protests against the real and perceived encroachment of communism in Little Saigon communities. The demonstrations against the Hi Tek video store were by far the best known and best attended in the United States, but they were hardly the only ones.

In the end, diasporic anticommunism is traced back to political competitions during late colonialism and decolonization, especially during the August Revolution, which saw intra-Vietnamese violence favoring the Việt Minh. Anticommunism intensified during the Vietnam War and took another turn after the fall of Saigon. Postwar policies, especially the incarceration of South Vietnamese government officials and military officers, diminished the hope for national reconciliation and validated wartime beliefs about the inhumanity of Vietnamese communism. The carceral experience convinced prisoners and their families that the VCP was not capable of change in any meaningful way. Resettled abroad, they supported anticommunist activities by establishing political networks, organizing public protests, and contributing to diasporic media. Anticommunism in Little Saigons existed long before their migration, but it is they who shaped diasporic anticommunism as we know it today.

PART II

EXPLORATIONS OF
VIETNAMESE AMERICA

5

BUILDING A PLACE IN THE

SPACE OF LOS ANGELES

Vietnamese Refugee Community Creation, 1975–1990

Elwing Suong Gonzalez

Introduction

The Los Angeles area drew the largest number of Vietnamese refugees in the first decade of resettlement in the United States. Vietnamese refugees resettled in Los Angeles and almost immediately began to eke out a place for their lives in pockets of settlement that became a networked community—one that sought to transverse space and place to connect as a web of multiple locations, united by a common language, culture, status, and history.[1] As Vietnamese refugees moved to create community and worked to maintain (or recreate) cultural institutions and practices, the refugees also had to reconcile their understanding and expectations with those of U.S. resettlement policy and governmental systems. Refugees used the tools provided to them and drew on their own resources to create spaces in community organizations, religious institutions, and schools, as well as via ethnic entrepreneurship.

In 1986, the Unified Vietnamese Community Council (UVCC) of Los Angeles hosted a four-year anniversary celebration. This organization comprised a coalition of Vietnamese refugees in Los Angeles who led a variety of groups and organized events, including the 1982 *Tet* (Vietnamese New Year) celebration that gave birth to the idea of a central, united organization to represent the Vietnamese of Los Angeles. UVCC held the event at the International Institute of Los Angeles (IILA), a service provider organization that received government funding to assist in the resettlement of Vietnamese refugees and that acted as a fiduciary agency for the UVCC. The event program included an introductory "retrospect" section written by then UVCC chairman Sang Quy Do. Do was a refugee who had arrived in the United States in 1975. After being resettled in Ohio, he had initially created an organization called the Vietnamese Community in Greater Cleveland. Like many other refugees, he soon migrated to California. He then worked to establish himself within the local Vietnamese community, helped to create the American Indochinese Association of the San Fernando Valley, and was later elected as the first president of UVCC.

In his reflective historical overview of community efforts at organizing, Do provided many insights into the inner workings and challenges of building a space and creating collaborative efforts in the context of Vietnamese refugee resettlement in Los Angeles. Apparent in all of the difficulties he listed were the inherent tensions that had underscored the entire U.S. military campaign in Vietnam and the refugee resettlement project. The tension grew out of the United States' fluctuating positions as both injurer and rescuer, both providing support for and maintaining control over the refugees. The constant tension of differing expectations and the hovering hand of governmental agencies both helped and hindered refugee community development in Los Angeles. With or without government or volunteer agency (VOLAG) sanction or funding, the refugees themselves organized around their own goals and used their own networks to work toward their own vision of community.

Of course, the Vietnamese refugee population was and is not a monolith, nor was it a population without internal conflict. Vietnamese refugees shared a displacement and migration experience, as well as national origin, and these commonalities alone prompted refugees to find one another and create networks. However, the very nature of Vietnamese refugee making also resulted in frictions and factions within the refugee population. The political and historical context that created the refugees, resettlement policies, refugees' own desires, and the sprawling landscape of the Los Angeles region caused both the concentration of refugees in Los Angeles and the splintering and creation of multiple communities within the same region.

Vietnamese refugees, especially those who arrived in the United States in and just after 1975, often had had much exposure to and sometimes deep connections with America. They had also experienced much trauma and dislocation, and many challenges and upheavals, due in large part to the U.S. military and imperial project in Southeast Asia. It was a project that had entwined the Vietnamese with the United States. The effects of U.S. involvement in Vietnam were built on the legacy of decades of French colonization and within the Cold War context. U.S. military intervention and the U.S.-backed South Vietnamese government greatly shaped the experiences of the Vietnamese population and subsequent refugees. Even within the context heavily shaped by the United States, the refugees had their own very distinct ideas about what they wanted and expected from life (and the U.S. government), about what resettlement should be like and how it should work, and about what their new identity and community would look like.

Here, I examine some of the efforts of those within the Los Angeles Vietnamese refugee community to actively organize themselves to meet their own needs, as well as the barriers they faced in doing so. I look at specific mutual assistance organizations (MAAs)—like UVCC—and their aims and interactions with government institutions and agents, as well as their contact and conflicts with one another. I set this examination in the context of the tensions that frame the entire refugee resettlement and are ever-present in the uneven relationship between the Vietnamese refugees and the U.S. government and its agents, a relationship that is shaped by the legacies of U.S. imperialist intervention and Cold War politics.

The Demands of U.S. Refugee Resettlement Policy

That the Vietnamese were refugees specifically of a Cold War conflict that the United States had been embroiled in for two decades had profound impacts on the types of resources the Vietnamese were granted and the expectations imposed on them by the government. The conflict between the refugees' simultaneous dependence on the government and expectations for their independence from government was manifest in the controlling and stifling hand of the VOLAGs and the government entities that controlled government funding directed at assisting Vietnamese refugees in attaining self-sufficiency.

The two main aims of Vietnamese refugee resettlement policy were refugee economic self-sufficiency and assimilation. To produce a successful resettlement that would validate American involvement in Vietnam, refugees were expected to accept their placement with sponsors, become gainfully employed, and acclimate to American society. Key to the success of this rewriting was the production of what scholar Yen Le Espiritu refers to as the "good refugee"—the trope of the refugee who expressed gratitude for rescue, dutifully adhered to government expectations—namely by accepting the parameters of federally outlined resettlement—and then became a self-sufficient and productive new member of American society (Espiritu Y. L. 2006: 412; Espiritu Y. L. 2014: 8). The federal government feared that impediments to assimilation, such as refugees who were on welfare or were concentrated in a few geographic locations, would undermine a successful refugee resettlement that could rewrite a positive ending for the otherwise disastrous and divisive American war in Vietnam, validating American military interventions and imperialism during and after the Cold War.

Despite government attempts at controlling refugee resettlement, tensions rose to the surface and manifested in various forms of refugee resistance. Though welfare use was discouraged and stigmatized, a large proportion of Vietnamese refugees used public assistance during their resettlement. The federal government also promised the public refugee dispersal via the refugee sponsorship program, to be carried out by the VOLAGs contracted by the federal government. However, California, and in particular Los Angeles, became the site of the largest concentration of Vietnamese refugees in the United States within the first year of refugee resettlement. And though VOLAGs and local governments tried to control the development of the Vietnamese American refugee community, refugees directed their own resettlement and created enclaves and organizations to further their own personal, political, and cultural visions of life in America.

At the behest of the U.S. government, the volunteer agencies tried to drive refugee resettlement along the lines of a specific vision, in which the central tenets were control of the refugees, minimization of refugee impact on Americans, and the production of successful refugees, which thus acted as a validation of Cold War policy. Refugees' rejection or renegotiation of the help they received highlights the tension between the expectations and the reality of Vietnamese refugee resettlement in the United States. Resistance to the external forces attempting to shape the resettlement experience and the refugee image are manifest in many of the actions of Vietnamese refugees who wanted to determine their own course of resettlement. Reframing the narrative of refugee crisis and American humanitarian rescue as one in which Vietnamese refugees used the resources that were available to them, at times manipulating them or rejecting them altogether, creates a very different story.

In the introduction of the UVCC event brochure, Do expressed the mixture of resentment and appreciation Vietnamese refugee community leaders had felt about the assistance and services provided by the VOLAGs. Do described the VOLAGs as having "formidable influence to keep the community under their shadow . . . their towering influence suffocat[ing]." At the same time, the VOLAGs often provided the necessary foundational support to the refugees in both resettlement and the organization of trained leaders "to understand the rules of the 'game (Do Q. S. 1986).'" This conflict and tension was visible in multiple aspects of the refugee resettlement project, as with refugees who were using government-provided tools to create community organizations and who chafed at the amount of control resettlement agencies exerted over their trajectories.

Mutual Assistance Associations: What Did Vietnamese Refugees Really Want and Need?

Almost immediately on arrival in the United States, Southeast Asian refugees began organizing around different issues relevant to their relative communities. And for specific networks of individuals within the Vietnamese refugee community, creating private, nonprofit associations served as a means of meeting a variety of pressing needs. These grassroots efforts were organized around accessing social services, cultural preservation, religion, special interests, economic development, and political activism, or simply around the general needs of the broader Vietnamese refugee community. These refugee-created and refugee-led efforts eventually came to be called mutual assistance associations (MAAs).[2] Some MAAs established physical locations for their organizations and functioned for years, while others existed in name only (Do Q. S. 1986: 2). Because these organizations were established and run by refugees who themselves identified with the particular experiences and circumstances of resettlement and spoke the same language as those seeking services, those organizations that sustained longevity were unusually successful in assisting refugees with services (Rutledge 1992: 57–8). The most successful MAAs (in terms of finances and longevity) were often those that carried out functions that aligned with official resettlement goals: namely economic self-sufficiency via vocational training, English-language instruction, and job placement. Those MAAs that existed to meet refugee needs and desires outside of the primary government objectives and fulfilled needs such as social support, cultural maintenance, and familial or professional networks were often edged out of government funding and relied on member dues and donations.

Before federal or even local government became directly involved in funding, contracting, or even acknowledging Vietnamese MAAs, individual refugees were already networking to organize and fulfill needs within specific subsets of the broader refugee community. The creation of professional, elderly, religious, regional, cultural, and veterans' associations grew out of friendships and connections within the Los Angeles refugee community. Those who started early MAAs that evolved into functional organizations in more than just name often possessed relatively high levels of cultural capital. English-language ability, familiarity with American government or social structures, or personal or professional connections with government or resettlement officials helped certain leaders transform specific MAAs into more stable organizations that developed relationships with governmental institutions or business interests.

Some refugees who had worked in media or journalism banded together to assist one another in getting back into their former professions. A group of volunteers established the Vietnamese Refugee Communication Center in Hollywood in an attempt to centralize job information for refugees.[3] Journalists and media producers worked to create radio and television stations directed by and for the local Vietnamese refugee population. Originally based in Los Angeles, Saigon TV was founded and directed by April Tran Hoang

Ngu to produce Vietnamese-language programming to broadcast via Los Angeles public access channel 18.[4] Los Angeles is a place of central importance within American media, and many first-wave Vietnamese refugee journalists had connections with U.S. news agencies from wartime work. These connections facilitated the creation of media-related professional organizations specifically for Vietnamese refugees in Los Angeles and contributed to the development of enduring Vietnamese-produced and Vietnamese-focused media. Today, Saigon TV still broadcasts throughout Southern California, along with nine other local Vietnamese-language television stations.

Elderly Vietnamese refugees needed additional support and a central location for meeting with other seniors, establishing social networks, and addressing their lack of employment, extra difficulty in gaining English-language skills, and increasing seclusion when family members were at work and school. Paul Tran Nguyen, a former province chief and candidate for president of South Vietnam, had resettled in Los Angeles in 1975. Using his leadership experience, position as a prominent member in the refugee community, and English-language ability, he established the Vietnamese Elderly Association in Koreatown and in Chinatown. The organization operated a nutrition program and social events for elderly Vietnamese refugees and provided a space where elders could be consulted about cultural rituals and provide "mutual psychological support (Do Q. S. 1986: 3, 5)."

The most famous Vietnamese actress among the refugee community in the United States, Kieu Chinh, likewise resettled in Los Angeles. In the late 1970s, she worked through the Catholic Conference and Los Angeles City College (LACC) to eventually establish a Vietnamese arts and cultural center at the college. Vietnam House, housed in the LACC library, served Vietnamese students as "a home, a place where we could meet, in which we could come together and speak our own language . . . a place to experience the Vietnamese culture. . . . It is important that our cultural traditions be maintained and that our traditions find a place in this multi-ethnic American culture."[5] As a very visible and notable member of the refugee community in Los Angeles, Kieu Chinh was able to gain funding from the United Way, office space at LACC, and the endorsement of government officials and honorary board members, such as state secretary of the California Department of Health and Welfare Mario Obledo and Los Angeles mayor Tom Bradley.[6]

Los Angeles Government and the Vietnamese Refugee Community

While Los Angeles's civic leaders, such as Mayor Tom Bradley, and local government bodies and service provider agencies helped facilitate refugee resettlement and community development, they also maintained an unequal relationship with the Vietnamese refugee community. By deciding which leaders and organizations would receive official validation and funding, county and city government had a strong hand in shaping the development of the Vietnamese refugee community. Much of the funding that was available for community development was funneled from the state and federal government through the county in the form of grants and contractual program funding. Therefore, the organizations that most closely aligned with government goals and the focus on economic self-sufficiency received grants and contracts from the county.[7] As much as Vietnamese refugee leaders lamented the uneven distribution of funds and the unequal role in decision-making that privileged government representatives and their narrow goals of economic self-sufficiency, they also regularly sought official validation and recognition and regularly petitioned for more government assistance in building their organizations.

In response to the ten-year anniversary of the beginning of the refugee influx from Southeast Asia, in 1985 the County of Los Angeles Board of Supervisors declared April as a commemoration month for Indochinese refugee residents. Spearheaded by the office of Edmund D. Edelman, supervisor of the county's Third District, where the largest concentration of Vietnamese refugees resided and sought county services, the county also hosted a commemorative event at the County Hall of Administration. Notes and press releases in preparation for the event provide a small glimpse into the aims and views of Los Angeles County efforts toward Vietnamese refugee resettlement. County officials were interested in presenting a specific vision of refugee resettlement, one that often aligned with federal resettlement goals and the traditional narrative of refugee crisis, assimilation, and success.

In correspondence between staff members in Edelman's office, the event is referred to as "a good idea, and good press" that would "give a boost to many of the Indochinese emigres here in Los Angeles and the Third District," and "if handled right, it can be a day to give some reflected glory on all the refugees and immigrants who are part of this diverse community."[8] The program agenda consisted of remarks from Edelman and "people involved in refugee resettlement," including Lavinia Limon, the chair of the Los Angeles County Refugee Forum, which helped coordinate county resettlement efforts. Many of the talking points revolved around lauding the efforts of the county in facilitating successful resettlement, recognizing the refugees' struggles and endurance in establishing a community in Los Angeles, and acknowledging the importance of tolerance and acceptance in the changing and diverse cultural landscape of the region.

Refugee voices appeared within the program, but local officials chose which individuals would represent the Southeast Asian refugee community and what they would briefly talk about. Edelman's office arranged for one refugee speaker from each of the Southeast Asian nations that refugees came from (Vietnam, Cambodia, and Laos) to "share their stories of escape from their homes and beginning new lives in the United States."[9] The foci of the event—and the narrative of Southeast Asian refugee flight and successful resettlement in the United States and of refugees as part of the diverse community of Los Angeles—were delivered through specific refugees from refugee programs that worked with or were funded by local government institutions. In contrast with the UVCC event, the county event was organized by nonrefugees and acted as both a validation of the role of government in that resettlement and as a vehicle for the promotion of the vision of a multicultural Los Angeles.

Without a doubt, the efforts and resources channeled to the Vietnamese refugee community through Los Angeles city and county officials reflected true concern for both the refugees and the broader population of Los Angeles and assisted in the successful implementation of many necessary programs and services. However, like VOLAGs, local government used refugees and refugee organizations to implement programs designed by nonrefugees. Local officials incorporated refugee input insofar as it kept the overall goals of local government in place. Though these goals sometimes conflicted with those of the refugees, Vietnamese refugees used the opportunities and resources made available to them in Los Angeles but continued to push at the boundaries for fulfillment of their own vision of resettlement, using limited entry points into the local infrastructure to voice their concerns, demands, and expectations.

The city council and mayor approved and provided funding and permits for various events that Vietnamese refugee community leaders requested, such as a flag-raising ceremony at city hall during the first *Tet* that Vietnamese refugees would celebrate in Los Angeles in 1976. The city council also issued a resolution to use the opportunity very early on in refugee resettlement in Los Angeles "to recognize and welcome Vietnamese-Americans on the occasion of the holiday of Tet."[10] In the resolution of official city support for the Vietnamese refugees in Los Angeles—a group the city council took the liberty of labeling as "Vietnamese-Americans" in January 1976—city officials ascribed two mutually reinforcing narratives. In the announcement, the Los Angeles City Council resolution extended an official welcome to the refugees, which employed both the narrative of the good refugee who sought freedom and desired to live in the United States and the narrative of the United States as a land of opportunity that had a legacy of welcoming people from all over the world, discursively establishing the Vietnamese refugees as simply the newest group to be incorporated into the local cultural landscape.[11]

While the support from Los Angeles city officials for the Vietnamese refugees was politically motivated as part of a broader Cold War anticommunism, it was much more a part of a regional climate of official civic accommodation of the refugees in a rapidly changing and diversifying Los Angeles. This zeitgeist in the local government was not necessarily present in other parts of the United States where Vietnamese had concentrated. Even greater than the official shows of city support for the refugees were the efforts of the County of Los Angeles, which was vested with the task of directly providing social services to the Vietnamese refugees. The supervisor of the downtown and central city district in which most Vietnamese initially settled became one of the strongest and most visible government advocates for the Vietnamese (and broader Southeast Asian) refugee community. Serving on the Los Angeles County Board of Supervisors from 1975 to 1994, Edmund D. Edelman was a popular former city councilmember who had very publicly advocated for the needs of the most vulnerable in the county and who had a history of advocating for and initiating services for the Los Angeles Asian American community as well.[12] Especially with the beginnings of the second wave of refugees into Los Angeles in 1978, Edelman voiced concern that the county services available to them were not easily accessible or made known to those who needed them.

The Los Angeles County Indochinese Refugee Services Center and Refugee Advocates

In 1979, Edelman presented a proposal to the board of supervisors to better coordinate services for Southeast Asian refugees in Los Angeles County. He proposed a task force made up of representatives of various government agencies providing services to the refugee community, and an advisory council of leaders from within the Southeast Asian refugee community to strengthen and formalize ties with county and city governments and provide a "cultural, recreational, and social outlet which will facilitate the mental well-being, ethnic identification and new hopes for building their families in the United States."[13] The greatest part of his proposal was the creation of a county-sponsored Southeast Asian refugee center as an outstation centralizing the most relevant county services in one accessible location.[14] After months of meetings between county officials and members of the Indochina Refugees Referral Center's advisory council, the Indochinese Refugee Services Center (IRSC) opened in November 1979 on the outskirts of Chinatown in a county-owned building with staff to act as a liaison between public and private agencies.[15] As time went on, the center hired refugees as staff members and relied on interagency networking with local MAAs and refugee staff at other organizations to organize and make accessible city and county services.

Once the center began operating, its staff brought to light many complaints about county services, from both refugees being served and the VOLAGs referring the refugees. The issues were mainly the lack of bilingual staff, difficulty in accessing information about services, and lack of coordination with private hospitals providing medical health services to refugees.[16] The center provided both organized momentum and a physical space in which various interests related to the provision of services to Los Angeles Southeast Asian refugees could come together. By 1982, IRSC was serving its purpose as a "one-stop center" for refugee services, having assisted more seventeen thousand clients via the Los Angeles City School Indochinese Vocational Project, fourteen thousand clients with the Women, Infants, and Children (WIC) nutrition program, and about seven thousand clients with health and mental health services, and with various Department of Public Social Services (DPSS) programs.[17]

Various leaders from within the refugee community, especially founders and directors of MAAs and those who had worked closely with private and public resettlement agencies, sat on the Los Angeles County Indochinese Advisory Board for the center and were actively involved in county actions affecting the refugee community. Representatives of major service provider organizations, such as Pacific Asian Consortium on Employment (PACE) and the International Institute of Los Angeles (IILA; a major local immigrant assistance nonprofit organization), and VOLAGs, like the Catholic Welfare Bureau, met with representatives of smaller refugee MAAs and Buddhist temples. The representatives networked and advocated for their constituents at board meetings to voice concerns and complaints to the county and state.

Local refugee community leaders provided input on the types of services the center could provide and began to advocate via the center and the Los Angeles County Board of Supervisors for specific types of funding and services and to voice opposition to county actions they deemed harmful to the refugees. Paul Tran Nguyen—the founder and director of the Vietnamese Elderly Association, a relatively small MAA that had a lot of leadership value in the community because many members were respected elders—sat on the advisory board for several years. Nguyen used his positions on the board of both the Indochinese Refugee Service Center and of the Asian/Pacific Counseling and Treatment Center (APCTC) to advocate for broader refugee community involvement in the 1983 decision to consolidate the Indochinese Mental Health Unit, which was more ethnic-group and refugee specific, into the broader APCTC.[18] Like Nguyen, leaders of smaller MAAs used their place on larger local government advisory boards to channel refugee input into decisions made by government agencies and their service providers.

While the Indochinese Refugee Service Center was intended to exist as a central hub for Los Angeles refugees and was an expression of official support for the refugee community, the center was ultimately an externally created government entity directed and operated by county officials and staff. Even if the center was staffed with refugee employees and volunteers, had input from an advisory board that included refugees from the community, and provided services built around refugee needs, the effort was not refugee led. Instead, those individuals and efforts acted more as a facilitator for county services that were provided within the parameters of the federal government's vision of successful resettlement. In proposals and reports, both county officials and various leaders of the Vietnamese refugee community continually emphasized the argument that despite obstacles and challenges, the refugees could become and were becoming productive members of society. Ultimately, those Vietnamese refugees and organizations with visions that aligned with the federal and local governments' focus on economic self-sufficiency and assimilation were the ones that gained access to funding and therefore furthered their vision. This manifested in the lion's share of funding going to programs that facilitated vocational training and education programs.

While government programs and funding laid the foundation for much of the early Vietnamese refugee community in terms of generating guidelines for providing services and organizing for group funding, money for refugee services in Los Angeles County and across the nation began to dry up in the late 1980s. In addition to federal tax cuts and changes in refugee policy, the sense that, as a group, the Vietnamese refugees had achieved relative success was generated by media depictions of the Vietnamese as the newest model minority (Espiritu Y. L. 2014: 94–96). As funding decreased, government-contracted service providers put even greater emphasis on on-the-job and industry-specific vocational training. This move resulted in funding cuts to nonvocational education programs, English-language instructional programs, and social and cultural organizations.[19] At that point, VOLAGs and local funding providers directed many refugee-led MAAs that had depended on government support to "move towards a system of diversified funding which could possibly cushion the loss," without any true explanation of how to do so.[20] To the federal government, the sense that adequate economic self-sufficiency and assimilation had been achieved for at least the first wave of the Vietnamese refugees resettled in the United States meant that the refugee crisis had been resolved, regardless of the real needs that continued to exist in the refugee community.

Struggle and Negotiation for MAA Funding and Support

As a second, larger wave of Southeast Asian refugees began to flee and seek asylum in the United States beginning in 1978, the once ad hoc decisions to admit and provide funding for those refugees dramatically changed and were codified to both reduce government spending on refugee programs and move away from large-scale refugee admissions. The Refugee Act of 1980 and its 1982 amendments codified many of the priorities and actions that had previously been produced by ad hoc presidential decisions. While a new, larger annual ceiling for refugees was created and a process for raising that ceiling was put in place, many of the same priorities and objectives that undergirded the first wave of Vietnamese refugee resettlement became official and systematized. Refugee dispersion, focus on economic self-sufficiency, monitoring of refugees and their resettlement, provision of funds to states for resettlement services, and the utilization of public and private nonprofit agencies to facilitate resettlement were all written into law.

Additionally, one of the biggest points of conflict within refugee resettlement—welfare—was also addressed in the new laws. The limiting of cash assistance to refugees was clearly stipulated in the act, as was a limit to the amount and length of funding to states for refugees. As funding was reduced, and with the prevailing emphasis placed on self-sufficiency, the task of meeting refugee community needs was moved away from federally funded private service providers and government agencies toward MAAs, in which resettlement officials "wield a unique influence in shaping community attitude and behavior regarding welfare and employment" (Coleman 1982). The tension between dependency and independence continued as the government worked to shape Vietnamese refugee resettlement and community outcomes at the local and federal levels. MAAs were then seen as a vehicle for the federal government to deter dependency on government assistance, while the MAAs themselves depended predominantly on government funding.

Early MAAs were sometimes financially or otherwise supported by VO-LAGs and later by grants from local and state governments but were able to maintain relative autonomy.[21] After the Refugee Act of 1980 established the Office of Refugee Resettlement (ORR), the federal government also began providing financial grants and contracting with MAAs for refugee services. In Los Angeles, though a host of organizations existed and were tapped to provide various services to the refugee community in the first years of resettlement, they were mainly VOLAGs and nonprofits that served refugees and immigrants in general, or the broader Asian American community. Vietnamese-specific MAAs initially were very small and usually revolved around a very specific issue and group of people, often replicating the extended family networks that refugees desired to recreate or maintain (Le X. K. and Bui D. D. 1985: 223–224). As some MAAs grew, they were contracted to facilitate and act as liaisons for local and government institutions that provided services for refugees. MAAs also worked to facilitate social inclusivity and provide a cultural space that would eventually, in some cases, create a platform for cultural empowerment and political expression and representation (Tran T. N. 2007: 106–107).

Early on, many VOLAGs and related government institutions (such as the Metro North and Inglewood branches of the Department of Public Social Services) hired refugees as case workers, interpreters, and program coordinators to address the needs of the Vietnamese community.[22] Each of the VOLAGs working on resettlement in Los Angeles hired at least a secretary or interpreter to provide translation for incoming clients. Similar positions at various agencies such as the Asian American Mental Health Research Center,[23] the Interagency Forum on Resettlement,[24] and the International Institute of Los Angeles were filled by refugees who had training in the medical field or who had a good grasp of the English language.[25] Refugee leaders were also invited to serve on advisory boards for a variety of county and service provider agencies and of community organizations. From those positions and from the knowledge gained by volunteering in efforts led by those organizations, local Vietnamese refugee leadership emerged to establish MAAs and organize events coordinated by the Vietnamese for the Vietnamese, although these associations and events still rested on a foundation of government funding, oversight, and interaction.

The MAAs were financially supported primarily by the federal government. Throughout the first decade of official MAA contracting and funding through government sources, MAA leadership lamented the lack of diversity of funding sources and options as one of their major concerns.[26] This funding relationship represented a continuation of the enmeshed position of U.S. government control and its underwriting of Vietnamese refugee resettlement and community development. And, as scholar Jeremy Hein explained in his examination of the role of the modern state in the development of ethnic organizations, the government utilizes its political and fiscal power to shape the boundaries and rivalries of ethnic groups in the interest of social cohesion (Hein 1997: 280). In the case of the Vietnamese refugees, there was a federal government effort to control not only how and where the community would develop but also what problems and issues the community could actively address and how they could do so. By channeling federal money toward MAAs that provided social services, and contracting them to do so, the state directed refugees to address problems via a coethnic intermediary, both privileging Vietnamese community groups that aligned with state goals and further erasing the visible presence of the federal government in refugee resettlement.

Conflicts about and between Los Angeles MAAs

Although working with American agencies and government institutions created certain types of conflict or uneasy relationships, working from within the Vietnamese community was also not without conflict. Tensions developed as organizations competed for legitimacy and recognition not only from government bodies that controlled resources but also from the Vietnamese refugee community itself. In the event program for the celebration of the UVCC, Chairman Sang Quy Do pointed to internal issues and conflicts within the refugee community that he saw as deterrents to the creation of a unified community. Do described the enduring refugee trauma and lack of trust in the leadership as great hindrances. The issue of trying to regain status for those who had been government and military leaders in Vietnam sometimes impaired community organizing. Do recalled that "any attempt to represent the community would be shut off as many potential 'leaders' and rivals seemed unable to compromise" and that "public gatherings always resulted in angry debates and personal attacks (Do Q. S. 1986: 1)." Additionally, both the dispersal of the refugee population throughout sprawling Los Angeles County and also the ethnic and religious divisions that contributed to the creation of different concentrations constituted obstacles to a unified community in Los Angeles.

The earliest efforts to organize within the Vietnamese refugee community were meant to fill specific cultural and social needs that only the refugees could address. Small, localized networks of refugees providing social interaction, cultural and religious events, and specific services such as rotating credit or professional contacts cropped up around Los Angeles. Larger efforts, however, were less likely to develop apart from the VOLAGs and service provider agencies, which did not really allow for truly autonomous MAA development. After the beginning of the second wave of refugees, it became clear to both Vietnamese refugee community leaders and the local government that there was a definite need for more intensive and sustained services, and governmental programs did not have adequate representation by Vietnamese or Vietnamese-language staff to fully accommodate refugee needs.[27]

In 1982, after nomination and election at an announced, open meeting of the Refugee Mutual Assistance Coalition, officials selected two Los Angeles MAAs, UVCC and the Southern California Indochina Chinese Association (SCICA),[28] to represent the local Vietnamese refugee community in the county Refugee Targeted Assistance Program (RTAP). RTAP was a federal program enacted by the Office of Refugee Resettlement to channel moneys directly into localized service provider programs that could facilitate the overarching goal of refugee self-sufficiency. The main objective of granting money to counties was to specifically assist refugees to "find and retain jobs, increase their employability potential and/or enhance their job market possibilities" as the key components of self-sufficiency and the vision of successful resettlement.[29] After the adoption of the California State Master Plan for refugees, Los Angeles County formed RTAP to meet the state goal of refugee social and economic self-sufficiency. The county brought both UVCC and the SCICA on board to advise and act as a liaison between the Los Angeles Vietnamese refugee community and the county services that primarily revolved around employment training and placement and medical and mental health services.

Aside from providing a seat at the table and access to funding to work in referring refugees for county services, inclusion in RTAP and Los Angeles County funding helped UVCC, SCICA, and other MAAs to grow as organizations. However, this opportunity often came at a cost. Organizations that had addressed multiple issues in the Vietnamese refugee community sometimes tailored their programming to fit into grant requirements that maintained the federal government focus on self-sufficiency via vocational training and English-language instruction. Additionally, MAAs had to partner with an established service provider organization that would act as a fiduciary agency on their behalf.

Both UVCC and SCICA partnered with the International Institute of Los Angeles (IILA), an organization that had worked with immigrant communities in Los Angeles for decades. In recounting the joint venture of IILA and the Vietnamese refugee MAAs, Sang Quy Do stated that the relationship eventually became an unhappy one, as the IILA, or "mother agency," "became the owner of the [UVCC]" and "the community felt they existed only in name (Do Q. S. 1986: 5)." Many of the decisions and program implementations that UVCC had envisioned were subsumed by the IILA. And, because of its financial stability, refugees who had been working as volunteers for UVCC accepted paid positions at IILA. After two years with IILA, "UVCC still held an empty bag," and it came close to collapsing. Eventually, UVCC and SCICA both struck out on their own, using volunteer labor and member donations to continue operating without a larger "mother" organization to oversee them. Both organizations eventually managed to tap into small grants directly from the county and became refugee service providers through their own offices in Los Angeles's Chinatown.

A similar situation occurred with another service provider in Los Angeles, the Special Service Group (SSG), and the newly formed Vietnamese Chamber of Commerce (VCC). SSG was an organization that had grown out of the United Way, and like the IILA, it had a long history in Los Angeles working in underserved communities, eventually becoming a service provider for refugees. As VCC partnered with SSG, the smaller organization became subsumed by the larger, with "the mother agency unwilling to recognize the identity of its partner . . . and members of the Vietnamese Chamber of Commerce lost their enthusiasm and dedication. Existing staff evolved [sic] themselves to work directly with the mother agency (Do Q. S. 1986: 4)." The VCC never recovered from the loss of volunteers and staff to SSG, and because of the inability to establish autonomy and attain funding, it eventually ceased to exist.

While the issues of organizational and funding competition and control had a hand in destroying the VCC, the location and nature of Los Angeles resettlement also helped lead to its demise. Sang Quy Do also commented on the scattered and sprawling nature of settlement in Los Angeles County, where "the leadership [of] the Vietnamese community got lost in the vast cluster of small towns and cities (Do Q. S. 1986: 2)." The fact that Los Angeles Vietnamese refugees and their businesses were much more dispersed throughout the county and that their various concentrations were located in other ethnic enclaves deterred the Vietnamese refugees from developing a single unique location for a Vietnamese business district. Additionally, the rapidly growing and concentrated Little Saigon Business District in Orange County began attracting more attention and patronage. There, in 1985, the Vietnamese refugee community officially established the Vietnamese American Chamber of Commerce (VACOC), an organization that grew out of the Orange County chapter of the Los Angeles–based VCC (Day and Holley 1984: A1). Shortly afterward, the VCC in Los Angeles collapsed, while the VACOC went on to become the largest Vietnamese chamber of commerce in the United States.

Some of the first-wave refugees' aversion to organizing came out of a distrust for the motives of leaders, which had carried over from the experiences of government corruption in Vietnam and of those who had been cheated or robbed during the course of flight and resettlement. Sang Quy Do described some of the dynamics within the Los Angeles Vietnamese refugee community that had deterred larger organizing efforts, including infighting and competition for leadership roles that prevented talented and qualified potential leaders from getting involved (Do Q. S. 1986: 3). Do pointed to issues that came directly out of the nature of refugee resettlement—namely trauma and displacement—noting that "self-alienation, low self-esteem and face loss . . . all seemed to be very devastating to the reformation of the Vietnamese sense of community." Do also commented on the desire of those of higher status to reclaim their positions of power, which meant that "a couple of dozens of associations came into existence, mostly to satisfy the needs of founders rather than to actually activate the community to provide services to other refugees (Do Q. S. 1986: 1)." Former high-ranking military officers and government officials, who wanted to forcefully regain their status among the refugee population, were some of the most vocal leaders in the refugee community. This group included leaders who sought to organize anticommunist demonstrations against the new regime in Vietnam. These demonstrations often tapped into the refugee desire to return home and channeled organizing energy and refugee donations toward return to Vietnam, rather than resettlement in the United States.

A small group of such individuals also formed homeland liberation groups (HLGs) with the explicit goal of returning to a noncommunist Vietnam. The most popular of these groups was the National United Front for the Liberation of Vietnam, an HLG that sought to organize guerrilla fighters to invade and retake Vietnam (Getlin 1983: OC_A1). While many MAAs and VOLAG-aligned Vietnamese refugee groups could not or would not officially back these HLGs, individuals who worked for those organizations openly supported the movement (Holley 1983: OC_A1). The hope to return to and reclaim Vietnam, and the channeling of funds and energy to that end, directly conflicted with the aims of refugee resettlement expected from VOLAGs and government entities but aligned with some of the core desires of a large swath of the Vietnamese refugee community.

In contrast to leaders of MAAs, who focused on setting down community roots in the United States, HLG leaders viewed "all overseas Vietnamese as political sojourners who needed to channel their time, energy and resources towards a separatist agenda" (Tran T. N. 2007: 158–159). Do described some of these individuals as "a few vocal persons [who] had been kicking around with abrasive and abusive language and attitude" in response to the efforts at less political events and association organizing (Do Q. S. 1986: 1). Though Vietnamese refugee anticommunism seemed in line with American foreign policy, these particular manifestations of this specific ideology did not find a niche in the more left-leaning local politics of Los Angeles. Some organizers of Los Angeles MAAs and student groups did work on organizing pro-American and anticommunist events and rallies, but more extreme demonstrations were rejected because they challenged the expectations of acceptable refugee expressions of their particular and unique views.

Such was the case of Dr. Nguyen Thai—founder, president, and executive director of Thanks America Day Inc. Nguyen Thai was based in Los Angeles County and hoped to organize a 1989 event called Thanks America Day, similar to several Orange County rallies and events, such as a 1985 event similarly called Thanks, America (Jarlson 1981: OC_A1; Landsbaum 1985: OC_A1; Duarte 1985: OC_A1). Thai wrote letters to Los Angeles County officials and agencies requesting official support for his event. UVCC advised county officials not to support the effort, as other Los Angeles MAAs and refugee groups would not participate, because of "Dr. Thai's dramatic, flamboyant . . . overzealous approach to 'thank America.'"[30] The same type of "flamboyant" demonstration of anticommunism and support for the United States that flourished in more right-wing Orange County (Ong and Meyer 2008: 78–107; Nguyen Phuong Tran 2017) met resistance in the more liberal left-wing county and city government of Los Angeles and was weeded out from the Los Angeles Vietnamese refugee community by lack of support from both local government and the established organizational leadership of the MAAs. The local government vision of a Los Angeles Vietnamese community was built upon assimilation into a specific multicultural vision and did not make a space for all the sentiments and political opinions that existed in the Vietnamese refugee population, even the loudest and most prevalent ones.

Conclusion

As the first wave of Vietnamese refugees began to put down roots and develop a community in Los Angeles in the late 1970s and early 1980s, the refugees not only had to maneuver through their negotiations of Vietnamese and American culture and systems but also had to balance the expectations of both Americans and Vietnamese involved and invested in their resettlement. Because of the nature of Vietnamese refugee resettlement—its roots in American imperialism, the legacies of VOLAGs and American institutions in Vietnamese American resettlement, and the internal conflicts bred out of the war and Vietnamese history—the refugees found themselves forced to navigate a complex web of expectations and power dynamics. Utilizing various tools and resources their status offered them, and at times repurposing or manipulating them, Vietnamese refugees made choices of which obligations and identities they would accept and reject. And while the social, cultural, and political landscape of Los Angeles offered many opportunities, ultimately, the seized opportunities did not coalesce into a broader, unified Vietnamese community. They did, however, produce lasting impacts on the development of Los Angeles and set the stage for the later growth of Vietnamese communities and enclaves throughout the Los Angeles region.

The growth of mutual assistance associations to further a variety of goals and visions for the Los Angeles refugee community, the creation of specific spaces and expressions of Vietnamese culture and ideologies, and the development of niche economies revolving around ethnic and cultural demands and desires were manifestations of the will to build community. But the entangled nature of the refugee-government relationship and the legacies of the Vietnam War, coupled with social and cultural changes in Los Angeles, heavily shaped visions of a Los Angeles Vietnamese community. Much like federal refugee resettlement, assistance from local government and institutions in Los Angeles was a double-edged sword that provided necessary resources and guidance but that also imposed control and expectations on the refugees. As Vietnamese refugees utilized government funds and resources in their own resettlement, they eventually became free agents with a variety of tools and visions that resettlement policy and authorities had not foreseen or considered, and they ultimately charted their own numerous and varied paths.

Archives

- *Los Angeles City Council Public Record*, Los Angeles City Archive.
- *Mayor Tom Bradley Administration Papers*, UCLA Library Special Collections—Charles E. Young Research Library, UCLA.
- *Papers of Edmund D. Edelman, 1953–1994*, Huntington Library—Manuscript Department.
- *Southeast Asia Resource Action Center Records*, MS-SEA004, UC Irvine Libraries, Irvine, California—Special Collections and Archives.

6

VIETNAMESE AMERICANS
AND THEIR HOMELAND

Transnational Advocacy Efforts and Diasporic Ties

Ivan V. Small

Introduction: The Vietnamese Diaspora, Origins, and Return

The Vietnamese global diaspora is significant, estimated to be around 4.5 to 5 million. But unlike many other diasporas, the origins of much of this exodus is primarily rooted in refugee, rather than migrant, mobility in the aftermath of the so-called Vietnam War. From around the late 1970s to the early 1990s, thousands of Vietnamese, especially from the former Republic of Vietnam, chose to leave Vietnam by boat. The country's long coastline, as well as its network of inland rivers leading to the ocean, facilitated this mode of escape. Vietnamese would crowd small fishing boats meant for offshore fishing, plying the Eastern (South China) Sea with crude navigation technologies to reach refugee camps elsewhere in the region, from the Philippines to Indonesia. There refugees were screened in camps and then sent to processing centers, where they awaited permanent resettlement in countries such as the United States, Australia, Canada, France, and Germany. Receiving camps even included Hong Kong and Macao, where eventually some of the arrivals were found to be from more proximate northern Vietnamese departure points, especially Haiphong, blurring the definitional line between political refugees and economic migrants and eventually leading to the closure of camps in the 1990s. By this time, the United States had also instituted the Orderly Departure and Humanitarian Operation Programs allowing for the direct flight out of qualifying refugees.

As many refugees were resettled into third countries of permanent resettlement, they faced a plethora of challenges and struggled to adapt to their new circumstances. While these are well documented, and while a broad swath of American sociological studies in the 1980s dedicated themselves to analyzing assimilation potentials in new immigrant environments, an analytical framework oriented toward the nation-state and the nuclear family household led to the de-emphasis of transnational and extended kin ties and concerns, especially in the formulation of applied social work policy recommendations (Haines, Rutherford, and Thomas 1981). As Vietnam's economy further suffered under command economy socialism and an ongoing U.S. embargo, everyday living conditions deteriorated rapidly. By 1986, Vietnam was rated as one of the world's poorest countries. With the elimination of market-based farming-production incentives, Vietnam's staple rice supply plummeted, leading to severe food and nutrition shortages (Kerkvliet 2005). Among the refugee community that had safely made it abroad, there was immense concern about the living conditions of family members left behind. These individual and collective concerns laid the foundation for what would become vibrant and sustained diasporic remittance and humanitarian-aid flows from across the globally dispersed diasporas back to the Vietnamese homeland, now estimated at greater than 17 billion U.S. dollars annually.[1]

Humanitarian Outreach

The humanitarian concerns that catalyzed diasporic aid flows channeled back to Vietnam in a variety of creative ways, often initially depending on networks of Vietnamese contacts located across different geographies. In the case of the United States, where the largest community of Vietnamese outside of Vietnam has resettled, sending monetary assistance to Vietnam was severely hampered in the 1970s and 1980s by the embargo restrictions imposed by the U.S. government, including a block on financial channels. In the 1980s, Foreign Assets Control Regulations in the United States limited remittance transfers to not more than $300 to an individual in Vietnam within any consecutive three-month period—a tiny amount, much of which would disappear to rent-seeking government officials and middlemen. Many Vietnamese Americans in the early years therefore relied on a network of diasporic contacts to get money and letters back to family in Vietnam. A central node in this network was France, where a Vietnamese community had existed for many years, going back to the colonial period, and which maintained diplomatic relations with Vietnam after the American war. Diasporic remittances were also sent to Vietnamese stuck in refugee camps, especially those that had been "screened out" following the 1989 Comprehensive Plan of Action, whereby asylum seekers were either accepted as political refugees or disqualified as economic migrants and therefore placed in limbo to be repatriated to Vietnam (Lipman 2020).

Remittances from the Vietnamese diaspora to Vietnam or to refugee camps were mostly directed to individuals and family households at the beginning. Remittances were intended for economic survival, and they often took material form—both because financial channels were limited and also because of widespread scarcity in Vietnam's postwar economy. Vitamins and medicines, a common form of aid sent back to Vietnam, could address family health concerns or be traded in Vietnamese black markets for foodstuffs (Đặng P. 2000). Collective action among the diaspora to support Vietnamese in Vietnam, beyond individual remittances, slowly began to emerge in the 1980s. This paralleled secondary migration processes in which previously isolated families were able to move to more concentrated Asian American community nodes in places like California and Texas, where they could reconnect with extended kinship and ethnic networks and turn their economic attention beyond immediate survival to humanitarian concern for other Vietnamese in the diaspora and homeland. These ranged from advocacy for Vietnamese in refugee camps and political lobbying against human rights abuses within Vietnam to fundraising for anticommunist groups focused on regime change in the homeland. Direct humanitarian aid to Vietnam was still difficult to organize, but an array of seeds for action were being laid. The catalyzing agents for these were diverse and cross-generational, from former ARVN veterans to hometown and alumni associations and college students. The forms they took and the support they garnered depended in part on the social, cultural, economic, and political conditions in places of resettlement.

Diaspora Politics

The Vietnamese American population is often stereotyped as largely anticommunist and politically conservative, with a much larger percentage leaning Republican than other Asian American groups. As discussed in the Introduction to this volume, this may be a generational phenomenon. The fact remains, however, that the majority of Vietnamese American elected officials affiliate with the Republican Party. This is generally attributed to the political sentiments and affiliations of the first wave of high-ranking ARVN officer refugees who came directly to the United States in 1975. A number in this first wave arrived in the United States with expectations that their exile would be temporary and that regime change in Vietnam was a serious and imminent possibility. South Vietnamese political elites played a formative role in shaping the diasporic politics of communities of initial resettlement. This includes the substantial Vietnamese American population of Orange County, California—which, distributed between the two municipalities of Westminster and Garden Grove, has come to be collectively designated as Little Saigon. The naming of Little Saigon has sometimes become a political statement in municipalities with large Vietnamese populations, as choosing such a name, as in the case of a similar attempted designation of the San Jose, California, Vietnamese business district in 2008, may be associated with more contentious conservative politics. In many communities in the Vietnamese American diaspora, the flying of the former Republic of Vietnam flag is widespread. Activist groups demanding recognition have circulated petitions and successfully lobbied for local municipal regulations to replace the Vietnamese government's yellow-star-on-red-background flag in public settings and recognize the former RVN flag, with its yellow background and three red stripes, as the official "Heritage and Freedom" symbol representative of diasporic Vietnamese.[2]

Anticommunism among the diaspora is also entangled with a complex politics of history and demands for recognition in the U.S. resettlement context (Vo Dang 2005; Ong and Meyer 2008). The Vietnamese diaspora in the United States is a direct legacy of American involvement in Vietnam and the U.S.-RVN alliance. Many refugees feel doubly betrayed by the communist takeover of South Vietnam and the shift in U.S. policy in the 1970s under Nixon that led to the perceived abandonment of its Vietnamese ally. Conjuring memories of the collective alliance against communism can therefore serve as a means of staking claim in American society, reminding empathetic Americans of the common Cold War cause that both countries fought and ultimately lost. This can be seen, for example, in anticommunist protests among Vietnamese Americans where signs in English remind onlookers of the fifty thousand American soldier casualties, without referencing the far higher South Vietnamese death toll incurred over the course of the war. In Australia as well, where domestic politics have generally been more conservative and immigration policy more restrictive, anticommunism appears to be a more significant facet of Vietnamese diasporic expression, mirroring cultural politics in geographies of resettlement.

In other countries such as Canada, the prevalence of anticommunist community politics is less visible, and one is less likely to see, for example, the yellow RVN flag that is so ubiquitous in America's Little Saigons flying in Vietnamese shopping malls and community centers. This also extends to Vietnamese communities in Europe. In France, there has long been a relatively even division between more conservative anticommunist refugees and left-leaning members of the diaspora that preceded the refugee exodus (Bousquet 1991). Germany, with its own history of Cold War division, also brings together disparate elements and politics of the diaspora, including former war refugees to West Germany and former North Vietnamese labor migrants to East Germany. Serious divisions among the population segments based on politics, regional origin, and time frame of arrival linger. Other Eastern European countries, such as the Czech Republic, Poland, or Russia, with Vietnamese immigrant populations inherited from socialist-era labor-migration policies also have different political orientations, as well as more northern regional origins (Schwenkel 2017). Resultant political affiliations extend even into religious ritual forms and symbolisms (Hoskins 2021).

All of this has directly or indirectly affected transnational ties between the diaspora and Vietnam over the years. While the Vietnamese government has long highlighted the humanitarian contributions from the Vietnamese European diaspora in its publications, such as Quê Hương (Homeland) of the State Committee for Overseas Vietnamese Affairs, it has been more cautious in identifying aid flows from the United States. Indeed, for many years any collective aid to Vietnam beyond individual and household remittance flows was largely discouraged or at least kept discreet in many Vietnamese American communities. As one reporter for a Vietnamese-language media outlet in Orange County, California, described, "it was only in the 2000s that we could start to announce fundraisers for humanitarian aid efforts in Vietnam, before then there was suspicion that individuals and businesses that supported such benefits were sympathetic to the communist regime in Vietnam." Fundraisers for humanitarian organizations note that attitudes have changed over time and that in the last generation support for efforts that are clearly not linked to politics, such as raising money for educational scholarships or orphanages, has become more mainstream. But still, any appearance of communist sympathy can easily sabotage the efficacy of such efforts, and anticommunism has also been used as a distracting foil attached to interpersonal conflicts and rivalries. For such reasons, some organizations in the Vietnamese American community that raise money for aid efforts in Vietnam do not register for 501(c)(3) nonprofit status as they do not wish to attract too much attention, despite the tax-exempt incentives in the United States for doing so. But they also express agency in doing what they feel is right for Vietnamese left behind, even if such activities ruffle more conservative feathers within diasporic communities.

Homeland Politics

Politics in Vietnam has also had an effect on the visibility and effectiveness of humanitarian aid efforts from the diaspora. Just as there is mistrust of the Vietnamese government among a significant sector of the overseas Vietnamese population that fled as refugees after the communist victory in 1975, there is also ongoing suspicion by the Vietnamese state of elements of the Vietnamese diaspora that may continue to explicitly or implicitly advocate for regime change in Vietnam. Supporters of the Republic of Vietnam are considered in Vietnamese state historiographies to have been on the wrong side of history. Until recently, government officials of the Saigon regime were widely referenced as *"nguy,"* or puppets, in official narratives of the war. Since some former RVN officials and veterans did actively pursue an anti-revolutionary agenda of reversing the communist victory in the years after 1975, including maintaining governments in exile, there is an anxious history of the socialist Vietnamese state attempting to keep anticommunist sympathizers out of the country.

Starting in the early 2000s, official attitudes toward former political refugees began to soften. Vietnam was becoming a tiger economy and had achieved normal trade relations and diplomatic recognition with the United States. In 2004, the Vietnamese Politburo passed Resolution 36, which symbolically affirmed Vietnamese located anywhere in the global diaspora as integral members of the nation, whether a former political refugee in California or an ethnic Vietnamese in Cambodia. This was followed by the creation of "Overseas Compatriot" organizations (*Hội Kiều Bào*) designed to encourage state linkages with overseas Vietnamese communities. In 2007, Prime Ministerial Decision 135 offered five-year visa waivers for overseas Vietnamese, which have been popular among the diaspora and which facilitate repeated entries and returns. In 2008, the amended Vietnamese Nationality Law extended Vietnamese citizenship on the basis of the principle of consanguinity to any overseas Vietnamese born in Vietnam or descended from a Vietnamese national. A series of property-ownership legislative measures have also been enacted, and the government regularly offers workshops for overseas Vietnamese entrepreneurs interested in investing in Vietnam. This latter group has emerged in recent years as an important new source of support for humanitarian philanthropy.

When it comes to humanitarian aid from the diaspora, any projects that bring in development assistance from abroad fall under the oversight of the People's Aid Coordinating Committee (PACCOM). This in itself creates challenges for many humanitarian organizations. To work most transparently and effectively, an aid project must be registered with the government and work together with state as well as local officials and mass civil society organizations, such as the Women's Union, to implement their projects. PACCOM's three stated criteria for NGO project approval are no politics, no religion, and no profit. From PACCOM's perspective, it is important that all NGOs, overseas Vietnamese or otherwise, work closely with local organizations and agencies to coordinate their efforts. They offer the example that in times of natural disaster there are often many groups pouring into the affected locale to provide relief, but without effective coordination and the fair and equal distribution of resources, such aid can potentially aggravate community tensions and divisions. According to PACCOM, aid projects should also be all inclusive and not have hidden political or historical agendas. This latter point reflects a bias that many diasporic NGOs confront when trying to conduct work in Vietnam, one that at times discourages them from attempting to formalize their presence. Relatively local organizations largely driven by distributing donations that may already be under the nonprofit radar abroad, relying primarily on part-time volunteers and without local staff in Vietnam to manage cumbersome activity and financial-reporting requirements, may avoid the bureaucratic, oversight and political suspicion hurdles of PACCOM registration. Indeed, a PACCOM affiliation itself may hamper fundraising efforts among the overseas diaspora if a nonprofit organization appears to be working too closely with Vietnamese government officials and Communist Party mass organizations.

Alliance Building

The operational confusion that inevitably ensues when humanitarian impulses and fundraising visions translate to messy on-the-ground project logistics and management have led to various attempts to build alliances among diasporic Vietnamese organizations over the years. Such efforts seek to channel aid and share expertise more efficiently but also help navigate Vietnamese bureaucratic oversight requirements for their operations. One of these is the Vietnamese American NGO Network, which brought together a confederation of official and unofficial NGOs (with varying levels of 501(c)(3) and PACCOM registrations) in the mid-2000s.[3] It received foundation seed grants in the United States during a time when there was heightened foundation and official aid interest in mobilizing diasporas to assist with homeland development as part of the gray-matter and Home Town Association models promoted by development economists. The network organized a series of workshops in the United States and in Vietnam to discuss strategies for more effective development impact and local capacity building. Part of the impetus for this group was to establish an official recognition of the alliance itself as a PACCOM-registered NGO, under whose auspices some of the smaller organizational members could then operate in Vietnam without the extra hassle of individually navigating Vietnam's overseas development-aid bureaucracy. For a number of reasons, this vision never panned out, although the alliance continues as a knowledge-sharing network among diasporic individuals with a history of transnational engagement and advocacy in Vietnamese development aid.

There have also been attempts to build transfer-of-knowledge projects. An initiative of the United Nations Development Programme, called the Transfer of Knowledge by Expatriates Abroad (TOKTEN), was designed in the 1990s to create a roster of overseas Vietnamese experts that could assist Vietnam through technical knowledge. It was eventually closed, with the understanding that the Vietnamese government's Committee for Overseas Vietnamese Affairs and Fatherland Front had created similar parallel initiatives, such as the Vietnam Union of Science and Technology Associations (VUSTA). Indeed, across the global diaspora one can find various confederations of academics, scientists, and other experts, often consisting of alumni groups of students originally sent abroad, that seek to contribute their talents to Vietnam's development in areas such as engineering, education, economics, and entrepreneurship. An October 30, 2020, conference in Ho Chi Minh City, for example, focused on the role of diasporic expertise in promoting digital transformation and overcoming the challenges of COVID-19 for Vietnamese development.[4] About five hundred overseas Vietnamese are estimated to return to Vietnam on a regular basis to provide consultation services to the government. There are also similar associations of current students studying overseas who intend to return to Vietnam, whose members are encouraged to be more visible—often with ceremonial handovers of funds at embassies abroad—by the Vietnamese government. Humanitarian fundraising frequently targets more immediate emergency-relief causes such as flooding and typhoons, an increasingly common disaster scenario in low-lying regions susceptible to global warming. Overall, the Overseas Vietnamese Committee's work under the Ministry of Foreign Affairs has been primarily to document existing efforts and celebrate the work of diasporic humanitarians, rather than to directly coordinate and facilitate their efforts, but such documentation depends on the willingness of project organizers to make their work publicly visible to the state.

On the fundraising side, there have been many well-intended efforts over the years, especially by younger members of the diaspora, to help channel donations intended for humanitarian aid to appropriate and well-managed projects within Vietnam. Because younger diasporic Vietnamese, unlike their parents' generation, often do not have many personal connections within Vietnam, especially in rural areas where poverty is most entrenched, finding target destinations for meaningful and effective charitable-giving efforts has been a significant interest. While these efforts wax and wane, they have ranged from employing technology and building websites and databases intended to connect donors across the global diaspora with development projects in Vietnam to mobilizing social networks for public fundraising campaigns. The latter take such forms as music and fashion shows or happy hours to solicit support from professionals and community members both among the diaspora and among diasporic returnees working in Vietnam. One such group that was active in Saigon chose a different charity to highlight and raise funds for at each of their monthly events. Returnees are of increasing importance in contemporary Vietnamese society when it comes to connecting business success and social activism. While there has been a lot of energy invested in such efforts, their drive has often not been sustained over time as organizers move on to other interests and locations.

Beyond specific Vietnamese diasporic fundraising efforts, many Vietnamese American professionals also participate in pan-Asian philanthropic initiatives. A number of these are institutionalized and actively cultivate community by organizing events like giving circles and galas. Targeted efforts to develop relations with individual high-value donors are also a key philanthropy strategy. A number have offered matching funds to encourage organizations to promote greater support from their smaller donors. These initiatives, while effective, tend to be a step further removed from the projects they are raising funds for, and the motivations of givers are often as much connected to cultivating social relations and community-building interests among other Asian Americans as to specific advocacy for and knowledge of on-the-ground humanitarian projects, which often span Asian and Asian American causes. When it comes to building relations, knowledge exchanges, and humanitarian aid connections with other members of the diaspora based in non-U.S. locations, there has been relatively little in the way of formal efforts to coordinate such work, beyond the efforts of the Vietnamese government to track them. However, a great deal of diasporic aid directed to grassroots projects is motivated by informal hometown and personal connections. In this sense, the local community groups that receive such money play an important role in tracking donors across the global diaspora and helping to facilitate their reconnection with one another once they return, often to gauge and celebrate the humanitarian and development impact of the projects their donations have funded. Maintaining not only globally dispersed kinship but community connections over the years therefore has been an important aspect of expanding Vietnamese remittance giving into the collective charitable arena.

Motivations

What is it that personally, collectively, ethically, and otherwise motivates Vietnamese Americans and other members of the global Vietnamese diaspora to turn their attention back to Vietnam and to give—beyond the immediate familial obligations that characterize the most commonplace remittance patterns? In the realm of fundraising, personal benevolence as well as social recognition and reputation are contributing factors, as the actions and responses of many attendees of such events attest. But for the humanitarian actors who channel such funds back to Vietnam and oversee their implementation for development assistance and relief to the poor, what drives them to set aside time, often on a volunteer basis, to conduct and sustain such work in fields such as educational, medical, and environmental aid?

In research conducted with Vietnamese American NGO workers and volunteers in Vietnam, volunteers were motivated to give to Vietnam because (1) they recognized the uneven economic differentials between the United States and Vietnam as well as within Vietnam and wanted to directly address poverty reduction and social justice issues, and (2) the process involved some form of (re)connection to a place of origin and the reestablishment of identities dispersed through migration.[5] Collective philanthropy or social remittances of this sort have been identified by analysts as "identity maintaining mechanisms" (Najam 2006). However, for younger volunteers such work was often less about maintaining and more about constructing connections with a homeland with which they had little or no experiential connection. Many arrived in Vietnam with idealistic ambitions; some stayed for a few months or a year and then returned home to jobs or graduate school. Others stayed on in Vietnam, often moving to more urban areas and finding other opportunities in Vietnam's fast-growing economy. A group of college summer volunteers I met reflected on how coming to Vietnam in a service capacity offered a chance to see Vietnam on their own terms, rather than through the lens of their parents' historical and political memories or through the filter of family visits that were limited to particular locales and people. For them, humanitarian work offered an important form of agency that allowed them to explore their ethnic roots and decide for themselves what kind of relationship they wanted to have with an inherited "homeland" and its complex histories of war and exodus.

For some older volunteers, humanitarian relief work offered an opportunity to fill an emotional hole. For many years after migrating abroad, they were unable to return to Vietnam. There was little room to think about broader collective and ethical concerns in an environment of raising families, working jobs, and sending family remittances to support basic survival. There was nonetheless a lingering sense of guilt and awareness of how the stark economic differences in the West and in Vietnam shaped opportunities and futures. Now older and more established, and with the lifting of travel restrictions and embargoes of the past easing return to Vietnam, they are able to not only reconnect with communities of origin but also develop new relations in which there is a felt value that they can bring to the exchange. For example, a doctor returns regularly on medical missions to central Vietnam to provide health clinics in underserved rural areas, addressing issues ranging from cleft palates to leprosy—health challenges that can be addressed with some medical care and resources. A former teacher raises money for pedagogy workshops in the Mekong Delta, promoting more interactive learning styles. Another volunteer in the same program raises money to buy bicycles so that children can reach their schools more easily, making it easier for them to continue their education while also returning to their family farms to help out their parents. A former chef helps open a cooking school in Ho Chi Minh City where rural-urban migrant youth can learn practical culinary and service skills in order to find jobs in the city's high-growth and high-income restaurant sector. Another volunteer raises money for learning materials for a school serving disabled children in a small coastal town, allowing them to participate in meaningful activities rather than being relegated to isolated lives at home. Yet another pools resources from former U.S. veterans to buy books for a mobile book library that travels from school to school in Huế, where media resources are otherwise limited. In the same city, a California-based volunteer raises diasporic funds abroad for solar-powered cooking stoves that can be distributed to households with limited resources for equipment or fuel. A number of volunteers are involved in scholarship programs providing grants for students to continue education from elementary school to university as well as encouraging their families to support their children's educational pathways, a challenging proposition when weighed against the potential household revenue lost from not working full-time, even if only at marginal subsistence jobs.

In some cases, NGO workers of this generation said that they purposely avoided projects that involved or were proximate to extended family members, as giving to them always felt like an obligation and detracted from the rewarding feeling of altruistic charity. One man in his sixties told me how his humanitarian efforts in Vietnam caused tensions and ultimately ruptures among his extended family relations in Vietnam. "They [my family members] say why do you give to all of these people you do not know but not to us, your own family? I try to explain to them that the people I help are in much greater need, but they do not understand. Over time I have stopped telling them when I return to Vietnam. But it feels much more rewarding that I am giving to people truly in need, rather than just giving out my money because of obligations even when my family no longer needs it." Again, there is an important dimension of felt agency that drives much giving among this generation. This sentiment was widely expressed among a significant representation of female project directors who have chosen to foster flexible career paths out of the humanitarian aid, fundraising, and grant-writing skills they have developed in humanitarian project management.

In addition, a significant segment of 1.5-generation Vietnamese Americans expressed that returning to Vietnam was fulfilling in that it allowed them to navigate skill sets to more effectively bridge two cultures. They had Vietnamese linguistic capacities and cultural affinities that exceeded those of their second-generation counterparts, as well as English-language, American-cultural, and international-business familiarities that helped make their organizations more legible to the kinds of international donors and publicity campaigns that were necessary to promote and fundraise for humanitarian work in Vietnam. Andrew Lam, a 1.5-generation Vietnamese American author who has been a vocal advocate for diasporic humanitarian causes in Vietnam, captures the sentiments of the diaspora, but especially this generation, in an edited volume of Vietnamese American literature in his reflections: "Among Vietnamese, a collective understanding assumes that we have all suffered an epic loss, so it is pointless to ask . . . when we set foot on the American shore, History is already against us. Vietnam goes on without us. America goes on without acknowledging us" (Tran D., Lam A., and Nguyen H. 1995). For this generation, the bridging work of navigating dual trans-Pacific cultures also helps foster important notions of agency, belonging, and appreciation in which one no longer remains forgotten, bypassed, or unacknowledged. Indeed, across generations, there was a strong sense that humanitarian aid served as a form of gift giving, reflecting a long-standing philosophical recognition of how in gift relations the felt agency of the gifter may be elevated, as opposed to the obligatory sense of remittance fatigue, in which the agency and origins of giving are lost amid cycles of filial duties and reciprocal expectations and demands (Mauss 1967; I. Small 2019).

Most of the diasporic organization representatives I interviewed were characterized by the charismatic leadership, founding vision, and management oversight of their directors. Board members, where they existed, were often long-standing friends, and projects relied on a network of personal connections, in some cases going back to relationships and community connections preceding refugee migration. A number of organizations, as discussed, chose not to officially register with the government. In many cases, the humanitarian aid involved an annual trip to distribute relief supplies or an in-person volunteer project by overseas Vietnamese with a finite timeline and service-output agenda. Offices were sometimes run out of hotel rooms or the homes of local staff members. While those organizations that had chosen to formalize could expand their sources of revenue by not only distributing funds raised abroad but also applying for large foundation and overseas development-aid grants to support their operations, in many cases the part-time nature of an organization's staff led to a preference for informality. Projects ranged from poverty reduction to community development, scholarship assistance and education, labor and sex trafficking, school building, disaster relief, and environmental conservation. While some relied entirely on diasporic contributions and volunteers, a significant number played a bridging role to help channel relief money—in some cases from former American military veterans or activists who felt remorseful about the wartime destruction of Vietnam—back to local projects in their hometowns. Organizations tended to expand or decline in their services over time depending on the sustained energy and commitment of their leaders. Few were highly bureaucratic, which reduced overhead but also limited institutional continuity and impact.

Many of the groups had close linkages with the communities they worked in and felt that their direct service and personal passion made their work more effective than that of larger bureaucratic international organizations and NGOs that channeled their money to mass organizations managed by inefficient or sometimes corrupt government social workers. Because there is no clear tax-exempt status for nonprofit organizations in Vietnam, there was additionally less incentive to go through the lengthy paperwork and bureaucratic hurdles of formally registering their organizations, an issue that many community-based organizations in Vietnam find challenging. If they did need to expand outreach, such organizations had working relationships and linkages with larger established organizations that could help them to further channel and distribute their aid. Many such organizations, despite the encouragement to formalize their operations on both the donor-sending and service-receiving sides, preferred to maintain informal operations and a lower-key presence.

Development, Religion, Philanthropy, and Corporate Social Responsibility

Over the years, diasporic outreach to Vietnam has taken a variety of forms. The more political ones that include demands for democracy and human rights generally find that an overt message makes it difficult to conduct work within Vietnam. Much of their advocacy remains outside of the country, including lobbying in countries of resettlement for international diplomatic policies demanding more accountability from the Vietnamese government. Human rights were for many years linked to U.S.-Vietnam trading relations under the Jackson-Vanik Amendment and the annual renewal of normal trade relations prior to Vietnam's accession to the World Trade Organization. The salience of human rights as a critical political and diplomatic tool has declined in recent years, potentially hampering the ability of such efforts to effectively reach their intended legislative audiences. Organizations that pursue more seemingly apolitical humanitarian projects, largely within the realm of poverty alleviation and economic development, have been able over the years to develop working relationships with local individuals, community groups, and government officials inside Vietnam. These in turn have allowed them to sustain and expand their operations. For such groups over the long term, humanitarian relief has given way to strategic development aid, as many such organizations strive to teach fishing rather than to give fish, as one put it. Among many of these groups, capacity-building workshops have been one of the primary ways that diasporic Vietnamese volunteers have attempted to play a role in building up local project efficacy and leadership.

However, humanitarianism has always been a crucial foundation and continuing motivation for much diasporic giving, especially when it comes to religious giving. For many in the diaspora, long-standing relations with local temples and churches, especially in rural areas, are the most trusted way to channel money directly to communities in the greatest need. Across Vietnam, one can find freshly rebuilt and expanding religious buildings adorned with donor placards and bench inscriptions attesting to the financial support of the diaspora. For some donors to religious organizations, motivations go beyond altruism. In many cases, diasporic donors describe such donations as a way of giving back, of expressing gratitude for divine intervention that may have helped them to safely escape abroad, especially during the years of precarious boat refugee flight, and to find economic security and social stability in their places of resettlement. Donations also serve to remember the loss of and pay homage to other family and friends who were not so fortunate. In some cases, religious giving is attached to politics, as a number of Buddhist, Catholic, Cao Đài, Protestant, and other religious subdenominations are not officially recognized in Vietnam and their leaders and followers have often been arrested or harassed. Members of these denominations overseas tend to also lobby for reforms to Vietnam's state policies on religious freedom. Over the years, a transnational circulation of monks, nuns, and priests has emerged across the many communities of global Vietnamese, whereby diasporic donors give directly to trusted religious leaders who will shepherd their funds back to meaningful social assistance projects in Vietnam. As with NGOs, the growth and revival of temples and churches in Vietnam has led to a situation where many are unregistered. Smaller-scale religious groups in many cases do not find it worth the time and effort to get official recognition for their status, especially if they have working relationships with local officials, and like NGOs, there are not necessarily the same financial incentives that there are in the United States to register a religious group. Diasporic Vietnamese also frequently direct remittances to older relatives, often women, who in many cases decide to allocate such funds to religious organizations with which they are involved. As one woman who receives money from her son in California explained, "I am old now and do not need many material things. But the temple gives me spiritual peace, and they do many good deeds to help those who are much poorer and need the help. Giving to the temple makes me happy." Indeed there is a long-standing tradition of charitable (*từ thiện*) activity in Vietnam, and for many in the diaspora, it makes the most sense to tap directly into existing projects (Nguyen P. A. and Doan D. 2015).

Studies on the state of Vietnamese philanthropy reveal that large donors play increasingly significant roles in driving humanitarian assistance in Vietnam, a phenomenon confirmed by many NGOs.[6] Many such philanthropists hail from across the diaspora, but also increasingly from among successful Vietnamese and permanent diasporic returnees who have relocated their personal and business operations to Vietnam. Vietnam's fast-growing economy has led to unprecedented prosperity for quite a few entrepreneurs. Overseas Vietnamese capital played an important role in a number of start-ups and joint business ventures, and those who were able to build their businesses early on in Vietnam's market liberalization and economic transition have benefited tremendously. Many wealthy Vietnamese across the diaspora as well as diasporic returnees in Vietnam are now playing significant roles in directing some of their newfound wealth to support humanitarian projects in the country. According to the State Committee for Overseas Vietnamese, in 2019 there were about three thousand overseas-Vietnamese-led enterprises in Vietnam, with registered capital of US$4 billion. This coincides with a period in which overseas development aid to Vietnam is on the decline as Vietnam climbs into the ranks of middle-income countries, while the Gini coefficient is rising, reflecting growing income inequality. Some philanthropists and business leaders have set up challenge grants, encouraging NGOs and community-based organizations that are vying for their money to match their donations through additional fundraising. Across Vietnam, it is clear that a new philanthropic culture often connected to reputational branding is emerging, and it is especially prominent in Saigon/Ho Chi Minh City, Vietnam's largest city and a key driver of the country's economic growth. Many diasporic philanthropists expressed that giving back is personally fulfilling, reminding them that their motivations for returning were never solely about accumulating profit in an emerging market.

However, the most significant development that parallels Vietnam's economic growth is the expansion of corporate social responsibility as a major source of funding for humanitarian and development projects (Nguyen Minh, Bensemann, and Kelly 2018). While the majority of the international NGOs in Vietnam are based in the capital, Hanoi, and a significant proportion of community-based organizations in the north are dependent on or an indirect outgrowth of such organizations, in Ho Chi Minh City many community-development initiatives have fewer government connections and less support. Yet with a number of companies looking to polish their image in Vietnam and attract a growing base of ethically and environmentally conscious consumers, there is a clear move toward corporate social responsibility (CSR), or corporate citizenship, as some companies call it. With increasing formalization of Vietnam's tax code, there are also some allowances for charity deductions following the 2008 Corporate Income Tax Law. Ironically, concurrent with the formalization of Vietnam's economy, CSR initiatives rely on finding officially registered humanitarian organizations to direct their money to. There is growing realization that with the right combination of corporate financial support, government connections and access, and official NGO registration and institutionalization, charitable organizations can mobilize significant resources and recognition for their humanitarian work, creating possibilities for further expansion and greater impact. To this end, there have been capacity-building workshops to help recognize and strategize the potentials of such cross-sector partnerships. With regard to the humanitarian landscape of Vietnam today, the most significant development when it comes to diasporic advocacy has been the growth of a new class of overseas Vietnamese business leaders who are mobilizing their own personal resources through philanthropic giving as well as those of their companies through corporate social responsibility.

Transnational Orientations

The Vietnamese diaspora is spread globally, and in many ways, it remains scattered on the basis of the particular political, economic, and cultural dynamics of host countries of resettlement. Over the years since 1975, however, this diaspora has matured and exerted significant collective agency to reorient itself back to Vietnam, not simply from a distance but increasingly through in-person return, now estimated at over half a million annually, as well as through investment. Transnational advocacy among the diaspora to influence Vietnamese affairs has diversified from political lobbying for human rights and democratization at a macro yet physically removed policy level to more direct and personalized humanitarian engagement through strategic development assistance and philanthropy. These activities are varied in scale and intention, often gendered and generational, and challenging to track because of varying degrees of formality. While the Vietnamese government has noted these diasporic aid flows with interest and has sought to intervene in the management and oversight of such funds, many groups understandably choose to remain below the radar, and because of that, they may also be relatively unknown to one another.

While there have been occasional attempts to create alliances among such humanitarian groups, they quickly diverge along the specificities of issues and geographies. At the end of the day, hometown affiliations, but not necessarily associations, are the primary liaison for diasporic reconnections with the homeland. There are also in many cases unspoken political and personal divisions between and within organizations. Ironically, China's aggressive security stance toward Vietnam in recent years, particularly in the Eastern (South China) Sea, has emerged as a point of shared ethnonationalism across interest groups in the diaspora and within Vietnam. As one large-scale Vietnamese American philanthropic donor explained his rationale for giving to humanitarian causes in Vietnam, "When I see the poverty in Vietnam and limited choices that people have to make because of that poverty I feel ashamed, especially as China has become wealthier and bullies Vietnam even more. I hope through my and others' efforts that Vietnam can eventually grow stronger and prouder. Even though I live in America and have earned my wealth there, I am always a Vietnamese."

The organizational structures of most diasporic NGOs, formal and informal, are relatively weak compared to better-funded and permanent fully staffed institutions with larger bureaucracies and more significant overhead costs. They are often driven by personal connections and trust networks that, depending on the situation, may or may not enhance the effectiveness of their aid and development projects. More generally, overseas Vietnamese humanitarian organizations are in part driven by a degree of diasporic nationalism that strives to help the Vietnamese nation, even if not necessarily the state, all while cultivating pride in and awareness of the various forms of Vietnamese diasporic identities that have also emerged outside the country's geographic boundaries. There is a widely expressed sense that Vietnamese culture (*văn hóa*), wherever it unfolds, is something to be proud of and to share across the diaspora and homeland. Although there remain holdouts among some overseas refugees who refuse to return, there are now a much greater number who view the diasporic relationship with the homeland as no longer one of permanent exile but one of cautious and anticipatory engagement and, through such engagement, eventual social and political reform. The transnational orientation of much of Vietnam's diaspora, as this volume emphasizes, is helping bring a new generation of scattered offspring back together in the homeland to reimagine Vietnam's postcolonial possibilities. Through such agential efforts come new realizations that the long-term effects of Vietnam's tragic civil-cum-global war, while producing untold hardships and bitter memories that will not soon go way, have also produced, two generations later, a variety of unanticipated opportunities. For many, such opportunities offer optimistic horizons in which reconciliation, reconnection, redemption, and renewal on their own terms appear to be emerging outcomes.

7

VIETNAMESE AMERICAN POLITICS

Evolution at the Grassroots, 1981–2020

CHRISTIAN COLLET

Introduction

This chapter traces the forty-year evolution of Vietnamese American politics, emphasizing the strategies undertaken by activists to gain support for an ambitious dual agenda: the incorporation of Vietnamese Americans and the democratization of Vietnam. I examine this American-politicization dynamic by focusing first on the concept of Little Saigon and then on activism in two realms: civil and electoral. In terms of civil activism, I illustrate how protest events, organizational development, and transnational activism at the grassroots worked to provide resources, strengthen group identity, and raise the salience of Vietnamese American and Vietnam-related issues. In terms of electoral activism, I discuss efforts since the 1990s to gain access to U.S. institutions—primarily through voting and candidacy—in order to address domestic inequalities, institutionalize community symbols, and contest the Vietnamese government. I conclude with a consideration of the future trajectory of Vietnamese American politics and the potential impact of subsequent activist generations on democratization in the United States and Vietnam.

Little Saigon: Imagination, Identity, Issue

The chapters in this volume underscore the need to recalibrate Vietnamese American history to an alternate chronology that focuses on life and agency under the Republic of Vietnam. Building on this, I argue here that the starting point for any chronicle of Vietnamese American politics is Little Saigon, a concept shaped by two currents of history: one in Vietnam, the other in the United States—"from above" by the dynamics of geopolitics and global economics and "from below" by those who fled/migrated and the localities with which they engaged. The critical macro-level event is the collapse of the Republic of Vietnam (RVN) regime and the transition of its capital, Saigon, to communist forces in April 1975. The critical micro-level event is the long-term disrupture and displacement of refugees. Before Saigon's fall, the Vietnamese population in the United States numbered less than thirty thousand, with a presence in Orange County, California, of perhaps several hundred. Today, Vietnamese America stands close to two million, with about one in ten living in Orange County alone.

It is sometimes forgotten that Little Saigon was never intended to be, and, despite its establishment across many American localities, it remains somewhat of a controversy. As postwar resettlement policies sought to disperse "new arrivals," Washington endeavored to minimize the politics it figured would ensue from immigrant enclaves and, in doing so, accelerate the spread of a certain brand of de-ethnicized civic Americanization. What happened instead was the transformation of a conservative area in central Orange County into the first "capital of refugees" ("thủ đô tị nạn," in the phrasing of Người Việt Daily News) and, over the following decades, the creation of kindred areas in San Jose, Houston, Falls Church, Boston, and elsewhere. Standing today as the hub and spokes of diasporic power, Little Saigon is both an officially designated space and a community of the imagination—a constellation of sites for tourism, commercial exchange, social support, and cultural preservation, as well as, for many, a collective object of ethnic identification and ontological security. In this way, Little Saigon serves to render an ideal—representing not only defiance of assimilation and the reclamation of self-determination in America but also resistance to the erasures and co-optations of the communist regime in Vietnam.

On a more practical level, history will likely see Little Saigon as an important territory that facilitated the initial development of community politics. The first organized claims made by Vietnamese Americans on local government occurred in the early 1980s, as first-generation leaders negotiated with the city of Westminster over the demarcation of what was officially called the "Little Saigon Community Planning Area." It was from that point that "Little Saigon" became a brand that would evolve into a vehicle for political ambition and then into its own political cause. Through the 1980s, signage followed on Westminster's Bolsa Avenue and local freeways to attract consumer activity to the area, and more businesses incorporated Little Saigon into their names. In 1990, Little Saigon Television began evening news broadcasts in Vietnamese, and within a few years, Little Saigon Radio was syndicating its Orange County–produced programs to stations in San Jose and

Houston. This was before the age of broadband internet, and while *Người Việt* was having a huge impact in the Southern California region, Little Saigon Broadcasting helped to link the diaspora with programming that, when combined with print media, contributed to a growing, and distinct, political identity.

The growth of Little Saigon during this juncture, fueled by subsequent waves of refugees, émigrés, and ex-prisoners of reeducation camps, coincided with monumental changes in the Vietnamese Communist Party (VCP) and the diplomatic relationship between Washington and Hanoi. As I explain below, it was then that the banal offices, strip malls, and parking lots in suburban Orange and Santa Clara Counties and elsewhere served as the locus of growing organization, fostering various groups, from the paramilitary to the partisan to the purely charitable, whose work would result in an assortment of political projects. What is important to recall in retrospect is that the street-level dynamics of Little Saigon politics during this time were irreducibly intertwined with those "from above" between the American and Vietnamese governments and within the VCP internally. When the effort to impose socialist economics and rewrite history in Saigon proved disastrous in the years after the war, the VCP turned under *Đổi Mới* to the growing capital of the diaspora, who had long been sending, in the face of a crippling U.S.-led embargo, millions of dollars in parcels and remittances to families left behind. To attract Vietnamese Americans to return to Vietnam and make investments to rebuild the country, the VCP undertook a challenging project: to convince the former "reactionaries" and "traitors," so denounced by the late secretary general Lê Duẩn, that they were now welcomed back as "part and parcel of the Vietnamese nation."[1] While many quietly responded to the overtures by booking trips and wiring money, political activists—still influenced by an aging RVN elite—amplified their pushback against the VCP by sanctioning those who publicly welcomed the new embrace and by initiating new projects to strengthen the community's identity and voice.

It is at this point, as the century turned and bilateral relations normalized, that the 1.5 generation came of political age—and incorporation into local political structures took center stage. Until then, public opinion among Vietnamese Americans had not only been hostile toward the VCP but favored its overthrow, seemingly out of a lingering belief fueled by former RVN leaders like President Nguyễn Văn Thiệu ("the responsibility to liberate [Vietnam] is ours")[2] that with sustained pressure the regime's days were numbered and return would be imminent. With Hanoi now on the relative upswing, backed in full by debt forgiveness and bilateral trade with Washington, attitudes in Little Saigon started to change. The communist regime continued to be publicly despised—even more so now that there were more transnational engagements and opportunities for Vietnamese Americans to

TABLE 7.1 GROWTH IN SOCIOECONOMIC STATUS OF VIETNAMESE AMERICA, 1980–2019					
	1980	*1990*	*2000*	*2010 (ACS)*	*2019 (ACS)*
Total Population	262,125	614,547	1,122,528	1,625,365	1,873,707
% living in California	34	46	40	37	36
% living in Santa Clara or Orange County	12	21	22	19	18
Socioeconomic Characteristics					
Median household income	$12,545	$29,772	$45,085	$52,153	$72,161
% on public assistance	28	25	10	5	3
% college graduates	13	17	19	25	32
% employed in management, professional, or related occupations	13	18	27	30	36
% homeownership	27	50	54	64	68
% foreign-born U.S. citizens	11	44	58	74	75
Note: Vietnamese alone.					

interact with the state firsthand—but diplomacy, not force, became the preferred course of political action. A poll conducted for the *Orange County Register* in 2003 found a majority saying that, even if Vietnam democratized, "home" was in the United States.[3] A decade prior, only 39 percent had said so.

These changes in macro-level politics and micro-level sentiments, combined with demographic transformation—as Table 7.1 shows, a majority in the 2000 Census became homeowners and U.S. citizens—resulted in a strategic shift among activists from exile to identity politics. In the sections below, I describe how this new climate gave rise to a wave of first-time candidates who, in turn, helped to grow and consolidate an ethnic voting bloc that today wields significant influence in certain local elections. But with the basic goal of local representation achieved, activists sought to further institutionalize Vietnamese American culture and, in doing so, demarcate a boundary between the overseas community (primarily in the United States) and the VCP. It was in this vein that an international grassroots movement arose that not only gained formal recognition for the former RVN flag (described further below) but in some instances saw activists attempting to *displace* the official banner of the Socialist Republic of Vietnam (SRV). Coupled with this were efforts to identify Vietnamese business and residential concentrations around the United States as Little Saigons. In the established "capital" of Westminster and Garden Grove, young Vietnamese American officials helped to erect "Welcome to Little Saigon" street signage (adorned with the RVN flag) and declare the cities "Communist-Free Zones." In San Jose, a protracted legal and political battle ensued over the name "Little Saigon" itself (Collet and Furuya 2010).

Now at the point where efforts are made to draw lines around it, whether by city ordinance or in the mind, Little Saigon, four decades on, is transcending its origins as a center for commerce and culture. It is, and in retrospect always has been, a fundamentally political entity: a symbol of identification and agency, of security and controversy, and, more recently, a *cause* that has prompted movements for its recognition, promotion, and defense. While there is little doubt that Vietnamese Americans would have had a significant impact on government without the concept of Little Saigon, the community's political trajectory has been irrevocably shaped by it. As a site for activism and a vehicle for incorporation, it has not only provided critical infrastructure for organizational development but also brought more Vietnamese Americans into the civil and electoral spheres.

Activism in the Civil Realm

The Symbolism, Logic, and Evolution of Protest Events

Much as the history of Vietnam has been shaped by resistance movements, Vietnamese America—from the initial days in refugee camps to today's Little Saigon—has been animated by diverse acts of protest, ranging from small uprisings, street demonstrations and rallies, to other organized forms of sociocultural public expression, like ceremonies and commemorations. Quan Tue Tran demonstrates later in this volume how these events collectively shape what she terms "Vietnamese American memoryscape." Regardless of whether they have been overtly partisan-political,[4] they often share common symbols and familiar rituals; make salient the history and consciousness of the diaspora; and convey the goals and messaging of organizers. The English-language corporate media tends to give these events outsize attention in ways that frame Vietnamese Americans as politically volatile, socially at odds with assimilation expectations, and in conflict with values like tolerance and the liberal exercise of First Amendment rights. What scholarship emphasizes instead is that a logic among activists, left and right, prevails—and that the symbolic act of demonstration, in the end, serves an instrumental purpose. "Protest," write Nhu-Ngọc Ông and David Meyer,

> can offer clear benefits as part of a larger political strategy, producing benefits beyond enhancing political leverage to influence policy. At

once, colorful protests [allow] a relatively small group to project its
concerns to a larger audience . . . and to instill feelings of political
efficacy and collective identity among participants. Beyond the instrumental impact of a protest event, participation in assertive action can help individuals maintain the commitment to continue their
efforts in other ways . . . [and provides] a means of socializing and
encouraging them. Protest is also a means of winning political recognition and relevance for an otherwise excluded community . . .
[and] provide an attractive contrast to the politics of their home-land.
Protest demonstrates not only the openness of American politics but
also, by contrast, the repressive nature of the regimes they fled. (Ong
and Meyer 2008: 79–80)

If one looks broadly across the last four decades, the contours of this style
of grassroots activism come into relief. Figure 7.1 displays the total number
of coded protest events identified in three Southern California media sources—the *Los Angeles Times, Orange County Register,* and *Người Việt*—between
1981 and 2019 (N = 141). The number of events in a given year are indicated
on the vertical (y) axis. Each event is represented by a dot, and each dot is
colored by the entity (typically the state) that was the target of the event. A
special category, "Little Saigon," refers to events where community institutions or Vietnamese Americans themselves were targeted. The dots are scaled
in size by the estimated length of the event. Thus, the larger the dot, the longer
the event lasted in days.[5]

Since the first documented "rally" in 1977—intended, as explained by its
organizer, Father Đỗ Thanh Hà, to "make more people aware of the plight
of prisoners in South Vietnam" (*Santa Ana Register* 1977)—an average of
about three protest events occur in and around Orange County annually.
Spikes in activity typically coincide with larger events playing out on the
international stage. The normalization of U.S.-Vietnamese ties (culminating
in the lifting of the U.S.-led trade embargo) generated at least ten protest events
each in 1994 and 1995; the announcement of a bilateral trade agreement in
1999 produced eight. The most enduring events, depicted in the figure as
large yellow dots, have targeted Vietnamese Americans or community institutions.[6] The most publicized of these occurred in 1999, when thousands
gathered outside Hi Tek Video in Westminster in response to the proprietor's
display of a portrait of Ho Chi Minh commonly found in storefronts in Vietnam. Portrayed as internecine dramas, these events typically reveal Hanoi
as the real target behind the personalized local object—an inference strengthened by the observation that about half of the events (N=69) over the thirty-
eight-year time frame have focused directly on the Vietnamese communist
regime. From time to time, organizers have turned their focus to peripheral

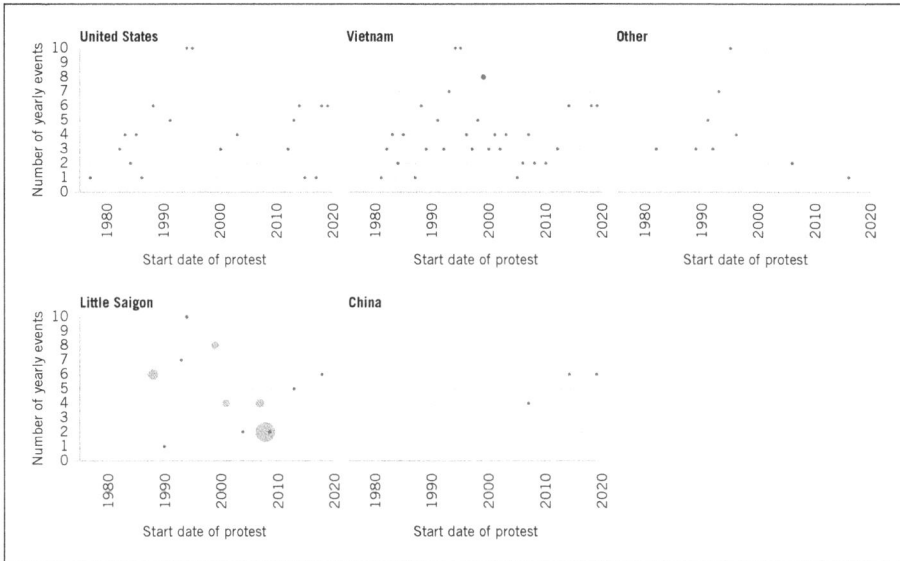

Figure 7.1 Vietnamese American Protests in Orange County, 1981–2019. Dots scaled by length of protest. *(Orange County Register, Los Angeles Times, Nguoi Viet Daily News)*

actors, such as when Presidents Xi Jinping and Barack Obama met in 2013 or when Seoul detained a member of the now-dissolved exile group Government of Free Vietnam. But, in the broadest sense, the aims of Vietnamese American protest over the years have remained the same: to strengthen group identity, to symbolically display social status, and to gain political leverage.

While the logic of protest remains consistent, the substance appears to be evolving. As Figure 7.1 shows, events since 2010 continue to be influenced by foreign affairs but now reflect a wider range of ideologies and a more complex set of issues. This could be, at least in part, a function of community demographic shifts, the rise of the 1.5 and second American generations into political activism, and a more diverse information landscape. At the same time, changes in Vietnam and the geopolitical dynamic are clearly at play: namely, the assertion of Chinese territorial claims in Southeast Asia and the deepening of U.S.-Vietnam defense cooperation. Although signs of ideological diversity began to appear in Vietnamese America during the normalization period in the mid to late 1990s, it did not become fully apparent until 2013 and 2014, when media began to cover events like the demands of a Westminster group, Viet Rainbow, to allow LGBTQs to participate in the area's annual festival for Tết or the hundreds who traveled to the Chinese consulate in Los Angeles to protest Beijing's claiming of the Spratly (Trường Sa) and Paracel (Hoàng Sa) Islands in the South China Sea (Kopetman 2013; *Người*

Việt 2014).[7] Efforts by the Trump administration in 2017 to suddenly deport refugees with long-standing protections under U.S. law to Vietnam triggered further activism that eventually revealed a split between those repelled by the president's actions and those attracted to his jingoistic tone and confrontational stance toward China.[8] Thus, where protest through the first quarter century of Vietnamese American refugee history could safely be characterized as consistently anti-regime and, by extension, aligned with the anticommunist conservative right, events since have revealed a more complex political DNA in the community—one that also contains ample strands of progressivism and Vietnamese nationalism.

Organizational Development and Netroots Activism

The incorporative building blocks of street-level activism derive from the resources gained through socioeconomic advancement, social capital, and social organization. While some watershed protest events, like Hi Tek in 1999, may have spurred group formation, the history of Vietnamese American politics teaches us that organizations—social, business, religious, or civic in nature—grow out of domestic and transnational social networks: some, as Van Nguyen-Marshall argues in this volume, predating the migratory experience; some extending from families and connections in refugee processing camps; others being forged subsequently in the course of American life. Networks spur organizations, which, in turn, lay the foundation for the realization and propagation of political claims. Interacting with identity and in response to domestic and international events, organizations have fostered the collective expressions that have shaped the community's political trajectory.

In Orange County, evidence suggests that the first formalized social organizations appeared roughly a year before Father Đỗ's rally in 1977. In Santa Ana, a few miles east of today's Little Saigon Business District, a former student protestor in Paris and Army of the Republic of Vietnam (ARVN) officer, Lê Quý Biên, helped to form the Vietnamese American Refugee Club in a small strip mall labeled by local newspapers as "Vietnam Town." From available records published in a directory by the subsequently formed Vietnamese Chamber of Commerce (itself claiming to be "the oldest and largest non-profit organization of its kind")[9] and then by the *Người Việt Niên Giám* yearbook, it appears as if the number of listed (Hội Đoàn) civic associations in the area grew rapidly from 33 in 1986 to 119 in 1990, in line with the significant population and economic growth brought by the second, boat people, wave of immigration. Since that time, Vietnamese organizations have proliferated, across the United States and around the world, constituting a

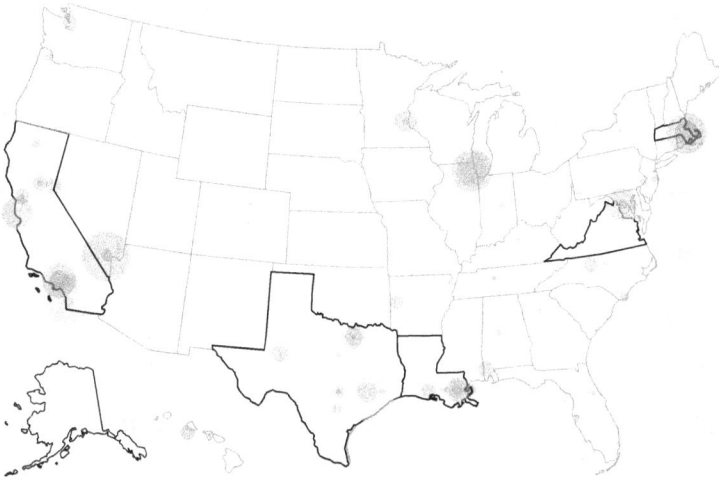

Buddhist ■ Other

A

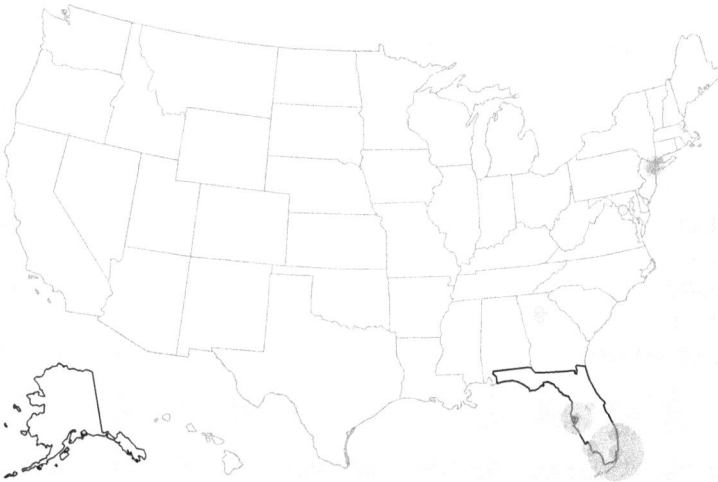

B

Figure 7.2A Vietnamese American 501(c)(3) Organizations, 2019–2020. Dots scaled by the group's number of assets in dollars. *(National Center for Charitable Statistics)*

Figure 7.2B Cuban American 501(c)(3) Organizations, 2019–2020. Dots scaled by the group's number of assets in dollars. *(National Center for Charitable Statistics)*

genuine diaspora network capable of influencing public opinion and policy in a variety of domestic and international locales.

The nature of Vietnamese American organizational development can be seen through a simple comparison with Cuban Americans, a community similarly shaped by exile and multiple waves of refugee immigration but also seen as a potent "ethnic lobby" with considerable political influence. Compared to Cubans, Vietnamese Americans channel greater resources into tax-exempt 501(c)(3)s than into political action committees (PACs) or other 527s. According to an analysis of 2020 data maintained by the National Center for Charitable Statistics,[10] 905 Vietnamese organizations filed for nonprofit status, 333 in California alone (37 percent). By comparison, the data show about 175 Cuban organizations across the United States, with 102 (58 percent) residing in Florida (see Figures 7.2A and 7.2B). Taken together, the 905 Vietnamese groups reported a combined $68.5 million in income and assets of $116.4 million. The 175 Cuban groups report $23.2 million and $25.4 million, respectively. Vietnamese groups are also distinguished by a large number of churches and religious entities—several of the most well-heeled groups being Buddhist (e.g., the Sugarland, Texas–based Vietnamese Buddhist Center and the Vietnamese Buddhist Meditation Congregation centered in Anaheim).

The diffuse and diverse array of Vietnamese American organizations have, after forty years, given its politics the feel of a grassroots social movement aiming for broad, systemic change, as opposed to an interest group seeking instrumental, incremental gains in the corridors of Washington. This is not to suggest that the latter is either absent or unlikely—consider, for example, the efforts of the Human Rights for Vietnam PAC (HRV-PAC) in the mid-2010s, backed heavily by the Saigon Broadcasting Television Network, or Vietnam Advocacy Day, an annual event organized by Virginia-based Boat People SOS (BPSOS) in which hundreds descend on congressional offices to lobby for human rights (Dinh C. and Nguyen B. 2015).[11] Rather, it is to suggest that geographic dispersion, social inequality, and ideological diversity appear to have led groups to maintain a more socially welfare-conscious and partisan-transcendental posture. The American party system, increasingly polarized since the 1970s, offers two basic routes to influence; Madisonian pluralism and geographically based representation reward demographic concentration and professional candidates capable of raising huge sums of money. While this has offered Vietnamese Americans significant opportunities to influence local policy making, as I explain below, it has also compelled organizations with broader ambitions to seek an end run around the roadblocks in the American system.

Such groups have strategically adapted to domestic constraints by creating virtual spaces that employ the language of democratization and deploy campaigns of mobilization. The goals are broad and simple: to influence public opinion internationally and Vietnam's civil society directly. The Long Beach, California–based Vietnamese Overseas Initiative for Conscience Empowerment (VOICE; vietnamvoice.org) offers one example. Emphasizing the transnational nature of their cause and a practical agenda to educate and train young activists, VOICE is a 501(c)(3) cofounded by Dan Hoang (Hoàng Tứ Duy), a financial officer-turned-activist whose earlier ventures involved the Vietnamese Public Affairs Committee (V-PAC), election fundraising, and rounds of congressional testimony. VOICE is linked to numerous other organizations on Facebook and other social media, among them, Việt Tân, a transnational party led by fellow V-PAC member Diem Do (Đỗ Hoàng Điểm). With over one million followers on Facebook and an active news site publicizing human rights–related issues (viettan.org), Việt Tân claims to be "actively promoting civil disobedience campaigns throughout (Vietnam)" and has been linked to protest events in San Jose and Ho Chi Minh City (Simonson 2016; Tuổi Trẻ Online 2016).[12] (Việt Tân's tactics are explored in greater depth by Duyen Bui in Chapter 11.) Hanoi, in turn, views Việt Tân as a foreign terrorist organization, listing Do and Hoang on the pages of the Ministry of Public Security website and running pieces denouncing "democracy" supporters in *Nhân Dân*, the official newspaper of the Vietnamese Communist Party (VCP; *Nhân Dân* 2020).[13]

Activism in the Electoral Realm

The line between "freedom fighter" and "foreign terrorist" can be thin, depending on the ideology and security of a domestic state. From the viewpoint of political science, Do and Hoang would likely be seen in more benign, behavioral terms as "complete activists"—Vietnamese Americans who have come to politically engage (in their case, with considerable risk) in a variety of modes in pursuit of their cause. This makes them exceptional. While Vietnamese American public opinion has consistently viewed the VCP unfavorably, supported human rights issues, and shown more inclination than other groups to engage in protest, majorities have also undertaken transnational economic and social practices in everyday ways that keep politics out of public view (Furuya and Collet 2009; see also Ivan Small's chapter earlier in this volume). Moreover, many in communities like Orange County and San Jose choose independence over partisanship. This tells us that for most Vietnamese Americans most of the time, political expression takes place within the ordinary confines of U.S. representative democracy: registering to vote, donating money, and, particularly over the last twenty years, running for office. This transition toward formal political incorporation, "from protest to (electoral) politics" in Bayard Rustin's terms, has been one of the defining stories of the community's four-decade history.[14]

The Evolution of an Ethnic Voting Bloc

An important chapter in this story took place in the summer of 1992, when Tony Lam (Lâm Quang), a former U.S. government contractor in Saigon and community restaurateur, ran for the Westminster City Council. Lam was one of three Vietnamese, and of several Asian Americans, contesting for area office that year. Despite being a Republican in a predominantly conservative area, Lam faced considerable headwinds. He later wrote:

> When I ran, the Republican hierarchy did not encourage or endorse the candidacy of Vietnamese Americans . . . Asian Americans were perceived by party leaders as inexperienced and unreliable. (But) I had always been successful at raising money for (Little Saigon) community projects as well as for refugee assistance. This gave me high visibility as a spokesperson for Vietnamese Americans. . . . My affiliations with various community groups, business leaders, and members of the Vietnamese community brought in $60,000 during my first political campaign. (Lam T. 2002: 159–160)

At the time, most Vietnamese Americans who were registered to vote in Orange County were affiliated with the Republicans, but the bigger problem facing Lam was that coethnic voters constituted only about 9 percent of the Westminster electorate. As a result, he employed two consultants—white and Vietnamese American—who helped position him as a middleman/pathbreaker on one hand and "tax fighter/crime fighter" on the other, one who would give Vietnamese Americans a representative voice but would also defend elderly white people living in the area's numerous trailer parks. Spending more than ten times his nearest rival, Lam prevailed in the six-candidate race by only 132 votes out of nearly 28,000 cast. An analysis of his vote shows only a weak relationship between his precinct-level support and the proportion of registered voters with Vietnamese surnames. In other words, some of his most significant support came from neighborhoods that were predominantly non-Vietnamese.

Lam would win reelection twice by continuing to dramatically outspend his opponents, but by the time of the Hi Tek incident in 1999, Little Saigon had grown significantly, as noted above, and its politics had begun to place demands on his business-oriented approach. What emerged from the prolonged protests was an assertion of younger voices, an affirmation of a Vietnamese *American* identity, and a movement to organize energies into electoral politics. Between 1998 and 2002, the number of voters in Orange County with Vietnamese surnames (or listing Vietnam as their place of birth) had grown from 41,793 to 67,449, a 61 percent increase, with particular gains in Democratic and independent ("decline-to-state," or DTS) registrations

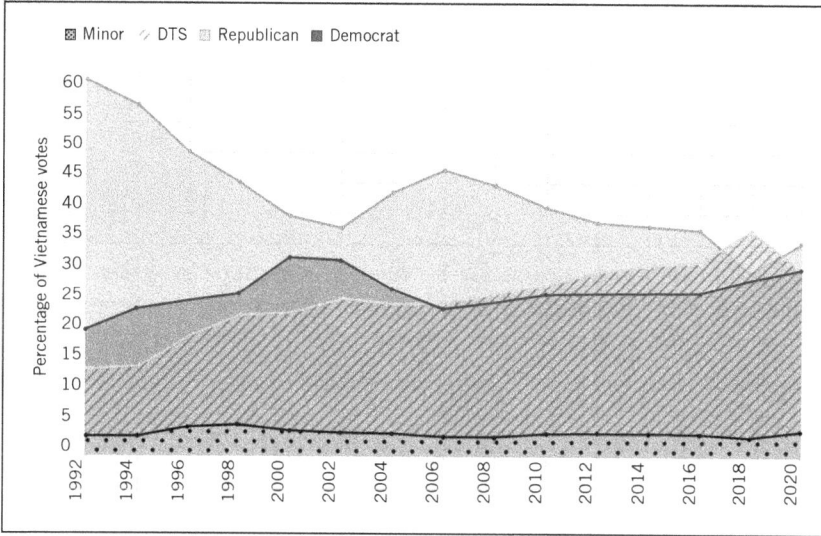

Figure 7.3 Party Choices of Registered Voters in Orange County, California, with Vietnamese Surnames or Listing Vietnam as Their Place of Birth, 1992–2020.

(Figure 7.3). A slate of young, 1.5-generation politicians emerged to compete for the new votes, eventually tripling in four years the number of Vietnamese Americans serving in local elective offices.

What is striking about this period is how, despite emerging partisan divisions, the Little Saigon electorate solidified into a cohesive voting bloc. Even before Hi Tek, analysis showed the support for Lam in his last reelection bid starting to rely more heavily on Vietnamese-dominant voter precincts. But by 2000, it became evident that coethnic support could be *the* driving force behind local political incorporation. When Van Tran (Trần Thái Văn) and Lan Nguyen (Nguyễn Quốc Lân) were elected to the council and school board in the City of Garden Grove in 2000, respectively, their precinct-level support aligned almost perfectly with the proportion of Vietnamese American voters—suggesting that the new electorate was making a critical difference in the community's empowerment (Collet 2005). Yet even as these gains furthered the reputation of Little Saigon as an electoral power broker, they also indicated that racially polarized voting could potentially define campaigns where future Vietnamese American politicos would be pitted against white and Latino candidates. As Lam's experience would suggest, this would mean having to confront a burden familiar to other Asian American and immigrant candidates: the need to raise vast amounts of money for messaging that mobilizes coethnic people but assuages out-group voters to avoid backlash (Collet 2008).

Running for Office: Strategies and Successes

Reflective of the community's strengthening identity, the campaigns that marked the new wave of 1.5-generation candidates into state and local politics in the 2000s featured a distinct turn toward the emerging symbols of Saigon nationalism.[15] The most potent of these, by a distance, was the Vietnamese American Heritage and Freedom Flag, named by activists as they mounted grassroots efforts in jurisdictions throughout the United States, as well as Canada and Australia, for its official recognition. The yellow banner itself, with three red horizontal stripes, was aesthetically unchanged from the same flag that first flew during the post–World War II period under the brief regime of Chief of State Bảo Đại and eventually served as the symbol of the Republic of Vietnam. Yet, much as it did then, when it became a vehicle for leaders from President Ngô Đình Diệm of the First Republic to President Nguyễn Văn Thiệu of the Second Republic to build a new southern identity, the resurrected flag came to represent something larger for the diaspora: an independent political consciousness, an aspiration for incorporation, and a defiance toward what Ling Chi-Wang would call a "dual domination" of a racially hierarchical American society and an erasure/exclusion by the post-unification VCP (Jessica Chapman 2013; Wang L.-C. 1995).

It was also great politics for young candidates in need of elderly votes. Two campaigns—Van Tran's in the Republican primary for the California State Assembly in 2004 and Madison Nguyen's (Nguyễn Phượng) for the San Jose City Council a year later—typified the new style. In Tran's case, the flag served unabashedly as a Saigon nationalist backdrop for a call to group mobilization; facing racist attacks on his registration efforts from his white conservative opponent, Tran, speaking through Vietnamese media, urged his coethnics to resist "political factions that want to oppose the rights and growth of the community" and "to actively participate . . . in full numbers in order to protect (its) voice and future."[16] In Madison Nguyen's case, the flag would become even more central as an issue as she and her second-generation opponent, Linda Nguyen, contested a runoff as a flag resolution was being considered by the council (Collet 2008). Still others, following Tran, introduced measures to restrict the visits of VCP officials (thus establishing "Communist-Free Zones") and to erect "Welcome to Little Saigon" signage that would incorporate the yellow flag. Even as these efforts generated intense debate in the media, polls showed them to be popular among Vietnamese Americans themselves, with nearly three in four in Orange County saying the yellow RVN flag should be the only one recognized and fewer than one in six saying the red SRV flag should be recognized along with it. The strongest support for the Heritage and Freedom Flag came, in fact, from the oldest members of the community and those most active in, and attentive to, the political system (Furuya and Collet 2009).

All of this was not lost on non-Vietnamese incumbents, as more found themselves at community events in *áo dài*, waving miniaturized versions of the banner and distributing mailers arguing that they, too, were "standing up for the Vietnamese community" by (in the words of then congresswoman Loretta Sánchez [D-Santa Ana]) "pushing the government of Vietnam to respect basic human rights, accept a multiparty system and restore the right of the Vietnamese people to vote in free and fair elections."[17] In fairness to Sánchez, her rightist predecessor (Robert K. Dornan) and several of her House colleagues had long embraced human rights in Vietnam as a consonant ideological issue and, in turn, courted relationships with the community by appointing young Vietnamese Americans (like Van Tran) to entry-level staff positions.[18] But as more of those aides began to seek office themselves, and as relations between the United States and the SRV strengthened under bipartisan administrations, the co-optation of human rights and anti-Hanoi rhetoric would pose a strategic problem for those wanting to move up the ladder. How to continue to mobilize a coethnic bloc of voters and donors while, at the same time, reaching toward a larger "mainstream" electorate?

One part of the answer would be found in the mythology of the American Dream. As they articulated the rationale for their candidacies, toggling between coethnic and non-Vietnamese partisans, 1.5-generation activists began to draw on the narratives of immigration—touching repeatedly on themes of "hard work," opportunity, and gratitude even as they attempted to assuage nativist fears by emphasizing their "experience," well-worn American roots, and professional qualifications. But what might be seen critically as a negotiation between model-minority expectations and pure racism was, at the same time, an opportunity to articulate the shared struggle of the refugee and minority experience—stories familiar to Vietnamese American voters irrespective of generation.

Consider:

Janet Nguyen (Janet Nguyễn), Republican candidate for the California state senate, in a 2006 letter:

> I believe in the American dream, and that's why I have decided to dedicate my life to serving our community. . . . Growing up, my family got our clothes at the Salvation Army until my parents were able to save up enough money to open their first business. My father was a bus boy/cook at the community college so that he could attend class to learn English. Our Christmas gifts came from the church. I was working for my cousin cleaning homes at 12 years old. While I was in college, I had three jobs.
>
> My parents taught me that in America, hard work was rewarded. They also instilled in me a set of values: freedom, family, respect and love for our country.

Hon Lien, Democratic candidate for San Jose City Council in 2007, on the home page of her campaign website:

We will never be able to repay our parents for the wonderful gift they gave us when they loaded our family into a small boat to escape the communists in Vietnam and started our journey to America to start a new life.

But I am determined to repay our nation for the opportunity to live free. I believe in the American dream, and that is why I have decided to dedicate myself to serving our community.

Life has taught me that in America, hard work is rewarded. I believe that most of the people who live in our district share this belief.

From the website of conservative Republican Tri Ta (Tạ Đức Trí), in his campaign for Westminster City Council in 2006:

I've always admired the beauty of cultural diversity in the United States—the land of hope and freedom for many immigrants. We as Americans all share one dream of making this country a better place to live and to love. And I pledge to do just that for the city of Westminster should I become an elected official.

From the campaign site of Hong Tran (Trần Hồng), a Democratic candidate for the U.S. Senate in Washington State, also in 2006:

In the Spring of 1975, as the Viet Cong entered the city of Saigon, my family and I fled to the boat docks . . . I was eight years old and I can still recall the sights and sounds of that turbulent time. We were lucky. . . . After several days at sea, our barge was spotted by a US naval ship . . . they fed us, sheltered us and provided us with a sense of hope and security.

I love my adoptive country. As an immigrant, I have an additional responsibility to ensure that the United States remains a place of hope for all people. As a citizen of the most powerful country in the world, I want to ensure that we remain a beacon of hope for all nations.

The toggling strategy often proved fruitful (Collet 2008). Over the twelve-year period between 2004 and 2016, Van Tran and Madison Nguyen won their respective races and were successfully reelected; Vietnamese majorities emerged on the Westminster and Garden Grove City Councils; Tri Ta and Bao Quoc Nguyen won the mayoralties in both cities; Janet Nguyen became the first Vietnamese American woman elected to the California legislature and, at the time, the highest-ranking Vietnamese elected official in the country. The most stunning result came outside of California when, in 2008, one-time seminarian Joseph Cao (Cao Quang Ánh) was elected to Congress after upsetting an African American incumbent in a New Orleans district that hadn't sent a Republican to Washington since 1892. Upon winning, Cao told his supporters, "The American Dream is well and alive."[19]

Conflict, Competition, and the Paradox of Concentration

Despite the numerous breakthroughs, to which Democrat Stephanie Murphy (Đặng Thị Ngọc Dung) added in 2016 by defeating a Republican incumbent in Florida's Seventh Congressional District, the wave of progress also revealed ample strife. Joseph Cao, Madison Nguyen, Janet Nguyen, and Tri Ta, along with fellow Westminster councillors Kimberly Ho (Kimberly Hồ) and Charlie Nguyen (Charlie Nguyễn Mạnh Chí), all survived recall attempts;[20] a number of races in Orange County and San Jose found multiple Vietnamese American candidates competing against one another—splitting an electorate that, just years before, had coalesced around the argument for incorporation and need for greater representation. The divisions were ostensibly ideological—in Madison Nguyen's case, the fury arose, prima facie, from nationalist sentiment to name a proposed commercial area the Little Saigon Business District—and frequently corruption was alleged and faithfulness to the community's trust was invoked. Yet the lines could be crosscutting, complex, and deeply personal, reflecting well-rooted grievances between partisan and candidate-driven factions as well as generations seeking mutual respect. As one Garden Grove activist admitted at a public meeting in which flag-waving elders threatened to recall Bao Quoc Nguyen, "We recognize the main reason (for our criticism) is that you're too young, too inexperienced, too arrogant, too naïve."[21]

As the images of these local dramas seared Vietnamese America's Sturm und Drang into the broader public consciousness, it became clear by the 2010s that coethnic competition could threaten the community's incorporative ambitions. Liberals faced relentless pressure to defer to elderly elites and adhere to the unstated tenets of Saigon nationalism—promote the Heritage and Freedom Flag and the "territory" of Little Saigon and confront perceived efforts to co-opt, divide, or distort it. Conservatives found themselves struggling to balance their identities and ambition with ideological purity in the face of rising Republican nativism. Across the spectrum, from Bao Quoc Nguyen to Joseph Cao, officeholders sought to exercise a certain independence as they weighed broader public policy needs for their diverse and oftentimes poor constituencies with the narrow demands of symbolic representation. As they

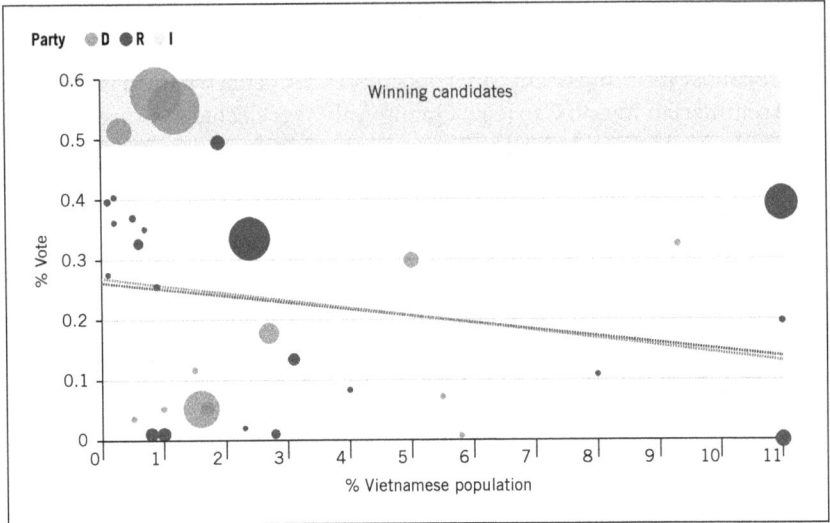

Figure 7.4 Vote for Vietnamese American Candidates for the U.S. Congress by Size of Vietnamese American Constituency, 1994–2020. Circle scaled by the amount of money raised by the candidate.

did so, they confronted severe headwinds that in some cases would significantly reroute their political careers and, in others, would end them.

Figure 7.4 illustrates the paradox. The figure plots the vote of thirty-four Vietnamese Americans who ran for U.S. House and Senate elections between 1994 and 2020 (*y* axis) against the proportion of Vietnamese Americans residing in the constituency (*x* axis). As a proxy for the seriousness of the campaign, the points are weighted by the total amount of money (in USD) raised by the candidate in that particular election cycle.

As the figure makes clear, there has, at least thus far, been little relationship between the potential size of the Vietnamese American electorate and the proportion of votes Vietnamese American candidates have received. In the two winning cases (involving Cao and Murphy and her two reelections) seen in the upper left corner of the plot, the Vietnamese community (at the time of the election) constituted no more than 2 percent of the constituency. In contrast to these are multiple cases where candidates in predominantly non-Vietnamese areas did well and those in more concentrated areas did poorly. Perhaps most striking among these are four underfunded Republican candidates (in Florida and North Carolina) who won nearly 40 percent in constituencies where the Vietnamese American population was less than 1 percent. Equally striking are the cases on the right side of the graph, where three Vietnamese Americans competed against one another in the Republican primary for California's Forty-Seventh U.S. House District, with 11 percent Vietnamese population. In the end, Van Tran, the eventual nominee, mustered 39 percent against Sánchez and decisively lost the general election. Having raised over $1.1 million in individual donations (doubling that of Murphy in 2016), Tran later told reporters that the loss was "a sobering moment for anyone who wants to run in this district. I think gerrymandering has a lot to do with it" (Irving 2010).

His reference to the Democratic leaning of the Forty-Seventh brings attention to the lack of a "Vietnamese district" in the central Orange County area—and the community's inability to persuade state mapmakers to refrain from "cracking" Little Saigon across multiple constituencies. Again, the comparison with Cuban Americans is instructive. While the two districts with the largest concentrations of Vietnamese voters in California were represented in the 117th Congress by a white liberal and Korean American conservative, respectively, all three Miami area districts (where 40 percent of Cuban Americans reside) were represented by a Cuban American Republican. As with Vietnamese American organizational development, size and financial strength do not necessarily or directly translate into political influence. The growth and diversity of the community combine to produce a politics that, while formidable and in many ways pathbreaking, at the grassroots level, continues to encounter barriers as electoral stakes increase—and the need to assemble broader coalitions becomes critical.

Conclusion: The Future of Vietnamese American Politics

In 2018, in her first bid for reelection, Stephanie Murphy ran much as she did two years prior, drawing heavily on centrist themes and projecting the image of a pragmatic, problem-solving mom. Touting her "work with both parties," Murphy's ads referred to bills she introduced on lobbying bans and congressional pay. A 650-word biography on her website noted in underlined bold how she "has been consistently named one of the most effective and most independent members of Congress," and according to voteview.com, her first term voting and cosponsorship record confirms the claim. In some detail, Murphy listed her service on House committees and to the party's leadership; only in passing does she mention that "she is the first Vietnamese-American woman to serve in Congress," and she does so by also noting that she is the first woman to ever represent Florida's Seventh Congressional District.[22] Of the $1.5 million Murphy raised in individual contributions in that cycle, a mere $21,992—1.5 percent—came from donors with discernibly Vietnamese surnames. The contrast with Cao, an outspoken human rights advocate and VCP critic who, when faced with his own tough reelection drew deeply on Vietnamese American money, could not have been starker.

After she won the race, Murphy's tone began to shift. In late 2018, she evoked on Twitter her family's flight from "Communist Vietnam" in speaking out against Trump administration efforts to renegotiate a Washington-Hanoi agreement that protected pre-1995 refugees from deportation. A few months later, she penned a *Washington Post* op-ed in which she called herself a "proud capitalist" and worried "that some may take for granted the unique opportunities afforded citizens of this country, leading them to favor, or flirt with, socialist policies" (Murphy 2019). Following her second reelection in late 2020, in which she was increasingly rumored to be a challenger to Senator Marco Rubio, she began to attack Republicans for being weak on authoritarianism and, in light of the insurrection on January 6, 2021, likened the experience of escaping the Capitol mob to her family's flight from Saigon. A new biographic video saw the congresswoman saying:

> My family escaped communist Vietnam and we were rescued by the U.S. Navy and so I owe this country my life. My parents, facing a future (in Vietnam) where their children wouldn't have the opportunity of freedom or democracy, decided that we might die in search of light but that was better than to live on in darkness. I think if you've experienced oppression and you get a taste of freedom that's something that you never forget.[23]

Murphy's evolution, from pragmatist to partisan, as well as the fine lines she has drawn on identity and human rights issues, hints at the future texture of Vietnamese American politics. As it evolves, it seems likely to confront not only a more complex approach to U.S.-Vietnam relations but overall a further pluralization of interests driven by growing attachment to the American two-party system. Greater diversity and inclusion of interests is already apparent at the local level, where protest continues to be a staple of activism but is now instigated by a wider range of domestic and international issues and directed at a broader range of targets. Anger toward, and public distance from, the VCP seems likely to persist; at the same time, China may come to be seen as the more imminent threat. As 1.5 and subsequent generation candidates emerge and younger voters enter the electorate, it seems likely that partisanship will become as significant a fault line for future community politics as generational differences have been for its past. One could see how this could produce a more muted tone on identity issues and the overarching humanitarian aspiration for Vietnam's democratization. At the same time, in contexts where elections are competitive and ambitious candidates find themselves pitted against one another, as has been the case in Northern and Southern California, it is not difficult to also see how national polarization could exacerbate personal rivalries and escalate the community's temperature. It is in such situations that ethnic media become significant mobilizers and older voters are seen as potentially decisive, compelling public officials to distinguish themselves on international affairs to reach higher-propensity voters.

That said, the past four decades have also witnessed a distinct independent character emerging in Vietnamese American politics, illustrated by numerous efforts by activists to transcend the domestic political system altogether. This is exemplified by the influence of American-based, transnational NGOs on changes in Vietnam's civil society and has manifested further by the numerous, diverse, and sometimes well-heeled religious organizations operating in domestic space. Further evidence can be found in the significant proportion of Vietnamese American voters who register with neither political party as well as the campaign rhetoric and policy actions of leaders, Cao and Murphy being examples, willing to take visible positions against the partisan grain. This suggests that future Vietnamese American politics may be a mixture of the strongly partisan and significantly *a*partisan, defying easy labels for the community but suggesting that the constants of cultural preservation, identity, social welfare, and the improvement of human rights in Vietnam will remain salient on the activist agenda.

DIVERSITY IN IDENTITIES, INDUSTRIES, AND BUSINESS STRATEGIES

Female Vietnamese American Entrepreneurs

JENNIFER A. HUYNH

Introduction

On her iPhone, Gia Ly navigates a virtual tour that she designed to promote her family's businesses. The businesswoman contracts with the search giant Google to sell online tours to small businesses. Her marketing firm, Arrow GTP, prides itself on its multigender, multicultural, and multiskilled public relations team. One of its recent projects was a three-year public health campaign partnered with Boat People SOS, a nonprofit organization, devoted to Vietnamese American civic and political activism on smoking cessation. Other Arrow GTP clients include Kaiser Permanente and the Orange County Transportation Authority. Ly epitomizes Little Saigon's modern female Vietnamese American entrepreneur. Ly was the first female chairperson of the Vietnamese American Chamber of Commerce in its thirty-five-year history, which is the oldest and largest nonprofit organization of its kind in the United States. She grew up helping her parents with Zen, a Vietnamese restaurant in the heart of Little Saigon, which is indicative of the type of business that members of the first generation often open. Comparatively, Ly's multicultural marketing firm and former presidency of the Vietnamese American Chamber of Commerce are symbolic of the untold story of the power of Vietnamese women entrepreneurs in local ethnic politics and commerce.

Immigrants and the children of immigrants are founders of almost 45 percent of U.S. Fortune 500 companies. Entrepreneurship is also popular among Vietnamese immigrants. Between 2006 and 2011, the number of U.S. businesses owned by Vietnamese Americans rose 35.7 percent, to more than

300,000 firms with $34.6 billion in revenue, whereas the number of all U.S. firms increased only by 2 percent during the same period (Frauenfelder 2016). Entrepreneurial experience has transnational origins and ties to the Republic of Vietnam (1955–1975) and present-day Vietnam. As a place where Vietnamese first gained entrepreneurial experience in the homeland and today, refugees and second-generation diasporic Vietnamese engage in cross-border businesses.

What makes Vietnamese American entrepreneurship unique is the high rate of female business owners (nearly 50 percent of Vietnamese entrepreneurs are women).[1] Business ownership by women of color, especially the foreign born, is the fastest-growing business community in the United States (Pearce, Clifford, and Tandon 2011). This chapter centers on Vietnamese women entrepreneurs as agents of their histories by providing an intersectional analysis. It does so by analyzing how the complex web of ethnicity, class, and generation shapes Vietnamese business owners' experiences in the United States.

A Brief History of Ethnic Entrepreneurship among Vietnamese Americans

The history of the ethnic economy and entrepreneurship among the Vietnamese is commonly told from transnational men's perspective, often leaving out or erasing Vietnamese women entrepreneurs' stories and their contributions to ethnic entrepreneurship and the ethnic economy. U.S. intervention in Southeast Asia contributed to a large exodus of Vietnamese to the United States after the end of the U.S.-Vietnam war in 1975. The community's size, geographic concentration, residential segregation, and mode of economic incorporation are significant. The story of ethnic entrepreneurship among Vietnamese Americans first begins in Orange County in Southern California, the largest Vietnamese community outside of Vietnam and the first ethnic community of Vietnamese.

Many of the first Vietnamese exiles were of the professional class and intellectuals, and they mobilized their skills and networks to begin new enterprises and entrepreneurial endeavors. The social and economic diversity of the Vietnamese population played a critical role in building Little Saigons across the United States (Vo L. T. and Danico 2004). Vietnamese immigrants included skilled and well-educated professionals with invaluable entrepreneurial experience in the homeland. This helped create the array of professional and service businesses in the United States serving coethnic clientele. However, this was not a direct translation of skills, as many first-generation Vietnamese at first faced what Pyong Gap Min describes as "status inconsistency" (Park 1997) in their being forced to initially take low-paid, low-status jobs.

As discussed in the Introduction to this volume, migration from Vietnam to the United States took place in diverse waves. The earlier waves of Vietnamese immigrants had higher human capital and included the entrepreneurial class from Vietnam (see Table 8.1). That, in combination with transnational social capital, created the necessary sources for the ethnic communities to grow. The first substantial wave of Vietnamese immigrants—comprising mainly former military and government officials from relatively privileged class backgrounds who were sponsored by U.S. government programs—began in 1975 (Bloemraad 2006). An estimated 20 percent of immigrants from the first wave had a college education, compared to just about 1 percent of the population in South Vietnam. A second wave of refugees, comprising approximately half a million individuals, began in 1978. The forced closing of businesses owned by ethnic Chinese living in Vietnam, in addition to the nationalization and redistribution of land, created a mass displacement of boat people who left the country during this wave. Motivated to leave Vietnam as a result of the new government's implementation of drastic political, economic, and agricultural policies, many immigrants from the second wave were also compelled to leave after having witnessed soldiers being arrested and held in detention in prison and reeducation camps (Bloemraad 2006). In the early 1980s, these Vietnamese immigrant entrepreneurs helped transform Bolsa from a street "lined with bean fields and half-empty shopping centers" into the "Vietnamese Capital of the United States" (Nguyen Phuong Tran 2009: 11).

The building of the vibrant ethnic economy in Southern California relied both on the entrepreneurial experience and human capital of the first and second waves of migration and on the transnational capital from developers in Hong Kong and China; a study by Aguilar-San Juan estimates that 33 percent of the second wave were ethnic Chinese who had entrepreneurial connections with China and other Chinese communities in Southern California. Many of the first entrepreneurs—and notably the future "Godfather of Little Saigon," real estate mogul Frank Jao—were Vietnamese of Chinese origin who had owned businesses in Vietnam. Many spoke fluent Cantonese, which opened the door to Chinese customers and business contacts all over Asia and North America (Aguilar-San Juan 2005: 37–65; Gold 1994: 196–226).

The rapid development of Little Saigons across the United States includes the role of transnational entrepreneurs from China, Taiwan, and Vietnam. For example, in 1981, Roger Chen, a young Taiwanese developer, and Frank Jao bought properties on the 9000 block of Bolsa Avenue in Westminster (Nguyen Phuong Tran 2017). Around the same time, Duong Chuong, a pharmacist in Vietnam, opened up the largest Asian supermarket in Orange County. He originally opened a small grocery store in Inglewood in 1979 with $5,000 he managed to smuggle out of Vietnam (Nguyen Phuong Tran 2015). By 1984, along with Chinese coethnics in Taiwan, Thailand, and the United States, he opened an import-export business that supplied more than one hundred grocery stores in Southern California.

Between 1976 and 1984, investors from Hong Kong provided more than $10 million in development along Bolsa Avenue, paving the way for the first Little Saigon's future growth. Ethnic entrepreneurship burgeoned during this time as more immigrants settled in the United States. Between 1982 and 1987, the number of Vietnamese-owned businesses increased from 4,989 to 25,671, a 415 percent increase, far exceeding the 135 percent increase in the Vietnamese population during the same time period (Nguyen Phuong Tran 2017). In the span of ten years, ethnic entrepreneurship grew to 7 percent of Vietnamese immigrants in 1990, as compared to 3 percent in 1980 (Zhou 2010). Chain migration produced new residents, entrepreneurs, and workers moving from Vietnam and from other states to Southern California and powered the area's expansion (Aguilar-San Juan 2009).

The presence of transnational behemoths and the exiled entrepreneurial Chinese class spearheaded the development of Little Saigons across the United States. Vietnamese-run firms grew nationwide from an estimated 59,674 in 1992 to 312,881 in 2012.[2] California has the largest number of Vietnamese-owned firms at 68,812, with the Los Angeles-Orange County area having the largest number (32,356), followed by Houston (16,982) and Dallas (12,038) (Frauenfelder 2016). Aggregate receipts of Vietnamese firms in Orange County were $13.4 billion in 2007. By 2010, the rate of self-employment per 1,000 employed persons nationwide was 94.4; for the Vietnamese, it reached 142.9. These numbers undercount the vast number of businesses that operate by cash only or that are not formalized businesses.

Spatial segregation of ethnic businesses is as evident for Vietnamese today as it was in the past, and so is residential segregation; a study by Logan and Zhang found that the index of dissimilarity for Vietnamese is similar to that of Black people, with little change over the last twenty years. Vietnamese are likely to live in highly segregated neighborhoods (Logan and Zhang 2013). A similar study by Walton using census data in Northern and Southern California found that immigrant enclaves are overrepresented among Vietnamese American ethnic neighborhoods (Walton 2015: 490–515).

The history of residential segregation, ethnic economy, and entrepreneurship among the Vietnamese is told from the lens of transnational capital and familial resources. This chapter focuses on gender and Vietnamese entrepreneurs' stories and contributions to contemporary ethnic entrepreneurship. Vietnamese women entrepreneurs are found in a multitude of industries and occupations beyond traditional service industries such as nails, restaurants, and beauty salons. While the history of women in the building of Little Saigon is often overlooked, the presence and importance of women in Little Saigon today is unquestionable.

Methods

This chapter draws on data from the U.S. Census Bureau and the Southeast Asian archives at the University of California, Irvine; more than ten years of ethnography in Southern California; participant observation in three Vietnamese American communities; and in-depth interviews with fourteen Vietnamese women entrepreneurs.

I draw on two key sources of nationally representative survey data to analyze demographic trends in immigrant entrepreneurship. First is the American Community Survey (ACS). Data on self-employment is demarcated in two types: general and incorporated. Unincorporated businesses include sole proprietorships and partnerships that make up the majority of small businesses. Incorporating a business can provide legal protections for its owner, yet not all self-employed individuals find incorporation beneficial, and it may lead to a higher tax liability (Christnacht, Smith, and Chenevert 2018). A second important source of data is the Survey of Business Owners (SBO), which the U.S. Census Bureau conducts every five years. The data set is unique because it provides detailed information about sex, ethnicity, race, and business characteristics.

The qualitative section draws on fourteen in-depth interviews with Vietnamese women entrepreneurs between 2010 and 2020. When requested, names of businesses and individuals have been changed to protect their privacy. I include interviews with different generations of Vietnamese to showcase the diversity of Vietnamese women entrepreneurs. The first generation is defined as those who immigrated to the United States when they were at least eighteen years old; the 1.5 generation, defined as immigrants who arrived in the United States as children under the age of thirteen; and the second generation, defined as children born in the United States with at least one immigrant parent (Portes and Yiu 2013: 75–95). Researchers show that those who immigrate at younger ages are more likely to resemble the native-born in values and attitudes since they are socialized into the new society to which their families migrated (Portes and Rumbaut 2001). Focusing on those who immigrated as adults reveals the values and characteristics of those who experience ties to both the United States and to Vietnam. When possible, I also make distinctions for those who identify as Chinese Vietnamese since they have a different history of immigration to the United States. All first-generation immigrants that I interviewed came before 2012 and as refugees, which is true for most Vietnamese who came to the United States. Criteria for inclusion included participants who were at least eighteen years of age and whose business was at least three years old. Respondents varied from twenty-four to sixty-two years of age, with a median age of forty-six years. Interviews were open-ended and semi-structured to cover seven topics, including family history, employment history, intersectionality, social capital/networks, transnationalism, ethnic identity, and work experience.

Using reputational snowballing, I initially knew only three of fourteen interviewees, or 20 percent of the sample, from volunteer work or community organizations. This chapter intentionally includes a diverse range of entrepreneurial businesses and locales to highlight the diversity of female Vietnamese entrepreneurs. Census data shows that female Vietnamese entrepreneurs have opened professional businesses in corporate finance, international trade, law, marketing, and traditional service industries (hair salons, restaurants, nail salons), among others. The realities and lived experiences of female Vietnamese entrepreneurs are complicated and nuanced.

Trends in Self-Employment for Vietnamese and Selected Immigrants

This section answers the question of who is entrepreneurial among immigrants to the United States. What are the key industries and businesses that Vietnamese women in the United States create? How does this relate to the scholarly literature on immigrant entrepreneurship?

Immigrant entrepreneurship is a social mobility strategy (Gold 1994: 196–226; Portes 1987: 340–372; Zhou 2010). Social scientists have amassed a large body of evidence indicating how ethnic entrepreneurship benefits many immigrant groups and communities in the United States (Dhingra 2012; Min 1990: 436–455; Zhou 2004: 1040–1074). However, some scholars view self-employment as a survival strategy, while others explain it as a means of collective and individual success or mobility (Portes and Yiu 2013: 75–95). Nevertheless, entrepreneurship is popular among immigrants. The opportunity structures available in the country of immigration and the coethnic context within which the actors operate are two critical variables for female entrepreneurs and entrepreneurs in general (Chreim et al. 2018: 210–222). Globally, female immigrant entrepreneurs are underrepresented in certain countries, depending on their embeddedness in economic and social contexts (Brieger and Gielnik 2020: 1–25). The United States has created a relatively welcoming atmosphere for immigrant entrepreneurs, including particular entry and visa requirements to entice immigrant entrepreneurs (Fairlie and Robb 2007: 225–245).

Table 8.1 describes the different rates of entrepreneurship among contemporary immigrants to the United States by gender and race. The most recent data shows that foreign-born Vietnamese women are highly entrepreneurial. Vietnamese immigrant women have higher rates of self-employment than U.S. Black people, U.S.-born white women, U.S.-born white men, and female immigrants from China, Mexico, and El Salvador. Vietnamese immigrant women are even more likely than Vietnamese men to be self-employed as general small business owners (9.82 percent to 9.44 percent, respectively). Vietnamese women are also more likely to incorporate their businesses compared to white women (4.35 percent to 2.69 percent, respectively). What could explain Vietnamese women's high rates of entrepreneurship? Race and ethnicity grant significant access to resources tied to social capital (Valdez 2016: 1618–1636). Social capital fosters ethnic resources such as knowledge, values, information, and business networks, which facilitate ethnic enterprises (Valdez 2016: 1618–1636). It is not surprising then that Vietnamese women can easily and readily be absorbed into local ethnic economies or ethnic niches, as the Vietnamese are the sixth-largest immigrant group in the United States and are highly concentrated in particular industries (see Tables 8.2 and 8.3). Researchers have cogently written about the successful entrepreneurial experiences of Cubans, Chinese, and Koreans who use ethnic networks and niche economies (Min 2008; Portes 1987: 340–372; Zhou 2010).

Theories that explain entry into immigrant entrepreneurship include labor market discrimination. For example, many Vietnamese indicated that they experienced labor market discrimination because of limited English proficiency and language skills and because American employers do not recognize their educational credentials from Vietnam (Le C. N. 2007: 15–28).

In terms of women-owned businesses, Korean business owners earn the highest reported income, followed by Chinese business owners and then white owners. Regardless of race, male business owners incorporate their businesses at a higher rate than female owners. As prior research indicates, for both men and women, self-employed incorporated workers earn more than self-employed, unincorporated owners (Valdez 2016: 1618–1636). Other researchers also found that refugees and forced migrants have high rates of entrepreneurship, which this data confirms when one examines rates of entrepreneurship for Vietnamese and Cubans (Kosten 2018). The gender wage gap that exists in the mainstream economy replicates itself in the entrepreneurial world.

The most recent data from the SBO, from 2012, is presented in Table 8.2. It shows the number of firms owned by select racial and ethnic groups, the number of firms per 1,000 population, and their business receipts, including sales, receipts, or values of shipments for each racial and ethnic group. The data also separates firms without employees and those with at least one employee. It is also important to point out that the majority of U.S. businesses are considered small businesses. The U.S. Small Business Administration

TABLE 8.1 EMPLOYMENT TYPE AND INCOMES FOR SELECTED ASIAN AND LATINX IMMIGRANT GROUPS, U.S.-BORN WHITES, U.S.-BORN BLACKS, 2018

Characteristics	Natives			
	White		Black	
	Male	*Female*	*Male*	*Female*
Type of employment				
Waged/salaried worker (%)	87.0	91.2	92.5	95.7
Self-employed—general (%)	7.7	6.1	5.0	3.1
Self-employed—incorp. (%)	5.3	2.7	2.5	1.2
Annual income—mean	68,412	44,965	43,654	37,303
Waged/salaried worker	67,076	44,815	43,330	37,259
Self-employed—general	50,907	25,639	28,690	20,641

Characteristics	Immigrants							
	Chinese		Korean		Vietnamese		Mexican	
	Male	*Female*	*Male*	*Female*	*Male*	*Female*	*Male*	*Female*
Type of employment								
Waged/salaried worker (%)	88.2	90.4	80.0	85.0	85.5	85.8	89.5	91.7
Self-employed—general (%)	6.2	5.8	9.9	8.3	9.4	9.8	8.2	6.8
Self-employed—incorp. (%)	5.6	3.8	10.1	6.7	5.1	4.4	2.3	1.5
Annual income—mean	81,119	61,072	79,033	55,069	57,758	43,132	39,941	29,547
Waged/salaried worker	81,150	61,332	79,143	55,459	57,527	43,142	39,509	29,485
Self-employed—general	53,225	28,137	58,801	35,620	41,242	21,079	37,505	16,388

Source: 2018 ACS 5-year PUMS estimates.

Note: Sample excludes under 16/unemployed. Waged/salaried workers include individuals who work in private for-profit and private not-for-profit companies, as well as local, state, and federal government employees. Figures in the table are adjusted using person-level analytical weights.

TABLE 8.2 FIRM OWNERSHIP AND SELECTED PERFORMANCE INDICATORS, 2012

Groups	All Firms				Firms with Paid Employees			
	Total number of firms	Firms per 1,000 population	Sales, receipts, or value of shipments ($1,000)	Mean gross receipts per firm	Number of firms	Firms per 1,000 population	Sales, receipts, or value of shipments ($1,000)	Gross receipts per firm ($1,000)
Asian								
Korean	224,891	142.40	107,813,236	479.40	81,902	51.86	99,194,346	1,211.13
Asian Indian	377,486	134.40	227,148,254	601.74	137,720	49.03	209,778,561	1,523.22
Japanese	119,163	113.28	44,243,189	371.28	23,906	22.72	39,990,633	1,672.82
Chinese	528,702	155.75	210,062,246	397.32	139,016	40.95	190,602,834	1,371.08
Filipino	193,336	69.23	25,845,518	133.68	24,548	8.79	20,460,768	833.50
Vietnamese	310,864	204.23	34,649,696	111.46	37,015	24.31	24,193,204	653.60
Latin American								
Cuban	281,982	173.56	92,600,303	328.39	32,037	19.71	84,298,660	2,631.29
Mexican	1,624,617	71.70	204,712,259	126.01	141,764	6.25	156,210,266	1,101.90

Source: U.S. Census Bureau, 2012 Survey of Business Owners.

(SBA) estimates that there are 30.7 million small firms, which account for approximately 99.9 percent of all small businesses in the United States. More than 70 percent of small businesses had no employees in 2019.

Firm ownership also varies by gender among various racial and ethnic groups in the United States, as shown in Table 8.2. On the basis of population, Vietnamese women are the most entrepreneurial group compared to all other female Asian immigrant groups and Vietnamese men. Another possible explanation for high rates of entrepreneurship among Vietnamese immigrants is transnationalism. A strong tradition of entrepreneurship in Vietnam may also be a pull factor for female Vietnamese entrepreneurs in the United States. Theories that explain female Vietnamese entrepreneurship transnationally include the fact that "31.3% of businesses in Vietnam are owned by women, placing Vietnam at sixth among the 53 surveyed economies, ahead of most of Europe, the United States, China other Asian nations."[3] A study of female Vietnamese entrepreneurs in Vietnam found that the top five motivators are higher incomes, independence, securing family jobs, utilizing experience, and job safety (Perri and Chu 2012: 93). Only 28 percent of female participants cited a push factor, such as unemployment, as motivation for starting their businesses, as opposed to 72 percent who were motivated by good opportunities or their qualifications (*International Labor Organization Office in Vietnam* 2007). Vietnamese entrepreneurs' most common challenge in Vietnam is financial constraints on business expansion (Nguyen H. A. et al. 2020: 215–226). Small businesses in developing countries, especially those owned by women, often have less access to financial capital (Wang Q. 2013: 299–321). This limited opportunity structure is weakened in the context of the United States. Because the initial costs to start a business are typically low in the United States, female Vietnamese entrepreneurs rely on family and friends rather than banks for start-up capital. This is consistent with a study that found family and friends to be the most common business capital source for male entrepreneurs (Zhu et al. 2015: 103). Nevertheless, female Vietnamese business owners still face considerable challenges, including implicit biases, institutional racism, language barriers, and restricted capital access.

While self-employed women earn less than men across all categories, much of the difference can be explained by industry choice and women's higher burden of household tasks (Hundley 2001: 817–829). If we consider sales and gross receipts per capita as an indicator of business performance, South Asian Indians' enterprises lead in having large sales volumes, followed by Koreans. This is not surprising given that Asian Indians are highly selected immigrants in terms of education and income in the United States. Generally, firms that have employees often have larger payrolls and sales; therefore, they are considered separately (Wang 2013: 299–321). In terms of firms with paid employees, South Indians and Chinese have the largest sales receipts.

Industry Concentration of Vietnamese Female Entrepreneurs

The most popular type of business to be operated and owned by a female Vietnamese entrepreneur in the United States is a nail salon, followed by beauty salons and restaurants (Tables 8.3 and 8.4). There is, however, a growing number of businesses outside these traditional ethnic niches, which includes professional services, creative arts, and finance. Data from the 2018 ACS shows that dentistry is the fourth-largest incorporated business industry for foreign-born female Vietnamese entrepreneurs. For U.S.-born Vietnamese women, the third-most-popular incorporated industry includes independent artists, writers, and performers. Studies show that gender (men) and marital status (married) are often positively related to entrepreneurship. Ethnic entrepreneurship is frequently a collective family affair (Zhou 2010). However, contemporary reality shows that immigrant women are opening businesses that go beyond family enterprises and transforming traditional mom-and-pop restaurants (De Luca and Ambrosini 2019: 201–215).

Finding myself in one of the many cafés on a sunny Southern California afternoon, I spoke with Phuong, a first-generation immigrant who owns a lucrative phở restaurant called Phở Kim Quy or Phở Kimmy. Why? I ask her. Well, "it's easy—if you were a good cook at home, you can cook here." Restaurants dominate Little Saigon with names that illustrate the restaurant's specialty and region of the cuisine or ethnicity found in Vietnam, such as Bún Chả Hà Nội (a type of grilled pork dish unique to the northern capital) or Cơm Tấm Nha Trang (a beef/pork rice dish from Nha Trang, a city in central Vietnam) or Triều Châu Restaurant. Restaurants from the 1.5 or second generation are anglicized, with names such as Garlic and Chives or Mama Tieus, or use fusion Vietnamese, such as Silk Noodle, to appeal to non-Vietnamese. Mama Tieus includes a ragù bread bowl topped off with cheese alongside a watermelon basil lemonade and traditional Vietnamese fare like pho and banh mi sandwiches. Many 1.5- and second-generation restaurants also offer happy hours, with happy hour banh mi bites. Their restaurants are also made to appeal to non-Vietnamese. Entrepreneurship is an economic strategy for female Vietnamese immigrants and the U.S.-born. The most striking result of the quantitative data analysis is that female Vietnamese immigrants are much more likely to be entrepreneurs than white women or other selected immigrant women.

Table 8.3 shows industry concentration, comparing men and women in incorporated businesses, and Table 8.4 shows industry concentrates for those in unincorporated businesses. The ACS data shows that, among self-employed workers, female-owned Vietnamese businesses share common industry concentrations in food, retail, and personal services such as beauty salons. Male

TABLE 8.3 INDUSTRY CONCENTRATIONS OF SELF-EMPLOYED
VIETNAMESE IN INCORPORATED BUSINESSES

Industry	Male				Female			
	Native %	Margin of error +/-	Foreign born %	Margin of error +/-	Native %	Margin of error +/-	Foreign born %	Margin of error +/-
Construction	3.54%	0.50%	7.08%	0.29%	0.00%	0.00%	0.53%	0.09%
Lessors of real estate & offices of real estate agents & brokers	2.56%	0.43%	1.50%	0.14%	5.55%	0.95%	3.05%	0.21%
Dentists	2.64%	0.44%	4.70%	0.24%	4.79%	0.89%	4.04%	0.24%
Restaurants & food services	9.49%	0.80%	7.20%	0.29%	6.45%	1.02%	7.34%	0.31%
Beauty salons	1.44%	0.33%	4.61%	0.24%	8.55%	1.17%	11.34%	0.38%
Nail salons & personal care services	8.53%	0.76%	18.61%	0.44%	20.29%	1.68%	33.83%	0.57%

Source: U.S. Census Bureau, 2018 American Community Survey.
Note: Data are based on a sample and are subject to sampling variability. A margin of error is a measure of an estimate's variability. The larger the margin of error in relation to the size of the estimates, the less reliable the estimate. This number, when added to and subtracted from the estimate, forms the 90 percent confidence interval.

Vietnamese business owners tend to be distinctly concentrated in construction, utilities, and wholesale trade. Vietnamese male- and female-owned businesses are frequently found in a few industrial sectors, as shown in the table. This includes service industries like beauty salons, nails, and restaurants. Tables 8.3 and 8.4 illustrate the types of businesses that female and male Vietnamese entrepreneurs enter. Hum holds that certain economic sectors and markets offer easy entry but also include high risks of failure for first-generation immigrants (Hum 2004: 25–55; Le C. N. 2007: 15–28). However, businesses that provide professional services, as in the legal, financial, educational, and technical fields, are also found. These types of professional services are beginning to proliferate among U.S.-born Vietnamese women and the 1.5 generation. The top ten industries for U.S.-born female entrepreneurs outside those listed in Tables 8.3 and 8.4 include accounting and tax preparation, educational support services, outpatient care centers, and independent artists, writers, and performers. This diversification in professional services and creative arts entrepreneurship is common among second-generation and 1.5-generation Vietnamese.

The creation of restaurants was a survival tactic of the first generation. For those linguistically isolated with little transfer of skills from the home

TABLE 8.4 SELF-EMPLOYED IN OWN NOT INCORPORATED BUSINESS, PROFESSIONAL PRACTICE, OR FARM

	Male				Female			
Industry	Native %	Margin of error +/-	Foreign born %	Margin of error +/-	Native %	Margin of error +/-	Foreign born %	Margin of error +/-
Construction	14.60%	0.84%	13.72%	0.29%	0.00%	0.00%	0.71%	0.07%
Lessors of real estate & offices of real estate agents & brokers	2.83%	0.39%	1.95%	0.14%	1.43%	0.31%	2.25%	0.12%
Landscaping services	0.98%	0.23%	5.80%	0.23%	0.32%	0.15%	0.25%	0.04%
Restaurants & food services	5.59%	0.55%	6.33%	0.24%	4.68%	0.55%	5.73%	0.18%
Beauty salons	44.50%	1.18%	0.39%	0.06%	15.92%	0.95%	14.90%	0.28%
Nail salons & personal care services	9.25%	0.69%	23.60%	0.42%	21.10%	1.06%	43.00%	0.39%

Source: U.S. Census Bureau, 2018 American Community Survey.
Note: Data are based on a sample and are subject to sampling variability. A margin of error is a measure of an estimate's variability. The larger the margin of error in relation to the size of the estimates, the less reliable the estimate. This number, when added to and subtracted from the estimate, forms the 90 percent confidence interval.

country to the new country, starting a restaurant in the community was an easy way to make money. For 1.5- and second-generation female Vietnamese entrepreneurs, the motivations for starting businesses are described not only in terms of economic strategy but in terms of a creative enterprise. The profile of those who start businesses and were born in the United States tends toward college-educated with greater capital (Portes and Yiu 2013: 75–95). Accounts of neoliberalism see the rise of entrepreneurial activity as directly related to the informalization of labor and the dismantling of the traditional workplace over the past few decades (Harvey 2007; Peck 2010; R. G. Smith 2015). Deindustrialization and the creation of the hourglass economy have resulted in new challenges and a shrinking middle class. Today, economists estimate that 16 percent to 32 percent of Americans make their living through nontraditional employment, with the sharpest increases in "alternative work arrangements" (Katz and Krueger 2019: 382–416). Alternative work arrangements include self-employed entrepreneurs who work as independent contractors or freelance workers (Katz and Krueger 2019: 382–416). For those working in professional and business services, health and education represented half of those engaged in alternative work arrangements. The above data presents a national and quantitative portrait of trends among male and female Vietnamese entrepreneurs.

Entrepreneurial Strategies of Female Vietnamese Entrepreneurs

My qualitative interviews indicate that several of the strategies mentioned, including transnational strategies and human capital attributes, are not as gender specific as they would appear in the literature on immigrant entrepreneurship; however, the literature to date has primarily privileged the narratives and voices of male Vietnamese entrepreneurs. It is also important to note that the strategies are not mutually exclusive, as many are used in combination.

"My Mom Ran Her Own Business"

Family business experience and the coethnic community play instrumental roles for female Vietnamese entrepreneurs. Over 60 percent of my interviewees had mothers who owned businesses, including restaurants and nail shops, or worked informally in a market in Vietnam or in the United States. Participants also often mentioned experience working in their parents' business as children. Children with self-employed parents are more likely to become business owners themselves, with only a small percentage of those businesses being inherited (Fairlie and Robb 2007: 225–245). One person described how, as a child, she worked in her parents' business in Vietnam at the marketplace selling cloth and vegetables: "I worked at the Vuon Chuoi Market near our home. My older brother also told me, 'I am a son but this is war time, so I have to accept that reality. I leave the family's business in your hands.'"[4] Kien Tam Nguyen opened her own wig salon in her home in Saigon and then to run one of the largest beauty schools in Southern California with her husband and children. The beauty college estimates that it has graduated more than forty thousand students and has more than forty employees with two locations. Kien's business experience in Vietnam, along with the support of her partner, shaped her desire to open a beauty school in the United States in the Vietnamese community:

> My husband taught at one (beauty) school. That was the time when the Vietnamese students started coming to the American school in droves. On principle, he couldn't teach without a teaching license, but he could teach by interpreting English into Vietnamese or translated teaching material into Vietnamese so others could teach. There was

one school that was closed to move to a different location. An instructor there told my husband about it so he decided to purchase the place.

The importance of family and social networks cannot be understated. Female Vietnamese entrepreneurs can draw on coethnic resources, including advice, labor, and marketing products, or resources within the community, and outside the community, they can market to the mainstream client base (Dhingra 2012; Piperopoulos 2012). Family members can play an important role in offering advice and support and passing on informal knowledge. As one second-generation female Vietnamese entrepreneur owner of an import-export company explained:

> They [My parents] were actually super supportive when I wanted to start my own business, I think because both of them, since they came to the U.S., they're both business owners. . . . So that's been their pathway, it has been to really create their own means. And I see it as very instrumental to my journey because, you know, they have a lot of business advice and insight and they know a lot about just how to manage relationships, how to navigate different transactions, how to navigate different relationships.

The resources and social capital derived from belonging to a particular ethnic group include ethnic resources such as access to labor and supplier markets, as well as knowledge that enhances start-up and success (Zhou 2010). This is true for some female Vietnamese entrepreneurs who decide to stay in the same industry as their parents. One 1.5-generation entrepreneur described her familiarity and comfort with opening a nail shop after working in her mother's shop:

> My mom opened her own nail shop. When my sisters were still in high school, they would work on weekends at my mom's shop. They went to college and they still worked part-time at the nail shop. My second sister graduated with a BA and she worked for a few times, but she did not like it, so she came back to work with my mom until now. My youngest sister is a lawyer and she went to law school, so she stopped working at my mom's shop. My family has a lot of people with nail licenses. I think nails is a perfect career.

Researchers show how coethnic businesses serve as places for training and teaching entrepreneurial skills to recently arrived members or younger generations; this is sometimes referred to as a stepladder hypothesis, where entrepreneurship allows for role models and informal training systems (Aldrich and Waldinger 1990: 111–135; Portes and Yiu 2013: 75–95; Raijman and Tienda 2000: 682–706). Ethnic controlled economies, like nail shops, functioned as a resource for Vietnamese entrepreneurs. Scholars defined the ethnic controlled economy as significant and persistent economic power exercised by ethnic employees in the mainstream economy, with ethnic entrepreneurs clustering in the same occupations or fields (Light 2005). Examples abound, including motels owned by Guajarati Indians, Korean grocers, Cambodian doughnut shops in Los Angeles, Chinese and Korean apparel manufacturing, and the Vietnamese nail industry (Tseng 1994: 169–189; Curtis 2013: 13–29). However, while ethnic entrepreneurship also is common among first-, 1.5-, and second-generation women, there are generational distinctions in terms of business operations and client bases, including the expansion of the customer base beyond the ethnic community.

"No Brick or Mortar Business": Media and Technology Enabling Client Expansion

Unlike the first-generation women-owned businesses that I encountered, many second-generation and 1.5-generation female Vietnamese business owners did not have a brick-and-mortar establishment. Instead, their businesses included an online presence targeting pan-ethnic Asians and millennials to expand their customer base. Many used new media technologies like Instagram and TikTok to advertise and create hype and market products beyond the ethnic community.

Traditionally, the literature in ethnic entrepreneurship shows that women-owned businesses are more likely to be based in one's home than those owned by men (Wang 2013: 299–321). The in-home business option is partially explained by the gendered inequality in household responsibilities and care work for women (Long 2012). However, the internet and social media new ways to reach audiences beyond the ethnic community. Loan Nguyen is creator of The Loop, which sells made-to-order churros with fanciful toppings and glazes. At the store fronting a strip mall in the heart of Bolsa's Little Saigon, Loan said that "80 to 90% of her customers aren't Asian. We wanted to come up with a dessert that appeals to everybody." Featured in *Cosmopolitan* magazine, Instagrammable desserts like her "mermaid glazed churro which features blueberry glaze and a mermaid sparkle sugar" come at the price of five to eight dollars per churro. The new ethnic business owners use social media like Instagram, Facebook, and Twitter to appeal to trendy millennial audiences. Millennials are a potent economic force in the United States today, representing 30 percent of total retail sales. Forbes reported that millennials like sharing experiences with friends and are 13 percent more likely than Generation X to broadcast what they buy on social media. Businesses using new technology market themselves to nonethnic people. The stereotype is that gender and minority identity may constrain entrepreneurs' advancement, but it can also generate innovation and creativity (Pio and Essers 2014: 252–265).

"A Strength in My Journey": Ethnicity, Gender, and Race as Assets in a Multicultural Marketplace

Many female Vietnamese business owners described their multicultural perspectives as a strategic advantage to being a female Vietnamese entrepreneur. As one second-generation coffee-company owner explained:

> So my identity as a Vietnamese American woman offers, in my experience as a woman, offers me this lens and this perspective, that I feel like it's so enriching, it is so powerful that it helps, that it shapes everything I do in a way that I feel is really unique and also a really high impact and really effective for the world that we live in. Because the world that we live in is a globalized world, is a diverse world with many, many different perspectives and experiences. I think having the ability and the emotional capacity and also the heart and the awareness to understand and appreciate diversity is a huge advantage for anyone who is trying to navigate the future of our world.

Female Vietnamese entrepreneurs described their positionality as a strength in multiculturalism and a privileged perspective knowing both the coethnic market and also the host country market (Essers and Benschop 2009: 403–423; I. Small 2019). This is also true for Darla, a second-generation Vietnamese restaurant owner in Brooklyn, New York, who has broadened her customer base beyond the ethnic community:

> Yeah, I guess just growing up with the food and the culture, being familiar about it and feeling like the ambassador of pho and (Vietnamese dishes) gives us an authenticity for sure. But on the other side of the coin, we have an American chef, Antonio, who's spent some time in Vietnam. His Vietnamese is impeccable, his palette is a true Vietnamese palette, so us being Vietnamese definitely helps but I don't think it's an end all be all.

Transnational Marketplace

Many female Vietnamese entrepreneurs described transnational business opportunities with Vietnam as an untapped resource. Many interviewees saw transnational business exchange activities as opportunities for personal career development and a new mode of labor market integration; Vietnamese can capitalize on their bilingualism and cultural fluency in both the United States and Vietnam to start an international corporation or to pursue transnational entrepreneurship. One telling example involves the workings of a transnational organization, the Vietnamese American Chamber of Commerce. At a summer 2019 public event, the president remarked:

> Because of the US trade war with China, a lot of US manufacturers are asking if it's OK to move our supply chains to Vietnam. I want to tell you that this is a good time for Vietnam and this is important especially important if you're looking to expand your small business market. There are currently 326 industrial parks with 43 foreign direct investments already doing business. Vietnam is the 17th largest trading partner of the US, and the US is the first largest trading partner of Vietnam. This is an excellent time. . . . There are already a lot of Vietnamese returning and we have a demographic advantage since there is a wide variety of bilingual trade services and a large multicultural consumer market in California.

The forum sponsored by the Vietnamese American Chamber of Commerce included a panel speaker from the U.S. Small Business Administration. The forum advertised the U.S. government's recent $18 million grant to support small business trade growth in global markets. Another group of studies has focused on the migration of U.S.-born second-generation to Vietnam, pushed by the globalization of work opportunities (I. Small 2019). Research shows that highly skilled Vietnamese Americans who returned to Vietnam constructed symbolic boundaries that distinguished themselves from both foreigners and locals, instead occupying a third space (Nguyen-Akbar 2016: 96–121). This requires active ethnic renegotiation of identity across multiple spaces and the use of cultural and social capital in the process of negotiating situational identities (Nguyen-Akbar 2016).

"Tenacity, Resilience, and Discipline"

A poignant question presented to my sample asked what business skills women Vietnamese entrepreneurs believe they need to become entrepreneurs and where these skills are acquired. Hard work, discipline, and flexibility were key attributes described; as one first-generation nail-shop owner mentioned, "I work 12 hours a day, 7 days a week." Other characteristics included tenacity, resilience, and commitment. Long hours seemed to be a common characteristic shared by female business entrepreneurs. Another entrepreneur explained, "Owning a nail shop—I like to joke about it—we work 7 days a week. So yeah, life is hard, that's the irony. I've become my mom." A survey of 170 male Vietnamese American entrepreneurs similarly found that the most common challenges faced by entrepreneurs included "long hours required by this role and too little time to interact with their family" (Jabeen, Faisal, and Katsioloudes 2017). This second-generation entrepreneur's mother owned a nail shop, and her aunt owned a restaurant, which provided role models, but she said there were generational differences:

> Their minds are very influenced by going through a war. So for them it's all one-sided like "Why are you not at the restaurant? Why are you not at the restaurant?" They want us to do every job and not hire employees because they think that if we work really hard and do the work ourselves we would save more money and have less overhead by hiring less employees, but I would argue that although my mom is a good businesswoman and she works so hard, she was never able to scale her business or had the desire to scale it because she had to do everything herself. Where our point of view is work smarter and technically not harder although we are working our asses off. So it does take a little bit to explain that to them. They think that because I'm not managing the restaurant on a certain day that we're not working hard enough.

Much of this knowledge regarding business operations and these characteristics came from family but also via informal mentors, coethnic business organizations such as the Vietnamese Chamber of Commerce, or women-led groups focused on entrepreneurship and business.

Challenges: Microaggressions, Sexism, and the Need to "Speak Out"

None of these businesses grew without challenges. Several respondents reported microaggressions and bias in how their perceived identities as women and minorities shaped their everyday interactions with customers and operations. Many said that they were never subject to outright racism; rather, racism was subtler. One owner explained her mistaken identity:

> I would say that people don't like to take me seriously as a woman business owner. Like I have a lot of vendors come by, people to fix the dishwasher, they always come up to me and say, "Can I talk to your boss?" And I just find it exhausting that I have to correct people all

the time, so yeah, that is disheartening, exhausting, but it's something that I experience, and it's something that my partners do not have to experience. Or if a locksmith comes up I know that I'll have a higher quote than my husband will.

In response, business owners developed strategic communication strategies to negotiate their multiple identities and to respond to implicit biases and subtle racism in the workplace. As one respondent explained:

> It's this subconscious challenge, because it's like you have to do more work mentally to convince yourself that it's possible because we live in a very heteronormative, patriarchal society that constantly sends messages to women that it's not possible or you're not valid or you're not valued or you're not powerful, strong enough or not good enough. Those are the kinds of messages that I myself as a woman in general, let alone women entrepreneurs, though the messages I've gotten my whole life and I still encounter, because that's just that's our society. . . . And then all of these ideas feed into an agenda in a very general sense. They feed into other people's minds. So at any point in my business, my experience as a business owner, when I'm interacting with somebody, whether it's a vendor, whether it's a client, whether it's a contractor, whether it's a partner. Right. Sometimes I have to encounter their preconceptions of biases rooted in sexism, whether it comes up in their communication style, whether it comes up in the communication style, could be layers of gaslighting. It can be manipulation. It can be patronizing and can be condescending.

As a result, the interviewee gave an example of an interaction with the business accountant and discussed the role of bias in language and societal expectations or stereotypes of business owners:

> He was a white man who I was having issues with. I would catch errors in my account and then he would say things to me like, "I'm just so impressed that you're so diligent with your books." You know, that's not a compliment. Right. It's a total insult. Because why is it so impressive that I care about my business? Why it's so impressive that I would be diligent with the books. It's my money, right? . . . And he would just say, "I'm just so impressed that you actually built something that has legs here." Right. Again, this level of "I'm so impressed" that comes from a level of I don't really think women are capable, like inherently it in his mind, like you would never you would never track

it back to that. But it's in his brain. . . . I have to spend the mental and emotional bandwidth to react to respond to this person. And it's just annoying and it's frustrating.

As a response to the subtle sexism and racism and microaggressions, business owners—especially second-generation women—explained the importance of not conforming to traditional gender roles for Asian American women:

> My advice would be don't dim your light, or don't be less outspoken and don't be kind of quiet. Don't be all the other stereotypes of what Asian women are, be outspoken, you don't have to be likeable. Be loud, be aggressive. . . . I think just growing up with my family, my parents, we're always taught to assimilate, to not stick out. To always be agreeable, smile, be nice, be sweet, which I think in this day and age you don't have to be. You can be outspoken; you can speak your mind. You don't have to be agreeable. You can be rude and tell them "Hey I am the owner."

Many first-generation Vietnamese business owners spoke less about the challenges of being a woman and instead focused more on the challenges of being Vietnamese in America. The largest challenge many mentioned was overcoming the language barrier. One interviewee described how, after working for fifteen years to learn English, she still sometimes found it hard to communicate with customers. She described being mocked in her nail shop by her clients, and even by her husband, who blamed her for her poor English when business was bad. Research indicates that language challenges disappear for the children of immigrants, as shown above in the quotes that are more focused on sexism and U.S. racial hierarchies as challenges (Dhingra 2012).

Motivation for Starting a Business: Agency and Autonomy

The decision to start a business is a risky one. What motivations or reasons did these women entrepreneurs give for taking the leap into business ownership? A repeated theme in the stories included the desire for creativity and agency. As Sahra, a second-generation business owner, explained:

> My motivation was the idea of creating my own lane. I like the idea of bringing something to life that doesn't exist already, whether it's a product or a brand or a vision. I get to do a lot of those things with Nguyen Coffee Supply. I get to celebrate my culture and my family. Like my family roots and my family name. I get to tell stories about

today's Vietnamese food and culture and coffee culture all through producing and sharing a product being Vietnamese coffee that is actually not widely accessible or available on the market. So, it's just like this feeling of creation and bringing added value to the world that is fully controlled by me. I think having that level of agency and autonomy and like designing and creating this.

The primary motivational factors for Vietnamese American businesses included the chance to "be my own boss," job security, and experience and training (Zhu et al. 2015: 103). This was also true for the women Vietnamese entrepreneurs interviewed. Many second-generation entrepreneurs are more likely to concentrate on the creative arts and industries, including newspapers and journalism; entrepreneurship becomes a form of the creative class. As Karen, a restaurateur, explained:

I think, well in my mind, second generation we are the first ones born here. So, we're all second generation and I find that if we never became the doctors and lawyers that our parents wanted us to become, we escaped to New York to become creatives. . . . The Vietnamese community in New York right now are all transplants of Vietnamese kids I guess, that grew up in other Vietnamese communities (across the nation) all coming together in New York and kind of just finding each other.

The range of female Vietnamese entrepreneurs includes a mix of those leaving professional jobs to enter the community and those without professional credentials. Many of the female business owners I interviewed explained that they first entered professional careers in technology and medicine and then turned to entrepreneurship because they found their jobs unsatisfying and because of layoffs in 2008 that resulted from the financial crisis. These jobs in the professional fields were seen as part of the mainstream economy that their parents believed would buffer their immigrant children from discrimination and provide stability. Other scholars of Asian American studies have written about how Asian parents perceive blocked opportunities and racial discrimination in the United States and hence encourage their children to pursue education as a defensive strategy. For example, immigrant parents encouraged their children to choose technical fields to circumvent discrimination in the labor market (Louie 2004). This rang true with many of my interviewees. A key reason for entering professional jobs was stability. Most second-generation female Vietnamese business owners indicated that their parents wanted them to have a stable career and that professions provided that route. This often meant that they hesitated to tell their parents about their entrepreneurial work. One successful entrepreneur explained that, after a request to open a chain abroad, she finally told her parents: "We didn't tell our parents that we quit our daytime jobs until we had three chains." Or as one freelance photographer explained:

> My mom finally came on board but it took years. She finally saw that I made it when clients would fly me all over the world to photograph their weddings. She would brag to friends and her clients at the nail salon when I photographed Justin Timberlake. I know because she has the photographs from wedding magazines at her station that I've done.

She further explained the reason she entered entrepreneurship:

> I worked at an architectural firm and I also had a blog for fun. I worked at the firm for five years and then with the economy crash in 2000, I was laid off, which was a blessing in disguise. I haven't looked back. I love it. It's a lot of work [owning her own firm]. It's more work than I've ever done in my life.

Sociologist Patricia Fernandez-Kelly noted that there is a pattern in second-generation entrepreneurship. She coined the term "expressive entrepreneurship" to describe "the ways in which children of immigrants seek to circumvent labor market uncertainties through business ownership" (Fernandez-Kelly and Konczal 2005: 1155). Second-generation immigrants desire recognition and wealth. Entrepreneurship becomes a new mode of labor-market integration to circumvent weak labor markets and generational rises in aspirations.

Other female business owners, especially first generation, described entrepreneurship as an economic strategy that stemmed from a desire to help their families in Vietnam by sending remittances to Vietnam or employing recently arrived relatives in restaurants and nail shops. Studies suggest that female business owners are motivated to start their own businesses for independence, to be their own boss, to increase income, to overcome job dissatisfaction, and to use previous experience (Perri and Chu 2012: 93; Perri and Chu 2018).

"Representation Is Really Powerful": Conclusions

This chapter provides an important and overlooked aspect of Vietnamese American integration—the role of women Vietnamese business owners. What are the outcomes for women-owned businesses? If we are to imagine—on a societal level—the outcomes of immigrant female entrepreneurship, one is the power of representation of women in leadership positions who act as role models to other women (Dhaliwal and Kangis 2006). As one owner explained:

> I think representation is really powerful. Representation can be a really simple yet effective form of validation and affirmation. It's like if you see something and you kind of believe it's more possible because there's such a huge lack of representation of women in all industries, specifically in high positions of leadership or positions of decision making, positions of power, authority, influence.

Studies show that female entrepreneurs are more likely to employ other women from similar backgrounds (Chreim et al. 2018: 210–222; Tariq and Syed 2018: 495–513). In this chapter, I present contemporary demographic trends in entrepreneurship among immigrants and the gendered patterns of business ownership. Through qualitative stories, I also center voices of female immigrant entrepreneurs as active agents with diverse histories, stories, and ties to the Republic of Vietnam and South Vietnam today. There is a dearth of studies that focus on women Vietnamese American entrepreneurial endeavors. Instead, Vietnamese entrepreneurs and female Vietnamese entrepreneurs are often lumped under the broad category of Asian American entrepreneurs. Pan-ethnic categories obscure the diversity of the Vietnamese American experience in entrepreneurship, ignoring interethnic or generational distinctions and thereby preventing a deep understanding of the intersections of multiple identities like class and gender. Future research should look at the role of women Vietnamese immigrants in the founding of Little Saigons across the United States and perform a deeper analysis of contemporary transnational Vietnam-U.S. businesses spearheaded by women.

9

TRAPPED WITHIN THE WHITE FRAME

Vietnamese Americans in Post-Katrina New Orleans

NGUYEN VU HOANG

Introduction

New Orleans is well known as a city in which the majority of the population is African American. As in many areas in the southern United States, its African American population suffered from severe racial discrimination during slavery and the Jim Crow period. The Civil Rights Movement during the 1960s ended Jim Crow but did not eliminate subtle and covert forms of racism against African Americans. Ten years after the peak of that movement, New Orleans received thousands of Vietnamese refugees after the fall of South Vietnam in 1975.

Following their resettlement, Vietnamese refugees had many new experiences, such as driving cars or working with people of other races. They also learned many new ideas, such as the legal system and the color-blind ideology. Mutual misunderstandings were common and resulted in sometimes violent conflicts that were viewed in racial terms. For one, the influx of Vietnamese Americans in New Orleans in the late 1970s caused a job crisis for the city. While they took part in the local job market, many African Americans could not get jobs, and they blamed Vietnamese refugees for "stealing" jobs from them. This perception resulted in a long, hostile relationship between Vietnamese Americans and African Americans.

Another example of those early misunderstandings involves some African Americans' complaints that Vietnamese refugees were receiving too much support from the U.S. government at their expense. Dr. Vu, a medical doctor, remembered showing some checks with tax-deducted amounts to some local African Americans to prove that he did pay taxes here. After some time, African Americans learned that Vietnamese people also had to work and worked very hard to earn money. Then they stopped making those complaints.

Still another example concerns many Vietnamese fishermen who fished in the Gulf of Mexico but did not know the fishing traditions and rules in the United States. Because they did not understand private-property signs marking the fish farms of other people, their fishing led to violent clashes with American fishermen. Initially thinking that the latter were discriminating against them for their race, the Vietnamese fishermen gradually learned the fishing rules and the property signs in the Gulf Coast. Then fewer clashes happened.

In general, Vietnamese Americans experienced many conflicts when they resettled in New Orleans. While they tried to adapt to the new life, they also faced hostilities from the settlement society. Many of the aforementioned early negative experiences contributed to the formation of Vietnamese people's racial perceptions. By 2005, this population had grown to about 15,000. Vietnamese Americans accounted for less than 5 percent of the city's population (383,997), whereas 54.2 percent of the population was African American and 32.9 percent was white.[1] This chapter examines the racial views prevalent among New Orleans's Vietnamese Americans. I agree with Eduardo Bonilla-Silva (2001: 138) that "Doing ideological analysis about race then is not a matter of finding 'racists' but rather an attempt to uncover the frames, racetalk, and storylines that help lubricate a racial order at a particular historical juncture." Beginning with a discussion of security issues in Village de l'Est, the first section explains how many Vietnamese Americans formed racial stereotypes against African Americans through daily activities. The chapter then turns to racial issues in public and in the workplace. It argues that while experiencing mistreatment, many Vietnamese Americans developed a stereotypical view of African Americans that made them not only the victims of racial discrimination but also discriminators in the white racial frame. Hence, the daily practices of these Vietnamese Americans in New Orleans show a strong conformity to white supremacist ideology.

Theoretical Perspectives on Race and White Supremacy

In American society, immigrant groups may be seen and positioned within a racial hierarchy that is shaped by the white supremacist ideology. These immigrant groups are racialized according to the categories defined by white supremacy. Under white supremacy, racial groups other than white people are considered subordinate. The history of white supremacy can be dated to when Europeans set foot on the American continent. With power at hand, white settlers established a system that ensured the privileged position of white people. In this system, race is constructed to rationalize white supremacist ideology. From the end of the Civil War in 1865 until the Civil Rights Movement in the 1960s, the white supremacist system shifted from using coercion to devising legislation that legalized white people's privileged position and allowed discrimination against people of color in public places, education, and housing.

People of color continued to be discriminated against despite the Civil Rights Act of 1964 and the Voting Rights Act of 1965. The term "color-blind racism" was coined by Eduardo Bonilla-Silva (2001). Many Americans believe that racism is a set of ideas that produces and reproduces individual prejudices toward an entire group of people, causing members of the dominant race to discriminate against racial minorities. Calling this "the idealist view," Bonilla-Silva argues that this reduces racism to psychology and offers a materialist interpretation of racism. According to Bonilla-Silva, the white supremacist system has shifted from overt to covert discrimination, meaning that post–civil rights discrimination against people of color has been subtle and difficult to recognize. Racial inequality has never ceased to exist, and white supremacy continues to haunt American society. Comparing the racial structure of the Jim Crow period with that of the contemporary United States, Bonilla-Silva (2001: 48) argues that "the persistent inequality experienced by Blacks and other racial minorities in the U.S. today is due to the *continued* albeit *changed* existence of a racial structure."

To Bonilla-Silva, although color blindness sounds progressive, "its theme, style, and storylines are used to explain and justify racial inequality. By supporting equality, fairness, and meritocracy as abstract principles but denying the existence of systematic discrimination and disregarding the enormous and multifarious implications of the massive existing racial inequality (particularly between blacks and whites), whites can appear 'not racist.'" Eventually, "the political beauty of color blindness as an ideology is that it allows Whites to state their racial views as if they were principled, even moral positions." Bonilla-Silva (2001: 264) also presents African American views of racial discrimination. Interestingly, the work points out that, while Black people "believe discrimination is real and central in shaping their life chances and that government must intervene in a number of areas to guarantee equality among the races," they are still influenced by many of the frames of color blindness, directly and indirectly. Bonilla-Silva underscores "the large indirect effect of the frames of color blindness on blacks and how this blunts the oppositional character of their perspectives on racial matters."

Bonilla-Silva only focuses on the relationship between Black and white Americans regarding the new racist form. In contrast, Claire Jean Kim (1999) maps the racial positions of white, Black, and Asian Americans on the two axes of the racial triangulation perspective: *inferior-superior* and *foreigner-*

insider. This perspective suggests that Black people are considered to have insider status compared to the perpetual foreigner status of Asian Americans. However, they are seen as inferior to Asian Americans. Above all, the racial triangulation perspective helps to explain how white racial power can continue to thrive in the United States. Kim (1999:129) shared with Omi and Winant that subordinated groups continue contesting imposed meanings through political struggle and argues that "racialization is clearly a reflexive as well as externally imposed process." Her racial triangulation perspective suggests a framework to analyze how groups of color contend with the white racial structure of opportunities, constraints, and possibilities.

However, like Bonilla-Silva, Kim fails to consider the position of Native peoples in the United States and the role of colonialism. Andrea Smith (2006; 2010) proposes three primary logics of white supremacy in the United States. The first pillar is the logic of slavery, which is the anchor of capitalism. The second pillar is the logic of genocide, which is the anchor of colonialism. The third pillar is the logic of orientalism, which considers Asian Americans to be a constant threat to the well-being of empire. These three pillars are based on three distinct racial groups of Black people, indigenous peoples, and Asian Americans. Smith argues that these groups' survival strategies and resistance to white supremacy are built by the white supremacist system itself. Smith (2006: 69) shows that all non-Native peoples are promised the ability to settle colonized indigenous lands; all non-Black peoples are promised a higher position than Black people in the racial hierarchy; and Black and Native peoples are promised that they will have better economic and political positions if they join "US wars to spread 'democracy.'" Smith (2010: 3) suggests that, in this model organized around shared victimhood, people "are not only victims of white supremacy, but complicit in it as well." In other words, what keeps people of color trapped within the pillars of white supremacy is that they are "seduced by the prospect of being able to participate in the other pillars."

The idea that people of color may be complicit in white supremacy while also being its victims is related to the myth of the model minority, which many scholars consider as a means to rationalize Black people's subordinate position. The model minority is a theoretical perspective that developed in the 1960s to describe the success of Japanese Americans. It is considered a response to the 1960s Civil Rights Movement as African Americans fought for equal rights and racial desegregation. By indicating that other minority groups, such as Japanese or other Asian Americans, could succeed in the United States, the myth suggests that instead of blaming the system, African Americans should focus on education and work within the system to lift up their communities. Through the lens of the white supremacist ideology, the model minority myth offers a rational reason for other minority groups to accept the supremacy of white people. However, by considering one group as the model minority, it also causes racial hostility and discrimination between them and other people of color. Moreover, it is possible to fall into the trap of not seeing the painful and racial mistreatments that members of the idealized group face in everyday life.

In her work, Mia Tuan (1999: 154) studies Asian Americans in California and argues that "not only is racism still an issue haunting middle-class Asian ethnics, the particular strand that plagues them also involves xenophobic elements that play up the notion of being foreign. Their class status has done little to validate their authenticity as long-time Americans in the eyes of the public." Like Tuan, Rosalind Chou and Joe Feagin (2008: 215) also shed light on how this stereotyping of Asian Americans misses the discriminatory character of many U.S. institutions. They concluded that "being viewed individually or collectively as a 'model minority' does not save them from racial hostility and discrimination" from a wide range of white people of different ages, genders, and classes, in every social setting, and at various degrees, from overt to subtle and covert acts.

Although both Tuan and Chou and Feagin capture the hardship of Asian Americans in everyday life, they only see how Asian Americans suffer from being labeled the "model minority" and from white Americans' discrimination. However, the question of how Asian Americans perceive themselves in relation to other minority groups has not been addressed adequately. Indeed, if there are Asian Americans who fulfill the expectations of a model minority, the model minority position may have effects on how these Asian Americans perceive other minority groups. Do they really conform to the white American ideology and act as if they are honorary white people to other people of color?

These questions are relevant to the case of Vietnamese Americans in New Orleans because the city's population has a majority of African Americans. If Vietnamese Americans in New Orleans have been successful, how do they perceive African Americans in the city? Do they suffer from racial hostility and discrimination? If yes, who makes them suffer? How do Vietnamese Americans fit into the white supremacist ideology?

Everyday Racism in the Neighborhood

Security was the first concern that local residents shared when I arrived in Village de l'Est in July 2010. By analyzing how Vietnamese Americans in New Orleans perceived the security in their residential neighborhood in relation to the presence of low-income African Americans, this section acknowledges a racial prejudice of Vietnamese Americans that is similar to that of white Americans. In April 2010, the BP oil spill in the Gulf of Mexico caused joblessness for thousands of people. Vietnamese Americans in New Orleans were also severely affected by the oil spill because a significant number of them relied on the seafood industry in the Gulf Coast. During the first months of the disaster, the Catholic Charities of New Orleans provided food vouchers of $100 USD per week each for seventy-five families on a first-come, first-served basis. People who were seeking vouchers had to line up for hours before the office opened. I heard several Vietnamese people, both men and women, complain about the risk of getting robbed by *"Mỹ đen"* (Black Americans) if they went alone in the early morning.[2] The women also questioned the office for using this method of voucher distribution because it was unfair to women, especially women with small children.

Many people in the village compared the security situations before and after Hurricane Katrina. The seventy-year-old Mr. Doan affirmed: "About security, in the past when there were a lot of Black Americans, there were a lot of robberies, especially in the Versailles Arms apartment area. After Black Americans left, the situation was better. Mainly Vietnamese people, only some Black Americans and Mexicans are living here." However, among Vietnamese Americans, there were different perceptions of security before and after Katrina. Mrs. Van, a lady in her sixties, explained to me:

MRS. VAN: I don't dare to go to church alone in the morning because I am afraid of Black Americans.
HOANG: Why are you afraid?
MRS. VAN: Nowadays, Black Americans in Versailles are mainly renters, not homeowners [*chủ nhà*]. Last year, I heard some cases of people who got robbed and raped behind the small church [in Versailles]. Therefore, even when I go to local Vietnamese grocery stores, I have to look around before getting out of my car. We used to be afraid of only Black Americans, and now we are afraid of Mexican immigrants too. We can't get close to them because we are weaker than them.
HOANG: What do you mean when saying that you are weaker than them? I think there are more Vietnamese than Blacks in Versailles.
MRS. VAN: Yes, we have more Vietnamese here, but Vietnamese are not really united. They just live for themselves [*mạnh ai người nấy sống*]. Therefore, we have to find ways to protect ourselves.
HOANG: When did you know about this insecurity?
MRS. VAN: It has been like this for a long time. Old people don't know the language [English], so they cannot do anything. If young people see it [a robbery], they would call the police. It's not safe in this neighborhood. After Katrina, three cars were stolen from my family. Before Katrina, this street was very safe because the owners stayed in their houses. White Americans have moved out com-

pletely after Katrina, and Black Americans together with Mexican immigrants have rented these houses. This area has become insecure.

During this interview, Mrs. Van did not refer to any bad Vietnamese individuals or gangs. She only focused on African Americans and later Mexican immigrants when stating the cause of her fear. Her conclusion was drawn from both local rumors and her own assumptions. Although she did not know who stole her family's cars, she accused Black Americans of stealing them. To Mrs. Van, the neighborhood became insecure because of the white flight and the influx of Black American and Mexican renters.

Mr. Trong, a Vietnamese fisherman, shared Mrs. Van's insecure feelings regarding the newcomers. As a homeowner who had lived in Versailles for more than thirty years, he expressed his concerns about the renters.

TRONG: People are moving out [of the village]. Just look at my neighbors' houses, I am fed up with living in this area. In the past, people who lived in the houses were owners. Now, they . . . have sold their houses to other people. . . .

HOANG: Who have bought the houses, Vietnamese or [non-Vietnamese] Americans?

TRONG: Vietnamese.

HOANG: What's wrong with the Vietnamese new owners?

TRONG: Yeah, they have bought the houses and rented them out to Mexican [and] Black American strangers. Living here is not good anymore. I think this area is insecure because the majority are renters. . . .

HOANG: Are there many renters in this area?

TRONG: Not in the past, but now they have been moving in, probably next month my neighbor will rent out his house. White Americans used to live here a lot. The house next to mine is owned by Black Americans, but they are good because they own the house and they have jobs.

HOANG: Yes, many Black Americans also own houses.

TRONG: In general, people who live in their houses care more about their properties. The houses for rent may be rented to many different people in one year. Some renters have jobs, some don't, some take drugs and drink.

HOANG: Have you ever talked to Black Americans and White Americans?

TRONG: Yes, I meet a lot. I say "hi," "Morning" to them. There are good and bad people.

According to Mr. Trong, the neighborhood had been safe before Hurricane Katrina because there were more homeowners regardless of whether they were white, Black, or Vietnamese. However, after Katrina, more white Americans sold their houses to Vietnamese people, and the new owners rented out the houses to people who needed housing. Mr. Trong considered African American and Mexican renters to be transient, jobless, and mostly drinkers and drug users, who made the neighborhood unsafe. In the interview, he not only compared owners with renters but also subtly expressed his nostalgia of the time when "white Americans used to live here a lot."

Nevertheless, not all African Americans living in Versailles were renters. I met several Black American homeowners in local meetings and in daily life activities. Mr. Edward Blouvin lived in Versailles from 1980 onward. Although his house was located on a street with four Vietnamese American households, they did not know one another well. On Sunday, he went to a Catholic church for English mass because the mass at 11:00 A.M. in Mary Queen of Vietnam Church was too late for him. Although he did not have much interaction with Vietnamese, he had a positive view toward them: "Vietnamese people are nice but shy." He could only say "hi" to his four old Vietnamese neighbors. Yet Mr. Blouvin was very active in community activities. He was a member of the executive board of Village de l'Est improvement group that aimed to improve the neighborhood's living conditions. Mr. Blouvin owned his house, and it was broken into three times in 2011–2012. He told me that his house was located "adjacent to the houses of some thugs" and he could not do anything but set "up more security systems in the house."

To deal with this security issue, most people set up alarm systems for their houses, like Mr. Blouvin, and chose to go by car or in group, like Mrs. Phuoc. According to her, "When I go jogging around Versailles, I always go with a group of Vietnamese friends. Not only because it is more fun to go with friends, but it is also safer for us." When I asked if she had any experience with robbery or the like, she replied: "I have not had any, but a friend of mine living in the next street just got robbed by Black Americans right in front of his house a few weeks ago." Regarding her own solution, she told me: "Since I serve in the church's choir, I have to practice singing with the choir every Saturday evening. I always walk to the church because my house is close. When the rehearsal is done, I go back home alone on the road. Sometimes I am afraid but I know that my friends are driving behind me, so I think that if anything happens my friends would call the police or do something." Although Mrs. Phuoc had not experienced robbery, the example that she cited was attributed to African Americans.

Being nice to African Americans was also a way to overcome the fear. Mrs. Ngoc, who was in her early fifties, shared her way of dealing with her fear of African Americans. For her, saying "hello" and asking about their health was a way to be treated nicely. Therefore, whenever she saw African Americans on the road, she started smiling at them, waving her hands from far away and actively talking to them when approaching or passing them. Although this method may not help, it functioned as a psychological support for her when walking in the village.

In August 2012, the Mary Queen of Vietnam Church organized a meeting about local security. According to the pastoral priest, this was the first time the parish had put the security issue on the table. In the past, there were robberies in the Versailles Arms apartment area, but nobody stood up. He called for a way to make conditions in Versailles more secure for local residents as well as for visitors. Tuoc Tran, a Vietnamese police officer who served in the New Orleans Police Department (NOPD), conducted a crime review of Village de l'Est neighborhood from January 2012 to August 2012 for the meeting. According to the review, twenty-three houses were broken into, thirteen cars were stolen, nineteen cars had broken glass, and there were also six robberies, one rape, and three murders. This detailed review received much attention from the audience. About ninety to one hundred people, mostly elderly men and women, attended. In this presentation, Mr. Tran did not use any specific terms to describe the criminals or their race. He played a neutral role as a knowledgeable rapporteur with Vietnamese people regarding crimes in the neighborhood. Only one time did he say: "A problem in our neighborhood is that nowadays, less Vietnamese, but Mexicans and people of color hang out on Alcee Fortier Boulevard." Mr. Tran explained to the audience that NOPD police officers could neither stop them from going around nor do ID checks unless people violated the law. The meeting ended with a number of suggestions on how to enhance community solidarity.

In general, since Vietnamese Americans in New Orleans East lived in a suburban area, their lifestyle limited their interactions with people of other races. This factor greatly contributed to the shallow contact and occasional misunderstandings among the people living in the same neighborhood. For three decades, there was no time that people of different races built close friendships until in the aftermath of Hurricane Katrina.

For the second generation, the local news about criminals and crime rates contributed to their prejudice against African Americans. Thuy, thirty-five years old, shared her perception of local safety:

THUY: It is [not safe] for the whole city, it's worse in certain areas. Anywhere you go in New Orleans East, it's scary. A couple of months ago, they found a lady that was dead right there at the local market. Before that, they had found another dead lady near where my mom has always been walking.

HOANG: So why do they still want to stay here, if this area is not safe?

THUY: Because of the church, that's why they stay here.
HOANG: Do you think the Westbank area is safer?
THUY: Westbank is not really safer either. I've heard a lot of crimes too, on news.
HOANG: Which race is most mentioned?
THUY: I think more [about] Blacks.
HOANG: Before Katrina, the security in this area was worse than now, is that true?
THUY: Now is worse. I remember when I was younger, I lived in the place down there, I always played outside. We didn't have to worry about anything. But now, when I walk the dog, I get scared. Just because, you never know. I wasn't scared when I was young. You know, we used to go for Halloween, walked all around in the neighborhood. But they would do that no more. Very rare, because it's more dangerous.

In sum, some Vietnamese Americans seemed to hold certain negative stereotypes of African Americans, which came from rumors and incidents in the community as well as from their own experiences. While the first and 1.5 generations of Vietnamese Americans pointed out a potential threat from African American tenants, the second generation, who grew up with African Americans, tried to maintain a neutral view toward them. Interview quotes also reveal that only low-income African Americans caused anxiety for Vietnamese American residents, who did not behave differently from Mr. Edward Blouvin in this respect. This class dimension influenced how Vietnamese Americans positioned themselves in relation to low-income African Americans.

Public Places

This section investigates Vietnamese Americans' perceptions about other races in public places such as police departments, entertainment centers, and even the roadside. Village de l'Est is often mentioned as a Vietnamese enclave in New Orleans because about 44 percent of the population is Vietnamese. At the community meeting of the Mary Queen of Vietnam parish discussed above, Mr. Tho, an elderly participant, complained that the police discriminated against this neighborhood, "because if people in Versailles called the police, it took them a while to come to the area. However, if people who lived on Bullard Avenue, just 3 miles away from Versailles, made a call, the police came right after. Vietnamese people here don't call the police because they have got frustrated with the slow response of the New Orleans Police Department (NOPD)."

Chou and Feagin (2008: 29) attribute such complaints to the fact that "many Asian Americans are immigrants who distrust the police and have a limited understanding of U.S. laws." However, more examples from other Vietnamese Americans in New Orleans suggest that there was more than just distrust or lack of understanding. Agreeing with Mr. Tho, Mr. Minh recalled the day when he was robbed in front of Winn-Dixie, the biggest supermarket in the area. After he called 911, he was taken to the local police department and was asked to wait. After several hours of waiting, he walked upstairs and saw some police officers watching football on TV. He concluded: "Do not believe the police here, they discriminate against us!"

While Vietnamese Americans felt that the police discriminated against them, they treated Black people differently from white people. Many of my interviewees acknowledged that Vietnamese Americans used racial slurs for African Americans and looked up to white Americans. Mr. Tuc Nguyen, who was born in 1952 and arrived in the United States in 1975, affirmed that he had not been mistreated by Americans and that Vietnamese discriminated against African Americans.

HOANG: Do you think the position of Vietnamese is higher than that of African Americans in the society?

TUC: Yes. [Black] Americans don't discriminate, but Vietnamese are the ones who discriminate [against them]. Vietnamese people like to go shopping in white American areas and entertainment centers, and avoid going to Black American areas.

HOANG: Why is that?

TUC: Partly because of the safety, but the main thing is that we look down on (chê) Black Americans. We discriminate against them by only going to white American areas. Good-income people also like to buy houses in white American areas for more safety. Nobody dares to go to Black-American-dominated areas in the evening. If we want to find a place to entertain, we would go to white American areas even if Black Americans organize something in the weekend.

The behavior Mr. Tuc described seemed common among Vietnamese Americans in New Orleans. They were very concerned about security not only in their neighborhood but also in the whole city. While it was a matter of choice that they went to certain places, Mr. Tuc's comment indicates that they preferred to live with white lifestyles and liked to hang out in white entertainment and shopping areas.

Further, some Vietnamese Americans also looked down on African Americans when they stereotyped their tastes in comparison to those of white Americans and themselves. Tac Nguyen, who worked for a medical laboratory, had both Black American and white friends. They occasionally asked him to go out for lunch or dinner. He commented:

> White Americans do not like to go to buffet restaurants because they want the service more than the quantity of foods. They think that they pay the money for what they want. Especially for their birthday, they do not want to have buffets in which people have to go back and forth. They want to have a birthday in a restaurant in which they are served by waiters/waitresses. However, Black Americans think differently. They want to go to the place that they can eat as much as possible, until [they are] full.

These stereotypes became the basis of Mr. Tac Nguyen's choices whenever he went out with friends of different races. He said: "I go along with the friends I hang out with." By going out with his white American friends, he learned about the quality of the services and highly preferred the services of American restaurants to those of Vietnamese restaurants in New Orleans.

The discriminatory behaviors of Vietnamese Americans may also be seen in daily incidents. The seventy-year-old Minh Nguyen said: "White Americans are diverse, but they consider us better than Blacks, especially on the security issue. We are not disordered like Blacks. We live peacefully, never do anything wrong. If we did something wrong, we would be punished by the laws." In agreement with Mr. Minh Nguyen, Mr. Tac Nguyen also thought: "White Americans like us because we [Vietnamese Americans] don't do that many crimes or felonies." By presenting a view of white Americans toward Vietnamese people, Mr. Minh and Mr. Tac seemed to accept the white-dominated racial hierarchy in which Vietnamese Americans were considered better than African Americans.

In sum, race was present in Vietnamese Americans' everyday activities. From police departments and restaurants to the roadside, Vietnamese Americans always saw and judged people of different races. In return, they were also judged and treated differently on the basis of how others perceived them. While some Vietnamese Americans still found themselves mistreated by individual Black or white Americans in certain cases, and while they were well aware of the government's poor investments in their neighborhood, many Vietnamese Americans also held a prejudicial view against African Americans. On this issue, Father Nguyen, a Catholic priest in New Orleans, commented:

> I have a feeling that our Vietnamese people still bear the mind of slavery-colonialism. They generally respect Americans, white Amer-

icans, but only respect Black Americans who are in power. The ordinary and low-income Black Americans are disrespected more than
what they have done to us. Some people live with the other races because they have to accept it. There are no close friends between Vietnamese Americans and Black Americans, very few if it happens. But
Vietnamese Americans like to be friends with white Americans, and
there are a lot more.

If Father Nguyen's feeling was true, Vietnamese Americans' racism against
African Americans was caused by their unquestioning acceptance of the
slavery-colonialist ideology in the white-dominated American society.

Racial Hierarchy in Workplaces

In the Village de l'Est neighborhood, Vietnamese Americans seemed to have
limited direct contact with people of other races. However, at workplaces such
as offices, factories, and grocery stores, as well as in the fishing industry in
Louisiana, they had to find ways to get along with people of other races. Although Vietnamese Americans advanced in every job field, white supremacy
kept haunting their workplaces. Moreover, they still endured the suffering
of being an ethnic minority and being treated unequally at some point.

After arriving in New Orleans in 1975, many Vietnamese refugees who
resided in Village de l'Est began with oyster-shucking and shrimp-behead-
ing jobs at local seafood-processing factories. They went in groups to the factories in the early morning and got back home together at noon after finishing the daily shifts. Gradually, the first generation of Vietnamese people
became a significant labor force in the local seafood-processing industry.

Many of the local seafood-processing factories were owned by white Americans. Some of my informants worked for those factories and had good experiences with white people. Mr. Viet Nguyen, sixty-five years old, worked for
such a factory in his early days in Louisiana. He said: "In 1975 after I was
sponsored from Fort Chaffee camp, I worked for a seafood factory in Abbev-
ille, Louisiana. The owner promoted me to be the team leader although I had
been employed not too long ago. I didn't know why. After one week, he held
me warmly and gave me a [bigger] paycheck while the rest [twenty Vietnamese and thirty to forty American workers] got [regular] wages. After a few
months, I decided to leave the factory because I didn't like to be the target of
my coworkers' jealousy." Mr. Viet Nguyen later became a successful business-
man in New Orleans, owning several seafood stores, motels, and fishing boats.

Mrs. Sy Tran, seventy-five years old, was one of the first Vietnamese to
arrive in New Orleans in 1975. She worked as a dish cleaner, shrimp beheader,
and tailor for many stores and restaurants. She also held a positive view to-

ward white American bosses while being comfortable around her Black co-workers. She recalled: "When I worked for a seafood factory, there were white, African, and yellow Americans, I mean, Vietnamese. My salary was so low: weekly checks were a bit more than $90. Managers in the shrimp factory were two white Americans, very good people. They paid me $5 per hour while paying other people only $4 per hour. They said that I worked very well." During her nine years working for the seafood factory, she found it very comfortable to work with white and Black workers.

Mr. Lac Bui was a project leader who had worked for twenty years for a wood-processing company owned by a white American. He observed that his Vietnamese coworkers were more diligent than both their white and Black counterparts. Although his English was good enough for his job, he admitted: "Compared to white Americans, my English is not as good. Sometimes we have disadvantages. Therefore, in order to compete with white Americans, we need better working skills. If not, they would look down on us." Mr. Lac Bui further claimed that "Black Americans can never do better than us because they are not only lazy but also like to sue the boss. Mexicans are OK: They are physically strong but not as smart as Vietnamese. Therefore, if the boss has to lay off one worker, he would lay off the Black American first." In Mr. Lac Bui's view, white Americans occupied the top position in the hierarchy, followed by Vietnamese, Latinx, and African Americans. His view seemed to be in accordance with the white supremacist ideology that considers Asian Americans a model minority. In reality, compared to Japanese, Chinese, and Korean Americans, Vietnamese Americans were just recent refugees and had lower economic and social achievements (Tuan 1999).

White supremacy was evident when working well and getting promotions could not guarantee Vietnamese Americans' full acceptance by white colleagues. Mr. Tac Nguyen, who worked in a medical laboratory, described his experience as follows:

> Before Katrina, I worked as a supervisor at a hospital department with many white Americans [working under me]. Although they had to do [what I asked], they did it because of the salary, not because they respected me. It was because if they hadn't done it, they would have been fired. . . . Because no matter how good we were, they [white Americans] would not look up to us. They would ask why they were not appointed to be a supervisor, why a Vietnamese got it.

Tac Nguyen's perspective about white Americans' belief in white supremacy shared the same point with Bonilla-Silva (2010: 83): "When Whites do not get a job or promotion, it must be because of a minority. If they are not admitted into a college, it must be because of a minority. This story line allows

Whites to never consider the possibility that they are not qualified for a job, promotion, or college." In the cases of Mr. Lac Bui and Mr. Tac Nguyen, their narratives shed light on the racial barriers in the workplace. The barriers were not only set by the managers but also came from one's coworkers.

With white-collar jobs, Vietnamese Americans not only must work hard to hold their positions but sometimes have to endure jealousy from colleagues of other races. Mrs. Mary Bui, who worked in the back office of a credit union for seven years, shared her work experience with me:

> HOANG: Have you experienced any kind of discrimination at work?
> MARY: Yes, certainly, when I work better than them [my colleagues], they would treat me badly. They would despise me. But I would not be disappointed by that attitude. I would show them that Vietnamese people do not easily accept being mistreated. I would try to make them understand me by working harder and better. Once they understand me, they would need me.

Another form of discrimination at the workplace comes from the unfair distribution of daily tasks experienced by Vietnamese Americans working in the service sector. For example, many Vietnamese American women in Village de l'Est were hired to work as housekeepers in luxurious hotels in New Orleans, but some quit their jobs after only a few weeks. A woman who quit her job complained that the supervisor for the cleaning service was African American and kept closer rooms for her Black friends and let Vietnamese workers do the more distant rooms. She mentioned other Vietnamese women who were hired for cleaning jobs, but only few continued to work after some weeks. Ultimately, she blamed the Black supervisor for discriminating against the Vietnamese workers by assigning more difficult and tiring tasks to them than to her Black colleagues.

Similar racial discrimination and tension also existed in the fishing industry in Louisiana (Tang 2011: 143). A large number of Vietnamese came to live in New Orleans because fishing had been their livelihood. Father John Nguyen recalled: "Of the fishermen in the 2000s, about 70% of the fishing boats in the Gulf Coast belonged to Vietnamese people, and the competition caused [non-Vietnamese] fishermen to feel uncomfortable. It was rumored that the U.S. government bought the boats for Vietnamese people. But actually, the boats were the shared properties of Vietnamese fishermen." However, the fact that Vietnamese Americans kept fishing productively and that the number of their fishing boats increased significantly endangered the domination of non-Vietnamese American fishermen in the Louisiana seafood market. According to Father Michael Tran, "[non-Vietnamese] American fishermen who felt threatened by Vietnamese fishermen . . . found ways to harass the latter. In fact, some Vietnamese fishermen were threatened or even killed with a statement, 'you guys came to steal from us.'"

Mr. Thanh, a shrimper, shared Father Tran's view when sharing his own experience of shrimping in the Gulf of Mexico: "Sometimes they [non-Vietnamese fishermen] hated us and used their larger boat to block our way. Vietnamese fishermen like me didn't want to be in trouble. So we just tried to find other ways to avoid any clash, partly because we lacked English proficiency." A friend of Mr. Thanh had his long-line tuna fishing tool cut and stolen in the Gulf by another fishing boat. When his friend discovered the theft, he could not communicate with the owner of that boat and just let it go. According to Mr. Thanh, a ten-mile long-line fishing tool cost about $3,000 to $4,000 USD and was a significant asset.

In general, both inland and offshore job sectors in New Orleans contained racial barriers for Vietnamese Americans. Many managed to overcome the barriers and advanced in the workplace. However, many others could not stand the racial barriers and left their jobs. For Vietnamese Americans, being successful depended on how each individual thought about and resolved the racial barriers.

For Vietnamese Americans of the second generation who had been born in the United States, I found their perception of race in the workplace to be somewhat different. Young Vietnamese Americans who had not had working experiences in American mainstream jobs expressed a relatively positive view regarding the labor market. Linh Tran, twenty-three years old, thought that employers would look at the applicants' qualifications rather than race. He said: "I think race doesn't matter. It's all your résumé, your college transcripts, GPA." Sharing Linh Tran's view was Thuy Nguyen, thirty-six years old, who worked as an X-ray technician in a medical clinic for five years before moving to work in a hospital. Thuy Nguyen said: "When I was hired here, I didn't see my supervisor as a racist. He's white American, but you can tell from somebody's personality if he or she is racist or not. He wasn't because he looked at my résumé, he saw my experience, and there were other candidates that applied for the same job as me. But he chose me because I had more experience, and he liked my personality." Both of my young interviewees thought that the application process was fair for everybody and that no racial preference was set. Thuy Nguyen believed that the two jobs she had had were the result of her competitive qualifications.

Despite the apparent fairness in the job application and recruitment process, Thuy Nguyen did feel some racial barriers in the workplace in general. She thought that the racial hierarchy was everywhere and that Vietnamese Americans had to work harder than people of other races.

HOANG: So, are Vietnamese Americans really at the bottom of the racial hierarchy?

THUY: They have a harder time getting to the top. They have to work harder. I feel like, you know, that's how it is in this society. You have to work harder to get there. But mainly if you are Black or white Americans, you don't need to work as hard to get where you need to be. I don't know why, but that's how it is.

HOANG: Do you mean you have to work harder to prove yourself?

THUY: Right, work harder to prove that you can do as well what they do, maybe better [than them].

Some other young Vietnamese Americans also recognized certain racial barriers and tensions in workplace settings. Xuan Lan, who worked for a local Vietnamese American organization, presented her position:

My friends [Vietnamese Americans] in their jobs, I don't know, there was never any proof. A friend would be doing all the work, or doing a better job than coworkers of other races in order to get a promotion. You know, in an office job, a lot of time, they [Black and white Americans] get more advantages because they know more people, they have more connections. I think there are more barriers in the office field [for Vietnamese Americans]. If you work in a bigger corporation, it's harder to move up if you don't have connections.

Although Xuan Lan's stories might not be true for every office, her opinion was shared by many Vietnamese Americans of the second generation. Even those whose careers went smoothly might feel a racial barrier at the workplace. T. Phan, thirty-six years old, got her current job for the U.S. Internal Revenue Service (IRS) after earning her MBA from the University of New Orleans. Before that, she had worked for a Medicaid office in Louisiana as an interpreter. According to T. Phan, the language barrier was a hindrance in the workplace for the first generation of Vietnamese Americans. She continued: "I don't know about younger people, I think it's a bit easier. You were born here, you know the American culture more. So, it's a little bit easier." Working for the IRS for more than thirteen years, T. Phan reported not having faced any discrimination at her office. However, she felt something that she could not even express. The following interview excerpt demonstrates that feeling:

HOANG: Do you see any Vietnamese Americans working in your department?

T. PHAN: Yes, there are about four Vietnamese American colleagues out of 300 coworkers.

HOANG: Do you see any racial structure in your workplace?

T. PHAN: No racial structure in my workplace. I think that the majority of Vietnamese are *siêng năng* [diligent]. People see it too. So
they don't discriminate against us. I think I am fortunate too, just
kind of luck, too.

HOANG: Luck? So, do you think there are still barriers?

T. PHAN: There are . . . I am not sure. . . . I am not sure about that. I
am thinking there is, but . . . I am not sure . . . what could that be?

HOANG: So you feel it, but you can't say it?

T. PHAN: I can't describe it. I don't feel it personally, so I can't speak
for others. I am pretty sure there are, but I can't describe.

T. Phan had such a good experience in her career that she saw no barrier
in the workplace for Vietnamese Americans, yet she could not deny its existence for others. Her way of thinking implicitly demonstrated an argument
by Chou and Feagin (2008: 139) that "Asian Americans have gained some
degree of acceptance into white social worlds because of their adoption of
white framing and folkways." Because she grew up in the United States, had
an MBA degree, and spoke a second language (Vietnamese) well, T. Phan's
résumé seemed even better than that of many white Americans. Her academic and career success may have reinforced the white frame in her mind
so that she could not even recognize that she had conformed to it. In the interview excerpt, although she found "no racial structure" in her workplace,
her statement that "the majority of Vietnamese people are diligent. People
see it too, so they don't discriminate (against) us" revealed that she was complicit in the white frame.

The perception of many second-generation Vietnamese Americans indicates that white supremacy not only is omnipresent in the workplace but
also permeates their minds. The inequality that Vietnamese American youth
may face does not occur at the time of job application. But this inequality
surfaces and becomes more intense when they begin to work in a place dominated by white workers, forcing them to work harder and perform better.
As a result, the more diligent minority employees only receive recognition
equal to that of those employees of the dominant race who are less diligent.
Importantly, many people of the second generation see no racial hierarchy
between white and Vietnamese Americans because they have fully conformed
to the white supremacist ideology.

In sum, Vietnamese Americans have contributed to the labor force of
American society for the past four and a half decades. Of the three generations examined in this section, each generation was exposed to a different
extent of racial barriers in the workplace. Although Vietnamese Americans
have advanced in every job field, they still hold the feeling of not being treat-

196 / Nguyen Vu Hoang

ed equally at some points. Even when not experiencing overt acts of racism at work and in public places, many are trapped in the white supremacist ideology. By looking up to white Americans and looking down on African Americans, especially the low-income ones, these Vietnamese Americans in New Orleans continue contributing to the model minority myth and therefore unconsciously accept the white supremacist ideology.

Conclusion

This chapter has provided a detailed account of many racial aspects in the everyday life of Vietnamese Americans in post-Katrina New Orleans. It suggests that Vietnamese Americans continued to be haunted by white supremacy in the United States after more than forty years of resettlement. Everyday racism was observed in all settings, such as neighborhoods, public places, and workplaces, regardless of the education and economic achievement they obtained. The chapter illustrates a view toward racial and ethnic relations in the United States and the intergenerational conflicts within a Vietnamese American community. Although there was less overt racial discrimination and few acts of extreme racism, Vietnamese Americans were both racial discriminators and victims of racial discrimination. The case studies show that many Vietnamese Americans were trapped within the dominant ideology of white supremacy.

In addition, a class dimension is observed in the racial stereotypes held by some Vietnamese Americans against the African Americans in the city, especially in their residential neighborhood. The Vietnamese American–concentrated neighborhood of Village de l'Est created an environment for them to live in an ethnic enclave in New Orleans. The Mary Queen of Vietnam Catholic parish and their lifestyle allowed local Vietnamese residents to have minimal contact with their neighbors of different races. Therefore, security incidents related to African Americans led to the high vigilance of Vietnamese people at home or on the street. Vietnamese Americans attributed the community security problems to low-income African Americans, who often resided in subsidized housing projects. This point indicates that many Vietnamese Americans shared a view congruent with that of white Americans toward low-income African Americans.

PART III

PARADIGMS OF DIASPORIC KNOWLEDGE

THE UNRECONCILED

Phan Nhiên Hạo's Poetry of Diasporic Testimony

Hai-Dang Phan

Introduction

The routes of diaspora are many.[1] In April 2007, when I was a doctoral student at the University of Wisconsin, I drove down from Madison on a cold spring day to the city of De Kalb in northern Illinois to meet for the first time the poet Phan Nhiên Hạo. There were still patches of snow in the stubby fields on both sides of the highway, I remember, and areas of dense fog that made driving more difficult than it should have been. Using my dissertation research as a pretext for our meeting, I was simply excited just to have the opportunity to spend some time with a poet whose work I found to be courageous and revelatory. He came out to meet me at the local gas station, and then we drove ten minutes to the University of Northern Illinois campus, where we walked through the mostly empty and quiet floors of the university library to reach his office. Pausing in front of his office, he then said something that would stay with me in the many years to come: "They don't know about my secret life as a poet." What did he mean, "they don't know about his secret life"? In the immediate context, I knew he was referring to his colleagues at Northern Illinois University. He had just been telling me about his new job as the curator of the Donn V. Hart Southeast Asia Collection, considered one of the major Southeast Asia library collections in the United States. Still, I could not help hearing a more somber truth behind his words. I knew that his poems, because he was an overseas Vietnamese, remained unpublished and censored in Vietnam, where the state-run publishing houses ultimately controlled who and what was printed and sold in bookstores. I also knew that because he wrote in Vietnamese, his poems were unlikely to reach a broader American readership. I also had read enough of his poetry to hear in the word *secret* a key word or code word that appeared frequently in the translated poems I read in *Night, Fish and Charlie Parker* (Phan N. H. 2006). For years now, the poet Phan Nhiên Hạo has been creating a distinct body of poetry that transmits a vital signal from the diaspora—sorrowful, humorous, resilient, and unforgettable—though that signal has been carried and received by far too few. The signal has something to do with exile—not only what it means to be a poet writing under new forms of banishment and regimes of censorship but also a critical and creative act of resistance and freedom—it has something to do with not being at home.

I first read Phan Nhiên Hạo's poetry in the exciting translations by Linh Dinh, translations of poets who represented "the fringe and vanguard of Vietnamese poetry" (Dinh 2002). At the time, whatever Linh Dinh wrote or translated, I read with great anticipation. In 2006, when I was finishing my coursework, a full-length volume of Phan's poems in translation was published. The dual-language edition of *Night, Fish and Charlie Parker*, with Phan's original poems in Vietnamese enfacing Dinh's English translations, would become a touchstone. Encountering Phan Nhiên Hạo's poems was like reading the confidential documents from an estranged older brother speaking in a private language. His poems spoke like a phantasm across the table, communicating through image and metaphor, trying to get something off its chest, keeping secrets and telling them too. The poems dug up the psychic debris left in the wake of war and immigration, and they told the open secrets of Vietnam's postwar realities. It was as if his poetic vision was trained to the shadows and his poetic ear tuned to the lower frequencies of the dark time he has escaped.

What are the conditions of writing poetic testimony from, about, to, and through the diaspora despite or because of the lack of a public sphere? Phan performs a counterpublic witness that attempts to document injuries and losses, inflicted in the past and accrued in the present, for a future form of redress. His powerful work represents an already-existing enactment of Yen Le Espiritu's (2005) call for Vietnamese American writers to "become tellers of ghost stories" by drawing attention to "what modern history has rendered ghostly." His diasporic poetics similarly articulates historical and cultural perspectives on the war and its aftermath that have been missing from prevailing Vietnamese homeland and U.S. representations: namely the lives of Vietnamese from former South Vietnam and the experience of displacement. The political edge of Phan's poetry emerges in and through these acts of counterpublic witness, which begin the work of articulating an alternative form of redress and an emergent diasporic poetics. Working in the obscurity of a poet exiled from his primary audience, Phan nevertheless gives testimony through his poetry to the historical and cultural perspectives on the war from the vantage of a southern Vietnamese of the postwar generation now living in the diaspora.

Literature in the Age of Reconciliation and Economic Normalization

Phan Nhiên Hạo's life and work capture part of the predicament of writing in, to, and from the Vietnamese diaspora. Born 1967 in Kontum, Phan came of age in a postwar Vietnam shaped by the new regime of the Vietnamese Communist Party. Set against the scarred cultural and political landscape of postwar Vietnam, Phan's childhood memories greatly affected his consciousness. Border wars, food shortages, social marginalization, boat people and immigration, cultural amnesia, and regimes of censorship are just some of the things that a young Phan witnessed and experienced firsthand before his immigration to the United States at the age of twenty-four. These historical changes contextually frame the paradoxical features of his poetic style.

Phan's first collection, *Thiên Đường Chuông Giấy* [Paradise of Paper Bells] (Phan N. H. 1998), written mostly during his first six or seven years in the United States, introduced to Vietnamese-language readers the work of a younger, postwar-generation writer whose poetry was a mix of native and foreign influences and the product of his own imagination. His imagistic and elliptical short poems captured the everyday surreality of being a Vietnamese immigrant in the United States during the 1990s. About half of them were written while the poet was living in Seattle, and the other half when he was living in Southern California. Many defining features of Phan's poetry are already present in these earlier poems: the homespun resourcefulness; the swerves of the surreal within the real; the plainspoken voice; the commitment to a South Vietnamese refugee memory; the sorrow, the humor, and the toughness. His following collection, *Chế Tạo Thơ Ca 99-04* [Manufacturing Poetry 99-04], published in 2004, shows a poet willing to write more outwardly, more boldly and dangerously, taking not only thematic risks but formal ones as well. Phan experiments with collage techniques and longer forms, while sharpening the speed and attack of shorter poems. Many of the poems address specific historical events, cultural myths, and symbols and are often pierced with laughter, sarcasm, and disgust. Phan published poems, as well as essays and translations of modern and contemporary American poetry, in the leading overseas Vietnamese literary journals, in print and online, in places like California-based *Hợp Lưu*, Sydney-based *Tiền Vệ* and Berlin-based *Talawas*—these names may mean next to nothing to Anglophone readers, but to Vietnamese-language writers and readers they represented what was most vital and urgent in contemporary Vietnamese literature and culture. Even just to sketch the outline of Phan Nhiên Hạo's life and poetry within this context, as I have tried to do here, is to glimpse the vitality of another literary history existing and evolving alongside the emergence of a new wave of Vietnamese American writing in the decade after 1995.

Vietnamese American literature for me began in 1998 when a high school friend, returning from a trip to San Francisco, gave me a book full of poetry and prose by contemporary Vietnamese American writers. This was *Watermark* (1998), the anthology published that spring by the Asian American Writer's Workshop, which included many of the poets and fiction writers I—and I imagine many other Vietnamese Americans—would read with urgency and gratitude in the coming years. Poets like Linh Dinh, Mong Lan, Bao Phi, and Truong Tran; lê thi diem thúy's novel *The Gangster We Are All Looking For* (2003); Monique Truong's novel *The Book of Salt* (2004); Andrew X. Pham's travelogue *Catfish and Mandala* (2000); and more—to name these names, to list these works, is to recall a period of great possibility, of many voices. And these were only the Vietnamese American writers whose works were written in English and found success in being published with major and independent U.S. publishers.

In her seminal work of literary history on Vietnamese American literature, Isabelle Thuy Pelaud (2010) identifies a "First Generation" and "A New Era" of literary works by Vietnamese in the United States, with 1994 marking the hinge year. Pelaud observes that "America's return to Viet Nam through the market economy facilitated the entry of Vietnamese American cultural production in the U.S. national narrative," and specifically "the emergence of what would become a relatively popular genre, the Vietnamese American memoir" (Pelaud 2010: 27). Pelaud attempts an overview of the "diverse and heterogenous" literature, marking off three major phases and articulating key themes and issues (Pelaud 2010: 22). The first generation of post-1975 Vietnamese American writers, the years between 1979 and 1984, mark a transitional period, with writings by Vietnamese mostly for Vietnamese, remaining within an ethnic enclave. The "new era" was ushered in by a second generation of works by Vietnamese American literature in English, attracting more critical and popular attention from the large publishers. Where in this literary history of post-1995 literature would we place Phan Nhiên Hạo? A poet like Phan Nhiên Hạo, living in the United States since 1991 and writing in Vietnamese, shared with these other diasporic writers over a decade of literary production, parallel yet separate and virtually unknown. What would it mean for Vietnamese American literary studies to include not only poets and novelists writing in English but also those writing in Vietnamese?

These were also the years of reconciliation and normalization of relations. Since the early 1990s, attempts were made on both sides to understand the war from a more balanced perspective. In 1994, the United States lifted its thirty-year trade embargo on Vietnam, setting the stage the following year, on July 11, 1995, for the formal normalization of diplomatic relations between the two countries. In 1995, the first English translation available in the United States of Bảo Ninh's novel *The Sorrow of War* was published (Bảo Ninh and Palmos 1995). Those years also saw a concerted engagement on the literary and cultural front, with the appearance of numerous publications and projects working toward the aim of reconciliation and of "coming to terms" with the past through the work of fiction, poetry, and memoir, which not only featured American authors but also included Vietnamese authors, many or most of whom were also veterans of war. Representative of these projects is *The Other Side of Heaven* (Karlin, Lê, and Truong 1995), an anthology of postwar fiction by authors who were also North Vietnamese and American veterans. These collaborative literary projects often framed themselves as works of reconciliation stemming from a "compulsion to see the human in the other" and "coming to terms" with the past.[2] As cross-cultural acts of remembrance and mourning, these reconciliation projects sought to heal the wounds of war through literature. These literary reconciliation projects were notable, among other things, for their omission and general exclusion of Southern Vietnamese voices and, consequently, for the erasure of South Vietnamese accounts of the war in U.S. history. Not only were American veterans of the war returning and writing about that experience but so too were Vietnamese Americans.

Vietnam War representation, as numerous literary and cultural critics have argued, is part and parcel of an ongoing struggle over the cultural and historical significance of the war. *Tangled Memories*, Marita Sturken's specific and historically situated argument about the production of cultural memory in the United States during the 1980s and 1990s, remains a critical touchstone in this regard. Defining cultural memory as "a field of cultural negotiation through which different stories vie for a place in history," Sturken observes how Americans in the aftermath of the Vietnam War "interact with cultural elements to produce concepts of nation, particularly in events of trauma, where both the structures and the fractures of a culture are exposed" (Sturken 1997: 1–3). "Attempts to rescript the Vietnam War," according to Sturken, "have been as much about healing, with its bodily metaphors, as they have been about smoothing over the disruptions of the war's narratives" (Sturken 1997: 16). Despite the increasingly transnational conditions of literary and cultural production about the Vietnam War and its legacy since normalized diplomatic ties in 1994, the literature of reconciliation reified stereotypes and reinforced false notions of national and cultural coherence both within the United States and within Vietnam, as well as in the Vietnamese diaspora. Recognizing who and what has been left outside or at the margins of this field of negotiation, scholars of Vietnamese American studies,

critical refugee studies, and Asian American literature draw critical attention to the absence of representations from Vietnamese and Vietnamese
American authors writing about the war.

Introducing a 2005 special issue of *Amerasia Journal* assessing the cultural and political legacy of the Vietnam War thirty years afterward, Yen Le
Espiritu reflects on the absence of Vietnamese perspectives on the war and
argues that artists and scholars who wish to look for and call attention to
these lost subjects of history "have to be willing to become tellers of ghost
stories." For Espiritu, telling and writing "ghost stories" means actively working through the past, "to pay attention to what modern history has rendered
ghostly, and to write into being the seething presence of the things that appear to be not there" (Espiritu 2005: xix). Drawing critical attention to the
experiential realities of the public and private lives that have been systematically hidden or erased in existing narratives about the war and its aftermath,
Espiritu outlines an interventionist project that seeks to recover past and
present voices from the margins. "As a consequence of U.S. history's erasure
of Vietnamese—especially South Vietnamese—accounts of the war in United States history," Espiritu argues, "we have only partial and imperfect recollections of the war" (Espiritu 2008: 1702). Faced with the haunting legacy of
the Vietnam War, Espiritu places writers and critics in the role of the witness
who must "look for the things that are seemingly not there, or barely there"
and, to quote sociologist Avery Gordon, must listen "to fragmentary testimonies, to barely distinguishable testimonies, to testimonies that never reach
us" (Espiritu 2005: xx). In speaking of the need "to write ghost stories," Espiritu enlists narrative for the political project of "looking for and calling
attention to the lost and missing subject of history" (Espiritu 2005: xx). Consequently, Espiritu sounds a rallying cry for scholars and artists alike to enter
the field of contested memory. This call would be echoed, amplified, and
answered many times over by many writers and scholars. Viet Thanh Nguy-
en, to name only the most prominent in recent years, would successfully
launch his own literary offensive in the arena of the novel with *The Sympathizer* (2015) and the parallel critical-memoir hybrid *Nothing Ever Dies* (2016),
in which he writes: "All wars are fought twice, the first time in the battlefield,
the second time in memory." Nguyen and others have suggested such wars
might be endless, forever, in part because of the nature of memory and the
"often irresolvable conflict over remembering particularly troubling events."

The literature of reconciliation offers us a prism through which to view
the struggles over the representation of the history, memory, and legacy of
the Vietnam War, then and now. What *was* reconciliation? The imprecision
with which it has been defined and the disparate uses to which it and its cog-
nates, such as "coming to terms," have been put calls for a situational awareness around the uses of the term. During the immediate postwar period be-

tween 1975 and 1995, the term was invoked mostly from the United States. It seems that no one can quite agree on what reconciliation is and what it might achieve. In the context of the war in Vietnam, peace and reconciliation would necessarily have to be shaped by many perspectives. John Borneman, a cultural anthropologist specializing in the theory and practice of reconciliation, offers a starting point for the broader assumptions and greater stakes of postwar reconciliation for Americans and Vietnamese. Borneman (2003: 204–206) observes that for Vietnamese and Americans, reconciliation starts from different premises, involves competing stakes, and produces ambiguous results. According to Borneman, nationalist agendas lie at the heart of reconciliation efforts. On the one hand, "U.S. efforts at reconciliation are largely an attempt to rehabilitate not the Vietnamese but the U.S. government as a moral interlocutor whom one can trust"; on the other hand, the ruling strategy of the Vietnamese government also shapes the discourse of reconciliation, in which case, "rebounding violence from the war experience is rarely expressed as hostility against either Americans or Chinese. Rather, it is part of a psychosocial process that infects the social and is directed against other Vietnamese." Borneman primarily addresses the South Vietnamese case for reparation after the confiscation of property, imprisonment, disenfranchisement, and persecution. Christina Schwenkel observes that Vietnamese perspectives on reconciliation and healing differ dramatically from American ones, so much that "the quest for healing and reconciliation that was so central to U.S. journeys was largely absent from Vietnamese perspectives" (Schwenkel 2006: 43). Schwenkel takes issue with Borneman's definition of *reconciliation* ("to render no longer opposed"), suggesting instead that reconciliation may not be "a politically neutral process or mutually inclusive negotiation." For Schwenkel, the memory work involved in *hòa giải*, or reconciliation, is a morally charged subject position. Yet both Schwenkel and Borneman share the same observation about who is not included in reconciliation projects, though they draw different conclusions. As Schwenkel (2006: 46) writes: "ARVN veterans were conspicuously absent from most of these reconciliation projects and healing endeavors," and in effect, "they were disregarded participants in a war that is often framed and reductively remembered as a conflict primarily between the United States and 'North Vietnam.'" This absence "serves to maintain a dominant historical discourse and memory of a past war as a war between communism and anticommunism (in U.S. historical memory) or, in Vietnamese official memory, as a war against American imperialism in which ARVN soldiers served merely as puppet troops" (Schwenkel 2006: 46). Furthermore, Borneman posits that "any attempt by southerners to seek redress for injury is understood by the Party not as a demand for justice but merely as a bid for more political power. The Party prohibits the media coverage (and hence public

discussion) of certain issues and historical injuries, a tactic that may transform aspects of the past into 'public secrets'—but does not make them go
away. They fester . . . in the political unconscious" (Borneman 2003: 208).
These studies of reconciliation projects alert us to reconciliation's *real-
politik*—the shaping presence of power and interest. The political implications of reconciliation can be further grasped in the context of Cathy Schlund-
Vials's work on Cambodian memory work in the wake of war and genocide
during the Killing Fields era. In *War, Genocide, Justice: Cambodian Memory
Work*, Schlund-Vials traces the "tactical forgetting of catastrophic upheaval"
and varied polemical attempts at Khmer genocide remembrance, calling
attention to the "strategic deployments, paradoxical conflations, and syn-
cretic collapses of two distinct US foreign-policy moments" that constitute
what she calls "the Cambodian Syndrome, a transnational set of amnesiac
politics revealed through hegemonic modes of public policy and memory"
(Schlund-Vials 2012: 6, 13). Against these nationalist frames of forgetting, she
insists that Cambodian American memory work is "the fight against state-
authorized erasures through individual and communal articulations about
the Killing Fields era" (Schlund-Vials 2012: 17). Schlund-Vials sees an elusive justice in this context, and Vietnam War reconciliation may have also
been an elusive chimera.

The dissident politics of Phan's poetry resounded precisely at a historical
moment in the 1990s when the United States and Vietnam were reestablish-
ing diplomatic and economic relations, and in the cultural and literary sphere
many of the most visible projects centered on peace and reconciliation. As
he shared with me in our interview the day I traveled down from Madison:

Reconciliation is a very complex topic. For one, the term "reconciliation" is projected by the Vietnamese government. They want us to
forget about the past if we are to cooperate. In other words, reconciliation on their own terms, which means you don't criticize, you don't
raise issues about human rights, or they just shut you out of the so-
called conversation on reconciliation. They will tell you that you can
write about anything you want—people, country, etc.—so long as you
avoid politics, so long as you don't criticize the government. That's
their reconciliation. Overseas Vietnamese writers are actually asked
to help. You should help, they tell us, you should reach out and put
Vietnamese writers in contact with the rest of the world. You should
be a bridge between Vietnamese literature and the "outside" world.[3]

Refusing to get with the political program, Phan was and remains a recalci-
trant voice, neither conciliatory nor nostalgic. While Phan may reject exist-

ing reconciliation projects, his poems perform alternative forms of witness and testimony. In poem after poem, he articulates historical and cultural perspectives on the war and its aftermath that have been missing from prevailing Vietnamese homeland and U.S. representations of reconciliation, and he continually affirms his own exilic existence as a poet in the diaspora.

The limits of postwar reconciliation call not for a wholesale rejection of such projects but rather for a reconceptualization of what it means to come to terms with the war and its aftermath and to continually ask *reconciliation about what* and *for whom*. In this regard, Michael Rothberg, a scholar of the Holocaust and memory studies, helpfully redefines the public sphere along the contours of what he calls a "multidirectional model of memory" to assert and create a space of political engagement for counterpublic testimony. Predominant conceptions of the public sphere, Rothberg points out, are based on a "competitive memory" model that "assumes that both the arena of competition, the public sphere, and the subject of the competition are given in advance," a "zero-sum logic of competition" where "memories crowd each other out of the public sphere" (Rothberg 2006: 161–162). What Rothberg calls the "multidirectionality of memory" instead "supposes that the overlap and interference of memories help constitute the public sphere as well as the various individual and collective subjects that articulate themselves in it."

The literature and politics of reconciliation likewise revolve around a "competitive memory" model in which both the space and the subject of reconciliatory testimonies are given in advance and where discordant perspectives—from dissident voices within the country and in the diaspora—are seen as competing forces. From Marita Sturken's definition of cultural memory as a "field of contested meaning" to Viet Thanh Nguyen's statement that "all wars are fought twice, the first time on the battlefield, the second time in memory," representation is figured as an endless war. Multidirectional memory looks similar to Christina Schwenkel's "recombinant history"—a term she uses for entangled, historical scripts and memorial practices, to suggest the "interweaving of diverse and frequently discrepant transnational memories, knowledge formations, and logics of representation" (Schwenkel 2006: 12–13). For Schwenkel, "recombinant history highlights how the reorganization of knowledge in Vietnam does not simply emerge from the intersection of diverse national and transnational memories or from the defeat or replacement of one historical narrative over another, but from an active, asymmetrical remaking and rearranging—a kind of co-production that is bound up in uneven relations of power and competing claims to historical authority and truth." Here, the life and poetry of Phan Nhiên Hạo offers one compelling case for such a literary practice of multidirectional memory and counterpublic witness.

Witnessing Vietnamese Diaspora through Poetry

Phan's artisan poetics of diaspora continues to take sides and to resist the reconciliatory impulse, refusing to forget the past and also, in what may be his poetry's distinct contribution to a framework for Vietnamese American studies, bearing witness to everyday life in the present. The ghost stories Phan's poetry tell are not those involving the past but rather the missing subjects of the present and the everyday, figured in the ordinary and everyday lives of his poems' speakers. His poems are not nostalgic and retrospective and past oriented but firmly, doggedly rooted in the present. Working in the obscurity of a poet exiled from his primary audience, Phan gives testimony through his poetry to the historical and cultural perspectives on the war from the vantage of a southern Vietnamese of the postwar generation now living in the diaspora. By thus "writing outside of the nation," to use Azade Seyhan's conception of diasporic writing, Phan's poetry represents a "a conscious effort to transmit a linguistic and cultural heritage that is articulated through acts of personal and collective memory" (Seyhan 2001: 12). His diasporic poetics performs a counterpublic witness that attempts to document injuries and losses, inflicted in the past and accrued in the present, for a future form of redress. Such poetry offers a melancholic witness for private, cultural, and historical legacies. By invoking the history of reeducation camps, hunger, and corruption, the poems bear witness to what southern Vietnamese would immediately recognize as collective and individual traumas of war. Two examples of these poems will show what a reconciliation worthy of its name and truth might include.

The first poem is "Portraits of Three Overseas Vietnamese (Who Are Not Quite Patriotic)" [Chân dung ba Việt Kiều (không yêu nước)], translated into English by Linh Dinh and included in *Night, Fish and Charlie Parker* (Phan N. H. 2006). Composed of three parts, "Portraits" depicts the lives of four different Vietnamese living in the diaspora: part one is a portrait of a former refugee named Ms. Ly who fled Vietnam by boat; part two is a portrait of an older Vietnamese couple who were able to immigrate to the United States through the Humanitarian Operation Program set up for former South Vietnamese who were affiliated with the prior Saigon government or worked for the United States; and part three is ostensibly a self-portrait of the poet. The title frames these "portraits" within the discourse of Vietnamese diaspora, or more specifically, within the specific cultural frame of reference invoked by the Vietnamese term *Việt kiều*.[4] The title's parenthetical remark about these Vietnamese, "who are not quite patriotic," functions as an ironic qualifier aimed at the rhetoric of betrayal surrounding *Việt kiều*. By making ordinary overseas Vietnamese the subjects of these biographical sketches, Phan insists and asserts the validity and significance of their suffering and their lives. Here are the first two "Portraits":

I
Ms. Ly lived for more than two decades in Colorado
where there were few Vietnamese and Winter was harsh
she was once a worker in a shoe factory
a packer in a meat plant
a caregiver in a retirement home
now 66 years old she has returned to warm California
she receives 610 dollars in social security a month
this small amount makes everything too expensive for her
when encountering a strange English word on the streets
she writes it down to look up in a dictionary at home
she said: "Only words are free."

Escaping by sea, in the Gulf of Thailand, she had to take it all.

II
Their hairs are completely white
the wife wears ao dais and the husband out of habit a suit
as when he was a judge in Saigon
they came to the US 15 years ago in the H.O. program
all of the husband's strength and youth were buried in the ground
along with manioc roots on the Hoang Lien Son mountains
in 1978 when he was in reeducation camp
the wife at home twice had to borrow money to buy insecticide
to cook a last meal for herself and their four children
a difficult period, no one had money to lend.

Even now her hand trembles each time she seasons while cooking.

1.
Bà Lý sống hơn hai thập kỷ ở Colorado
nơi ít người Việt và mùa đông dài ngập tuyết
từng làm thợ trong nhà máy đóng giày
gói hàng trong xưởng thịt
chăm sóc người già nhà dưỡng lão
bây giờ 66 tuổi bà về miền nắng ấm California
nhận trợ cấp xã hội 610 dollars một tháng
số tiền nhỏ bé này khiến mọi thứ đối với bà quá mắc mỏ.
Khi ra đường gặp một từ tiếng Anh không biết
bà viết vào tay rồi về tra tự điển
bà nói: "Chỉ có chữ là free."
Trên đường vượt biên, trong vịnh Thailand, bà đã từng lãnh đủ.

2.

Cặp vợ chồng này đầu bạc phơ
người vợ mặc áo dài và người chồng còn giữ thói quen mặc vét
ở Sài Gòn trước kia ông làm quan toà
họ đến Mỹ cách đây 15 năm theo diện H.O.
tất cả sức lực, tuổi trẻ, người chồng đã vùi xuống đất
cùng những gốc khoai mì trên núi Hoàng Liên Sơn.
Vào năm 1978 khi ông trong trại cải tạo
người vợ ở nhà hai lần mượn tiền mua thuốc trừ sâu
để nấu bữa cơm cuối cùng cho bốn mẹ con
thời buổi khó khăn, không ai sẵn tiền cho mượn.

Bây giờ bà vẫn run tay mỗi khi nêm nước mắm.

Written predominantly in a mode of social realism, both portraits swerve toward the lyrical and the subjective in their concluding lines. Part of the effect of this mixing of representational strategies is to trouble a clear distinction between the political and the nonpolitical. The poem gives voice to the lived realities of individuals who have experienced war and displacement. These first two portraits reference historical experiences of escape and immigration for Vietnamese overseas, using language and words that would sound recognizable in the diaspora, such as the word for "escape." In the first portrait of Bà Lý, we learn that she "escap[ed] by sea" [vượt biển] in the Gulf of Thailand, using the politically charged word for the mass exodus of Vietnamese boat people fleeing their homeland. In the second portrait of the older couple, we learn that "they came to the US 15 years ago in the H.O. program." These references historicize Phan's secondhand witnessing of Vietnamese diaspora by invoking postwar realities such as "reeducation camps." The biographical details connect the particular experiences of these individuals to a collective one. By poetry of witness, I have in mind something along the lines of Carolyn Forché (2011)'s definition:

In the poetry of witness, the poem makes present to us the experience of the other, the poem *is* the experience, rather than a symbolic representation. When we read the poem as witness, we are marked by it and become ourselves witnesses to what it has made present before us. Language incises the page, wounding it with testimonial presence, and the reader is marked by encounter with that presence. Witness begets witness. The text we read becomes a living archive.

I likewise read Phan's poetry as a living archive of poetic testimony, though I think his poems constantly remind us of their irrevocable status as written, mediated representations, in contrast to Forché's suggestion of the witness of literary art as unmediated "testimonial presence." For instance, while the first two sections of "Portraits" offer straightforwardly transparent biographical sketches, the final lines gesture toward what may be unavailable to the individuals themselves and resistant to representation. The biographical sketch of Bà Lý ends with a glimpse of her private life as a woman and immigrant still struggling with cultural, linguistic, and psychic dislocation, and the second portrait ends with the involuntary body memory of a trembling hand. The third portrait in the poem, beginning with details that resemble the poet's own life, extends this indeterminacy even further by infusing the biographical sketch with magical realism:

> *This young man is thirty years old*
> *in 1975 he lost his father and an album filled with photos of happiness*
> *in his own homeland he was branded an enemy*
> *on causes he did not contribute to*
> *this young man came to the US by swimming across the Pacific*
> *for more than a decade he swam during the day and rested on the bottom at night*
> *arriving, one of his lungs has turned into a gill, one into a leaf*
> *of a dead tree*
> *from then on he lived in a glass house*
> *next to jars of insecticide.*
>
> *In the next life he will come back as a boat.*
>
> *Người thanh niên này ba mươi mấy tuổi*
> *vào năm 1975 anh mất cha và cuốn album đầy những hình tuổi thơ*
> *hạnh phúc*
> *trên quê hương mình anh bị phân loại kẻ thù*
> *vì những lý do anh không can dự.*
> *Người thanh niên này đến Mỹ bằng cách bơi qua Thái Bình Dương*
> *suốt mười mấy năm ngày bơi đêm nghỉ dưới đáy*
> *khi đến nơi, một nửa phổi thành mang cá, một nửa phổi thành lá*
> *của cây rễ tàn.*
> *Từ đó anh sống trong nhà kính*
> *cạnh những bình thuốc trừ sâu.*
>
> *Kiếp sau anh sẽ đầu thai làm một con tàu.*

The matter-of-fact turn to the fantastic resists the realism of a unified history of diaspora and asserts an irreducible, irreconcilable difference.

Written with care for telling details, poems such as "Portraits" evince an intimate knowledge and connective imagination for the lives portrayed and offer examples of what critic Svetlana Boym calls "diasporic intimacy." For Boym, diasporic intimacy "can be approached only through indirection and intimation, through stories and secrets. It is spoken in a foreign language that reveals the inadequacies of translation. Diasporic intimacy does not promise an unmediated emotional fusion, only a precarious affection—no less deep, yet aware of its transience" (Boym 2001: 252–53). The loneliness and austerity of their lives in diaspora do not make them redemptive; neither can these subjects be easily assimilated into a narrative of "the gift of freedom."

Phan's diasporic poetry of testimony involves the reader in acts of secondhand witnessing. He dramatizes the position of the belated witness in another portrait of a diasporic Vietnamese in the poem "Meeting a Taxi Driver in New York City." As suggested by the title, the poem recounts a memorable encounter with a New York City taxi driver who turns out to be a Vietnamese man named Nguyen Van B.

The yellow taxi runs on roads ripped open
by earthquakes and never closed up
skyscrapers veer overhead
Nguyen Van B. has lived in New York for 28 years
he still can't speak much English
his French is better.

Three times robbed at gunpoint,
B. says: "Anything worth losing I've already lost,
country, youth, dreams
Once in Saigon my family had two servants
and one chauffeur
now I am the chauffeur for millions of people
In this city you catch a cab by whistling
just wave your hand I'll run up to you immediately
like a yellow dog called Taxi . . .

. . . don't worry, no need to tip me,
we're both Vietnamese, after all."[5]

Chiếc taxi màu vàng chạy trên những con đường nứt ra
từ trận động đất không bao giờ khép lại
phía trên là nhà chọc trời
Nguyễn Văn B. ở New York hai mươi tám năm

nói tiếng Anh không rành
(ông nói tiếng Pháp tốt hơn)

Ba lần bị kê súng vào đầu cướp sạch tiền bạc,
B. nói: "Những gì đáng mất tôi đã mất rồi,
đất nước, tuổi trẻ, mộng mơ,
xưa kia ở Sài gòn gia đình tôi có hai người giúp việc,
và một tài xế
bây giờ tôi là tài xế cho mấy triệu người
ở đây người ta bắt xe bằng cách huýt sáo
chỉ cần vẫy tay tôi chạy đến liền
như con chó vàng tên gọi Taxi . . .

. . . thôi, đưa tiền "típ" làm gì,
mình là người Việt với nhau."

Moving from the vertiginous view of the city from the car window to the cab driver, the poem swiftly positions us, another passenger in the back seat of this conveyance, to listen to Nguyen Van B.'s taxicab testimonial about his life and losses. That life story identifies Nguyen Van B. as part of a specific history of Vietnamese refugee flight and immigrant experience. Willing or unwilling witness within the confines of the taxi, the poet eventually turns the poem into a vehicle for diasporic witness. Giving half of its lines over to another voice from the diaspora, the poem takes Nguyen's taxicab testimony as valuable in and of itself as a narrative—a narrative that at once repeats familiar events and also resonates with idiomatic particularity. In writing the poem, Phan becomes a secondhand witness as he listens to Nguyen Van B.'s story, reframed here as reported speech, and extends the act of secondhand witnessing to the reader.

Yet mediating the taxi driver's claim of uncomplicated cultural-national belonging is the poet's uncertain and unspoken relation to rupture, dislocation, and vertigo, figured by the opening earthquake imagery. Though never explicitly acknowledged, the seismic upheaval of refugee flight and diaspora constitutes the unstated but implicit grounds for "Meeting a Taxi Driver in New York City"—that is, both the event *of* the poem and the event represented *by* the poem. For Nguyen Van B., the fall of Saigon is the constitutive cataclysmic event that continues to bind and identify the Vietnamese diaspora as such. But for the poet, the significance of the disruption is more difficult to pin down. "Diasporic writers all have particular subject positions in relation to war politics and war memory in their writing," as Mariam Lam (2008: 177) reminds us. "Some embrace the messiness and binary oppositions, others distance themselves from it entirely, and still others channel the painful complexity into the power of their pens."

Open Secrets, Secret Selves

For all of the secondhand witnessing they perform for the lives of others in the Vietnamese diaspora, Phan's lyric poems are remarkably elusive when it comes to testifying to the events and experiences that have shaped his own life. In his 2001 interview with Linh Dinh, Phan says, "April of 1975 also affected my family in a tragic way, and I think this has determined my consciousness." The child of an ARVN officer, Phan Nhiên Hạo was only seven years old when he was airlifted out of his hometown of Kontum with his mother and younger brothers. His father stayed back to fight and was killed in action. "No one witnessed my father's last moments," Phan writes in an unusually autobiographical essay from 2002. "I often imagine him dying at night, his wounds bleeding into the darkness. We have never found his remains." Giving voice to the predicament of the second generation, Phan states, "I had nothing to do with the war, but the war had everything to do with me." Phan's poems are also remarkable for how they resist the first-person confessional mode, even while they bear witness to everyday life in diaspora, as the titles often suggest: "Saturday, May 10, 1998," "At Home in the Summer with Remote Control," "Nights Working as a Custodian in Seattle."

In the face of anonymity and helplessness, Phan makes a tactical retreat into lyric poetry to continually test his freedom of expression and to affirm his sense of individual identity and political commitments as a Vietnamese writer living in America. Deeply private and introspective, his poems produce the effect of "overheard" conversation—to use John Stuart Mill's famous description of the lyric poem—of the poet speaking or thinking to himself or to an absent but intimate addressee. In the face of erasure and obscurity, lyric poetry offers a diasporic poet like Phan a durable form for the making or remaking of self. Phan's poems are short, often no more than a single page, nonnarrative works written in the first-person singular. Yet Phan resists the confessional mode with which much first-person poetry confronting historical and personal tragedy has become associated. The lyric, with its specific production of voice, temporality, and subjectivity, offers a formal strategy for the diasporic poet to rearticulate and reaffirm the senses of self and agency that have otherwise been silenced or neutralized in the poet's homeland and host country. The assertion of self is most directly articulated in a poem called "Sketch for a Self-Portrait" [Phác thảo cho một chân dung tự họa], a list poem that opens as follows:

This is my life: not beautiful but with some meaning.
This is my mother: also the mother of the sea.

This is my father: a dead man, the rifle next to his body still loaded.
This is my brother: an impotent and loud man.
*This is my big sister: half belonging to her husband, half to her under-
wear.*
This is my little sister: squashed by history and money.
This is my wife: my only friend.
*This is my daughter: from the darkness of her mother's womb she brought
light.*

Đây là cuộc đời tôi: không tươi đẹp nhưng có chút ý nghĩa.
Đây là mẹ tôi: cũng là mẹ của biển.
Đây là cha tôi: người đã chết, khẩu súng bên thân đạn vẫn còn đầy.
Đây là anh tôi: một người liệt dương và lớn tiếng.
Đây là chị tôi: một nửa của chồng, một nửa của đồ lót.
Đây là em tôi: bị đè bẹp bởi lịch sử và tiền.
Đây là vợ tôi: bạn duy nhất của tôi.
Đây là con tôi: từ bóng tối bụng mẹ nó ra đời mang theo ánh sáng.[6]

The poem continually affirms the autonomy of the writing self and the written self. The deictic marker and the possessive form firmly establish the poet's
claim to the aesthetic project of self-representation indicated by the "self-portrait." At the same time, as a "sketch," this representational project is prelimi-
nary, in progress and incomplete. The outlines of the self of the self-portrait
are drawn only in the interpersonal and intersubjective relation to others. The
"self" being sketched in the opening lines is not autonomous but is instead
presented in relation to others. This individual and group identity, however,
is problematized in the succeeding lines of the poem:

This is my language: half-underwater, half on the shore.
This is my people: all hatched from eggs.
This is my country: which country? I asked.
This is my enemy: identical to me, tired and rail thin.

Đây là ngôn ngữ tôi: một nửa dưới nước, một nửa trên bờ.
Đây là đồng bào tôi: tất cả cùng nở ra từ trứng.
Đây là đất nước tôi: Đất nước nào? Tôi hỏi.
Đây là kẻ thù tôi: giống hệt như tôi, mệt mỏi, gầy còm.[7]

These lines begin to question and perhaps undermine the project of self-representation by suggesting that the language and medium of self-representation possess an element of concealment, "half underwater, half on the shore";
the origin myth or creation myth of a "people" is challenged by the uncer-

tainty of "which country" the poet belongs to; and finally the troubling recognition of the identity between "enemy" and friend—these lines suggest that
any claim to a clear or self-apparent identity is always under the threat of
erasure, underscored by the poem's repetition to restate the seemingly self-
evident. The poem ends with a forceful statement of the poet's own stance,
"This is my life: not for sale" [Đây là cuộc đời tôi: không để bán].

This life and its partial and provisional representations are "not for sale,"
not to be sold and consumed within any totalizing economy, be it the politics
of reconciliation or cultural identity.

Drawing on the resources of the conventional lyric in such poems, Phan
uses secrecy as a means of asserting an impenetrable and inviolable subjectivity. The Vietnamese word for "secret" [bí mật], as well as related forms of
secrecy, such as invisibility, silence, and remoteness, pervade his poems. While
the existence of secrets is pointed to, the actual content or substance of those
secrets are not necessarily divulged or revealed. The insomniac voice of "Night's
Dawn" [Rạng Đông Của Đêm] offers one example:

Those are the invited secrets
in the middle of the night towards dawn
you tap the face of the clock with a hammer
the ceiling fan rotates beneath the moon
breathing in the smells of the city the way it was

Đó là những bí mật được gọi mời
lúc nửa đêm về sáng
em cầm chiếc búa gõ vào mặt đồng hồ
chiếc quạt trần quay dưới trăng
hít thở mùi đô thị cũ[8]

The poem continues with a sequence of other surrealist images; the poet also
speaks of missed opportunities and alternative routes: "There is another way
to step out of / the blinding roars / of the poisonous night / but you rejected
it"; "There is another way to stop / halfway between two asphyxiations / but
still you swim towards the sea / towards the secrets of the kelp" (Phan 2006:
11). Although other ways of escape from "the poisonous night" and "two asphyxiations" exist, the poet maintains a stubborn, militant, and even painful fidelity to this unnamed way he has taken. Finding himself "halfway between two asphyxiations," the poet is nevertheless committed to a kind of
endless task of "swim[ming] towards the sea / towards the secrets of the kelp"
(Phan 2006: 11). The poem's images challenge and thwart interpretation. The
poetic language and images attempt to give expression to the void of secrets
and the sea. In another poem, secrets are the object of a restless search: "We

live inside odd-shaped submarines / chasing after secrets and the darkness of the ocean" ("Inside Submarines"). In these lines, secrets are submerged in the watery realm of mystery. In "Autumn Song," the speaker seems to be in possession of a secret knowledge that he nevertheless is unable to keep: "I am not garrulous, it's just that I can't keep a secret / The hopelessness of unions makes me want to hear / Sounds of leaves falling on a chest / Of a man lying under a tree / With a hand grenade inside his pants pockets." The final image conceals one of the secret subjects of Phan's poetry in the figure of a dead soldier. In yet another poem, "To X. and I," it is the beloved addressee of the lyric—herself a figure of secrecy marked by "X"—who possesses the knowledge to secret meanings: "If I am an immoral sadness / then you are the old direction / maintaining the night flights / I walk on bridges connecting two alien shores / my hand holding an enduring curse / then you are a small dictionary / defining secret words for me" (Phan 2006: 15). All of these poems guard their secrets tightly in a private archive of image, metaphor, and allusion.

In his essay "On Lyric Poetry and Society" in *Notes to Literature*, Theodor Adorno offers a dialectical thesis of the modern lyric as "always the subjective expression of a social antagonism" (Adorno 1991: 45). The tropes of secrets and secrecy that pervade Phan's poetry are the most striking private expressions of an antagonistic relationship to a postwar society in both Vietnam and the United States that deprives diasporic subjects of agency and access to public history and discourse. Consequently, secrets and secrecy trouble the fundamental desire for transparency and disclosure in projects of reconciliation. While secrets are associated with the private space, testimony is associated with the public space. If reconciliation necessarily privileges communication, then secrets trouble those communicative ideals precisely because they suggest that something has not yet been effectively communicated or has been intentionally withheld. In the poem "As the Train Approaches" [Trong Khi Con Tàu Đi Tới], for example, the mission to address the lost and buried subjects of history is interrupted by the poet's reflections on language and identity.

> Growing up I thought speech could heal
> open a wound, disinfect, then re-bandage it. I thought . . .
> No, in this silence sometimes I see
> memory's two hands reaching out
> to clap violently without making a sound
> like the wind, like concealed hatred
> of souls buried in a mass grave.
> This silence exhausts me
> it does not forgive, it's like ants,
> patiently carrying red corpuscles from my body.

Khi lớn lên tôi tưởng lời nói có thể chữa lành
mở ra một vết thương, tẩy trùng rồi băng lại. Tôi tưởng . . .
Không, trong sự im lặng này đôi khi tôi thấy
hai bàn tay của ký ức vươn ra
vỗ vào nhau hung bạo không thành tiếng
giống như gió, giống như sự thù nghịch ngấm ngầm
của những linh hồn bị chôn chung.
Sự im lặng này làm tôi kiệt sức
nó không tha thứ, nó giống như kiến,
kiên nhẫn khiêng những hồng huyết cầu ra khỏi thân thể tôi.[9]

The poem's opening wound and the subsequent failure of language to open, disinfect, re-bandage that wound offers a corporeal metaphor of a fundamental inability of language to fully recover self and identity. Language is divested of the conciliatory power to "heal," and the poem itself becomes the figure of an open wound. The poem never identifies the reason behind the speaker's dramatic change of mind about the power of language, a silence that overtakes speech and overwhelms the speaker, as the poem quickly shifts from the past tense of the first two lines to the present tense of the remaining lines, from affirmation to negation. Unable to use the language of poetry to heal, the poet can only allude to these traces of history. The oblique references to "memory's two hands" and the "concealed hatred / of souls buried in a mass grave" and the earlier reference to "a coup d'état" invoke forgotten and repressed histories that await recovery and exhumation. Later, the poet's own "screaming voice" becomes drowned out as "the train lunges forward sounding a horn like thunders / making a mockery of my efforts" (Phan 2006: 40). Dominated by silence, concealment, and a sense of helplessness, the poem reminds us that our acts of representation—whether through speech or writing—are susceptible to change, shaped by silence, and in the end, unable to fully repair our literal and metaphorical wounds. The silences of Phan's poem are suggestive of what disrupts closure, an exhausting and unforgiving silence.

Phan's secret life in poetry can help us not only to understand the repressive dimensions of the official narrative of reconciliation but also to locate the expressive work of a diasporic Vietnamese American literature that, prohibited from public discussion, seeks counterpublic forms to give voice to the past and repair historical injuries. The speakers of Phan's poems are called to the witness stand, but their speech often slides into a private language unrecognizable in the public space of testimony. At other times, they speak in a public language, only to recognize the absence of an audience. What is mourned as the lost object is not only a suppressed, buried, or erased history—the alternative voices of diaspora as the "lost subjects of history," though it is also very much that too—but also a public that might receive such a testimony. Such poetry offers a melancholic witness that confronts history and politics without self-pity, the same history and politics that attempt to render the speaker's testimonial presence in the present as ghostly.

Exile with No Regrets

Early August 2019, when the long summer was suddenly approaching its terminus, I drove to the city of Geneva on the western side of the Chicago suburbs to visit Phan Nhiên Hạo again. This time, I was going as a translator and collaborator, and I brought with me the manuscript pages for what would become *Paper Bells* (Phan N. H. and Phan H.-D. 2020), a new volume of his poems published by the Song Cave. These poems represent the result of over ten years of literary collaboration and friendship. The previous April, fifteen years since his last book, Phan published his third collection of poems in Vietnamese, *Radio Mùa Hè* [Summer Radio] (Phan N. H. 2019). This most recent collection finds the poet leading an increasingly reflective life, with one foot in the present and one in the past. There is a more relaxed, retrospective cast to the poems. Chronic sorrow and loneliness are increasingly complicated by an insurgent anger and dark humor, evident especially in the acerbic portrayals of contemporary Vietnam. Here are the last two bitter quatrains of "This Country":

> *This country is a rusty bomb*
> *in a recycling plant owned by China,*
> *a deaf explosive*
> *taken apart and sold of scrap.*

> *This country is getting old,*
> *its fields battered patchwork, its rivers fraying threads—*
> *I've taken them off and left for another country*
> *Where I keep searching flea markets for something similar.*

> *Đất nước này là quả bom gỉ*
> *trong vựa ve chai của người Tàu*
> *chờ đợi được cửa ra đem bán*
> *bom có thể câm, có thể nổ.*

> *Đất nước này hơi cũ, đứt nút*
> *những cánh đồng miếng vá, những dòng sông chỉ mờ*
> *tôi đã cởi ra, để lại, bỏ đi*
> *đến xứ sở xa, tôi ra chợ trời tìm kiếm áo quần tương tự.*[10]

The poems return to Vietnam, not just through memory, as in earlier books, but now through Phan's travels back to his native land, and they return as well to refugee memories of his early years in the United States. There is also a renewed restlessness, an expanded geography of imagination, as the poet maps his own questions of travel in poems such as "A Travel Guide of Hue," "March in Atlanta," "Illinois, April 25, 2007," "Saigon on a Good Day," "Summer in Lisbon," and "In Berlin."

The poems are also finding new readers, in Vietnamese and in English. Reviewing the *Radio Mùa Hè* for the Vietnamese arts and culture magazine *Việt Báo*, Nina Hòa Bình Lê writes, "Đọc thơ Phan Nhiên Hạo, tôi nhận ra mình, tôi gặp lại quê hương của tôi, thành phố của bạn bè tôi, nghe được tiếng *"trời mưa từ sáng đến chiều."* Thơ anh mang thông điệp của một người đã qua bên kia bờ dòng sông, vẫn ngụp lặn tìm, những buổi sáng tỉnh dậy ở bên này, lồng ngực vẫn đầy những xáo động từ giấc mơ đêm qua bên kia" [Reading Phan Nhiên Hạo, I recognize myself, seeing again my own country and city, my friends, and hearing the sound of rain "from morning until afternoon." His poetry carries the messages of someone who has crossed to the other side of the river, but is still looking, waking up every morning here only to remember the commotions from last night's dreams of over there] (Lê N. H. B. 2020). Phan's poems continue to resonate for those in the diaspora whose own memories and dreams speak in Vietnamese. In translation, his poems are also reaching readers with fresh critical insights. As Ratik Asokan writes of *Paper Bells*: "Phan has made a virtue of displacement, finding a language for the strangeness of his exile, in which nothing can be taken for granted and the consolations of Western society ring hollow. At the same time, he satirizes all forms of oppression. . . . In this sense, Phan neatly inverts much ethnic literature, whose protagonists are forever striving to break into society, setting aside issues of morality and justice for the melodrama of identity" (Asokan 2021).

Phan hands me a copy of *Radio Mùa Hè* [Summer Radio]. The cover, designed by his daughter, features a simple and striking black-and-white design, a digital waveform that once turned ninety degrees looks like a Rorschach test. I see an unhealable rift in the black gash against the white background, and then it starts to look, a little comically, like a burnt corn cob. Flipping the book over, I see the waveform replaced by the poet's face, as if poorly photocopied, without a mouth. Where the mouth should be, small letters spell his name. I recite to myself the lines from the book's title poem:

This is the Voice of Solitude
from America, in the middle of a cornfield
on the channel of exile with no regrets.

Đây là tiếng nói cô đơn,
phát thanh từ nước Mỹ,
giữa đồng bắp miền Trung—Tây,
trên băng tầng lưu vong không hối tiếc.[11]

The two enduring themes of Phan's poetry remain: his American life as a Vietnamese refugee and exiled poet, and his commitment to a more just memory and history for South Vietnamese. Cultivating a scrupulous solitude, Phan expresses a world-weariness, existential exhaustion, and depletion of resources as a poet of exile. Yet he summons the strength to remember, just as he calls upon the strength to forget—long enough to sit down and write, with whatever materials and methods are near at hand, or as he puts it in "Manufacturing Poetry":

On an afternoon with nothing to do
I sit manufacturing poems
out of sixteen screws, two metal plates,
and four wheels. Poems fueled
by a mix of strife, hope, love, and futility.

Một buổi chiều không có việc gì làm
Tôi ngồi chế tạo ra thơ ca
chỉ bằng mười sáu con ốc, hai tấm kim loại,
bốn bánh xe. Nó được đổ đầy nhiên liệu
hỗn hợp của xung đột, hy vọng, tình yêu và sự vô ích.[12]

For the past thirty years, the poet Phan Nhiên Hạo has been living and writing exile with no regrets, off-center, in the shadows of no man's land, mostly invisible and unknown, undomesticated, and free. I remain a reader and a translator—and a witness.

DIASPORIC NATIONALISM

Continuity and Changes

Duyen Bui

Introduction

O n March 17, 1984, the Anaheim Convention Center in Southern California was packed to capacity. There were reportedly eleven thousand people in attendance for a Vietnamese music concert. Famous artists such as Khánh Ly, Lệ Thu, and Châu Đình An sang patriotic songs and pop hits for recent refugees who were grappling with the reality of a forced departure from their homeland in the aftermath of war.[1] Resettlement in a new country was a struggle at this time, and Vietnamese refugees were only beginning to gravitate toward areas where their coethnics lived after being initially dispersed to different parts of the United States. Southern California had one of the largest refugee populations at one hundred thousand people, so the fact that about one in ten individuals around the community attended this concert reveals the appeal of the event.[2]

Although some came to the concert mainly for the entertainment, others attended for another reason: to express a sense of diasporic nationalism for their homeland of Vietnam.[3] In the modern concept of a nation-state, geographical borders delineate the sovereign power of one state from another. Within those borders, people develop a sense of national identity and pride to unify. However, what happens to that sense of nationalism when a state collapses, forcing large numbers of citizens to find new homes and affiliations with different nation-states?

With the end of the Second Indochina War on April 30, 1975, many Vietnamese people living in South Vietnam became consumed with loss and confusion. The government system they knew under the Republic of Vietnam

(RVN) fell when military forces from the Democratic Republic of Vietnam (DRV) in the northern half of the country entered Saigon and gained control of the RVN's capital. Over the next two decades, more than three million people from the Indochina region of Vietnam, Cambodia, and Laos escaped their homelands as political refugees. Several hundred thousand perished on the treacherous journey to seek a better life. For those that survived, a majority resettled in the United States. The presence of several thousand Vietnamese refugees at an event—specifically organized to celebrate Vietnamese culture and support mobilizing efforts in the homeland—spoke to the profound role the Vietnamese nation still played in the refugee imaginary even if the state system they knew no longer existed.

This chapter introduces the concept of diasporic nationalism as an analytical framework that goes beyond identity formation. Through a movement-oriented lens, I employ this idea in multifaceted ways to demonstrate how people mobilize for collective action. Furthermore, I analyze historical and cultural conditions that influenced the development of diasporic nationalism within the Vietnamese overseas community. The process draws on symbols of the past—from sites that Quan Tue Tran (Chapter 12 in this volume) calls "memoryscapes"—and creates new forms of representation to produce a sense of solidarity in the community. Then, I explore how a Vietnamese transnational organization strategically developed and deployed symbols of nationalism to encourage community organizing for effecting change in the homeland. I focus on the activities of *Việt Nam Canh Tân Cách Mạng Đảng* [Vietnam Reform Party], hereafter referred to as Việt Tân.[4] This organization has genealogical roots that date back to the development of the Vietnamese diaspora. It also continues to be one of the few, if not the only, organizations from that time to currently engage in publicly known transnational activism campaigns within Vietnam and abroad, providing a long-term trajectory for analysis of continuity and change.[5] Breaking away from previous studies that categorized this form of organizing as primarily anticommunist, my research on diasporic nationalism reveals how nonstate actors can develop an idea of a nation outside of state control and use it as a tactic to contest state power.

Diasporic Nationalism in the Vietnamese Context

The music concert in 1984 was actually hosted by Mặt Trận, a more public-facing organization founded by the same people as Việt Tân.[6] At a time when coalition building was necessary for a movement based on people power for political change in the homeland, Mặt Trận, or the Front, operated as an umbrella organization that other groups could join, while Việt Tân was established to be a political party that took up the movement's mantle after collective action had succeeded in replacing the one-party Vietnamese state with a pluralistic political system.[7] In this regard, Việt Tân was clandestinely created by Mặt Trận's leadership with this future objective in mind, six months after Mặt Trận made its public appearance through a ceremony that announced the organization's Political Platform [*Cương Lĩnh Chính Trị*] on March 8, 1982.[8]

The event in Anaheim, California, was to commemorate the second anniversary of this political announcement, which was envisioned as a celebration not only for the organization but also for all Vietnamese people. In Mặt Trận's monthly newspaper, *Báo Kháng Chiến* [The Resistance Newspaper], a report on the music concert states, "This event also gives us a sense of pride. [We are] proud because we are united, and earnestly concerned about the future of our people."[9] The term "our people," or *dân tộc mình*, as an ethnic and nationalistic qualifier, was meant to refer not only to individuals in the diaspora but also to Vietnamese people in the homeland.

This allusion to the homeland was further reiterated in an opening speech at the music concert delivered by one of Mặt Trận's leaders, Phạm Văn Liễu, who shared the words of the organization's chairperson, Hoàng Cơ Minh. Phạm Văn Liễu stated, "The Chairperson has reminded us that our homeland will not push us away, will not abandon us. Comrade Hoàng Cơ Minh also reminded us that there has been no other time that we really need our homeland as we do today."[10] Although it had been nearly a decade since the RVN ceased to exist when the concert happened, the particular Vietnam the RVN represented was alive in the minds of these refugees. The collective imaginary fostered among these diasporic refugees, which I call diasporic nationalism, involved a nation they needed to defend but which was also a source of support. To understand this sense of diasporic nationalism, I incorporate into my analysis the framework Louis-Jacques Dorais uses to define the Vietnamese diaspora.

Dorais synthesizes a definition that Khachig Tölölyan explains was derived from analysis of the prototypical Jewish diaspora. The paradigm includes six criteria, which are:

1. The diaspora has its origin in the fact that a large number of individuals were *forced to leave* their country by severe political, economic, or other constraints.
2. Before leaving their country, these people already *shared a well-defined identity*.
3. Diasporic communities actively *maintain or construct a collective memory*, which forms a fundamental element of their identity.
4. These communities keep more or less *tight control over their ethnic boundaries*, whether voluntarily or under constraint from the host society.

5. Communities are mindful to *maintain relations among themselves.*

6. They also wish to *maintain contacts with their country of origin*, provided it is still in existence [emphasis added]. (Dorais 2001: 5; Tölölyan 1996: 12–15)

Applying this framework to the case of Vietnamese refugees, we already see that the experience of the community meets the first two criteria since the aftermath of war forced their dispersion away from the homeland and they had a common identity of being Vietnamese before leaving. Criteria three through six are also reflected in the Vietnamese case study. The aspect of collective memory and ethnic boundaries are addressed in this section, while relations among the overseas community and its homeland are explored in the examination of Việt Tân's activities.

As a conflict-generated diaspora, Vietnamese refugees left their homeland mainly for political reasons associated with the impending control of a communist state. Fear of political persecution and restrictions on liberties under the new government was a common reason millions sought refuge elsewhere. Testimonials from Vietnamese refugees often reflect the sentiment that they would rather risk their lives on the high seas rather than live another day under communist rule. In a book compilation about the boat people experience, a refugee named Nguyen Huu Bao explains:

Even though seeking Freedom was extremely dangerous and incurred a very high price, many people still wanted to risk their lives fleeing. Their reasoning was that they would rather die on the sea than live in a Communist, jail-like country. It sounded true. Ever since Vietnam was completely communized, re-education camps were like small prisons, while the entire country became a vast incarceration center. Those capable of an adventure felt happier dying on the sea than becoming a struggling bird in a cage. (Nguyen H. B. 2013: 95)

For Vietnamese refugees, the constraining environment under communism contrasted with the possibility of opportunities in a noncommunist state. These reasons for leaving the homeland developed into a collective memory of trauma, resistance, and resilience.

Previous scholarship on the Vietnamese community often concentrated on the anticommunist sentiments that motivated the escape and the development of an overseas community that countered the nation-building narratives of the one-party Socialist Republic of Vietnam (SRV). For instance, in a study on Vietnamese beauty pageants in the late 1970s, Nhi Lieu examines how the traditional Vietnamese dress, called an *áo dài*, was more than a cultural product to remind people in the overseas community of their heritage. At these pageantries, the *áo dài* not only produced a cultural nationalism within the community but also "became a symbol of Vietnamese American protest against the Communist forces" (Lieu 2000: 131). In particular, when the Vietnamese diaspora groups first organized these pageants, the SRV had imposed a dress code in Vietnam where people were forced to wear the basic work outfit, and the *áo dài* retreated from public view because it ran the risk of eliciting state surveillance and monitoring. The beauty pageants show a type of community organizing where the Vietnamese overseas community created an imagined nation that was an alternative to the SRV.

The predominant focus on anticommunism as a collective identity of the Vietnamese overseas community has sometimes limited the scope of what constitutes nationalism in the diaspora. First, there is an overemphasis on directly linking anticommunism with restoring the state system of the RVN, which disregards a history of building the modern Vietnamese nation that dates back to resistance against French colonization. For instance, in Tuyen Ngoc Tran's research on the political activism in California of the Vietnamese American community, Tran attempts to disrupt the monolithic narrative that the community only organizes as "outrageous and fanatical anti-communist vigilantes" (Tran T. N. 2007: 7). To show that there are different types of community organizing, Tran compares mutual assistance associations (MAAs), or self-help community groups, with homeland liberation groups (HLGs), or organizations attempting to return to the homeland. In Chapter 5 of this volume, Elwing Suong Gonzalez provides an in-depth analysis of MAAs in the Los Angeles area from 1975 to 1990. Gonzalez discusses how these groups helped resettle refugees and learned ways to negotiate relations with U.S. governmental institutions.

Although Tran and Gonzalez find that MAAs may lean anticommunist, Tran argues explicitly that the focus of MAAs is on the present issue of integrating the community into America while HLGs are "concentrated on the refugee's strong desire for reclaiming their national past" (Tran T. N. 2007: 7). For the latter group, Tran associates that national past with an attempt at "reestablish[ing] the South Vietnamese state as the legitimate and official government of Vietnam" (Tran T. N. 2007: 165). In a more recent study on the process of becoming American, Phuong Tran Nguyen explains how "residents of Little Saigon keep alive the symbols of the old regime" as a form of refugee nationalism (Nguyen Phuong Tran 2017: 2). Although certain groups used the collective action frame of connecting nationalism with the South Vietnamese government, closer examination of the dominant HLGs that existed at the time, such as Việt Tân, reveal other salient frames, such as concerns over human rights and democracy. Collective action frames "assign meaning to and interpret, relevant events and conditions in ways that are

intended to mobilize potential adherents and constituents, to garner bystand-
er support, and to demobilize antagonists" (Snow and Benford 1988: 198).
In other words, these frames not only represent the grievances of the movement actors, but they also ought to resonate with others to draw people toward the cause and away from the opposition.

The collective action frames connected to democratic principles have
roots in what a growing number of scholars identify as Vietnamese republicanism. This concept entered Vietnam during French colonization, when
ideas of nationalism began to spread in Japan and China at the turn of the
twentieth century. Peter Zinoman describes republicanism as celebrating
"liberty, equality and fraternity and promot[ing] democracy, science, education and the rule of law," which was a culture the RVN attempted to institute
despite the leadership's authoritarian tendencies, while such aspects did not
survive in the DRV (Zinoman 2022).

When analyzing Việt Tân's collective action frames, there are references
to republican ideals of liberty, equality, and democracy rather than allusions
to the South Vietnamese state. For instance, when the organization announced
the Political Platform in the early 1980s, it enumerated seven areas of development for rebuilding Vietnam to ensure it would be a country that is "independent, democratic, free, humane, and prosperous in harmony with its
neighbors" [độc lập, dân chủ, tự do, nhân bản và no ấm trong khuôn khổ hòa
đồng với các lân quốc].[11] These seven areas revolve around social, political,
economic, and foreign affairs. The recommendations often begin with what
must be reformed in the current system and then proposes what should be
added. The section about the economy contains an example. The first line item
explains that cooperatives and state-owned enterprises will be dissolved. Next,
property the Vietnamese Communist Party (VCP) confiscated will be returned to the people, and ownership rights will be reinstated. Since the document was written before economic reform in 1986, the Platform also emphasized that the country sans communism would promote free enterprise.[12]
Essentially, the program to improve Vietnam was concerned about counter-
ing existing policies of the VCP and suggesting new alternatives based on
the realities of the country rather than on ideology or a nonexistent South
Vietnamese government.

The second way scholars have analyzed anticommunism is as a tightrope
the diaspora must carefully tread, which leads to censorship in the community at best, and violence at worst. The HLGs are described in these studies
as representing the epitome of anticommunist organizing and are often depicted as antithetical to other forms of community building. Tran's comparison of MAAs and HLGs presented a dichotomy in which the former group
centered on building the future of the Vietnamese diaspora while the latter
focused on rebuilding the past. Similarly, Phuong Tran Nguyen explains HLGs

as ultranationalists for a homeland that is gone and thus a counter to the
project of refugee assimilation to the host country. In a study on transnational linkages with Vietnam, Kieu-Linh Caroline Valverde argues that certain staunchly anticommunist activities, such as boycotting a singer from
Vietnam in fear that she was "an agent of communist Viet Nam," created pressures to conform and hindered connections with the homeland (Valverde
2012: 14).

These scholars critiqued HLG activities in the context of a period in the
1980s when the unsolved deaths of at least five Vietnamese journalists in
America resulted in speculation that these incidences were committed by
anticommunist proponents tightening control over the ethnic boundaries.
In particular, it appeared that individuals who were sympathetic to the SRV
or who had criticized any of the dominant HLGs, such as Mặt Trận at the time,
could be harassed, assaulted, or killed. A group called the Vietnamese Organization to Exterminate Communists and Restore the Nation (VOECRN)
sent communiqués claiming responsibility for some of the murders. However, VOECRN never organized publicly within the community, causing people to cast suspicion on better-known HLGs, such as Mặt Trận, though the
FBI found no credible evidence against the organization during its fifteen-
year investigation.[13]

To understand the dangers of political rhetoric and identify areas the
community can improve, the divisive and unpleasant aspects of the Vietnamese diaspora's development must be highlighted. However, these analyses
relied on journalist investigations and police theories that individuals often
conducted without the cultural sensitivity and knowledge of the Vietnamese
community. Any entity mobilizing for political change in the homeland was
grouped under an anticommunist framework without consideration of the
varying political positions and organizational forms. For instance, although
there existed a self-described government in exile with hopes of reestablish-
ing the RVN, there were also political parties, nonprofits, advocacy groups,
and associations that more generally pushed for political pluralism inside
Vietnam. While the radicalism and even violence of some anticommunists
are undeniable, generalizing those examples across a wide range of actors
with diverse political and ethical views both whitewashes individual experiences and limits our analytical sophistication with regard to the complexities of that historic moment.

Moreover, the strategic approach of the HLGs was not thoroughly examined but instead subsumed under the notion that former members of the
South Vietnamese military were reengaging in militant actions to restore South
Vietnam. Refugees associated with the South Vietnamese government and
military did have greater political capital and experience with mobilizing,
but they alone did not determine the movement. For instance, when scholars

previously examined Việt Tân in connection with this period of organizing, they only highlighted that its first chairperson was navy rear admiral Hoàng Cơ Minh. Missing in this historical description was the role of Vietnamese students in Japan who were also part of the founding members of the organization (Bui D. 2020: 73–75, 83–91). In addition, reliance on depicting Việt Tân's past actions as part of the militant efforts to reclaim the homeland has left unexplained how it has been able to still mobilize in Vietnam and the diaspora. These scholars assessed that the anticommunist violence in the 1980s and the loss of Mặt Trận's top leadership during its ventures in Southeast Asia led to the organization's downfall, while others explained the public presence of Việt Tân in the early 2000s as evolution or reemergence (Le C. N. 2009: 197; Valverde 2012: 13; Nguyen Phuong Tran 2017: 95–96). Through examination of Vietnamese sources and in-depth analysis of the organization, we find that Việt Tân existed soon after Mặt Trận's public appearance. For two decades, the organizations mobilized in tandem, with one as the public face, to build up oppositional forces for a popular uprising in Vietnam and engage in community organizing and international advocacy efforts that are now better articulated to their audiences in the language of nonviolent struggle.

Conceptualizing anticommunism as a dominant identity practice in the Vietnamese diaspora has resulted in studies that observe individuals challenging the Vietnamese state as reactionary and conservative. But the complexities in the Vietnamese community led Thuy Vo Dang to apply the concept of cultural praxis to analyze anticommunism as a "productive and affective means for articulating stories" (Vo Dang 2008: 2). In this way, she can focus on ideas and practices of anticommunism that range "from paying respect to one's family and elders to educating the community and society at large about South Vietnam to maintaining a Vietnamese culture in diaspora." Anticommunism as an ideological perspective intermingles with cultural practices and signifiers to create a sense of belonging and conditions for collective action rather than only involving forceful constraints on the overseas community, as previous scholarships assert. Whereas Vo Dang's research navigates the realm of memory and meaning making, my application of anticommunism as a praxis examines how nationalistic sentiments in the diaspora are employed as collective action frames in the contention for political power between state and nonstate actors.

Diasporic Nationalism for Movement Mobilization

I now return to Tölölyan's definition of a diaspora by analyzing the last two criteria: maintaining intra-ethnic relations and preserving connections with the homeland. Examining Việt Tân's mobilization activities over the past four decades provides insight into the grassroots efforts of creating a sense of diasporic nationalism that also became a means to challenge the authority of the SRV state. An important factor to consider is the different political opportunities that arose during and after the Cold War that allowed certain symbols of nationalism to persist and change.

The concert at the Anaheim Convention Center in 1985 drew a large audience because most people in the Vietnamese overseas community felt a common grievance against the VCP since it was the cause that pushed them to seek refuge away from the homeland. The challenge for the organizers of the event was maintaining that support for the momentum of the movement. Whether in Vietnam or abroad, the formation of a collective identity constituted an important element in the process of mobilizing people into action. One of these identities powerful enough to inspire people to risk everything and sacrifice their life involved the concept of the nation (Anderson 1991: 7).

This concept of the nation exists within the imaginaries of all those who feel connected to that union. In other words, the geographical borders that delineate where the power of one nation stops and the authority of another one starts do not have to confine the sense of national pride that an individual feels. As a result, different nationalist symbols, practices, and feelings can produce different nationalisms, especially evidenced by political refugees, whose legal status is defined by estrangement from a nation. Consequently, Vietnamese diasporic nationalism is a long-distance nationalism built upon but not identical to the nationalism of the former RVN. Such long-distance nationalism transcends territorial boundaries and motivates people living afar—who may even claim the citizenship of another nation—into action for their homeland. Benedict Anderson, however, noted the lack of accountability for actors abroad since they are far away from the realities and threats of danger that those living in the homeland must face on a day-to-day basis (Anderson 1998: 74). Although that is a valid caution, Việt Tân built an interconnected network between the diaspora and the people in Vietnam for mass mobilization. Therefore, the overseas members have a sense of responsibility toward their counterparts in the homeland.

Because a conflict forced Vietnamese people to involuntarily leave their home country, they still longed for and were attached to it. To mobilize diasporic actors, Việt Tân needed to reframe nationalist symbols and feelings once tied to the RVN as a new diasporic nationalism that could build active support for efforts to overcome the authoritarian rule of the VCP. The task involved a multitude of community activities aimed at retaining the Vietnamese language, culture, and history. The plan was to develop a diasporic imaginary that could counter the Vietnamese state's attempts to project its legitimacy abroad. To understand this process of creating a sense of nationalism, I examine Việt Tân's initiative to celebrate *Ngày Quốc Khánh* [Vietnam's National Day], which is different from the one the Vietnamese state organized. Establishing an alternative National Day was not only a means to mobilize the diaspora together but also a tactic to diminish the legitimacy of Vietnam's communist state.

Declaring specific dates national holidays has been a state practice to unite the people under a common national identity. In particular, a National Day signals the beginning of the modern state and legitimizes the current political system. The VCP chose September 2 as the National Day when its leaders announced that Vietnam was free from French colonial rule in 1945 and established the Democratic Republic of Vietnam (DRV). The date marked the moment the VCP ascended to political authority. However, this was also the point when the communist leadership seemed to take political power away from noncommunist, nationalist forces who had been part of the same coalition that fought for Vietnam's independence from France. Not only did the communist leaders claim credit for Vietnam's liberation but they also engaged in a purge of noncommunist leaders in oppositional political parties and religious sects such as *Việt Nam Quốc Dân Đảng* [Vietnamese Nationalist Party], Cao Đài, and Hòa Hảo (Guillemot 2010: 236–237).[14]

Because of the historical divisions surrounding the September 2 date, Việt Tân saw an opportunity to challenge the narrative of the state and announced a National Day that represented the shared history of all Vietnamese people. In 1986, the leaders of Việt Tân proclaimed that *Giỗ Tổ Hùng Vương* [King Hùng Commemoration], which falls on March 10 of the lunar calendar, would be celebrated as Vietnam's National Day during this struggle.[15] Việt Tân chose a day that could unite the Vietnamese people and not invoke differing opinions of victory and loss. Furthermore, the leaders understood that a National Day should be a moment that awakens a sense of pride and has a genealogical history recognized by all Vietnamese people past, present, and future.[16] *Giỗ Tổ Hùng Vương* [King Hùng Commemoration] embodies these concerns because it has been a tradition passed on from generation to generation to pay tribute to the ancestors that formed Vietnam.

Contemporary Vietnamese history books, like the seminal collection written by historian Trần Trọng Kim, identified the dynasty of the Hùng kings as the start of the Vietnamese nation (Trần T. K. 1964: 23–25). Mixed with legend, the story described how king Lạc Long Quân, a descendant of dragons, fell in love with and married Âu Cơ, a descendant of fairies. Âu Cơ gave birth to one hundred children. Because their ancestral backgrounds proved to be too different, Lạc Long Quân told Âu Cơ, "You take fifty of the children to the mountains, and I will take the other fifty to the sea." The eldest son that went with Lạc Long Quân became the first King Hùng, and the dynasty lasted for nearly three thousand years.

A temple was erected in Phú Thọ province in the northern region of Vietnam to commemorate the dynasty of King Hùng. It was tradition for

Vietnamese people to pay homage to the site or hold small celebrations in their locality to remember their ancestors on this national holiday. However, when the French colonized Vietnam, *Giỗ Tổ Hùng Vương* [King Hùng Commemoration] was no longer officially observed. After the VCP came to power, this date was also not considered a national holiday until 2007, when Vietnam's National Assembly approved legislation for workers to take the day off in commemoration.[17] Việt Tân had recognized a day that represented the birth of the nation two decades before the Vietnamese government, contesting who better upholds Vietnamese values, traditions, and national identity.

Việt Tân employed several strategic tactics to challenge the Vietnamese state through the celebration of *Giỗ Tổ Hùng Vương* [King Hùng Commemoration] as *the* Vietnamese National Day. In the pamphlet given out at the yearly grand celebration of the event, an excerpt states, "Our ancestors have guided and nurtured us with love. Our ancestors did not drive their descendants out to sea, seeking refuge."[18] Without naming the VCP, Việt Tân alluded to how the communist leaders caused an exodus of over two million Vietnamese people that had not occurred before in Vietnamese history. In drawing on the historical folklore of Lạc Long Quân and Âu Cơ, Việt Tân also showed how the ancestors divided the first Vietnamese descendants to create the nation, not to force them to flee from their homeland as the VCP had done. These subtle comparisons between the VCP and Vietnam's ancestors attempted to show how the VCP's actions have been counter to the interest of the nation and, thus, reveal the VCP to be an illegitimate entity to govern Vietnam.

But in critiquing the VCP's leadership, Việt Tân tried not to corner all of its members. In another quote, the organization explained, "In selecting *Giỗ Tổ Hùng Vương* [King Hùng Commemoration] as the National Day, we call upon the members of the VCP to realize our same ancestral roots and defect from the source harming the country and return to be with the people."[19] This statement reflected Việt Tân's long-standing position on pulling disillusioned VCP members toward the movement. Việt Tân employed the *đấu tranh vận dụng* [mass mobilization] approach and drew on the frame of a common ancestry to encourage VCP members on the periphery to participate in the movement.

Aside from carefully conveying the significance of an alternative National Day for the struggle, Việt Tân also needed to create opportunities for people to become involved. From 1987 until 2001, Việt Tân organized one main Vietnam National Day celebration that rotated among major cities in Europe, North America, and Australia. In 1995, Asia was also host to one of the official celebrations, held in Tokyo, Japan.[20] Although local chapters of Việt Tân and community groups organized annual events, one destination was the focus each year because it would recognize the recipient of the *Giải Văn Học*

Nghệ Thuật Quốc Khánh Việt Nam [Vietnam National Day Arts and Litera-ture Award]. On September 22, 1986, the *Hội Đồng Kháng Chiến Toàn Quốc* [National Resistance Council] of Mặt Trận decreed that its homeland and overseas affairs department would recognize a project for an arts and lit-erature award presented at the annual National Day celebration.[21] The aim was to preserve and encourage creative forms of expression, in contrast to the Vietnamese state's censorship of information.

The first award was given in 1987 to Phan Nhật Nam, who wrote a mem-oir called *Tù Binh và Hòa Bình* [Peace and Prisoners of War]. The book was about his experience overseeing the exchange of prisoners of war in 1972 between North and South Vietnam.[22] When he was conferred the award, Phan Nhật Nam was still a political prisoner in Vietnam, imprisoned since 1975, and could not attend the event in Paris, France. Although he could not re-ceive his award in person, the organizing committee's recognition of his work helped highlight his case and bring international attention to what was happening inside Vietnam.

Over the fifteen years the event was organized, other recipients included poets, sculptors, musicians, and photographers, whose work reflected the theme of Vietnamese resilience and nationhood.[23] To celebrate these artistic and literary achievements alongside a day that commemorates Vietnam's ancestors, Việt Tân attempted to connect the past with the present and re-store a sense of pride in one's history, culture, and tradition. The purpose was to create a sense of community for refugees who had to leave everything fa-miliar behind to survive the aftermath of war. Furthermore, raising a na-tional consciousness different from the project of the VCP was an important process for mobilizing people in the diaspora to contribute to the struggle for political change in the homeland.

By the time Việt Tân became public in 2004, it had been a part of the community-building process that created a distinctive Vietnamese diaspora with cultural practices and productions often critical of the Vietnamese state but not the nation. Indeed, Việt Tân's strategy necessitated the development of a diasporic nationalism that imagined a Vietnamese nation both preced-ing the ruling stated and with greater authority, from which diasporic actors could claim legitimacy. Consequently, as advancement in technology and travel allowed for more transnational linkages to occur, Việt Tân was able to develop campaigns and strategic action that drew on a sense of national-ism that resonated with people in both the diaspora and the homeland in contention with the Vietnamese state. While newsprint once helped facili-tate the formation of an imagined community, social media platforms like Facebook created a digital experience that could build a sense of nationalism beyond borders, a "netroots activism," as Christian Collet discusses in Chap-ter 7 of this volume. Direct communication with people inside Vietnam through Facebook has allowed people in the diaspora and homeland to connect outside of government control and discuss issues related to the country. In particular, China's territorial assertiveness in the South China Sea has created a grassroots sense of nationalism that transcends borders and is in opposition to the state's foreign policies. This sense of nationalism also draws on a deep-rooted narrative that features the resilience of Vietnamese people fighting against several centuries of China's domination. Such national pride is embodied in how Vietnamese people today prefer to call this contested area the East Sea [Biển Đông].

According to the United Nations Convention on the Law of the Sea (UNCLOS), parts of the islands in the East Sea are within the two-hundred-nautical-mile zone exclusive to Vietnam. However, China argues that it has historical rights in the region. In 2009, China submitted to the United Nations a map with nine-dashed lines claiming ownership of a large area in the East Sea that conflicts not only with Vietnam's claims but also with those of Malaysia, the Philippines, Brunei, and Taiwan.[24]

In most instances, states attempt to build a sense of nationalism to defend against foreign aggression. However, several factors prevent the Vietnamese state from taking too strong a stance against China. A particularly apparent reason is their connection as communist states, through which there is a shared revolutionary past and mutual interest for both regimes to cooperate and resist pressures for democratizing (Vu T. 2014). Their geographical proximity to one another and China's looming territorial size against Vietnam have also produced an asymmetric relationship, in which the Vietnamese state has had to begrudgingly adhere to China's concerns over the years (Womack 2006).

On the other hand, the Vietnamese people have been more forthright about their resistance to China, often because of China's provocation. For instance, in the early 2000s, protest in Vietnam was rare, but it occurred after Chinese coast guards killed Vietnamese fishermen in 2005. These demonstrations happened again two years later when China began putting the contested islands under the administrative authority of Hainan Province. Over the next decade, protests to defend the nation from China occurred not only as a response to threats on the East Sea but also because of business ventures in Vietnam, such as bauxite mining or the possibility of extending land leases that could favor China. The cities of Hanoi and Hồ Chí Minh were the main centers of protests, but people also began to demonstrate in other big and small cities across the country, like Đà Nẵng, Phan Thiết, Tây Ninh, and Nghệ An.[25] Initially, the Vietnamese state allowed this display of nationalism for about one or two weeks. But when the Chinese government commented that these protests harmed Sino-Vietnamese relations, the Vietnamese authorities quickly stamped out the street demonstrations and detained activists.[26]

The increased repression against activists expressing their patriotism for the country backfired, and citizens began feeling disillusioned with the Vietnamese state. The phrase *hèn với giặc, ác với dân* [cowardly toward the enemy, brutal with the people] became a pithy way to describe the state's meekness in the face of China's assertiveness yet heavy hand in silencing defenders of the nation's sovereignty.[27] Those disillusioned with the state began to distinguish that nationalism entailed putting the country over obedience to the party in power.

As people in Vietnam were slowly becoming bolder and more vocal about their opinions against the VCP, the diaspora had long been critical of the one-party state's legitimacy to govern. Most diasporic groups have taken a confrontational or oppositional approach to challenge the authority of the VCP, while in Vietnam, tactics ranged from confrontational to more participatory means of engagement with the state (Kerkvliet 2015; 2019). But in 2015, a series of online and off-line actions revealed a convergence between diasporic and homeland sentiments critical of the VCP in defense of the nation.

To mark the fortieth-year commemoration of the end of the Vietnam War, Việt Tân launched a social media campaign called #40NămQuáĐủ [#40Years TooMany]. In other words, this campaign was a commentary that after forty years of the VCP rule, it was time for change. The campaign asked individuals in Vietnam to place this hashtag in any format and location that best represented its meaning. Then, participants would capture a picture and submit it online. According to the criteria of this competition, the submitter of the image with the most Facebook likes would receive an Apple watch to encourage participation.[28] Engaging in this campaign was an act of symbolic protest and noncooperation with the Vietnamese state. Viewers, who could be from Vietnam or the diaspora, were encouraged to take the extra step and like certain posts that resonated with them, creating a feedback loop so that submitters knew that their activism was gaining support. This campaign was a means to merge online and off-line action. It also became a coordinated effort between diasporic and homeland communities to challenge the state with limited risk of repression while symbolically showing that the people were publicly pulling away their support from the VCP.

At the end of nearly three weeks, there were 200 submissions. The image that received the most likes, at 7,888, was of an elderly woman holding a sign with the hashtag. The second-place winner was an image of a man wearing the mask of the activist hacker group called Anonymous with the hashtag written across his chest, while the third-place winner wrote the hashtag on a blackboard right underneath a picture of Hồ Chí Minh, the founder of the VCP. These latter two images received around 4,000 likes each. Việt Tân also announced a courage award for the first image submitted, which had the hashtag written on a public mailbox that contrasts with a state-sponsored billboard in the background.[29] The numbers of submissions and people liking their favorite image may not meet the threshold for mass mobilization, but they were high enough to show that the campaign was reaching people in Vietnam and encouraging small acts of disobedience.

Just a few months prior to the #40NămQuáĐủ [#40YearsTooMany] campaign, there was an initiative to post a selfie, or a picture of oneself, with a sign bearing the phrase #TôiKhôngThíchĐảngCộngSảnViệtNam [#IDon'tLike TheCommunistPartyOfVietnam]. Some participants also described why they disliked the VCP, which revolved around the themes of corruption, authoritarianism, police brutality, and the impoverishment of the country.[30] The online movement began in early January 2015, soon after state media reported that anyone speaking negatively about the VCP or the state would be heavily punished. To test the scope of this new policy, activist Lã Việt Dũng was one of the first to publish a picture of himself with the hashtag. He felt that if one critiques the state and it is the truth, then the state should listen and not threaten that person; therefore, if someone publicly exclaims they do not like something the VCP has done and it is the truth, then Lã Việt Dũng questioned whether that negative comment should result in punishment from the state.[31] Many of the participants in this campaign felt that expressing their like or dislike for the VCP was an opinion protected by the Universal Declaration of Human Rights and International Covenant on Civil and Political Rights, of which Vietnam is a signatory.[32] One of the significant aspects of this campaign was that the participants in Vietnam posted images of their face and name, despite possible repercussions from the state. Those in the diaspora also posted their picture in solidarity. This public display of discontent encouraged other disillusioned individuals to overcome their fears of repression and join the movement. In addition, the campaign's message reflected a growing body of people withdrawing their consent from the VCP, which is a sentiment that a nonviolent struggle attempts to develop to destabilize an authoritarian regime. The online nature of the campaign provided a platform for transnational participation between people in the diaspora and homeland, who created, consumed, and shared these hashtags that united people in the sense of nationalism against the VCP.

One other important hashtag that arose in early 2015 was called #ĐMCS, short for Địt Mẹ Cộng Sản [Fuck Communism]. This four-letter abbreviation drew inspiration from the title of a rap song by Nah, whose real name is Nguyễn Vũ Sơn. Nah was an international student at Oklahoma State University when he released the song—doing so despite the threat of repression since his family was still in Vietnam and he planned to return home after school finished in 2016.[33] He explained to *Radio Free Asia* how his time abroad allowed him access to information about the struggles in Vietnam, which he wanted to help resolve.[34] Although the rap song was arguably a more coarse

approach to express discontent toward the VCP, it attracted youth and encouraged them to realize that the state had suppressed them, caused them
to act as zombies, apathetic toward the political condition in Vietnam. The
hashtag soon spawned an avatar in the image of a zombie's face, which was
shared online and posted alongside the #ĐMCS.[35] The individuals involved
took their activism to the streets by mid-2015 and organized meetups for
the Zombie Movement. But local authorities quickly cracked down on these
gatherings, creating a challenge for the movement organizers to go beyond
online mobilization.[36]

These social media campaigns during the first half of 2015 drew on more
than a decade of strategic organizing for nonviolent political change in Vietnam. At times, certain issues like land rights or anti-China protests looked
to the Vietnamese authorities to resolve these concerns. But as the state repressed aggrieved citizens and patriotic protesters, people began to shift their
message in challenge to the VCP and in defense of the nation. The *#TôiKhô
ngThíchĐảngCộngSảnViệtNam* [#IDon'tLikeTheCommunistPartyOfViet
nam], #ĐMCS [#FuckCommunsim], and *#40NămQuáĐủ* [#40YearsToo
Many] campaigns reflected a growing boldness from the people to directly
critique the VCP. Nationalism, at this point, did not require Việt Tân to
create an alternative narrative to the state's nation-building initiatives. Instead, social media platforms like Facebook allowed Việt Tân to facilitate
connections between nationalist sentiments in the diaspora and those in the
home country.

At times, Việt Tân initiated a campaign to encourage protest and civil
disobedience, like the *#40NămQuáĐủ* [#40YearsTooMany]. Other times,
because people in Vietnam were becoming more disillusioned with the VCP
and less fearful of state repression, Việt Tân worked together with other activists to support and promote acts of civil resistance. In this sense, the past effort
to build a diasporic nationalism apart from the Vietnamese state's control
has expanded and connected with sentiments from Vietnam through the help
of digital technology. Applying a movement-oriented lens to analyze the
activities of groups that previous scholars consider HLGs provides a framework for reconceptualizing anticommunism as part of a diasporic nationalism where nationalist sentiments are developed and employed to maintain
relations among those in the Vietnamese overseas community and in the
homeland in contention with the Vietnamese state.

Conclusion

The Vietnamese overseas community is not only an ethnic group within a
particular host country. It is also a diaspora that spans several countries and
continents connected by an experience of being forced to depart from the

homeland while remaining bounded by a sense of nationalism to that home-land. This sense of nationalism often does not equate to support of the Viet-namese state, as Ivan Small also asserts in Chapter 6 of this volume. Instead, it involves maintaining traditions, creating cultural products, organizing events, and developing strategic actions that contribute to the progress of the Vietnam nation and the pride in being Vietnamese.

In Tölölyan's definition of a diaspora, the creation of collective transna-tional values and the mobilization of organizations are two aspects that help to maintain the linkages that occur within the overseas community and that arise with those in the homeland. When Dorais interviewed Vietnamese Ca-nadians to understand whether they felt there was a diasporic identity, his respondents' answers were focused more on familial and personal ties than on collective transnational organizing. Therefore, he could not conclude there was a Vietnamese diaspora but only that there was a diasporic dimension to the Vietnamese overseas community (Dorais 2001: 22–23).

However, through this study focused on Việt Tân, we see a transnation-al movement organization actively engaged in the creation of collective val-ues embodied in the concept of diasporic nationalism. What Dorais missed in his methodological framework is that individual opinion alone cannot indicate the presence or absence of shared transnational values among a dis-persed people. Rather, according to Tölölyan:

> Even when their number is small, diasporan activists may legitimate-ly be able to appeal to the minds and to tug at the heartstrings and purse strings of many kin. They can therefore have a considerable and mutually reinforcing impact on the community's perception of itself as well as the hostland state's perception of the community, and in-deed managing this game of mirrors is one of the chief skills of dia-sporan leadership. These activities are facilitated where there are deeply felt grievances in the community, and when the borders of the ethnodiasporan enclave are maintained by the majority's discrimi-natory behavior. (Tölölyan 1996: 19)

In other words, despite reflecting a small subset of the overseas Vietnamese population, activist organizations such as Việt Tân are important factors in developing and maintaining a diasporic identity.

The movement to defend human rights and advocate for democracy in Vietnam continues to encourage the diaspora to mobilize with activists in the homeland. These efforts were once labeled as "homeland liberation," under which the activities of Việt Tân fell. Through a movement-oriented analysis of Việt Tân's strategic activities from the years during and after the Cold War, this study reframed anticommunist organizing as part of a diasporic nationalism that over time has brought together the overseas community and people in the homeland to fight for the future of a Vietnamese nation in challenge to the Vietnamese state. Although different forms of state repression have attempted to silence critics, digital technology has offered a space for those in Vietnam and overseas to organize beyond borders. So long as there is still a sense of injustice or grievance against the Vietnamese state, the effort to contest the VCP persists, as we see in the formation of the next generation of transnational activist organizations, such as VOICE, *Hội Anh Em Dân Chủ* [The Brotherhood for Democracy], Vietnam Rise, Luật Khoa/The Vietnamese, The 88 Project, and *Người Bảo Vệ Nhân Quyền* [Defend the Defenders].

REMEMBERING WAR AND MIGRATION

Mapping the Contours of Diasporic
Vietnamese Memoryscapes

QUAN TUE TRAN

Introduction

Wars, regime changes, displacements, and migrations constitute significant events that shaped the second half of twentieth-century Vietnamese and diasporic Vietnamese histories. Emerging from these
developments are the formations of many Vietnamese communities across
the world, including in the United States. Within and across the Vietnamese
diaspora,[1] the past—animated by the dialectic of remembering and forgetting (Ricoeur 2004: 225; Nguyen V. T. 2016: 19)—manifests in tangible and
intangible forms.[2] For example, in Southern California's Little Saigon—also
known as "thủ đô của người tị nạn Việt Nam" [capital of the Vietnamese refu-
gees] and home to the largest overseas Vietnamese community—the past is
intimately tied to the defunct Republic of Vietnam (RVN) and the forced
migration following its collapse. It is palpable in the South Vietnamese flags
flying in busy plazas, in the music heard on the radio and inside beauty salons, in the memorials dedicated to the Vietnam War and the boat people
exodus, in the annual fall of Saigon commemoration, and in the silence that
stands between parents and children. In this Little Saigon and other similar
sites, the past seeps into the present, percolating across the fabric of contemporary life. This temporal commingling, along with its physical and abstract
manifestations, constitutes and enlivens the memoryscapes of the Vietnamese diaspora.

Examining diasporic Vietnamese memoryscapes reveals the dynamism,
complexity, heterogeneity, and multiplicity of Vietnamese refugees' "memory work" (Young 1993: x).[3] It further demands an understanding of Viet-

namese refugees as agentive actors rather than passive, homogeneous, and unwitting victims of historical events and forces. This chapter draws on existing scholarship concerning Vietnamese American memory practices in particular to show diasporic Vietnamese memoryscapes as multivalent, multilayered, multidimensional, and transnational sites of negotiation that simultaneously illuminate the contentious politics of memory and the positionalities of those who participate in explicit and implicit remembering and forgetting projects. The chapter first defines, maps, and situates diasporic Vietnamese memoryscapes. It then examines why Vietnamese Americans remember two defining events in recent Vietnamese and diasporic Vietnamese histories—the Vietnam War and the postwar exodus—arguing that Vietnamese Americans' remembering and forgetting of these events are not uniform and do not exist in a vacuum. Instead, they are heterogeneous and multiple and must be understood in relation to local, national, and transnational forms of remembering and forgetting. Vietnamese American memoryscapes are thus entangled in the memoryscapes of Vietnam, the United States, the international refugee regime, and the broader Vietnamese diaspora. Moreover, Vietnamese Americans' memories about war and forced migration, although seemingly scattered, localized, and ephemeral, are essential in shaping and sustaining Vietnamese refugee subjectivity, identity, culture, and community locally and transnationally.

Defining, Mapping, and Situating Diasporic Vietnamese Memoryscapes

In recent decades, scholars have noted the significance of the past and the politics of memory in contemporary Vietnam and the Vietnamese diaspora. In 2001, the anthology *The Country of Memory* features then emergent scholarship that examines different "sites of memory" (Nora 1989: 7) in late socialist Vietnam. In that collection, historian Peter Zinoman interrogates the political agendas that influenced the publications of Vietnamese revolutionary prison memoirs (Zinoman 2001b). Anthropologist Shaun Malarney shows how the Vietnamese communist state's acts of heroizing and martyrizing revolutionary soldiers who died in the French and American wars overlook the concerns of the deceased's surviving families, who care more about their loved ones' safe passage in the afterlife (Malarney 2001). Historian Christoph Giebel examines local claims to revolutionary past and prominence through the effort of erecting a shrine to honor Tôn Đức Thắng, a southern revolutionary leader who became the Socialist Republic of Vietnam's first president (Giebel 2001). Vietnamese historical memories are further negotiated in cultural, social, economic, and gender terms. Art historian Nora Taylor shows how *đổi mới*, or market-oriented economic reforms, redefined the memory politics surrounding revolutionary period paintings and their relevance to state as well as nonstate art publics (N. Taylor 2001). Scholars Laurel Kennedy and Mary Rose Williams examine how the fledgling Vietnamese tourism industry rescripts war memories to appeal to Western tourists in the post–*đổi mới* context (Kennedy and Williams 2001). Historian Mark Philip Bradley investigates war memories in Vietnamese revisionist films (Bradley 2001). Meanwhile, Hue-Tam Ho Tai, the anthology's editor and contributor, attends to both the presence and absence of women in the SRV's remembrances of the American War (Ho Tai 2001c).

While the abovementioned case studies focus on how Vietnamese state and nonstate actors remade memories of revolution and war to serve various concerns in late socialist Vietnam, the anthology ends with Ho Tai's call to "redefine the meaning of community and expand the geography of memory." She specifically names exile Vietnamese memory as "a truly contrapuntal voice to the official discourse" (Ho Tai 2001b: 229). In identifying the gaps in Vietnamese memoryscapes and acknowledging the need to include and engage with Vietnamese exiles' remembrances of historical events, Ho Tai positions diasporic memory both as outside and in opposition to Vietnamese official memory, reminding readers that the Vietnamese nation-state does not have a monopoly over the past. Indeed, as scholars of the Vietnamese diaspora have shown, diasporic Vietnamese memories constitute fertile ground to investigate competing claims to local, national, and international past, present, and future. A survey of these sites of remembering and forgetting illuminates the contours of the memoryscapes of the Vietnamese diaspora.

Broadly speaking, memoryscapes are physical and abstract as well as tangible and intangible sites of remembering and forgetting, where details and impressions about the past are both spontaneously recalled and carefully constructed, guarded and neglected, included and excluded to serve the needs of those who conjure them and to mark the absent presence of events and those who are not yet claimed/named. Memoryscapes are neither self-evident nor complete but fluid, dynamic, selective, nonlinear, and fragmented. If, as social theorist Avery Gordon asserts, life is complicated and personhood is complex, so too is what can be recalled of past experiences and events. According to Gordon,

> Complex personhood means that all people (albeit in specific forms whose specificity is sometimes everything) remember and forget, are beset by contradiction, and recognize and misrecognize themselves and others. . . . Complex personhood means that the stories people tell about themselves, about their troubles, about their social worlds,

and about their society's problems are entangled and weave between what is immediately available as a story and what their imaginations are reaching toward. (Gordon 1997: 4)

Gordon's words are instructive because they caution against the oversimplification of narratives and knowledge about the past, present, and future. Moreover, they acknowledge the inherent contradictions, biases, and tensions in individual and collective acts of (dis)engaging with such past, present, and future.

Memoryscapes are not enclosed bubbles of remembering and forgetting. Rather, they are ever evolving and entangled in the dynamics of local, national, regional, and global orders and overlapping networks of information and material representation and exchange. Social-cultural anthropologist Arjun Appadurai argues that the global cultural economy at the end of the twentieth and beginning of the twenty-first century necessitates interpretive frameworks that can account for the new global order's interconnectedness and disjunctures. He thus proposes "ethnoscapes," "mediascapes," "technoscapes," "financescapes," and "ideoscapes" as overlapping dimensions of cultural flows of humans, information, technology, money, and ideas that shape contemporary global relationships (Appadurai 1996: 33). It is productive to expand Appadurai's layered and relational use of the -*scape* suffix to examine memory as yet another site of interconnectedness and disjuncture that animates, constructs, and assembles contemporary social, political, economic, and cultural life on different but intersecting scales.

Along these veins, diasporic Vietnamese memoryscapes are complex, multifaceted, and multilayered. They comprise multiple overlapping and sometimes competing memoryscapes. For example, Vietnamese American memoryscapes are born primarily out of refugee experiences and grapple with memories of war, regime change, forced migration, and resettlement, among other things.[4] They expose social, cultural, and political ruptures and hauntings of lives and events marginalized and displaced by and in multiple nation-states. In attending to and negotiating fragments of the past, Vietnamese American memoryscapes crisscross many geographies and are at once visible and invisible, tangible and intangible, audible and inaudible, archived and ephemeral, mundane and spectacular. They also counter and corroborate with other intersecting memoryscapes, including those of the nation-states from which Vietnamese refugees have fled and in which they sought asylum and resettled.

Across the Vietnamese diaspora, those of refugee background have conveyed and wrestled with their complex and tumultuous past through a wide range of platforms, thus offering multiple access points into diasporic Vietnamese memoryscapes. In the United States, since the 1980s, volumes of oral histories have shed light on individual and collective experiences. Some of these oral histories emerged from collaborations between Vietnamese or non-Vietnamese scholars and their Vietnamese interview subjects. Examples of such collaborative efforts include James Freeman's (1989) *Hearts of Sorrow: Vietnamese-American Lives*; Mary Terrell Cargill and Jade Quang Huynh's (2000) *Voices of Vietnamese Boat People: Nineteen Narratives of Escape and Survival*; and Sucheng Chan's (2006) *The Vietnamese American 1.5 Generation: Stories of War, Revolution, Flight, and New Beginnings*. Other oral histories resulted from community organizations' and research institutions' concerted efforts to document, archive, and make available materials that can illuminate the spectrum of Vietnamese refugee experiences. The Viet Stories: Vietnamese American Oral History Project, based at the University of California, Irvine (UC Irvine), and the Texas-based Vietnamese American Heritage Foundation's 500 Oral Histories Project exemplify large-scale oral history collections that center Vietnamese American voices and memories. Since their inceptions, these projects and the multigenerational teams that have sustained them through grassroots labor have recorded, preserved, and proliferated hundreds of Vietnamese American personal narratives for research and future generations, making them physically and digitally accessible.[5]

Archives and museums are additional portals into diasporic Vietnamese memoryscapes. In the United States, physical and digital repositories spearheaded by Vietnamese refugees themselves actively collect and safeguard documents, narratives, and objects pertaining to various aspects of Vietnamese American past and present. The work of the Southeast Asian Archive at UC Irvine that Thanh Thuy Vo Dang discusses in this volume offers a glimpse into the significance and interventions of Vietnamese American archival endeavors. In some instances, such archival acts and spaces are tied to their sponsoring institutions' research agendas and receive institutional and professional support. In contrast, others emerged more organically out of the recognition that the double marginalization and erasure of Vietnamese American experiences in both Vietnamese and American institutional histories and popular representations necessitate grassroots acts of self-remembering and self-archiving.

The Museum of Boat People and the Republic of Vietnam, or Viet Museum, located at Kelley Park's History Park in San Jose, California, is a case in point. Operating since August 2007, this grassroots community institution materialized through the labor and vision of Vũ Văn Lộc and other sympathetic Vietnamese Americans. A former colonel in the Army of the Republic of Vietnam (ARVN) who resettled in San Jose after Saigon fell in 1975 and a community activist, Mr. Vũ in 1976 began collecting artifacts relating to the RVN, the ARVN, communist reeducation camps, and the boat people exodus, with the aim of establishing a museum dedicated to Vietnamese American experiences. As an amateur collector and curator and a living witness with deep knowledge about these topics, he operates on a shoestring budget to acquire most objects on display at the museum on his own time. He also relies on in-kind and financial donations and assistance from fellow Vietnamese Americans who share his sense of urgency. For over three decades, Mr. Vũ stored these materials in his home garage until he and his collaborators at the nonprofit Immigrant Resettlement and Cultural Center secured enough funding to install the collection in a more "official" and publicly accessible space at Kelley Park.[6] Since its opening, the Viet Museum, which has the distinction of being the first museum of its kind, has welcomed thousands of visitors from all walks of life, including Vietnamese Americans and non-Vietnamese Americans, young and old. Those visiting the museum are transported through time by the tangible objects and guided tours that impart specific knowledge and narratives about the RVN, the fall of Saigon, reeducation camps, and the boat people exodus.

Beyond museum and archival spaces, public commemorations, debates, and protests over historical symbols and markers further animate diasporic Vietnamese memoryscapes. Scholars have attended to the multilayered significance of the fall of Saigon/Tháng Tư Đen "Black April" commemorations in Vietnamese American communities in the United States. Thanh Thuy Vo Dang, for instance, examines how, among the Vietnamese American community in San Diego, Black April commemoration functions as a "technology of memory" that advances anticommunist narratives to counter the Socialist Republic of Vietnam's silencing of South Vietnam and refugee history. Vo Dang provides insight into how such commemorative acts are far from self-evident but must also contend with internal tensions arising from generational differences (Vo Dang 2008: 87). From a different angle, Karin Aguilar-San Juan traces how Vietnamese Americans in Orange County and Boston deploy memories and symbols of South Vietnam to enhance community-building and place-making efforts. Aguilar-San Juan argues that "strategic memory projects" such as Black April commemorations, heritage flag recognitions, Vietnam War monuments, anticommunist protests, and "Communist Free Zone" legislations enable Vietnamese Americans to "stay Vietnamese," define criteria for membership in their communities, and resist simultaneously the "master narratives" of American exceptionalism and immigrant assimilation as well as perceived encroachment of the SRV into diasporic spaces (Aguilar-San Juan 2009: 65, xxvii).

Diasporic Vietnamese commemorative practices and public discourses move beyond collective memories about war and the loss of South Vietnam. Memories of the postwar refugee exodus also factor significantly in diasporic Vietnamese memoryscapes. As I have written elsewhere, in the past two decades, diasporic Vietnamese, including Vietnamese Americans, have participated in pilgrimages to former Southeast Asian asylum camps and constructed memorials to the boat people exodus in the various geographies that have been touched by this mass migration, including Southeast Asia, western Europe, Australia, and North America (Tran Q. T. 2012). Similarly, scholar Linda Ho Peché also notes former refugees' returns to asylum camps to renovate refugee burial sites and to mourn and honor those who have died, ensuring that the deceased are not forgotten (Peché 2013). Rather than representing isolated and individualized pockets of recollection and remembrance, these collective acts of return, gravesite identification and renovation, and memorialization expand the contours of diasporic Vietnamese memoryscapes, revealing the expansive geography of the Vietnamese diaspora and the rich intra-diasporic networks that connect the widely scattered Vietnamese diaspora together. In this context, memories of the past and active attention to them serve as connective threads of transnational meaning making and community building (Tran Q. T. 2016a).

Aside from commemorative and memorialization practices in physical spaces, diasporic Vietnamese also grapple with the past in digital spaces. Growing internet access in the past two decades has enabled Vietnamese in the United States and elsewhere in the diaspora to assert, reconcile with, debate, preserve, and transmit individual and collective memories in cyberspace and thus transcend geographical limitations and democratize narratives and understandings of the past. For example, sociologist Yen Le Espiritu examines the creation and circulation of digital memorials to South Vietnamese war heroes such as the fallen Colonel Hồ Ngọc Cẩn as a means for Vietnamese Americans to pass on their war memories to future generations (Espiritu Y. L. 2016). Evyn Le Espiritu analyzes how the internet has enabled "radical re-mixing and re-purposing" of South Vietnamese histories and memories in the face of multiple state-sanctioned erasures and in gendered terms (Espiritu E. L. 2017: 5). The digital components of the aforementioned oral history and archival projects also attest to the digital preservation and proliferation of Vietnamese American memories. Furthermore, the twenty-first century has witnessed a memory boom that has resulted in numerous websites, blogs, and social media accounts dedicated to recuperating, crowdsourcing, maintaining, and sharing diasporic Vietnamese memories. Varying thematically, from memories of Vietnam during the French colonial era to memories of war and migration, to memories of school/hometown/military/refugee camp/professional affiliations, these grassroots efforts are created and curated by individuals and collectives, forming vibrant and diverse translocal, transnational, and transgenerational communities of remembrance across the diaspora and beyond. Such sites of memory wrestle control of narratives about the past from the monopoly not only of the Viet-

namese nation-state but also of the various asylum or resettlement countries. Moreover, they constitute extraordinary and expansive digital archives
of the Vietnamese diaspora and function as sites of decentralized collective
memory that not only preserve certain sets of knowledge about the past but
also document the formation and proliferation of diasporic knowledge and
communities in real time.

The public Facebook group Pulau Bidong Alumni_Tỵ Nạn Pulau Bidong
offers insights into the richness and dynamism of diasporic Vietnamese digital memoryscape. Created in 2007 by a small group of former Vietnamese
refugees who had spent time in the asylum camp on Pulau Bidong, Malaysia,
between the late 1970s and the early 1990s, this social media site is "dedicated to the people who have lived and know of someone who was on Pulau
Bidong and their friends and families."[7] At the time of this writing, membership to the group has surpassed ten thousand people, and those who have
joined sign in from a wide range of locations across the world, including
Vietnam. A scroll through the page reveals a trove of compelling posts and
exchanges written mostly in Vietnamese. The posted topics range from ca-
sual recollections of camp life to questions about the whereabouts of specific
individuals who might have shared the same escape boat or camp section or
who might have assisted the refugees at a particular point in time. Members
also voluntarily contribute numerous images taken by themselves or of them,
sometimes as refugees of yesteryear or in more contemporary moments. This
invaluable informal visual archive offers intimate glimpses into the complexity of refugee daily life and agency and also documents mundane moments and extraordinary events (e.g., a festival in the camp, arrival and departure scenes, and landmarks). Varied widely in contexts, some images are
annotated by the posters, while others are without captions, or are annotated
by another group member, thus affirming a shared memory/moment and il-
lustrating a process of collective memory making. In making public their
private mementos and memories, those who contribute contents and comments to the group actively participate in the organic reconstitution and affirmation of boat refugee memories, experiences, and communities on a daily
basis. As a result, they not only enliven this particular memoryscape but also
illuminate how memories and the act of remembering serve as powerful
threads that connect and foster truly diasporic community formations. As
a form of self-representation, a node among many others that indexes diasporic past, such space also makes visible the complexity, nuances, and diversity of refugee experiences and identity.

The prolific and dynamic cultural output both in physical and digital
spaces in the Vietnamese diaspora further reflects the depth and breadth of
diasporic Vietnamese memoryscapes and experiences. Memoirs, autobiog-
raphies, novels, graphic novels, short fictions, poetry, anthologies, blogs, films,

music, performances, visual arts, and more articulate the consequences and shadows of war, the loss of nation, postwar economic instability, political persecution, exile, migration, and resettlement. This incredibly rich and growing body of cultural production underscores the profound and transgenerational impact of these historical events, giving rise to a distinct set of refugee discourses and paradigms. In the United States, different Vietnamese American generations have taken up multiple questions about the past, each with their unique entry points and concerns. These divergent relationships to the past reveal the heterogeneity and multiplicity of diasporic Vietnamese memoryscapes.

For example, in studying Vietnamese American literature's merits and particularities, scholar Isabelle Thuy Pelaud delineates the weight of the past on distinct strands of Vietnamese American literary production. She notes that some first-generation Vietnamese Americans became writers "out of the intense desire to tell the public about the plight of the South Vietnamese people. . . . Their texts capture a deep sense of loneliness, anger, and alienation. The guilt of leaving loved ones behind in the midst of chaos and panic punctuate their narratives" (Pelaud 2010: 23). Pelaud further observes that the shared experiences of persecution and oppression in postwar Vietnam and the boat people exodus that ensued also reinvigorated the Vietnamese American literary scene. This literature, written in the Vietnamese language and intended for Vietnamese readership, remains "heavily invested in home politics and marked by an intense longing for a lost past," reflecting the desire not to forget Vietnam, postwar Vietnamese experiences, migration experiences, and those still left behind (Pelaud 2010: 24). These characteristics differentiate first-generation writers from those of their 1.5- and second-generation counterparts, as the latter write almost exclusively in English and for an English-reading audience. Some mobilize the past and Vietnam to shape and assert new claims to identity, home, belonging, and citizenship. However, for others, memories of war and displacement haunt "the lives of the narrators like ghosts, at times scary and at others comforting, driving both emotions and actions" (Pelaud 2010: 37). Such haunting and ghostly presence interfere and coexist with memories of assimilation, identity formation, and ethnic and racial tension while also nourishing ideas of returns to the Vietnamese homeland through the complex lenses of trauma, yearning, and nostalgia (Pelaud 2010: 29).

Vietnamese American cultural producers and consumers also invoke, confront, and consume difficult memories of the past through other modes of artistic expression, accentuating the aesthetic and sociality of diasporic Vietnamese memoryscapes. Scholars have noted the ubiquitous and powerful role of music and musical performances in conveying, preserving, and transmitting memories about war, migration, homeland, and resettlement among diasporic Vietnamese on local and transnational levels. Ethnomusicologist Adelaida Reyes notes how music and musical performances constitute both social acts and cultural objects that convey Vietnamese refugees' memories of homeland and social relations in asylum camps and the United States (Reyes 1999). Cultural studies scholars Nhi Lieu and Caroline Kieu Linh Valverde similarly assert that diasporic Vietnamese musical productions both circulate in a transnational niche entertainment economy and repudiate the deliberate forgetting of South Vietnamese music by the Vietnamese communist state. Through musical production and consumption, diasporic Vietnamese reconstruct shared memories and cultural experiences across borders and quotidian spaces (Lieu 2011: xxiv; Valverde 2012: 30). At the same time, as historian Phuong Tran Nguyen notes, music and musicians also perform "social work," enabling Vietnamese Americans to recast refugee memories in agentive light, make meaning out of their painful and melancholic past and exile conditions, and adjust to new life (Nguyen Phuong Tran 2017: 2).

Films produced in the diaspora further diversify diasporic Vietnamese memoryscape. As film studies scholar Lan Duong notes, Vietnamese American filmmaking engages issues of community and history. Therefore, such cinematic creations must be understood as meaningful cultural artifacts and archival sites, where South Vietnamese and Vietnamese American cinematic histories and memories are preserved, innovated, and disseminated (Duong 2020: 54–58). The preservation quality of Vietnamese American films as "archives of memory" is multifold (Duong 2016: 66). On one level, as Duong elaborates, "Virtual, decentralized, and provisional, this archive is vital to the remembrance of South Việt Nam" (Duong 2016: 65). On another level, Viet Thanh Nguyen's and Viet Le's studies of Hong-An Truong's film installations contend that the circulation and repurposing of old footage of colonial Vietnam and South Vietnam before and during wars survive the cultural purge in postwar Vietnam and take on new lives and meanings in diaspora (Nguyen V. T. 2006; Le V. 2011). On yet another level, diasporic Vietnamese films also preserve and circulate memories of the postwar migration and experiences of those in diaspora. Documentary and feature films produced, directed, and acted by diasporic Vietnamese grapple with the memories of these "new" experiences of displacement, which are censored and banned in Vietnam.[8]

Photography constitutes still another rich node and genre in the rhizomatic pattern of diasporic Vietnamese memoryscapes. For instance, Tieu-Khe Le's investigation of An-My Le's photography book *Small Wars*, which features reenactment photographs of various scenes and battles during the Vietnam War, shows how images of the war captured in documentary photography continue to be productive and contested sites of memory making and revisioning (Le T.-K. 2015). Thy Phu's scholarship on diasporic Vietnam-

250/ Quan Tue Tran

ese family photography shifts the focus away from the spectacular and oft-reproduced images of war to illuminate war's fraught and painful grip on the intimate and quotidian family photos of diasporic subjects (Phu 2014). Viet Le's examination of Dinh Q. Le's photo tapestries further illuminates how, when juxtaposed and woven together, documentary images of war, media-mediated narratives about Vietnam, and family photographs disrupt dominant narratives and expose ongoing struggles over who controls and has access to stories and representations about the past (Le V. 2005).

As Vietnamese American artists draw their inspirations from and meditate on the past in their work, they also offer new epistemological and aesthetic frameworks to rethink the past and raise new questions about refugee and diasporic subjectivity and identity. Yen Le Espiritu and Lan Duong's comparative study of artwork by Vietnamese American artists Trinh Mai Thach and Tiffany Chung alongside Syrian American artists Nisrine Boukhari and Ghalia Elsrakbi and Lauren Alexander arrive at a new theoretical insight, which they refer to as "feminist refugee epistemology." According to Espiritu and Duong, this epistemology reinterprets "war-based displacement as being not only about social disorder and interruption but also about social reproduction and innovation" (Espiritu Y. L. and Duong 2018: 588). In that context, like 1.5- and second-generation writers, Vietnamese American artists also push the boundaries of remembrances and forgetting beyond what is acceptable within their communities to arrive at new understandings. Sometimes, such transcendent acts ignite public protests, emphasizing the highly contested and negotiated nature of memory and community, especially along generational and gender lines. Caroline Kieu Linh Valverde's and Long Bui's analyses of various protests waged by some first-generation Vietnamese Americans against art exhibitions organized by younger members of the community in the past decades show just how diasporic Vietnamese memoryscapes can also be sites of exclusion and violence, which subordinate and "dismember," as Bui argues, those within the community who may not share the same dominant politics and investment in nationalist and masculinist memories of the past (Valverde 2012: 90–112; Bui L. 2018: 89–90).[9]

Public commemoration, cultural production, and community protests can privilege specific memories, inducing public silencing of the complex and diverse ways that diasporic Vietnamese address the past. These acts of simultaneous remembering and forgetting can also permeate diasporic domestic and spiritual spaces. Indirect and unspoken traumas of war and migration often inhabit Vietnamese American homes and affect intergenerational relationships, highlighting the invisible memories and struggles with the past. As Vo Dang poignantly writes, "Silence invokes postulations about what might have been and what is yet to come. Silence provokes inquiry into what is unknown and perhaps, unknowable. Silence also begets further silences as we continue to structure our lives around the gaps, sometimes forgetting that those gaps are even there" (Vo Dang 2008: 180). In some instances, language gaps and the seeming lack of shared experiences partly exacerbated such silences, facilitating the creation of what Yen Le Espiritu calls "refugee postmemories"—memories created by U.S.-born Vietnamese Americans of events that took place before they were born (Espiritu Y. L. 2014: 139). In other instances, silences are mitigated through familial and communal spiritual and ancestral worship practices, as shown in Linda Ho Peché's study of Vietnamese American home altars and the practice of caring for the graves of family members buried in former refugee camps. According to Peché, such sites and rituals of private worship and mourning function as "mnemonic experience and a new mode of cultural production that encourages the [second] generation to embrace the refugee legacy, despite having no firsthand experience" (Peché 2016: 161).

By no means exhaustive, this overview of Vietnamese American memoryscapes demonstrates that the past occupies a prominent and powerful space in the contemporary Vietnamese diaspora. Its invocations emerge on a wide range of platforms and at the intersection of factors diversified by differences across generation, gender, language, migration and resettlement experiences, geographical locations, and degrees of connections to the homeland and host country. Not free of biases, contradiction, and tension, diasporic Vietnamese memoryscapes operate within, across, and in between physical and abstract terrains, where, as Espiritu asserts, "public and private memories intertwine parallactically" (Espiritu Y. L. 2014: 108). Thus, the contours of diasporic Vietnamese memoryscapes include acts of remembering and forgetting that are publicly accounted for as well as those that are not yet or cannot be seen or articulated yet are still powerfully felt. Moreover, it is imperative to attend to what is being remembered and forgotten, by whom, and in which contexts such remembering and forgetting surface. In the next section, this chapter takes a closer look at the overlapping contexts that lead to the dominance of war and migration memories in Vietnamese American memoryscapes.

Contextualizing War and Migration Remembrances

Vietnamese American memoryscapes are not uniform, nor do they exist in a vacuum. Heterogeneous and multiple, they must be understood in relation to local, national, and transnational forms of remembering and forgetting. This section contextualizes why Vietnamese Americans remember and forget certain aspects of war and migration. Building on and complementing the rich scholarship surveyed above, I posit that Vietnamese Americans invoke memories of war and migration to address first and foremost individual and collective traumas and ruptures brought on by these events. Secondly, in their collective engagements with the past, Vietnamese refugees also seek to resist multiple forms of forgetting and reclaim control of narratives about themselves and about Vietnamese and diasporic Vietnamese histories. Lastly, although seemingly scattered, localized, and ephemeral, Vietnamese Americans' war and forced migration memories are also essential in shaping and sustaining Vietnamese refugee subjectivity, identity, culture, and community locally and transnationally. Entangled in the memoryscapes of Vietnam, the United States, and beyond, these memory sites offer and reinforce an origin narrative that anchors Vietnamese Americans in specific places and spaces, enabling them to carve out alternative local and transnational sites of belonging.

Vietnamese American war and migration memories comprise distinct and sometimes overlapping fragments. For example, Vietnamese American memories of war range from *wartime* military and civilian experiences and events that occurred in South Vietnam (e.g., enlistments; combats; the Tết Offensive; everyday life; and displacements caused by fighting, bombing, and population relocation measures) to memories of *end-of-war* experiences of migration (e.g., surrender, evacuation, the fall of Saigon, and transit experiences in refugee camps in Guam and later in the United States). These memories of migration differ from the memories of the migration that occurred in the *postwar* era, which encompass experiences of hardship and persecution (e.g., political "reeducation," social stigma and discrimination, cultural purges, and New Economic Zones) as well as "boat people" and "land people" experiences (e.g., boat escape journeys, escape journeys by foot through Cambodia to Thailand, and experiences in Southeast Asian and Hong Kong asylum camps). While, for the sake of clarity, this chronological and categorical approach underscores the specificities of war and migration memories and differentiates the mnemonic contexts, it is crucial to note that Vietnamese American memories of the past are compounds of multiple experiences that are deeply layered.

As watershed events in Vietnamese and diasporic Vietnamese histories, war and migration represent important ruptures that birth new forms, sites, objects, and subjects of remembering and forgetting. For Vietnamese Americans, the traumas, disruptions, and displacements caused by these events necessitate collective engagement with the past in order to make sense of them, to cope with the social, cultural, political, economic, environmental, and spiritual fallouts that they caused, and to recalibrate Vietnamese American identity and subjectivity. As those who lost the war, their country, and their loved ones and were forced out of their homeland by oppressive postwar conditions created by their compatriot victors, Vietnamese Americans and their memories of these losses are orphaned. They do not have the luxury of institutionalized and state recognition of their losses and wounds in either their home or host country or anywhere else. As scholar Thu Huong Nguyễn-Võ asserts, "Vietnamese Americans as refugees occupy the position of self-mourners because no one else mourns us. The accounts of boat people starved, drowned, raped at sea have been our own. We reenact them in plays at commemoration ceremonies, in photo-timelines that we exhibit, in stories that we write" (Nguyễn-Võ 2005: 170). It is in this position as "self-mourners" that Vietnamese Americans and their compatriots in the diaspora cobble together emotional and material resources in the places where they sought asylum and resettled to ensure that the pain and suffering they experienced and endured are not forgotten. However, as Nguyễn-Võ emphasizes, "For us, remembering in mourning, in commemoration, in symbolic local politics, is not a symptom of an incessant, pathological return to be cured with assimilationist remedies, but a way in which we can recover our histories which intersect, rather than coincide, with American nationalist history" as well as Vietnamese history and beyond (Nguyễn-Võ 2005: 159).

Vietnamese Americans' collective engagements with memories of war and migration also seek to resist multiple forms of forgetting and reclaim control of narratives about themselves and about Vietnamese and diasporic Vietnamese histories. As several scholars have pointed out, Vietnamese refugees and their memories of war and migration are triply erased from the public memories of the Vietnamese communist state, the American left, and the American right (Nguyễn-Võ 2005; Espiritu Y. L. 2014; Nguyen V. T. 2016). In postwar Vietnam, memories of South Vietnam, of those who fought to defend it, and of those forced to flee the liberated country have no standing place. Indeed, the Vietnamese communist regime's claim to victory and revolution is predicated on the forgetting and erasing of South Vietnam and South Vietnamese, both literally and symbolically. According to Nguyễn-Võ, violent acts committed by northern and southern communist troops during the war, as well as oppressive postwar policies against the southerners, such as reeducation camps, New Economic Zones, and cultural, political, and economic eradication, "remain unacknowledged to this day" (Nguyễn-Võ 2005: 160). Meanwhile, American public memories of the Vietnam War also omit Vietnamese refugees. On the one hand, aligning with revolution and liberation ideologies, American progressives dismiss Vietnamese refugees and their memories of war as reactionary and illegitimate (Nguyễn-Võ 2005: 161). On the other hand, American conservatives and others invested in upholding American imperial memories and anticommunist ideologies cast Vietnamese refugees to the side and only include the latter when it is expedient for them to do so (Nguyễn-Võ 2005: 162–167). Such selective acts of forgetting are most prevalent in American commemorations of the Vietnam War, as well in popular culture and discourse concerning the war.

It is worth noting that Vietnamese Americans also invoke memories of war and migration to combat internal forces of forgetting that evolve over time. Their prolific and active attempts to record, write, document, memorialize, and preserve knowledge about the past ensure that their stories of war and migration do not disappear once those who experienced these events firsthand inevitably pass away. This future-oriented goal of remembering reflects the ongoing precariousness of Vietnamese American memories in the present. Additionally, within Vietnamese American communities, forgetting also takes hold in the widening "generation gap" exacerbated by linguistic alienation and degrees of removal from direct displacement experiences created by war and migration. Diasporic Vietnamese in the United States and elsewhere must also contend with changes within their communities as second, third, and fourth generations come of age and are less preoccupied with their parents' and grandparents' past experiences. Moreover, new waves of Vietnamese immigrants bring with them different relationships to Vietnam, Vietnamese America, and the past. Some may not subscribe to the established set of memories and politics advanced by the Vietnamese refugee population, which could further contribute to the forgetting of Vietnamese Americans' refugee origin. The increasing transnational connections in the twenty-first century between the Vietnamese diaspora and Vietnam, a country that has undergone remarkable changes since the refugee era, has ushered in yet another set of potential amnesia. Thus, in actively remembering their past, Vietnamese Americans refuse both the forced forgetting committed by state and institutional entities that dominate conversations about the past and also forms of forgetting that stem from those within their own communities in the present.

Vietnamese Americans' war and migration memories powerfully shape and sustain Vietnamese refugee subjectivity, identity, culture, and community locally and transnationally—in spite of, and, perhaps because of, their precarity. As Hue-Tam Ho Tai notes, "If a community creates and sustains memory, the reverse is also true: memory creates and sustains the community" (Ho Tai 2001c: 227). Vietnamese Americans create and sustain specific memories of war and migration to define themselves and the boundaries of and membership in their community. In turn, these memories and their robust material manifestations (e.g., commemorations, physical and digital memorials, and cultural productions) forge a distinctive community of remembrance that stakes claims on multiple geographies. In privileging memories of war and migration, Vietnamese Americans affirm that their community stems from refugee roots. This refugee origin story enables Vietnamese Americans to negotiate their positionality and establish themselves in and stake claims to specific local and transnational places and spaces—Vietnam, the

United States, and the Vietnamese diaspora—entangling them in the memoryscapes of these entities. However, as mentioned earlier, the various tensions and contestations that arose over symbolism and cultural representation suggest that within Vietnamese American memoryscapes exists a hierarchy of remembering and forgetting that also obfuscates and silences other engagements with and narratives about the past.

As Vietnamese Americans labor diligently to ensure that their version of the past survives compounding ruptures, displacements, and erasures, their endeavor functions within a structure of mnemonic selectiveness that perpetuates what Viet Thanh Nguyen characterizes as unjust memory and forgetting. As Nguyen theorizes in his treatise on the ethics of remembering and forgetting wars, just memory and just forgetting entail the capacity and imperative to move beyond self-mourning and the mantle of victimhood to recognize the humanity and inhumanity of one's enemy, as well as one's humanity, inhumanity, and complicity in events of the past (Nguyen V. T. 2016: 283). Critical of all remembrances of the Vietnam War, including dominant Vietnamese American war memories, Nguyen leverages the following critique: "[Vietnamese refugees] have valid reasons to remember their past, but they also tend to forget, particularly in public commemoration, the venality of the southern Vietnamese regime, the violence committed by their own soldiers—who happened to be their fathers, brothers, and sons—and how their sentiments may be viewed from elsewhere" (Nguyen V. T. 2016: 280). This critique is a reminder that remembering goes hand in hand with forgetting and that it is crucial to never settle for any singular version of the past but to attend to and acknowledge the dialectical nature and the multiplicity of memory and what it makes visible and renders invisible.

Conclusion

In this chapter, I have synthesized existing scholarship concerning Vietnamese American memories of war and migration to identify the contours of diasporic Vietnamese memoryscapes. As discussed, Vietnamese American memoryscapes are complex, diverse, uneven, and contested. Anchored by memories of war and migration, Vietnamese American memoryscapes are born out of experiences of violence, loss, displacement, and erasure. These experiences generate a wide range of remembering and forgetting projects as Vietnamese Americans not only mourn their losses but also find in their experiences of displacement powerful sources of inspiration. Their attempts to remember and forget war and migration are both recovery and creative acts, recasting war and migration as points of diasporic origin and not just of death and loss. Different generations remember and forget war and migration uniquely, influenced by their diverse backgrounds and generational circumstances. In Vietnamese American communities, residual fragments of war and migration can be found in public and private spaces and continue to shape the present and future of Vietnamese Americans and beyond. Far from being uniform or free of contradiction and tension, Vietnamese American memoryscapes are ever evolving as their contours expand and constrict in relation to other memoryscapes.

DEVOTION IN DIASPORA

*Invoking Holy Mothers among Vietnamese
American Faith Communities*

Thien-Huong Ninh

Introduction

In October 2018, about one hundred Vietnamese Catholics coming from different countries congregated in Abu Ghosh, Israel, for the blessing ceremony of a newly installed statue of Our Lady of Lavang (*Đức Mẹ La Vang*). For many Vietnamese Catholics, this was a dream come true. The statue was unlike any other representations of the Virgin Mary in Israel, her birthplace. Our Lady of Lavang was in the image of a Vietnamese woman dressed in Vietnamese traditional attire (*áo dài*), and this distinctive representation was intentionally created and globalized by Vietnamese Catholics in the diaspora (Ninh T.-H. 2017).

About a month earlier, Vietnamese Caodaists from all corners of the world had also assembled for the annual Grand Ceremony for the holy mother of their religion, the Asian-looking Caodai Mother Goddess (*Diêu Trì Kim Mẫu*).[1] At her religious "home" based in the Caodai Holy See in Tay Ninh, South Vietnam, nearly one million Caodaists at the ceremony welcomed foreign dignitaries representing several overseas organizations, including Daesoon Jinrihoe from South Korea and Weixin Shengjiao from Taiwan. Meanwhile, their coreligionists outside of Vietnam congregated at various Caodai Mother Goddess temples for the largest annual Caodai event.

This chapter focuses on two cases of holy mother worship[2] among overseas Vietnamese: Vietnamese American Catholics and Vietnamese American Caodaists. In the aftermath of displacement from their homeland beginning in 1975, these Vietnamese faith practitioners had to overcome the forces of assimilation and social marginalization to continue such practices overseas. Yet by the 1990s, about two decades after the mass exodus of Vietnamese from their homeland, overseas Vietnamese have not only recentralized their fragmented communities by reviving devotion to Vietnamese holy mothers but have also played a pivotal role in popularizing these female religious figures across ethnic and national boundaries. As this chapter illustrates and as a part of an overarching argument of this volume, these "unpredictable" trajectories and transformations among overseas Vietnamese are not simply foreign produced but are anchored in the unique ideologies and values of South Vietnam, which they have brought to other parts of the world.

Theoretical Framework

Researchers on refugees and immigrants have posited that devotional practices that center female religious figures often revitalize and reinforce ethnicity locally and transnationally. Robert Orsi's *Madonna of the 115th Street* (2010), for instance, illustrates the yearly procession of the Virgin Mary as a central ritual for the identity of Sicilian immigrants. The event is an important opportunity for immigrant practitioners to legitimize their place in New York City and to showcase elements of their cultural traditions to the broader community. In this sense, Marian religious devotion is not only crucial for the literal and figurative reconstruction of dwellings and homes in the diaspora but also as a practice of belonging, placemaking, and innovation.

In a similar vein, Tweed (1997) argues that Marianism, through Our Lady of Exile, plays a crucial role in linking Cuban Catholics in Miami to their homeland. He contends that, through religious rituals such as prayers and elaborate processions and visual depictions of their exodus displayed at their site of devotion to Our Lady of Exile, they create a "transtemporal" and "translocative" space. In this liminal vibrant space of simultaneously "here and there," Cuban American Catholics reconfigure their history of displacement and envision a future in which they would return to their homeland. Tweed (1997: 87) asserts that in doing so they transpose the conditions of displacement into survival and aspirations, reinterpreting their painful past into a meaningful present and aspirational future in the United States and Cuba. Echoing Orsi (2010: 22–35), Tweed (1997) similarly identifies Marian devotion as a form of identity and social cohesion for immigrants and refugees. Other studies of Catholic immigrants in the United States have found similar patterns of ethnic orthodoxy at local and global levels (Castañeda-Liles 2018: 146–166; Ninh T.-H. 2017: 82–105; Horsfall 2000: 382–383).

In addition to the popularity of the Virgin Mary, studies have found intense devotion to female religious figures among Vietnamese American refugees outside of the Catholic faith. Among Buddhists, for instance, Truitt (2017: 83–107) has discovered that *Quán Thế Âm* (Guanyin or Kwan Yin) plays a central role in mediating their precarious positionality as refugees living outside of their ancestral home and on the margins of American society. Similarly, within the spirit-possession Vietnamese Mother Goddess tradition, Fjelstad and Nguyen (2011) have observed that the religion has become increasingly more popular in California as it becomes more communal. Traditionally, Mother Goddess rituals were clandestine, usually practiced individually or in small groups at private homes that were open only to invited individuals in the religion's tight-knit community. However, in the U.S. context, followers have slowly opened the walls of their underground temples to welcome initiated mediums as well as the curious. This openness creates a safe and inclusive space that has attracted many young Vietnamese adults who yearn to learn, maintain, and authenticate their cultural heritage with the blessings of religious mothers.

How and why do refugees and immigrants in the United States look to holy mothers as a modality to reconnect to coethnic coreligionists, locally and globally? Studies have found that religious mother figures emerge most vividly in the context of pain, suffering, and mourning associated with displacement, isolation, and migration (Castañeda-Liles 2018; Ninh T.-H. 2017; Truitt 2017; Fjelstad and Nguyen 2011). Suffering may be an individual experience, but spiritual mothers can conjoin refugees and immigrants across borders by facilitating sympathy, acceptance, and solace. This "borderless" outreach inflects healing and reconciliation that is unique to voluntary and involuntary migration experiences. In particular, the historical roots, ethnic underpinnings, and imagery of religious mother figures can create, relink, and solidify blood, cultural, and physical bonds among members of a shared ethnicity and faith.

Mother worship, therefore, is less bound to the commands of traditions than to the demands of contemporary life experiences and struggles. In front of religious mother figures, both men and women of different Vietnamese ethnic backgrounds can appeal for blessings, comfort, and guidance.[3] This attraction across gender and ethnicity partly explains why the Mother Goddess tradition has become rapidly popular within the past two decades in Vietnam and the United States. Whether the goddess is Liễu Hạnh in northern Vietnam, Thiên Y A Na or Po InâNâgar of central Vietnam, or the Black Lady or Our Lady of the Realm in southern Vietnam, she has summoned thousands of pilgrims from all over the world to her sacred homes (Salemink 2015; Noseworthy 2015; P. Taylor 2004; Fjelstad and Nguyen 2006; Pham Q. P. and Eipper 2009; Endres 2011). The transnational sphere created by religious mother worship is a unique and rare intimate point of juncture between Vietnamese followers in the United States and coreligionists in other countries, including their homeland. As Salemink (2015) has further elaborated, contemporary Vietnamese Mother Goddess worship enables practitioners to "connect worlds both vertically—the *Yin* and *Yang* worlds—and horizontally—the various lifeworlds lived in various countries in the region and around the globe" (Salemink 2015: 241).

Researchers have maintained that ethnic groups that participate in cross-border involvements motivated by a shared faith could reconstitute themselves into a deterritorialized nation in the diaspora. They have emphasized religion's transcendental characteristic as being efficacious for creating a collective identity across space and time and elevating that identity to a level of sanctity for communal worship (Baumann 2000; Smart 1987; Sokefeld 2004; Vertovec 1997, 2000). As practitioners must "do considerable ideological work" (Tölölyan 1996: 17) in order to commit themselves to this transnational collectivity, scholars have argued that practitioners intentionally resist being assimilated into their host societies or belonging to any one particular nation, including their homeland. Instead, through the "complementary disinclinations" (Sheffer 1996: 44) of belonging to only one place, diasporas have created their own alternative transnational community of belonging through their faith.

Historical Background on Catholicism in Vietnam

During the seventeenth century, about a hundred years after the arrival of Portuguese Catholic missionaries, French Catholic missionaries successfully made gradual inroads into Vietnamese society by acculturating Catholicism into the local culture (Dutton 2016: chap. 1; Keith 2012: 55–88; Phan P. 1991: 2–8). However, it was not until French rule (1887–1954) that Catholicism enjoyed full integration and acceptance into Vietnamese society. The Catholic Church flourished with the land and greater authority bestowed by the French colonial government. It built schools, churches, and medical centers, many of which remain standing today. However, its strength began to deteriorate beginning in 1954, when French colonial rule was replaced by Vietnamese communist control—first in North Vietnam and, by 1975, in South Vietnam (Chu 2008: 162–167). It was in large part because of these major political shifts that many Vietnamese Catholics had to flee from religious persecution: from North Vietnam to South Vietnam in 1954 and from South Vietnam to other countries in 1975 (Hansen 2009; Ninh T.-H. 2017; Hoskins 2012b).

Beginning in 1986, following policies of economic liberalization (*Đổi Mới*), the Vietnamese state slowly relaxed its control over religious practices (Fjelstad and Nguyen 2006: 9–11; P. Taylor 2004: 15–18; P. Taylor 2001: 23–30) and granted "qualified" religious freedom (Hansen 2009: 185–192). As of 2014, Catholicism is the second-largest religion of Vietnam, following only Buddhism. It has a following of approximately seven million (8 percent of

Vietnam's population of ninety million) and is heavily concentrated in the southern region of Vietnam.[4]

Historical Background on Caodaism in Vietnam

Through direct communication with God by the means of séances (direct possession), Caodaism (*Cao Đài*) was founded in 1926 in South Vietnam, when the country was under French colonialism.[5] It is formally known as the Great Faith of the Third Era for Salvation (*Đại Đạo Tam Kỳ Phổ Độ*). The religion encompasses teachings of tolerance that are aimed at creating universal harmony between Western and Eastern philosophies, traditions, and rituals. It believes that religions are different manifestations of the same truth and worships a common Supreme Being, from which all life originated. Through self-cultivation practices, such as meditation and vegetarianism, human beings may return to their roots and become united with the Supreme Being.

Caodaists utilize the Left Eye to represent the Supreme Being and as a symbol of their universal and inclusive faith, as the eye is not distinguishable by gender, race, or ethnicity (Hoskins 2015). Their religious pantheon includes Prophet Mohammed, Jesus Christ, Confucius, Li Bai (Lý Thái Bạch), Buddha, Lao Tzu, and the Bodhisattva Kwan Yin. Other saints include the Chinese revolutionary leader Sun Yat Sen, the French philosopher Victor Hugo, the Vietnamese poet Nguyễn Bỉnh Khiêm, the English playwright William Shakespeare, and the Russian political leader Vladimir Lenin.

Located in a once-deserted jungle area of the French-established Cochinchina colony, the Caodai Holy See (*Toà Thánh Tây Ninh*), the religion's headquarters, was built between 1932 and 1953. According to many Caodaists, the Holy See's eclectic and colorful architecture is a manifestation of the Supreme Being's culturally multifaceted and universally encompassing teachings. Its impressive structure and design have been replicated by Caodai temples throughout the world. The Holy See oversees all religious activities within the religion, from text publication to membership registration and religious ordination.

Caodaism flourished in its early years, although the French government kept a watchful eye on the new religion. In the 1940s, nearly 25 percent of the population in Cochinchina were Caodaists (Hoskins 2012a; Hoskins 2012b). Furthermore, the religion had attracted many Khmers in neighboring Cambodia. According to French colonial records, the number of Khmer visitors at the Caodai Holy See often outnumbered Vietnamese in the early years of the religion.[6] Caodaism's global outreach also included building relationships with Oomoto (a Japanese new religious movement that originated from Shinto) and making delegation visits to India.

Similar to the experiences of Vietnamese Catholicism, Caodaism was drastically repressed in Vietnam after 1975. Communism from North Vietnam took complete control of the Holy See, confiscated all of its properties, and banned nearly all religious activities, including séances, the Caodaists' fundamental mode of communication with their Supreme Being. The Vietnamese government also combined the Holy See's three administrative branches of "checks and balances" into a state-sanctioned Sacerdotal Council. All seats on the council and other leadership positions must be appointed by, or must have approval from, the government. This "secular" system of appointment replaced séance as the sacred procedure of direct communication with God for spiritual guidance, including leadership ordination. As of 2014, there were approximately 4.4 million Caodai followers (5 percent of Vietnam's population of ninety million), making Caodaism the largest Vietnamese indigenous religion and the third-largest religion in Vietnam, behind only Buddhism and Catholicism. Most of the Caodai followers are concentrated in the southern region of Vietnam.[7]

The Religious Significance of Holy Mothers: Our Lady of Lavang

Our Lady of Lavang is representative of the history of Vietnamese Catholics as religious martyrs and refugees constantly fleeing from religious persecution. According to an oral tradition, in 1798, the Virgin Mary appeared several times to a group of Vietnamese Catholics who were fleeing from anti-Catholic persecution in Lavang.[8] She comforted them and said, "My children, have faith and be brave. I have heard your prayers. From now on, I will grant the wishes of all who come to me" (Tran Q. C. 2009). Since then, Catholics and non-Catholics alike have sought refuge at the site of the apparition. Although the Vatican has not verified the historical accuracy of the apparition, Catholics and non-Catholics alike have continued to pray to Our Lady of Lavang. Except for a short hiatus due to war and violence during the 1970s, congresses have been held every two years to commemorate her apparition.

In 1901, when Vietnam was under French colonialism and Catholicism was better tolerated, the first Our Lady of Lavang church was built and completed on the site where faithful followers claimed that she had appeared. At this historic event, the local sitting French bishop placed a French-modeled statue of Our Lady of Victories (*Notre-Dame des Victoires*) to represent Our Lady of Lavang in the new church. The Virgin Mary was depicted standing and wearing a crown and a draped dress; her hands were positioned to the right, holding a crowned baby Jesus standing on top of a globe.

The Marian title Our Lady of Victories is old and tied to many names in the Christian world, most notably Our Lady of the Rosary (that is, victory comes from the power of the Rosary). While the veneration of the Virgin Mary may represent Catholic conquest over and absorption of paganistic goddess cults rooted in ancient Egyptian, Greek, and Roman cultures (Benko 1994: 5), the Marian imagery of Our Lady of Victories also embodies a distinctive French Catholic form and its political conquests.

Many French Catholics believed that the Virgin Mary intervened in the miraculous victory of the French over the Greeks in Constantinople in 1204, which marked the siege and sack of Constantinople in the culmination of the Fourth Crusade. Since then, they often appealed to Our Lady of Victories in times of political crisis and threats from religious heresies (Santoro 2011: 570). Despite or perhaps because of the French Revolution, which challenged the influential role of the Catholic Church, Our Lady of Victories during the nineteenth century became "a symbol of the aspiration of the [French] Catholic Church to roll back the evil forces of the French Revolution and to restore hierarchy, nobility, and authority" (Ashiwa and Wank 2009: 80–82). As the French spread its colonial power overseas, different French regimes more or less found the Catholic Church's religious authoritarianism useful in asserting and maintaining their power and dominance. Consequently, many statues and churches devoted to Our Lady of Victories can be found inside and outside of France. For nearly more than a century, this statue of a Western-looking Virgin Mary was associated with Our Lady of Lavang.

However, in 1998, upon the commemoration of two hundred years after the first apparition of Our Lady of Lavang was reported, Vietnamese Catholics replaced this Western image with a Vietnamese version created by Vietnamese American sculptor Nhan Van, who also made the first Vietnamese image of the Virgin Mary outside of Vietnam (Ninh T.-H. 2017). Portrayed as a Vietnamese woman, Our Lady of Lavang is dressed in a white traditional costume (áo dài) under a blue decorative cloak, adorned by a Vietnamese golden headdress, and holding a baby Jesus on her left arm. For the first time in history, a Vietnamese Marian icon of the Catholic faith was officially introduced to the global community, and during the same year, Pope John Paul II proclaimed Our Lady of Lavang as the patroness of the Catholic Church of Vietnam.

The Religious Significance of Holy Mothers: The Caodai Mother Goddess

Diêu Trì Kim Mẫu (Golden Mother of the Jade Pond), the Mother Goddess in Caodaism, is synonymous with Tây Vương Mẫu (Queen Mother of the West), a spiritual mother in Taoism who lives in a celestial garden that grows peaches of immortality. *Diêu Trì* or *Dao Trì* in Chinese refers to her spiritual residence. *Kim* means "gold" or "imperial." *Mẫu* is "mother" in Chinese and Vietnamese. Her other names include Buddha Mother (*Phật Mẫu*), Holy Mother (*Đức Mẹ*), Immortal Empress Mother (*Bà Chúa Tiên*), Birth Mother (*Me Sanh*), and Immortal-Fairy-Saint Mother (*Tiên Thiên Thánh Mâu*).

The Caodai Mother Goddess bestows one of the most important theological teachings of Caodaism, religious universalism, the idea that all are equal to one another as children of the supreme Caodai God. As reflected by a comment made by Phạm Công Tắc, one of the three cofounders of Caodaism, on January 10, 1947, "Inside the Caodai Mother Goddess temple, everyone has equal ranking, even if that person is the Pope or the Defender of the Religion, they must leave their uniform outside of the temple. One may rule the outside world but cannot do so with Mother as everyone is her child" (Phạm C. T. 1947). Since then, Caodai dignitaries have not been allowed to wear their rank-specific distinctive colorful uniforms during ceremonies and rituals devoted to the Caodai Mother Goddess. As with other Caodai followers, they wear a simple white Vietnamese traditional garment (*áo dài*).

The emphasis on equality, building bridges across social differences and strata, is an important theological tenet within Caodaism, and followers have demonstrated efforts to put it into practice. For example, unlike other institutionalized religions in Vietnam, including Catholicism and Buddhism, Caodai ecclesiastical hierarchy is open to women (Hoskins 2012a). Caodai women can reach the rank of cardinal (*Đầu Sư*), the third-highest position a living Caodaist can obtain.

Likewise, within the theology of religious universalism, the Mother Goddess holds equivalent and complementary status to the Caodai God or Supreme Being, whose energy is *yang* (*dương*), while hers is *yin* (*âm*). Caodaists have informed me that, while all living and nonliving things originated from the Caodai Supreme Being, the Mother Goddess created all things by unifying the *yin* (*âm*) and *yang* (*dương*) energy. Caodaists believe that as the creator and preserver of life, the Mother Goddess could protect them from secular materialistic seductions and return them to the right path of spiritual cultivation and unification with the Supreme Being.

In 1928, two years after Caodaism was declared a religion, the first Mother Goddess temple in Vietnam was built in Mỹ Tho, approximately 135 kilometers from the Holy See in Tây Ninh (Bui V. T. 1986). In 1951, the first original model of the Mother Goddess was created and displayed in the Temple of Gratitude at the Caodai Holy See. Although the Temple of Gratitude is only a temporary sanctuary for the Mother Goddess, Caodai cofounder Phạm Công Tắc's 1951 decree stated that only buildings within the Holy See compound can serve as the official Mother Goddess "temple" (*đền*) and that other devotional centers are simply "shrines" (*điện*). These shrines can only represent the Mother Goddess through four classical Chinese characters, 瑤池 金母 (Golden Mother of the Jade Pond, or *Diêu Trì Kim Mẫu*) and cannot display a statue of her. Moreover, according to Phạm Công Tắc's decree, Mother Goddess temples outside of the Caodai Holy See are prohibited from organizing the "official" annual Mother Goddess Festival.

Vietnamese Holy Mothers and Community Centralization in the Diaspora

As of 2016, there were more than two million Vietnamese Americans, most of whom had arrived in the United States as refugees after the fall of South Vietnam to communism in 1975 or were U.S.-born descendants of these Vietnamese refugees.[9] They were forced to flee their homeland for fear of political, religious, and economic persecutions.

Since their arrival, religion has constituted a visible presence within both the domestic and community lives of ethnic Vietnamese. In his 1980 survey, Rutledge (1985) has found that more than two-thirds of two hundred Vietnamese refugees in Oklahoma City regarded religion as "extremely important" or "very important." Religion has been one of the most important avenues for ethnic Vietnamese to cope with the challenges of migration and adaptation, particularly by creating liaisons and sharing resources with their coethnic faithful (Bankston and Zhou 1996; Burwell, Hill, and Wicklin 1986; Camda and Phaobtong 1992; Dunning 1982, 1989; Fjeldstad 1995; Hoang L. 2006; Hoskins 2007; Huynh T. 2000; Lewis, Fraser, and Pecora 1988; Nguyen N. 2001; Phan P. 2003, 2006).

At home, Vietnamese practitioners across different religious traditions have often set up altars devoted to gods, spirits, and ancestors (Peché 2012; Phan P. 2005; Huynh T. 2000). In the community, ethnic Vietnamese have regularly gathered to celebrate their religion and preserve their ethnic heritage, such as by teaching Vietnamese language classes and celebrating cultural festivals (Bankston and Zhou 1996; Dorais 2005; Hoang L. 2006; Phan P. 2003). Since the late 1990s, after the United States lifted its trade embargo against Vietnam, many of them have rebuilt ties with coreligionists in the homeland.

Compared with the percentage of Catholics in Vietnam (approximately 7 percent), Catholics make up approximately 30 percent of the Vietnamese population in the United States.[10] The overrepresentation of Catholics in the overseas Vietnamese population may be due to the fact that many had to flee Vietnam because of persecution against their faith. Moreover, a number of Vietnamese refugees converted to Catholicism during their flight and resettlement, especially those who were resettled by Catholic relief agencies (Hoskins 2007).

The largest number of Caodaists resettled in Southern California, but they were dispersed throughout the region. In 1979, through informal ties, word of mouth, and newspaper advertisements, a group of about five or six Vietnamese Caodaists reconnected with one another. Gradually, religious life and activities attracted an increasing number of Caodaists throughout Southern California. Currently, there are about fifty Caodai temples outside Vietnam, nine of which are in California. According to email exchanges with Kham V. Pham, the highest-ranking religious leader of the Diocese of California, there are approximately 1,350 Caodaists in the United States, more than 90 percent of whom belong to the Tay Ninh Caodai sect.

As refugees fleeing communism within the context of the Cold War, Vietnamese were welcomed by U.S. policies that, partly because of American military involvement in Vietnam, embodied ideals of moral responsibility, duty, and "multiculturalism." Their arrival even propelled the rewriting of the Refugee Act of 1980, which paved the way to open doors to more refugees, including the "boat people" and those who had served time in reeducation camps in Vietnam.

For many Vietnamese American Catholics and Caodaists, faith in their Asian-looking holy mothers played a powerful role in their experiences as refugees and ethnic minorities in the United States. Both Our Lady of Lavang and the Caodai Mother Goddess were certainly key figures in the religious life of the faithful in Vietnam. However, as a result of being forcibly uprooted from their homeland, Vietnamese American Catholics and Caodaists prayed to their holy mothers even more fervently as they sought comfort and solace in the strange land of their new home in the United States.

As I illustrate in the next sections, Our Lady of Lavang and the Caodai Mother Goddess have been instrumental in reconnecting them to their coethnic coreligionists and rebuilding their collectivity as a global community. At least once a year, Vietnamese American Catholics and Caodaists from different parts of the United States travel long distances to congregate and celebrate their holy mothers. These connections have extended across cities, states, countries, and oceans, mending the wounds of separation, isolation, and marginalization caused by religious persecution in Vietnam and forced assimilation in the United States.

Vietnamese American Catholics and Our Lady of Lavang

Since Our Lady of Lavang's "ethnic" transformation in the late 1990s, Vietnamese Catholics in the United States have increasingly popularized the symbolic coupling of the Virgin Mary and Vietnamese martyrs. Historically, for example, Vietnamese Catholic martyrs have often been depicted in paintings with an adult Jesus in the center. However, as the Vietnamese-looking Our Lady of Lavang became popular, she and the baby Jesus "displaced" the adult Jesus as the central figure in many of these religious artworks.

Similarly, representations of Our Lady of Lavang are often displayed within steps near large panels depicting graphic scenes of the public execution of Vietnamese martyrs. The martyrs are usually portrayed as the most helpless person, kneeling on the ground with their limbs restrained, and near them are tools of execution, such as swords, saws, and metal chains. The visual pairing of Our Lady of Lavang and Vietnamese Catholic martyrs can be found at many important Vietnamese Catholic sites in the United States, including the Vietnamese Marian pilgrimage center in Carthage, Missouri, which attracts nearly one hundred thousand visitors each year, and the Basilica of the National Shrine of the Immaculate Conception in Washington, DC.

Our Lady of Lavang's popularity in the United States is also represented by the growing number of sites and parishes named after her. When the local bishop gave them permission to have a church with a Vietnamese name in 2001, Vietnamese Catholics in Orange County chose to name the church after Our Lady of Lavang. The decision was nearly unanimous and was much anticipated by the community that has played a central role in globalizing the representation of Our Lady of Lavang as a Vietnamese woman. The same community recently raised $25 million to construct a monumental "Our Lady of Lavang Shrine" at Christ Cathedral, the seat of the Diocese of Orange County.

Meanwhile, Vietnamese Catholics in Silicon Valley are building a $45 million parish dedicated to "Our Lady of Lavang." Similar to the case of the Our Lady of Lavang Catholic Church in Orange County, the naming of the church after Our Lady of Lavang was welcomed unanimously by local Vietnamese Catholics. They had wanted to have a church with a Vietnamese name since as early as the late 1970s. After their original church, named St. Patrick's Proto-Cathedral, was heavily damaged by fire, they immediately mobilized to raise funds for the construction project. The new Our Lady of Lavang church was scheduled to open in 2021, but the completion date has been delayed because of several unexpected circumstances, including the ongoing COVID-19 pandemic.

Although there was some initial hesitation to accept the new Vietnamese ethnic image of Our Lady of Lavang (H. D. Nguyen 2007), this depiction has spread to many countries, including the Philippines, where local Catholics embrace her as patroness of Puerto Princesa and Palawan, and, most recently in October 2018, Abu Ghosh, Israel. Beyond her visual image as a Vietnamese woman, Our Lady of Lavang is important to many overseas Vietnamese because she represents their history of coerced displacement and global dispersion. This is clearly evidenced by the integration of the symbolically significant stars in her representations. In 2002, at the twenty-sixth Marian Convention in Lavang, Vietnam, the original Vietnamese-looking Our Lady of Lavang in Vietnam was replaced. The newer version depicts Our Lady of Lavang's headdress decorated with twelve stars. Vietnamese Catholics in Vietnam and abroad have interpreted these stars to represent the ones that Vietnamese boat refugees used to navigate the seas to safety. In the Chapel of Our Lady of Lavang at the Basilica of the National Shrine of the Immaculate Conception in Washington, DC, which was completed in 2005, the stars are decorated throughout the sanctuary as sacred reminders of the Vietnamese people's global dispersion.

Despite their geographical separation from one another, the Vietnamese-looking Our Lady of Lavang represents and facilitates the diasporic reconnection between Vietnamese Catholics around the world, including those in Vietnam. In 2010, a stone engraved with *Cộng Đồng Hải Ngoại* (Overseas Diocese) was placed at the Our Lady of Lavang pilgrimage center during the opening ceremony of the Holy Year. It recognizes overseas Vietnamese Catholics as the twenty-seventh diocese of the Catholic Church in Vietnam. The stone was later buried on the construction ground of a new church at the pilgrimage center, symbolizing the significance of overseas Vietnamese Catholics as a foundation of the Vietnamese Catholic Church in Vietnam and beyond. Meanwhile, a brick from the Basilica of Our Lady of Lavang in Vietnam has been on display at the compound of Christ Cathedral in Orange County, California, where a $12 million shrine for a 12-foot-tall statue of Our Lady of Lavang was installed and completed in 2021.

Today, statues of Our Lady of Lavang have become a popular diplomatic gift from one Vietnamese Catholic community to another in a different country, as I have observed in Germany, Taiwan, Japan, Belgium, the Netherlands, and France. In an email exchange, the former and last president of the Vatican-based Coordinating Office of the Apostolate of Overseas Vietnamese (*Văn Phòng Phối Kết Người Việt Hải Ngoại*) further affirmed that "Our Lady of Lavang . . . symbolizes overseas Vietnamese Catholics' connections to each other and to the Catholic Church in Vietnam." This transnational mediation through the Virgin Mary has also been observed by other studies of Catholic immigrants in the United States (Tweed 1997: 108–130; Horsfall 2000: 381–383; Castañeda-Liles 2018: 146–166).

Vietnamese American Caodaists and the Caodai Mother Goddess

Similar to the case of Vietnamese American Catholics and their holy mother, Vietnamese American Caodaists have turned toward the Caodai Mother

Goddess as a locus for reconnecting to other faithful and recentralizing their community. They revived and maintained devotion to the Mother Goddess overseas as early as the 1990s, nearly a decade before such practice would be allowed again in Vietnam since communism gained control of the Caodai Holy See and removed the recognition of Caodaism as a religion in 1975. In doing so, Vietnamese American Caodaists claimed that their beliefs and practices were "religiously pure," as they were not influenced by politics, as in the case of Caodaists in Vietnam.

In the early 1990s, Vietnamese American Caodaists constructed the first altar for the Mother Goddess in Southern California at the Lampson Temple. Although space in the temple was crowded because it was modeled from a garage attached to a small home, these Caodaists initiated the revival of Mother Goddess rituals in the United States. The altar shared the same space as another one for the Caodai Supreme Being, although normally these altars should be in separate rooms or buildings.

Their temple practices were simple, mostly consisting of chanting. Rituals and prayers were not accompanied by traditional music, a fundamental tool for inviting the Mother Goddess and her thirteen female companions to descend to the place of worship. Because they did not have enough members who could play various traditional instruments and properly form an orchestra, they could not organize a grand annual Mother Goddess Festival.

The second Mother Goddess shrine built in Southern California was completed on July 3, 1999, under the leadership of the Caodai Religious Province of California.[11] This shrine was larger than the first one at the Caodai Lampson Temple. It was able to comfortably accommodate more than two hundred people. It was located inside a Christian Church that was purchased as the new administrative headquarters for the Caodai Religious Province of California. Because the location was on Chestnut Street in Westminster, home of the largest Little Saigon Vietnamese ethnic enclave outside of Vietnam, it became popularly known as the Chestnut Temple. With the new Mother Goddess shrine located in a larger building, Vietnamese American Caodaists have been able to worship the Mother Goddess in a space appropriately separated from the Caodai Supreme Being. The altar is in the center of the room. Standing in the center of the altar is a plaque decorated with three vertical lines in classical Chinese characters. From left to right, the first line reads 九位仙娘 (Nine Immortal Maidens), followed by 瑤池金母 (Golden Mother of the Jade Pond or *Diêu Trì Kim Mẫu*), and lastly, 白云洞诸圣 (Sages of the White Cloud or *Bạch Vân Động Chư Thánh*). Normally, surrounding the altar are religious offerings, such as a vase with flowers, a cup of wine, a plate of fresh fruits, and an incense-stick holder. In front of and facing the altar is an open space of worship with rows of white pillows neatly arranged on the floor.

During weekdays at six in the evening and at noon on Sundays closest to the fifteenth and thirtieth of each lunar month, Caodaists regularly congregate at the Chestnut Temple for prayers. The ceremonies for the Mother Goddess and the Caodai Supreme Being are held at the same time. Usually, in Vietnam, the prayers occur at different times—at noon for the Caodai Supreme Being and six in the evening for the Mother Goddess—so that practitioners can participate in both rituals. However, according to my informants, most Vietnamese American Caodaists can only devote half of their Sundays to temple activities, and some must rely on other people's assistance for transportation to the temple. With the concurrent services, female Caodaists, more so than their male counterparts, tend to participate in rituals for the Mother Goddess.

As a part of its pursuit for religious purity, the Vietnamese American Caodai community has also been keen on reviving the annual ceremony for the Mother Goddess, which was prohibited in 1975 and only allowed to resume in 1998 by the Vietnamese communist government. They initially faced the challenge of not having enough members who could play traditional instruments and collectively form an orchestra. Once this problem was resolved as the community expanded and attracted more followers, Vietnamese American Caodaists immediately revived religious rituals for the Mother Goddess. However, because only the Caodai Holy See is allowed to organize the annual Mother Goddess Festival according to religious doctrines, they decided to initiate a new tradition as an offshoot. They called their celebration the "Observation of the Annual Mother Goddess Festival" (*Lễ Tưởng Niệm Hội Yến Diêu Trì*), which has been held on the fifteenth of the eighth month of each lunar calendar year.

Through the Observation of the Annual Mother Goddess Festival, Vietnamese American Caodaists have struggled to preserve religious purity as it was before Caodai religious life was repressed in 1975 under communism. As in Vietnam, they have embraced the Mother Goddess ceremony as the most important annual religious holiday even though attendance is not compulsory. Vietnamese American Caodai leaders put strong emphasis on rituals for the Mother Goddess Festival, replicating and reciting specific details as noted in Caodai religious books printed before 1975. As an informant explained to me, everything from the flower arrangements to the footsteps and hand gestures of ritual performers have to be carefully presented with precise accuracy to reflect the "beauty of the Caodai Mother Goddess."

Vietnamese Caodaists have been diligent in their quest for purity since they arrived in the United States, with the trauma of displacement further compounded by ethnic and religious marginalization. These Vietnamese Caodaists have transformed their refugee status into a privileged position in which they have been chosen by God to protect Caodaism from the impurity of communism in Vietnam. Although they could not organize the annual Mother Goddess Festival, an event that can only be hosted by the Caodai Holy See, this new tradition of "observation" of the celebration reflects Vietnamese American Caodaists' efforts to protect their religion from communist infiltration and disruption due to forced exodus.

Conclusion

The nation is a ghostly matter for Vietnamese (Kwon 2008; Ho Tai 2021). This is particularly so for Vietnamese Catholics and Caodaists who were forced to flee Vietnam as religious and political refugees (Nguyen Y. T. 2018; Nguyen N. H. C. 2009). They cannot claim Vietnam, or the United States, as home; both are sites of mourning and trauma that continue to haunt them and their descendants (Nguyễn-Võ 2005). Holy mothers, specifically the Vietnamese-looking Our Lady of Lavang and Caodai Mother Goddess, are the crucibles of faith for many Vietnamese Catholics and Caodaists. Following the fall of Saigon to communism in 1975, Vietnamese Catholic and Caodai refugees figuratively carried their holy mothers with them on their journeys of escape and transplanted their faith on new soil and in a new nation.

Vietnam is the gravesite of their dead country (the Republic of South Vietnam), one that they have not and cannot properly bury or forget. For both Vietnamese Catholics and Caodaists, South Vietnam under the Republic of South Vietnam government was a national haven where their religious practices flourished and were protected from communism. More than 70 percent of Catholics from northern Vietnam fled to the South in 1954 to escape communism (Hansen 2009). Meanwhile, the number of Caodaists surged as the religion worked toward harmonizing Western and Eastern religious teachings for a modern society (Hoskins 2015; 2012a; 2012b). The "death" of the Republic of South Vietnam and their inability to properly mourn for it because of the ensuing religious persecutions under communism have created a near-apocalyptic moment that continues to haunt them. As refugees and minorities in the United States, many Vietnamese Catholics and Caodaists have not been able to return to present-day Vietnam to reclaim the ghostly remnants of their past and to commemorate their dead nation.

Meanwhile, the United States has not fully integrated Vietnamese Catholics and Caodaists as citizens. Even though religious diversity and freedom constitute a fundamental right in American society, religion has become the proxy through which Vietnamese refugees are marginalized to the fringes of society as ethnic racial minorities (Ninh T.-H. 2017). As Catholics, they have been racialized in American society as ethnically unrepresentative of Catholicism or as not being "truly Catholic" because they are Asians practicing a "Western" religion. Meanwhile, their coethnic Caodai counterparts have been racialized as the only ones who could be "truly Caodaists" because their Vietnamese ethnicity is conflated with the religion. These processes of racialization have essentialized ethnicity and religion for the Vietnamese faithful, misconstruing the fundamental religious tenet and historical legacy of universalism in Catholicism and Caodaism, which both welcome followers across different ethnic backgrounds.

On the basis of ethnographic data collected in California, which has the largest overseas Vietnamese population, I argue that Vietnamese refugees and their U.S.-reared descendants have been able to recentralize their fragmented communities by innovatively adapting their devotional practices to holy mothers. In particular, Vietnamese American Catholics have transformed the image of Our Lady of Lavang into a Vietnamese woman and transplanted this image to other parts of the world. Meanwhile, their coethnic Caodaist counterparts have revived traditional religious rituals for the Caodai Mother Goddess, which were repressed and prohibited for many years by the Vietnamese communist government. Through their shared devotion to holy mothers, these Vietnamese American faithful have also rebuilt relations with coethnic coreligionists living throughout the world. For both the Vietnamese American Catholic and Caodai groups, holy mothers have emerged as emblems of their deterritorialized nation in the diaspora. From this positionality of "in-between-ness, in-both-ness, and in-beyond-ness" in relation to Vietnam and the United States (Fernandez 2003: 265), Vietnamese American Catholics and Caodaists have evoked holy mothers to reimagine their nation. Neither the country of resettlement nor the homeland constitutes their sole place of belonging. Instead, it is from this point of the plurality of vision, seeing these worlds as occurring together "contrapuntally" (Said 1984: 172), that they have reenvisioned their nation of belonging in contemporary global society.

14

THE PRESERVATION AND PRODUCTION

OF DIASPORIC KNOWLEDGE

Oral History and Archival Contributions

THUY VO DANG

Against Historical Erasure

n 2016, a small pocket diary, its cover still a vibrant shade of red despite having traversed rough waters, came to the University of California, Irvine (UCI) Libraries Southeast Asian Archive as part of James Schill's collection of photographs of Southeast Asian refugees.[1] The author of the diary remains unknown. Their journey is detailed meticulously in English, French, and Vietnamese. The first diary entry, made on June 17, 1979, provides the boat number and departure point—Cà Mau, Vietnam. This pocket diary fits neatly in the palm of my hand, yet its miniature size belies the weighty documentation of suffering and resilience of an individual during a monthlong journey in the South China Sea.

After some thirty days of boat travel that involved capture by Vietnamese authorities, two robberies by Thai pirates, water and food shortages, and stormy seas, the 403 passengers and two new babies born aboard arrived in Malaysia. The diary writer's multilingual ability might have positioned them to serve as boat spokesperson or translator, as a researcher might surmise after studying the diary entries closely. The diary writer was taken ashore along with a few other passengers and asked by the authorities to present their papers. Since they did not have any documentation, the writer reflected, "So we are illegal immigrants and must be punished . . . jailed."[2]

Because of the precarious nature of their journeys, refugees who have been displaced and exiled from their homelands often carry very few official documents and little material culture that might serve as evidence of their identities or experiences. As an archival object, this diary provides a firsthand account of a "boat person" experience. Its historical importance is clear. What may be less clear is the process of acquiring, preserving, and providing access to a record like this. Archival scholars and practitioners use the term *record* to mean a "written or printed work of a legal or official nature that may be used as evidence or proof; a document" (Pearce-Moses 2005: 326).[3] Thus, the privileging of the written record by governments and archives presents challenges and possibilities for populations forcibly displaced. Without the ability to validate their identities, some face tremendous barriers to proving their refugee status. Still, others might find a newfound liberation from the trappings of their former lives with the absence of such records. After this phase of reliance on the record for substantiating claims to personhood, the same population might find that such records become important in their struggle to preserve their history and challenge the historical erasure that often results from the loss of a homeland. This diary presents an interesting site of inquiry into the process of meaning making for Vietnamese refugee history. The diary's author is unknown, but the documentation of despair, struggle, loss, fear, and hope provides a rare and raw snapshot of a moment that has captured the world's fascination. Despite the anonymity of the diary's owner, this record provides a sought-after bottom-up perspective of an individual whose life was upended by geopolitical forces beyond their control but who also made choices and took action during their journey from Vietnam. From my time working with Vietnamese refugee narratives, I instantly recognized the research value this record would provide for the evolving scholarship on Vietnamese Americans.

Anne Frank and Dorothy Fujita-Rony argue that, "given the general marginalization of Vietnamese American issues in national media venues, the [Southeast Asian] Archive offers a critical intervention for all those who have a stake in Vietnamese American history" (Fujita-Rony and Frank 2003: 153–164). The "origin story" of the Southeast Asian Archive (SEAA) as a grassroots effort at the onset is parallel to many other projects to preserve and make available Vietnamese American history to a wider public. While this chapter does not cover all the institutional or grassroots repositories that preserve and provide access to Vietnamese diasporic history, it critically examines the role of archives and oral history projects in this important work of curating the past for future generations.

Since the moment the diary came into our custody at the UCI Libraries, it has been rehoused, described, and digitized. The surrogate is available online through Calisphere, a union database where archives and libraries throughout California can publish their digital or digitized assets.[4] Like many other primary source materials that provide insight into the Vietnamese refugee experience, the diary is part of a collection given to the SEAA by a non-Vietnamese collector. James Schill was a foreign service officer during the Vietnam-American War for the United States Department of State and USAID. He worked on Southeast Asian refugee resettlement beginning in 1975. At the time we acquired the collection of Schill's photographs, he signaled that there would also be a very special item—this anonymous pocket diary. He could not remember how he came to acquire this object. It is essentially an orphaned work, as the creator remains unknown. We decided to digitize this resource and make it available with the understanding that its owner might one day surface and request the scans be taken down from the website where it is available to the public, or even ask for the diary to be returned.[5]

In an often-referenced scene in *Star Wars: Episode II, Attack of the Clones*, Jedi archivist Jocasta Nu tells a puzzled Obi-Wan Kenobi that, "if an item does not appear in the record, it does not exist."[6] Her firm and resolute claim goes against the vernacular knowledge that Obi-Wan carries into the Jedi Temple Archives as he searches for a planet that has been deleted from the database. All over the internet, one can find this popular culture example used to critique history books and all they leave out. I often think of this moment in the film when I work with oral history and archival records of Vietnamese Americans. The Indochinese conflicts that produced the largest refugee exodus from Asia have been explored often by scholars and cultural producers, yet what Vietnamese American community members often express is their feeling of being left out of or misrepresented by this history. Perhaps, like the missing planet, the South Vietnam known to the Vietnamese American diaspora has been willfully deleted and to find evidence of its existence requires a deeper attention to the vernacular spaces where it may remain. Historians know well that archives are incomplete and are often created by those in power to further solidify their positions within the halls of history. Where do we look to find the narratives left out, erased, or maligned? When faced with historical erasure, cast as "losers," "puppets," or "victims" of the Vietnam War, the Vietnamese refugee community responded with local, grassroots efforts to preserve their stories for themselves and future generations. Their efforts to create new archives as interventions in the production of knowledge may be instructive for other groups faced with the tremendous challenge of documenting trauma, collecting materials that have been dispersed, and piecing together fragments of lives torn apart by war and displacement.

In the early years of diaspora, archives and other repositories of cultural memory for Vietnamese refugees were often initiated with materials collected by non-Vietnamese people who had some ties to the community or experience with the war. The SEAA reflects this history in the collections developed over the years. Founded in 1987 by Anne Frank, subject librarian for Orange County, California, in the UCI Libraries, it has since become an established repository of Vietnamese, Cambodian, Lao, and Hmong diasporic history. The alignment of these population histories through U.S.

militarism against communist revolutionary movements and the colonial occupation by France tie these diaspora communities together in significant
ways. Records created in the 1970s and 1980s often refer to peoples escaping
from Cambodia, Laos, and Vietnam as "Indochinese" refugees. Community
organizers and scholars of Southeast Asian Diaspora studies have pushed
back against this problematic formulation that centers the French colonial
legacy and advocated for ethnic specificity whenever possible or Southeast
Asian as the preferred collective descriptor.[7]

In 1985, Vietnamese American community members approached the libraries to start collecting materials that could help document the growing
population in the Orange County, California, region. Frank took on this daunt-
ing task in a slow and steady way, bringing in community members for their
valuable input and resources, particularly the donation of monographs and
archival materials. From a single desk drawer in her office, the SEAA grew
to claim a 645-square-foot reading room of its own and then became professionalized as a distinctive collection in Special Collections and Archives
around the mid-2000s. Frank retired in 2007 after twenty years of steadfast
stewardship of an archive that has often been taught as a model of a "community-based archives" (Wright et al. 2008: article 5). While housed and supported by a large institution, the SEAA can more accurately be described as
a "community-centered archives," advancing a model of archival work based
on collaboration with community stakeholders, critical interrogation of our
own collections and knowledge gaps, shared authority with communities,
and flexibility in how we work with diverse groups. Since its founding, the
SEAA has worked collaboratively with local communities and a network of
Southeast Asian Diaspora studies scholars to document their histories. Meaningful relationships established as a result of these community-university collaborations are driven by the need for Southeast Asian diaspora communities to take a prominent role in determining how to share their histories with
future generations. The establishment of the Orange County and Southeast
Asian Archive (OC and SEAA) Center in 2015 solidified UCI Libraries' commitment to fostering community-centered archives.

The Personal Is Archival: Reflections on Curating
Vietnamese Diasporic History

My first time entering the University of California, Irvine's Southeast Asian
Archive was during the summer of 2001, a few months before I began my
graduate program in Ethnic studies at the University of California, San Diego.
I was finally a bona fide researcher, being paid to conduct archival research
for my adviser. The reading room was located in a corner of the third floor

of Langson Library, the main library in one of the original buildings on campus, and it was often staffed by Anne Frank herself, along with a student assistant. Each time I visited the SEAA, I would write in my name and research purpose on a clipboard greeting patrons by the entrance. I pulled file folders from metal filing cabinets that lined one wall of the room and was allowed to take materials a few doors down to make photocopies. I read the *Người Việt Daily* newspapers stacked within large gray acid-free boxes and pulled periodicals such as *Thời Mới* and *Phụ Nữ Gia Đình* for closer examination.

After that initial summer, I gained confidence with navigating the physical holdings of the SEAA, and I would return a few years later to conduct research for my own work on Vietnamese American anticommunism (Vo Dang 2005: 64–86). The SEAA became essential for my journey as a scholar and community activist, providing access to Vietnamese language materials that I would be hard-pressed to find as easily elsewhere. As I conducted ethnographic and oral history research on the Vietnamese community in San Diego, I depended on this archive for historical context on the Vietnamese diaspora.

A decade after my relationship with the SEAA began, I was appointed the project director for Viet Stories: Vietnamese American Oral History Project (VAOHP), based in the Department of Asian American Studies at UCI under the direction of Professor Linda Trinh Vo. Viet Stories assembles the life stories of Vietnamese Americans in Southern California and involves university-community partnerships as well as a program for training undergraduate students, many coming from Vietnamese American families, to conduct and process oral histories. Since 2011, this project has collected over 450 oral histories through professional, student, and community volunteer interviewers.

By this time, the SEAA had undergone major transitions with Anne Frank's retirement in 2007; the reassignment of stewardship to Christina J. Woo, a research librarian with a portfolio that included many diverse fields; and the administrative transfer of the SEAA to its current position within the Department of Special Collections and Archives. As project director for the VAOHP, I worked closely with the head of Special Collections and Archives at the time. She provided technical expertise and the preservation and access vision for the partnership. We were building a "community-centered" collection of digital oral histories, with me working on the front line for engagement with the Vietnamese community to collect these stories and the SEAA (under the Special Collections umbrella) serving as the repository for preserving and providing access to them. This partnership produced fast results. We were able to launch a public access website with eighty processed oral histories within the first year of the project. Each oral history contained an audio recording, transcripts in Vietnamese or English, and narrator photographs. Each oral history had the appropriate consent and release forms to allow for perpetual stewardship by the UCI Libraries and wide access for the public.

Two years after I began my work on Viet Stories, I was appointed to steward the SEAA. I did not have formal training in library or archival studies, but my work with building a born digital oral history collection along with my subject expertise on Southeast Asian Diaspora studies enabled the transition into this role. I have grown in my role as curator for the Southeast Asian Archive, expanding my portfolio to include the role of research librarian for Asian American studies. The Asian American Studies Department at UCI was established just a few years after the SEAA, and the focus on knowledge production about historically marginalized communities aligns well with the work of community archives.

As a Vietnamese American child refugee, an oral historian, and a steward of archival collections, I have had many moments of profound privilege and joy and moments of grief and trauma that inflect my work on Viet Stories and in the SEAA. During an oral history interview, I was listening to a narrator share her story of life in 1940s Vietnam in a family headed by a wealthy patriarch, but as the child of a second wife relegated to the role of a household servant. During and after the interview, I felt deep appreciation for my role of stewarding a story and perspective I had not been exposed to before. And I wondered how many others would be able to learn from the resilience of this woman who sat before me describing the wet clothes she hung to dry each day after school because she only had two outfits to wear despite being the daughter of one of the richest men in Vietnam at the time. Knowing that her experience would be part of an archive, adding depth and nuance to the stories that would circulate about our community, I felt pride and joyful purpose. On other occasions, when I provide orientations or instruction to students and community members using materials from SEAA collections, I am often filled with a sense of purpose in this role. I remind students to be critical, peeling back the layers of archival work to reveal how decisions are made so that my listeners might have a better understanding of the famous concept that "who controls the past controls the future" (Orwell, Pimlott, and Davison 1989).

On Veterans Day in 2020, I received an email to my work address from a Vietnamese American, sharing a set of images from the Mỹ Lai Massacre in 1968 with a narrative that urged me not to forget the criminals among the celebrated veterans of the Vietnam War. Without a trigger warning, I saw violent images of mostly women and children, bodies splayed on the ground or in shallow graves, some close-up faces in excruciating pain and anguish. I felt sickened and enraged. I immediately recalled a book of photography gifted to me in college by a well-meaning friend. They were images taken by famous photographers of the Vietnam War. As I flipped through that book of photos back then, I cried until my body shook. I will never forget the emotional and physical toll of seeing such violence on bodies that look like my own, exhibited without a warning of the damage they might do. These types of materials serve an important role as records and archival documentation, but there should be an ethics and care that we take into consideration when we choose to provide access to them. Additionally, stewards of these visual materials should consider a critical engagement with how images have been deployed for memory projects.[8] Archival practitioners have written about "vicarious trauma" in this line of work, using a concept adapted from the mental health field that refers to ways in which those who work with people or materials affected by trauma are also affected themselves.[9] Whether it is vicarious trauma as an archives steward or inherited trauma based on my identity as a Vietnamese American that informs my response to these images, the more important point is how we might consider allowing for our hybrid identities to inform this work. Care for these historical records should also involve respecting and caring for the potential user communities, particularly the communities represented in the collection.

A few years into my work at the SEAA, we received materials from another former foreign service officer, Lionel Rosenblatt. His records were quite extensive, documenting the refugee camps throughout Southeast Asia. They also included state-sponsored materials created as training guides for working with refugees. As I selected materials from this collection for a class exhibit, I encountered a folder with images of deceased Cambodians at a refugee camp in Thailand. They were victims of brutality, likely at the hands of camp guards, as the redacted document included with the photographs suggested. Recalling my own encounters with such images, I flagged these few photos and worked with my colleagues to rehouse them into envelopes labeled with a trigger warning. This example might seem trite when we consider the widely circulated images of refugee suffering in the 1980s that contributed to the Western world's "compassion fatigue" toward Southeast Asians or even promoted "trauma porn," a perverse fascination with the suffering of others combined with inaction.[10] However, I believe that archival stewardship requires an ethics of care and empathy that challenges objectivity and neutrality as governing principles in archival work. Archivist Jessica Tai argues for a practice of cultural humility, which differs from the often-used concept of cultural competency because it "entails actively denouncing archival neutrality, requiring the continual and visible disclosure of one's own positionality" (Tai 2021: 3). Part of an emergent generation of archivists who insist that radical care be an embedded archival practice, Tai and others challenge me to consider how my situated knowledge informs my work as a steward of my own community's history. I take an approach that is consultative rather than authoritative, even when administrators or students might look to me to act as an authority on Vietnamese diasporic history. As with collecting oral histories from people or communities that have survived individual and collective trauma, we must "first, do no harm" and then consider and grapple with the context in which these materials were created and who their intended audience is/will be.

Multiplicity and Memory Work: Collecting Oral Histories of Vietnamese Americans for Public Access

"If I didn't define myself for myself, I would be crunched into other people's fantasies for me and eaten alive." While Audre Lorde spoke specifically of Black determinism, the quote suggests that what is at stake in the process of knowledge production is the misrepresentation or erasure of people's experiences and cultural memories, which likely leads to the circulation of more distorted histories.[11] Certainly for Vietnamese Americans, history has, more often than not, been written for us. While documentation such as news articles, government reports, organization records, and photographs could be collected in abundance as a result of the highly controversial and well-documented Vietnam-American War and refugee exodus, the narratives coming from Vietnamese refugees and immigrants themselves were not as readily available. For Vietnamese refugees (and other groups that have endured significant historical traumas), oral history has been an important method for the preservation of bottom-up perspectives, often left out of mainstream narratives in both the United States and a reunified Vietnam. Oral historians collect personal narratives for their potential to simultaneously broaden the lens on history by including a multiplicity of voices *and* zoom in on particular perspectives and experiences. Personal narratives, when combined with other primary and secondary sources, allow for researchers to understand the macro, meso, and micro scale of the Vietnam-American War, refugee exodus, and rebuilding of Vietnamese lives in diaspora. Undertaking an oral history project with Vietnamese Americans often requires a synchronicity of factors: timing, resources, and an understanding of the complexity of this identity—the ways in which it has often been tethered to anticommunism, indebtedness to the American nation-state, and the Asian American "model minority" myth in a racialized and stratified society.

Critical refugee studies scholar Yen Le Espiritu has insisted on a close examination of the workings of history and memory for Vietnamese Americans. She writes, "like other communities in exile, Vietnamese in the United States feel keenly the urgency to forge unified histories, identities, and memories" (Espiritu Y. L. 2014: 3). Similarly, Viet Thanh Nguyen has insisted that "all wars are fought twice, the first time on the battlefield, the second time in memory" (Nguyen V. T. 2016: 4). Indeed, the struggle over memory and history may take the form of archives creation, preserving Vietnamese American and South Vietnamese history, which has been maligned in mainstream narratives or erased in institutions in both the United States and Vietnam. These efforts to claim history have often adhered to strict limits of a Vietnamese diasporic identity rooted in anticommunist and heteropatriarchal values. Vietnamese diasporic anticommunism refuses the socialist regime in Vietnam and extends to a denouncement of China but has historically aligned with the U.S. empire. The extension of South Vietnam into the diaspora means that an extension of the allyship with the United States is fundamental to the narrative of why Vietnamese became Americans. Lan Duong and Isabelle Thuy Pelaud remind us that, "while U.S. empire and Việt Nam's human rights abuses should be critiqued, scholars also need to be critical of the Vietnamese diasporic community's efforts to construct a monolithic discourse about citizenship and cultural membership, one that complies with the disciplinary logic of being 'with' or 'against' one's community" (Duong and Pelaud 2012: 241–269). Heeding this call for more nuanced and inclusive representation in the work of archives creation, we must be ever mindful of how archives might reproduce dominant systems of oppression even as they attempt to counter the erasure of Vietnamese diasporic history.

Archives creation and oral history projects are nuanced and complex spaces for community members to intervene in public history.[12] The process of remembering the past to preserve it for the present and future is a political project involving struggles for power. Moreover, archives creators and stewards play key roles in determining what records have historical value, who should have access to them, and how they might be made discoverable. Transparency in archival work is essential, as others have argued, but is often a neglected part of the work.[13] Verne Harris, the archivist for Nelson Mandela's papers, explains the difference between remembering and "remembrancing." While remembering is a process that is imperfect, it allows for a multiplicity of narratives to emerge and often raises more complexity about documented events in the past. However, remembrancing is memory work that avoids complexity and often entails the use of memory as an instrument of power.[14] Collecting oral histories of Vietnamese American experiences with the end goal of making these stories publicly accessible is an example of how we might evoke remembering in our community. Projects that are organized around the recreation of an imagined heroic Vietnamese past, such as monuments or statues erected in sites around Vietnamese American strongholds like Little Saigon in Orange County, California, are remembrancing projects that attempt to reinforce heteropatriarchal power in the cultural history of the diaspora. In the Vietnamese American community, the flag of the Republic of Vietnam, adopted in many U.S. municipalities as the "Heritage and Freedom Flag" for the Vietnamese community, has often been wielded for the purpose of remembrancing. During the month of April each year, the flag is raised throughout Little Saigon to commemorate the fall of Saigon. First-generation Vietnamese Americans' longtime affiliation with the U.S. Republican Party and continued adherence to anticommunist politics have often been performed in public and used as mechanisms for policing parameters of Vietnamese American community and identity. For example, during the final months of 2020, Vietnamese Americans were featured in many mainstream media articles as outliers in their support of Donald Trump (Republican) while the majority of Asian American Pacific Islander communities leaned toward Joe Biden (Democrat).[15] Frequent rallies and car parades in Orange County's Little Saigon where Trump flags were displayed next to the Heritage and Freedom Flag prompted much debate, turmoil, and conflict in the community, and especially between the first and second generations. Much like the fissures during wartime Vietnam, when families had divided loyalties between North and South, tensions boiled over in Vietnamese America during the presidential election. The social media and ethnic media narratives that circulated in the community propped up Trump as a champion for freedom and democracy and a "strongman" figure who would stand up to China. Linking this narrative to a deeply entrenched history of anticommunism, their alignment with white supremacy was packaged as loyalty to their Vietnamese heritage, particularly in the way they claimed the South Vietnam flag. When attached to such political imperatives, the flag becomes an instrument of power rather than a prompt for remembering multiple, complex, and sometimes conflicting Vietnamese pasts.

Attending to these complexities must be part of any archival or oral history effort for the Vietnamese diaspora. As we build spaces for remembering to unfold in a way that can add more layers of meaning to the stories told about the Vietnam War, Vietnam the country, and the Vietnamese diaspora, multiplicity will allow for many truths to simultaneously exist and shape public discourse in the United States and the world. An understanding of the complexities of the Vietnamese American community requires a nuanced approach, radical empathy, and respectful care. Preserving history in this community requires not turning a blind eye to all the voices in our community, no matter how problematic they might be. In 2020, we confronted a global pandemic and the heightened awareness of anti-Blackness in American society. This context has reinvigorated my commitment to archives creation and to being more intentional in surfacing a multiplicity of narratives. The dominant community discourse on anticommunism might be questioned or challenged if we provide other narratives that push against this limit of community membership and meaning making.

Community archives arise from the need to address the silences of institutional memory projects. Inspired by the work of Verne Harris, Michelle

Caswell advances theories and approaches to community archives (Caswell, Cole, and Griffith 2018). Caswell uses the concept of "symbolic annihilation," drawn from feminist and media studies scholarship, to refer to the absence of disenfranchised groups from the historical record. When we do not see ourselves or people who look like us in the historical record, we feel that our experiences are not valid or important. Caswell argues that community archives can counter this marginalization and absence by fostering "representational belonging." Community archives provide a space for historically marginalized communities to see themselves in history. This recognition may foster a sense of belonging and provide Vietnamese in the diaspora with platforms for claiming space as well as the potential for alignment and allyship with other historically marginalized communities.

Collecting, preserving, and sharing historical materials and stories is often unglamorous hard work (and heart work) that has also disproportionately fallen on the shoulders of female or female-identified individuals. Whether in formal institutional archives or historical societies or among memory keepers for families or organizations, the work is often undervalued and underpaid (if paid at all). Replicating other divisions of labor in society, memory keeping has problematically become an extension of ways that women are expected to reproduce culture through maintaining our connections to the past. How do we continue to push back? In my experience, we must find multiple avenues, such as making visible these gendered expectations, insisting this labor be seen and valued, and claiming the intellectual contributions we make in the work of archives creation. For example, a SEAA collection of scrapbooks was donated by a former Hong Kong refugee camp director, but his wife created the six scrapbooks, meticulously assembling news clippings, photographs, correspondences, and other ephemera that documented a three-year period.[16] At the time he donated these scrapbooks, his wife had already passed away. While the materials highlighted his work, we named the collection after her, the creator, rather than him, the donor. It is important to consider how these practices of titling, attribution, and acknowledgments might call attention to the tremendous labor of those working "behind the scenes" to preserve cultural memory. Theorizing the intersection between cultural memory and feminist studies, Marianne Hirsch and Valerie Smith remind us to incorporate "feminist modes of knowing and listening that facilitate the work of memory and transmission" (Hirsch and Smith 2002: 1–19). In *The Memorykeepers*, Dorothy Fujita-Rony examines women's memory keeping across generations and contexts of migration. Fujita-Rony highlights ways this form of labor is gendered and argues that "women's memory-keeping creates an autonomous space for the critique of patriarchal structures and expectations" (Fujita-Rony 2021:93). Women make up more than 60 percent of the mainstream archival profession in the United States. Among Vietnamese diaspora memory keepers, there is a dearth of public data on how many open and accessible archival and oral history projects are conducted by female or female-identified individuals. Two prominent examples are efforts grounded in a community archives framework and headed or founded by women: Viet Stories: The Vietnamese American Oral History Project (VAOHP) originating in Southern California and the Vietnamese in the Diaspora Digital Archive (ViDDA) originating in Texas provide examples of the efforts by Vietnamese Americans to preserve and make available a multiplicity of sources and voices by the community, for the community. Emerging from sites with two of the largest diasporic populations, these projects collect, preserve, and disseminate life stories of Vietnamese Americans as an intervention in public history.

With public access as the ultimate goal, these efforts highlight how, when faced with a scarcity of primary sources, we must proactively create them ourselves. Using oral history as the methodology for building a record of Vietnamese American lives, these projects and others expand the avenues in historical research. Oral history has existed for much longer than the professionalized form it has taken since the 1940s in the United States. Oral traditions and storytelling practices are part of the rich heritage of cultures around the world. The modern approach, however, rests on the work of recording, preserving, and making available these stories. These three aspects are crucial to the way that knowledge about underrepresented communities can be circulated. The interpretive work that might arise from these oral history projects may include exhibitions, book publications, digital collections, and documentary films, to name a few examples. If the intentions behind these projects are to promote multiplicity in perspectives of the past, they have great potential to challenge the symbolic annihilation of marginalized communities from the historical record.

Examples of Vietnamese American/Diaspora Archives and Oral History Projects

The following is a curated list of oral history or storytelling projects and archives on Vietnamese Americans or Vietnamese in the diaspora, with descriptions pulled from their websites. This list is not meant to be comprehensive but may provide an access point for further discovery, research, and analysis.

> Viet Stories: Vietnamese American Oral History Project at the University of California, Irvine assembles, preserves, and disseminates the life stories of Vietnamese Americans in Southern California. http://ucispace.lib.uci.edu/handle/10575/1614.

The Vietnamese in the Diaspora Digital Archive (ViDDA) documents a grassroots collection of interviews conducted and supported through the Vietnamese American Heritage Foundation (VAHF) to provide oral history resources about the Vietnamese community living abroad for students, researchers, and the general public. https://vietdiasporastories.omeka.net/.

The Vietnamese Diaspora Project works to preserve the memories of those affected by the Vietnam War and the aftermath, which led to one of the most tragic diasporas in recent history. https://vietnamesediaspora.com/.

The Vietnam War Oral History Project (VNWOHP) gathers, documents, preserves, and disseminates recorded interviews, written records, and historical artifacts pertaining to the history and consequences of the Vietnam War. https://vietnamwarohp.com/.

The Arlington County Public Library and master's degree students from Virginia Tech's Department of Urban Affairs and Planning (National Capital Region) collaborated on a project to collect the stories of the Vietnamese community who immigrated to, shopped at, or owned businesses in Arlington, Virginia's Clarendon neighborhood when it was known as Little Saigon during the late 1970s and early 1980s. https://littlesaigonclarendon.com/.

Viet Chronicle is an ongoing oral history project that records and archives the life stories of Vietnamese Americans who settled in the New Orleans metropolitan area. http://hnoc.minisisinc.com/thnoc/catalog/3/26727.

The "Becoming Texans, Becoming Americans" Oral History Project documents the stories of Vietnamese refugees who arrived in North Texas after the fall of Saigon in April 1975. https://www.baylor.edu/oralhistory/doc.php/338760.pdf.

Project Yellow Dress is a storytelling platform that highlights the histories, voices, and experiences of the Southeast Asian diaspora. http://www.projectyellowdress.com.

Archives/Museums

The UCI Libraries Southeast Asian Archive collects, preserves, and makes accessible primary and secondary source materials documenting the history of the Cambodian, Hmong, Laotian, and Vietnamese diaspora. https://seaa.lib.uci.edu.

The Southeast Asian Digital Archive at the University of Massachusetts, Lowell seeks to collect, preserve, and share historical materials related to Southeast Asians in the Greater Lowell area, with particular focus on refugee resettlement and community building from the 1970s to the present. https://www.uml.edu/research/sea-digital-archive/.

The Viet Museum or the Museum of the Boat People and Republic of Vietnam is a museum dedicated to the history of Vietnamese Americans and their journey from Vietnam to the United States. https://www.sanjose.org/listings/viet-museum.

TIMELINE OF KEY EVENTS AND SELECTED MILESTONES IN VIETNAMESE AND VIETNAMESE AMERICAN HISTORY, 1900–2021

1904   Phan Bội Châu and collaborators founded Vietnam Moderniza-
        tion Society [*Việt Nam Duy Tân Hội*], launching the "Go East"
        movement to learn from Japan.

1907   A group of modernizing intellectuals founded Eastern Capital
        Public School [*Đông Kinh Nghĩa Thục*] in Hanoi to promote West-
        ern learning and westernization of Vietnam.

        Phan Châu Trinh published his open letter to the French gover-
        nor Paul Beau calling for French-Annamese collaboration to re-
        form the colonial system in the spirit of republican ideals.

1911–13 Phan Xích Long led a millenarian revolt near Saigon-Cholon.

1916   Young King Duy Tân led a failed conspiracy to oppose French
        rule.

1917   Lương Ngọc Quyến led a failed revolt in Thái Nguyên.

1919   Bùi Quang Chiêu announced the Indochinese Constitutionalist
        Party [Đảng Lập Hiến Đông Dương] to support colonial reform
        and greater Vietnamese political and economic rights.

        Phan Châu Trinh, Nguyễn Thế Truyền, Phan Văn Trường, and
        Nguyễn Tất Thành (Hồ Chí Minh) sent a petition to the Peace
        Conference in Versailles demanding political reforms in Annam
        in accordance with republican ideals.

1920   Trần Trọng Kim's *A Brief History of Vietnam* [Việt Nam Sử Lược] was first published. This was the first book of Vietnamese history written by modern methods.

1923   Hồ Chí Minh traveled to Moscow and attended the Stalin School, which trained communist revolutionaries for the Communist International.

1925   Lê Văn Trung founded the Cao Đài church [Đại Đạo Tam Kỳ Phổ Độ] in Tây Ninh.

1927   Nguyễn Thái Học and others founded the Vietnamese Nationalist Party [Việt Nam Quốc Dân Đảng].

1930   The Vietnamese Communist Party [Đảng Cộng Sản Việt Nam] (later changed to Indochinese Communist Party [Đảng Cộng Sản Đông Dương] on order from Moscow) was founded in Hong Kong by Hồ Chí Minh and other communists.

           The Vietnamese Nationalist Party launched a failed armed rebellion in Yên Bái and other towns.

           Villagers in Nghệ An, inspired by communists, revolted, forming "Soviet governments."

1932   Nguyễn Tường Tam (Nhất Linh) and his brothers and collaborators founded the Self-Reliant Literary Group [Tự Lực Văn Đoàn], leading an urban movement for cultural and political reforms.

1933   The Vatican ordained Fr. Nguyễn Bá Tòng as the first Vietnamese bishop.

           Young Emperor Bảo Đại formed a government with the aspiration to assert greater autonomy for the Huế Court vis-à-vis the French. Ngô Đình Diệm was appointed as minister of interior but soon resigned in protest of French policies.

1936–37   The Indochinese Congress was founded, bringing together Vietnamese Trotskyites, Stalinists, nationalists, and other groups to pressure the Popular Front government in France to carry out reforms in Indochina.

1940   The Indochinese Communist Party led a failed revolt in southern Vietnam.

1941   Hồ Chí Minh returned to Vietnam from Moscow via Yen'an, founding the Vietnamese Independence League [Việt Nam Độc Lập Đồng Minh or Việt Minh] in Cao Bằng.

1945 March 9: Japanese forces took control of French Indochina.

April 10: In Huế, Emperor Bảo Đại declared Vietnam independent and appointed Trần Trọng Kim to form a government. The Kim government lifted press restrictions, released political prisoners, instituted educational reform, and mobilized youth.

August 19: Việt Minh supporters seized power in Hanoi.

August 23: Trần Trọng Kim's government resigned, and Bảo Đại abdicated rather than suppressing the Việt Minh.

September 2: Ho Chi Minh declared independence, founded the Democratic Republic of Vietnam (DRV), and appealed to the Soviet Union and the United States for recognition. Hồ's government ordered the arrests and executions of numerous nationalists and Trotskyists. Civil war began between Việt Minh forces and other groups.

1946 March 6: Hồ signed an agreement to allow French troops to return to North Vietnam to replace Chinese nationalist troops.

December 20: Hồ's government launched attacks against French forces, beginning the First Indochina War.

1947 Bảo Đại and various nationalist leaders in exile met in Hong Kong.

1948 Bảo Đại signed the Élysées Accords with France to form a government of independent Vietnam within the French Union.

The State of Vietnam was established, with Bảo Đại as chief of state and Nguyễn Văn Xuân as prime minister.

1949 Hồ sent Việt Minh troops into China to help Chinese communists fight the Chinese nationalist government.

1950 January: Hồ traveled to Peking and Moscow, obtaining Soviet and Chinese recognition for his government. Communist China secretly sent military advisers and aid to help Hồ fight the French.

February: In response, the United States and allies recognized the State of Vietnam as the sole legitimate government of Vietnam.

1953 Hồ's government launched a class struggle in the countryside to eliminate landlords and rich farmers and to rally poor farmers' support. At least 15,000 landlords were executed by 1956 at the end of the campaign.

1954   July: French and Hồ governments signed the Geneva Accords. Vietnam was divided into two zones: the communist North under Hồ and the South under the French. The State of Vietnam refused to sign the accords.

Bảo Đại appointed Ngô Đình Diệm as premier.

August: The flow of more than 800,000 refugees began from North Vietnam to South Vietnam.

More than 100,000 communist cadres and troops in South Vietnam regrouped to North Vietnam, but about 30,000 remained with weapons.

1955   February: U.S. Military Assistance Advisory Group (MAAG) assumed training of South Vietnamese Army after command authority by French was relinquished.

April: "Battle of Saigon": Forces loyal to Ngô Đình Diệm defeated sectarian militias while opposing French attempts to retain control of South Vietnam.

October: Ngô Đình Diệm organized a national referendum that deposed Bảo Đại as chief of state. Ngô Đình Diệm became the founding president of the Republic of Vietnam (RVN) with Saigon as capital.

1956   The South Vietnamese government rejected holding general elections as suggested by the Geneva Accords. Ngô Đình Diệm launched the campaign to denounce communism.

1958   North Vietnam launched campaigns to emulate China's Great Leap Forward and authorized a limited communist insurgency in the South.

A large communist unit attacked a plantation north of Saigon.

1959   Hanoi began to build roads across Laos and Cambodia to send men and materiel to the South. North Vietnam also escalated the campaign to assassinate local officials in South Vietnam.

1960   April: Former government officials and opposition political party leaders called on the Diệm government to institute democratic reform.

November: South Vietnamese military officers launched a failed coup against Ngô Đình Diệm.

December: Under orders from Hanoi, the National Liberation Front (NLF) was secretly founded in South Vietnam to give a legitimate cover for the communist insurgency directed from Hanoi.

1961–62 American aid to the RVN increased. The number of U.S. military advisers in South Vietnam rose to 12,000.

The Diệm government launched the Strategic Hamlet Program to isolate and destroy communist guerrillas.

1963 April–June: a sudden surge of an anti-Diệm Buddhist movement.

November 1: a U.S.-backed military coup killed President Diệm and his brother, Ngô Đình Nhu.

November 24: Lyndon B. Johnson assumed the presidency after the assassination of John Kennedy and affirmed U.S. intention to continue its military and economic support of South Vietnam.

December: Hanoi leaders met and ordered a full military campaign to defeat Saigon in one or two years.

1964 January: General Nguyễn Khánh became the head of state in South Vietnam, lifting restrictions on press freedom and legalizing political parties.

August: U.S. Congress approved the Gulf of Tonkin Resolution, authorizing military action in Vietnam after North Vietnamese patrol boats fired on a U.S. Navy destroyer. North Vietnam sent its first full-sized army regiments into the South.

November: A civilian government under Chief of State Phan Khắc Sửu took power in Saigon.

1965 March: the United States sent first Marine units to defend U.S. bases in South Vietnam in response to rising communist attacks.

At Hanoi's request, Beijing sent troops into North Vietnam to assist in defense and construction. At its peak, the total number of Chinese troops in North Vietnam was at 170,000. They were joined by about 5,000 Soviet troops and 200 North Korean pilots.

June: Phan Khắc Sửu government resigned because of internal conflict, handing power to a Military Council under General Nguyễn Cao Kỳ and Nguyễn Văn Thiệu.

1966–67 U.S. troop numbers in Vietnam rose to 400,000, then to 500,000 the following year.

Thousands of South Korean, Thai, Australian, New Zealand, and Philippine troops joined the United States and South Vietnam in the battle against North Vietnam, now supported by troops from China, the Soviet Union, and North Korea.

The Military Council in Saigon authorized the elections of a Constitutional Assembly, which drafted and approved a new democratic constitution.

Nguyễn Văn Thiệu and Nguyễn Cao Kỳ became president and vice president of the RVN in the first democratic elections in Vietnamese history.

1968   North Vietnam broke an earlier promise and launched the Tết Offensive, a combined assault throughout South Vietnam. Communist forces suffered heavy losses and were defeated, but their ability to launch the large-scale offensive devastated U.S. international prestige and public trust in the U.S. government.

A U.S. military unit killed more than 500 civilians at Mỹ Lai, Quảng Ngãi, while thousands of government personnel and residents were arrested and massacred by communist forces during their monthlong occupation of Huế during the Tết Offensive.

1969   President Richard Nixon ordered the gradual withdrawal of U.S. troops as domestic antiwar sentiments grew.

President Thiệu launched the Land-to-the-Tiller policy, which provided legal ownership of land to millions of landless farmers.

1970   General Lon Nol carried out a coup to dethrone Cambodian King Sihanouk.

South Vietnamese military launched a raid across the Cambodian border to attack the communist base.

1971   South Vietnamese military attacked across the Laotian border to disrupt the communist supply route.

Professor Nguyễn Văn Bông, a leader of the National Progressive Movement [Phong trào Quốc gia Cấp tiến], was about to become prime minister when Hanoi ordered his assassination.

Nguyễn Văn Thiệu was reelected as president in an election in which he was the only candidate.

1972   North Vietnam's tanks crossed the 17th parallel while launching the Spring Offensive across three major fronts in South Vietnam.

With U.S. logistic support, the South Vietnamese military was able to repulse the enemy.

1973   Paris Peace Agreement signed; the United States withdrew its forces from Vietnam.

1975   April 30, communist forces invaded South Vietnam, captured Saigon. The South Vietnamese president ordered his military to surrender.

May: President Gerald Ford signed the Indochina Migration and Refugee Assistance Act of 1975, which granted the refugees special status to enter the country and established a domestic resettlement program.

A 1975 poll indicated that only 36 percent of Americans favored Vietnamese immigration.

More than 130,000 refugees fled from Vietnam, Cambodia, and Laos and were admitted to the United States.

The new communist regime began rounding up tens of thousands of politicians, officials, and military personnel tied to the South Vietnamese government and sending them to hard labor camps (called "reeducation camps"). Later, intellectuals, writers, artists, religious leaders, and leaders of ethnic minority groups were interned. Most were imprisoned in those camps for an average of 4 to 8 years. Some were incarcerated for as long as 17 years.

Approximately 40,000 Hmong refugees fled to Thailand in 1975 and more in the subsequent years. Between 1975 and 1997, 140,200 Hmong and other highland ethnics resettled worldwide, with the great majority in the United States. Between 1975 and 1995, approximately 360,000 Laotian refugees, including Hmong and lowland Lao, fled to Thailand. From 1975 to 1997, 183,907 ethnic Lao were resettled worldwide.

1976   The Socialist Republic of Vietnam was declared. Saigon, the capital of the Republic of Vietnam, was renamed Ho Chi Minh City.

The Vietnam Communist Party's Fourth Party Congress called for the revolutionary transformation of the southern economy into a socialist one, with mass relocation of people and forced collectivization of agriculture, small industry, and commerce. This soon led to a profound economic disaster and a famine, provoking new waves of refugees.

1977   Vietnam was admitted to the United Nations and turned down the U.S. offer for diplomatic normalization without any preconditions.

The Indochina Migration and Refugee Assistance Act of 1975 was amended (under the sponsorship of Senator Edward Kennedy [D-MA]) to permit refugees to adjust to a parolee status and later become permanent residents.

1978   Vietnam invaded Cambodia to topple the Khmer Rouge communist regime in response to the latter's border attacks on Vietnam.

A massive exodus of "boat people" from Vietnam, which lasted into the mid-1980s, marking the second wave of refugees from Indochina.

China canceled all aid to Vietnam partially in response to the latter's persecution of ethnic Chinese and seizure of their property and businesses in South Vietnam. Beginning in April, about 450,000 ethnic Chinese Vietnamese went overland to China or by boat to Hong Kong and Southeast Asian destinations as refugees. Many paid the Vietnamese government large sums of money to be allowed to leave semiofficially. 265,000 would be resettled in China.

Bidong Island, Malaysia, officially opened as a refugee camp for Vietnamese refugees fleeing Vietnam. It operated until October 31, 1991, and about 250,000 Vietnamese had passed through or resided in the camp.

December 15, Do Ngoc Yen established *Nguoi Viet Daily News*, the first, oldest, and largest daily newspaper published in Vietnamese outside of Vietnam.

1979   China, in support of Cambodia, retaliated and attacked Vietnam at the northern border.

The number of Vietnamese boat people leaving Vietnam increased dramatically, with more than 50,000 in some months.

At the First Geneva Conference on Indochinese Refugees, the United States, together with the United Kingdom, Australia, France, and Canada, agreed to be a country of resettlement and to establish an Orderly Departure Program (ODP) under the auspices of the United Nations High Commissioner for Refugees.

Under the ODP, from 1980 until 1997, 623,509 Vietnamese were resettled abroad, of whom 458,367 went to the United States.

Galang Refugee Camp was established and operated from 1979 to 1996 on Galang Island in the Riau Islands of Indonesia. An estimated 250,000 refugees passed through Galang during this period.

The Southeast Asian Resource Action Center (SEARAC) was established in Washington, DC, in 1979 as the Indochinese Resource Action Center (IRAC).

Giác Quang Temple in Oklahoma City, Oklahoma, became one of the first Vietnamese Buddhist temples built in the United States.

1980   The total population of Vietnamese Americans in 1980 was 261,729, according to U.S. Census.

The plight of the boat people compelled the United States to pass the Refugee Act of 1980, easing restrictions on the entry of Vietnamese refugees.

David Tran founded Huy Fong Foods, maker of Sriracha Chili Sauce, a hot sauce company in Southern California that has grown to become one of the leading and best-known hot sauce companies in the world.

Boat People SOS (BPSOS) was established as a nonprofit organization devoted to Vietnamese American civic and political activism, specifically to assisting people in Vietnam, on the high seas, in refugee camps, or after their arrival in the United States.

1981   Vietnam dissolved the autonomous Unified Buddhist Church of Vietnam (UBCV), the main Buddhist organization in South Vietnam before 1975, and replaced it with the government-controlled Vietnam Buddhist Church.

From 1981 to 1991, during the Vietnamese occupation of Cambodia, hundreds of thousands of Cambodians fled the country and resided in refugee camps in Thailand. About 260,000 eventually resettled abroad, more than half in the United States.

In Seadrift, Texas, American fishermen turned to the Ku Klux Klan to terrorize Vietnamese fishermen, claiming unfair competition. The Southern Poverty Law Center advocated on behalf of the Vietnamese refugees and won the case, securing protection from U.S. Marshals.

1982   The establishment of the Vietnam Veterans Memorial as a U.S. national memorial in Washington, DC.

Asia Entertainment was established as a Vietnamese American music program production company in Westminster, California.

The Venerable Thích Huyền Quang, the supreme patriarch of the UBCV, and Venerable Thích Quảng Độ, the second-highest figure in the church, were arrested by the Vietnamese authorities for calling for official recognition of the church.

Pastor Nguyễn Lập Mã, superintendent of the former Protestant Church of South Vietnam, was arrested by the authorities for refusing to hand over church buildings and to join the state-sponsored church. He was placed under permanent house arrest.

1983   The Vietnamese government formed the Committee for the Solidarity of Patriotic Vietnamese Catholics to separate the Vietnamese Roman Catholic church from papal authority. Philippe Nguyễn Kim Điền, archbishop of Huế, defied the formation of this committee and was later placed under house arrest until he died in 1988.

By September, the United States had received a total of 678,057 refugees from Southeast Asia, close to two-thirds of whom entered the United States between 1979 and 1982. Vietnamese refugees accounted for about two-thirds of all Southeast Asian refugees in the United States.

Lee's Sandwiches, a Vietnamese American fast-food restaurant chain credited with having helped to popularize Vietnamese sandwiches and iced coffee among mainstream American consumers, was founded. As of 2018, it has 61 locations in the United States.

Phở Hoà, a phở restaurant chain based in Sacramento but founded in San Jose, California. As of 2017, it has 72 locations across the United States, Canada, Indonesia, Malaysia, the Philippines, South Korea, and Taiwan.

The Tale of Kiều, translated and annotated by Huynh Sanh Thong, published. Thong was the first Vietnamese American awarded the MacArthur Grant (1981).

1984   Vietnamese American Thong Hy Huynh was stabbed to death by two white high school students in Davis, California.

Eden Center was established as the Vietnamese American strip mall in the Falls Church, Virginia/Washington, DC, area.

Thuý Nga [Trung Tâm Thuý Nga Paris] was established as a Vietnamese American entertainment company known for its Vietnamese-oriented entertainment, such as the variety show and direct-to-video series *Paris by Night*, and music released as part of the record label Thúy Nga Music.

1986   The Sixth Congress of the Vietnamese Communist Party convened and embraced market reforms.

Mary Queen of Viet Nam was built in New Orleans, Louisiana, becoming the first church built and owned by Vietnamese Americans.

1987   Congress passed the Amerasian Homecoming Act to resettle Amerasians, children of American servicemen and Vietnamese women. Under this act, approximately 75,000 Amerasians and family members came to the United States.

The Asian Garden Mall [Phước Lộc Thọ] opened by developer Frank Jao (Triệu Phát), becoming the first Vietnamese American business center in Little Saigon, Orange County.

The City of Westminster, California, officially called a part of the city Little Saigon.

1988   A freeway offramp sign was placed on the Garden Grove Freeway (State Route 22) designating the exits leading to Little Saigon.

The television documentary *Rescue Mission on the High Seas*, with Vu Thanh Thuy, was aired on national television, exposing the plight of Vietnamese boat people to the American public.

Tue Nguyen, 26, set a record at the Massachusetts Institute of Technology by earning seven undergraduate degrees.

1989   United States reached an agreement with Vietnam to allow political prisoners to immigrate to the United States, under the Humanitarian Operation (H.O.) Program.

The Comprehensive Plan of Action (CPA) was adopted by the Steering Committee of the International Conference on Indochinese Refugees, requiring asylum seekers from Vietnam to be screened for refugee status. In the next 10 years, over 110,000 are forced to return to Vietnam.

The musical *Miss Saigon* appeared on Broadway and quickly became a highly popular show. The play's racist and sexist undertones anger many Vietnamese and Asian American community members.

1990   The total population of Vietnamese Americans in 1990 was 614,517, according to U.S. Census.

Under the H.O. Program, the first group of former Vietnamese political and reeducation camp prisoners and their families is admitted to the United States. This kickstarted a new flow of Vietnamese immigrants into the United States.

Actor Dustin Nguyen starred on the popular television drama series *21 Jump Street.*

1991   The United States and Vietnam began a joint MIA effort designed to test Vietnamese willingness to cooperate and to begin a process that would lead to the normalization of relations.

1992   Luyen Phan Nguyen, 19, a University of Miami premed student, was chased down and brutally beaten to death outside a Coral Springs, Florida, college party by a mob of about 15 young white men. Six white men, between the ages of 18 and 22, were convicted of the hate crime and sentenced to 13 months to life in prison.

Eugene Huu-Chau "Gene" Trinh became the first Vietnamese American astronaut in space, as a payload specialist crew member on the STS-50/United States Microgravity Lab-1 Space Shuttle flight.

Tony Lam won a seat on the Westminster City Council, California, becoming the first Vietnamese-born and first Vietnamese American person to be elected to a political office in the United States.

Wendy Nicole Duong (Dương Như Nguyện) became the first Vietnamese American to hold judicial office in the United States when appointed associate municipal judge for the City of Houston and magistrate for the State of Texas.

1994   President Clinton lifted the 30-year U.S. trade embargo against Vietnam that had been in place since 1964.

1995   Vietnam and the United States restored full diplomatic relations. The U.S. embassy opened in Hanoi. Vietnam became a full member of the Association of Southeast Asian Nations (ASEAN).

1996   Malaysia and Indonesia closed their refugee camps, shipping their final boat people "holdouts" back to Vietnam.

18,000 Vietnamese were resettled under the 1996–2003 Resettlement Opportunity for Vietnamese Returnees (ROVR) for certain refugees still in asylum camps or recently returned to Vietnam.

Daniel (Danny) Peter Graves became the first Vietnam-born and Vietnamese American player in the history of Major League Baseball, as a member of the Cleveland Indians. In 2000, Graves earned his first All-Star appearance.

1997   Douglas ("Pete") Peterson, a former prisoner of war during the Vietnam War, was named the first U.S. ambassador to Vietnam since the War. Vietnam, in turn, named Lê Văn Bằng as its first ambassador to the United States.

The last Vietnamese boat people to voluntarily return home from Hong Kong refugee camps boarded a UN flight back to Viet Nam.

Thang Barrett became the first Vietnamese American judge to sit on a court of general jurisdiction in the United States, in Santa Clara, California.

Leyna Nguyen became the first newscaster ever to anchor the news on two stations in the same market. Nguyen is a three-time Emmy Award–winning journalist.

1998   Congresswoman Loretta Sanchez (D-CA) drafted and secured passage of legislation in the House National Security Committee honoring former Vietnamese commandos who worked for the United States during the Vietnam War, some of whom were imprisoned by the North Vietnamese for up to 25 years.

1999   Dat Tan Nguyen, the most productive linebacker in Texas A&M University, became the first Vietnamese American to be drafted, play, and be recognized as an All-Pro in the National Football League, representing the Dallas Cowboys.

A monthlong protest against a Vietnamese American videotape store owner, Tran Truong, who displayed the flag of communist Vietnam and a photo of Ho Chi Minh in his store in Westminster, California.

Three Seasons, a film directed by Vietnamese American Tony Bui and filmed entirely in Vietnam won both the Grand Jury Award and the Audience Award at the 1999 Sundance Film Festival.

2000 The U.S.-Vietnam Bilateral Trade Agreement was signed.

U.S. president Bill Clinton visited Vietnam, becoming the first U.S. president to do so since the Vietnam War.

Hong Kong closed its last Vietnamese refugee camp.

The total population of Vietnamese Americans in 2000 was 1,122,528, according to U.S. Census.

Vietnamese Americans Tawny Binh, Michelle Do, and Khoa Nguyen participated in the 2000 Summer Olympics in Sydney, Australia, as members of the U.S. Olympic Team in the sport of table tennis. Binh and Nguyen were gold medalists at the 1999 Pan American Games. Do, 17, was the 1998 Nationals Under-22 Women's Singles Champion.

Van Thai Tran was elected to the Garden Grove City Council with the highest number of votes in city history and became only the second Vietnamese American man to be elected to office in the United States (following Tony Lam in 1992).

2001 Saigon Broadcasting Television Network (SBTN) became the first 24-hour Vietnamese-language channel geared toward the Vietnamese diaspora.

Viet Dinh, a law professor at Georgetown Law School, appointed the assistant attorney general of the United States from 2001 to 2003, becoming perhaps the highest-ranking Vietnamese American official in the U.S. federal government. He was the chief architect of the Patriot Act.

2002 Between 2002 and 2021, the lobbying efforts of Vietnamese Americans resulted in the state governments of Virginia, Hawaii, Georgia, Colorado, Florida, Texas, Oklahoma, Louisiana, Ohio, California, Missouri, Pennsylvania, and Michigan recognizing the South Vietnamese flag as the symbol of the Vietnamese American community (Vietnamese American Heritage flag). At least 15 counties and 85 cities in 20 states have also adopted similar resolutions.

2003 The establishment of the Vietnam War Memorial in Westminster, California.

The Vietnamese International Film Festival (ViFF) was established as a biennial film festival.

The Union of North American Vietnamese Student Associations (UNAVSA) [Liên Hội Sinh Viên Việt Nam Bắc Mỹ Châu] was founded as a nonprofit, community-based organization for Vietnamese student organizations from across North America.

2004   Van Thai Tran was elected to the California State Assembly; Hubert Vo was elected to the Texas House of Representatives. Tran and Vo became the highest-ranking Vietnamese American elected officials in U.S. history.

Madison Nguyen became the first Vietnamese American to serve on the San Jose City Council. She was also the first Vietnamese vice mayor in the history of San Jose.

2005   Saigon National Bank in Westminster, California, became the first nationally chartered bank organized and owned by Vietnamese Americans in the United States.

The California and Ohio state governments enacted laws adopting the South Vietnamese flag as the symbol of the Vietnamese in the United States.

The city of Houston was home to 32,000 Vietnamese and Vietnamese Americans, making it the second-largest Vietnamese American community in the United States of any city, after that of San Jose, California.

2006   Nguyen Xuan Vinh, professor of aerospace engineering at the University of Michigan, was awarded the Dirk Brouwer Award for outstanding lifetime achievement in the field of space flight mechanics and astrodynamics.

Journey from the Fall [Vượt Sóng], a 2006 independent film by writer/director/editor Ham Tran, about the Vietnamese reeducation camp and boat people experience following the fall of Saigon on April 30, 1975, was released on March 23, 2007. The film is notable for having been financed entirely by the Vietnamese American community.

2007   Betty Nguyen was recognized by the Smithsonian Institution in 2007 as the first Vietnamese American to anchor a national television news broadcast in the United States.

The Viet Museum [Viện Bảo Tàng Thuyền Nhân Việt Nam], or the Museum of the Boat People and the Republic of Vietnam, opened on August 25, 2007, at the History Park at Kelley Park, San Jose, California.

2008   Westminster, California, became the first city with a majority Vietnamese American city council.

August 12, the City Council of Westminster, California, passed resolution 4257, recognizing that the last Saturday in each April will be "Vietnamese Boat People Day."

2009   Anh Quang "Joseph" Cao won a special election for a seat in the House of Representatives, representing New Orleans, Louisiana. He is the first Vietnamese American to serve in Congress, and at the time was the highest-ranking Vietnamese American elected official in U.S. history.

2010   The total population of Vietnamese Americans in 2010 was 1,548,449, according to U.S. Census.

The Vietnamese community accounted for a significant proportion of the population in Texas, particularly the Greater Houston area. Harris County had 80,409 ethnic Vietnamese, making up 28.7 percent of Asians in the county.

2012   Jacqueline Hong-Ngoc Nguyen became the first Asian American female to serve as a federal appellate judge of the U.S. Court of Appeals for the Ninth Circuit. She is also the first Vietnamese American federal judge and the first Asian-Pacific American female federal judge in California.

2014   Viet Xuan Luong became the first Vietnamese American general in U.S. history. He is also the U.S. military's first general born in Vietnam. Other Vietnamese Americans subsequently promoted to the rank of general included Lapthe Flora, John Edwards, William H. Seely III, and Huan Nguyen.

Janet Nguyen became the first state senator of Vietnamese ancestry in American history during the 2014 California State Senate election.

Ocean Vuong (Vuong Quoc Vinh), a Vietnamese American poet, was recipient of the 2014 Ruth Lilly/Sargent Rosenberg Fellowship from the Poetry Foundation, a 2016 Whiting Award, the 2017 T.S. Eliot Prize for his poetry, and a MacArthur Grant in 2019.

Tommy Pham became the first person of Vietnamese descent to play in Major League Baseball since pitcher Danny Graves; the first position player.

Bao Nguyen became the first Vietnamese American to become mayor of the city of Garden Grove, California.

Rise Inc., founded by Amanda Nguyen, a nonprofit organization which is aimed to protect the civil rights of sexual assault and rape survivors.

Viet Dzung Human Rights Memorial Highway in Orange County, California, was named after the Vietnamese American human rights activist Việt Dzũng.

2015   Kelly Marie Tran became the first Asian American woman to play the main role in a *Star Wars* franchise, *Star Wars: The Last Jedi*. In 2021, Kelly made history with the film *Raya and the Last Dragon*, voicing Raya, the first Southeast Asian Disney princess.

2016   The Museum of the Republic of Vietnam opened in Westminster, California. It is the first and only museum in the world dedicated to the history of the Republic of Vietnam and its military.

Viet Thanh Nguyen became the first Vietnamese American novelist to win the Pulitzer Prize for Fiction for his novel *The Sympathizer*. He received a MacArthur Grant in 2017.

2017   Stephanie Murphy (Dang Thi Ngoc Dung), the first Vietnamese American woman and the second Vietnamese American overall (after Republican Joseph Cao of Louisiana) to be elected to Congress, representing Florida's Seventh District.

Kathy Tran and Kelly Fowler were the first Asian American women to be elected to Virginia's House of Delegates in November 2017. Kathy Tran is the first Vietnamese American elected official on any level in the Commonwealth.

Dean A. Tran became the first Vietnamese American to hold an elected office in Massachusetts.

According to U.S. Census Bureau, in 2017 the median household income for Vietnamese Americans was $65,643, compared to $61,372 for the overall U.S. population. In 2017, 10.6 percent of Vietnamese Americans lived under the poverty line, lower than the poverty rate for all Americans at 12.3 percent.

Vietnamese living abroad sent nearly $14 billion in remittances to Vietnam via formal channels. Most of it came from Vietnamese living in the United States. Remittances tripled in the past decade and represented about 6 percent of the country's gross domestic product (GDP) in 2016.

2019   My-Linh Thai became one of the first two Vietnamese American legislators to be elected to the Washington State Legislature, alongside Joe Nguyen from the 34th district, following the November 2018 general election.

Pho 79, founded in 1982, became the first Orange County restaurant to win a prestigious James Beard Foundation Award.

2020   John Peter Pham was accorded the personal rank of ambassador, becoming the first Vietnamese American to achieve that rank.

Le Hoang Nguyen put up a bilingual English-Vietnamese billboard in Houston promoting the Black Lives Matter movement. The sign became a flashpoint within the community, and he received death threats and boycotts of his businesses.

2021   Dat Tran became the first Vietnamese American (acting) U.S. Secretary of Veterans Affairs, becoming perhaps the highest-ranking Vietnamese American official in the U.S. federal government.

During the 2021 storming of the U.S. Capitol, many South Vietnamese flags were seen in the crowd of rioters, inciting mixed reactions among many Vietnamese Americans.

Notes

INTRODUCTION

1. Approximately 2.1 million are spread across the fifty states and the District of Columbia, including a strong presence in California; Texas; Washington, DC; Virginia; New York; Pennsylvania; Massachusetts; Washington; Georgia; Louisiana; and Florida. "Asian and Pacific Islander Population in the United States," *United States Census Bureau*, April 30, 2020, https://www.census.gov/library/visualizations/2020/demo/aian-population.html.

2. The U.S. Census defines Asian as "a person having origins in any of the original peoples of the Far East, Southeast Asia, or the Indian subcontinent including, for example, Cambodia, China, India, Japan, Korea, Malaysia, Pakistan, the Philippine Islands, Thailand, and Vietnam." "Asian American and Pacific Islander Heritage Month: May 2022," *United States Census Bureau*, April 18, 2022, https://www.census.gov/newsroom/facts-for -features/2022/asian-american-pacific-islander.html.

3. One recent study that claims to provide a history of Vietnamese Americans lists "canonical texts on the Vietnam War" as including books by David Halberstam, Stanley Karnow, Frances FitzGerald, Neil Sheehan, and Gabriel Kolko. Note that the first four are journalists and the last one is a scholar but not a historian. All these books were published from the 1960s to the 1980s, and none of the five authors know Vietnamese. See Nguyen Phuong Tran (2017: 148, fn. 17).

4. Recent studies of South Vietnamese politics include Stur (2020); Vu T. and Fear (2020); and Luu T. and Vu T. (2023).

5. For example, see Kelly (1977); Liu et al. (1979); Stein (1979); Montero (1979); Haines (1989); Caplan et al. (1989).

6. Prominent examples are Kibria (1993); Freeman (1995); Zhou and Bankston (1998); McKelvey (2002).

7. An example of a genealogical memoir is Elliott (1999); on music, see Reyes (1999) and Pham D. (2000); on visual arts, see Le V. (2005: 21–35). For popular media, see Thuy Nga Paris and Asia Entertainment productions.

8. Also see Trinh M. H. (1989) as it applies to Third World writers.

9. In no way comprehensive, this list includes Truong Monique (2004); Lam A. (2005); Pham Q. X. (2005); Nguyen V. T. (2015), perhaps most notably recognized for the 2016 Pulitzer Prize for Fiction award to a 1.5-generation scholar and novelist.

10. More recent studies in this approach include Nguyen Phuong Tran (2017) and Bui L. (2018).

11. See the special issue edited by Nguyen M. and Fung (2016); also Nguyen V. T. (2016).

12. In his review of Espiritu's major work, Hao Jun Tam notes that "this study surprisingly does not include any extensive discussion of the communist regime's role in the refugees' flight." Tam (2016: 130).

13. For an analysis of the ideological contrast between the DRV and the RVN, see Dror (2018).

14. Others have divided these three waves into five waves. A more thorough explanation can be seen in Chan S. (1991; 2006).

15. "The Refugee Act," *Office of Refugee Resettlement*, March 17, 1980, https://www.acf.hhs.gov/orr/resource/the-refugee-act. For an analysis of national politics and policies toward Indochinese refugees, see Sutter (1990). On U.S. politics and policies toward Indochinese refugees, see Demmer (2017).

16. "H.R.3171-Amerasian Homecoming Act," U.S. Congress, August 6, 1987, https://www.congress.gov/bill/100th-congress/house-bill/3171/text.

17. For the remarkable role a Vietnamese American group played in the release and immigration of former political prisoners, see Demmer (2017) and Martin (2018).

18. Eleanor Hoover, "Vietnamese Settlers: Can They Adapt?" *Los Angeles Times*, May 27, 1975, quoting a State Department official. Cited in Nguyen Phuong Tran (2017: 33).

19. Vietnam began to open up its economy and legalize private enterprises in the late 1980s but maintained many restrictions on economic exchanges with the external world, especially on remittances by overseas Vietnamese deemed subversive by the communist government. The U.S. embargo also made such exchanges difficult until 1995, when U.S.-Vietnam relations were normalized. Official data shows that the remittance amount (by legal channels, not counting unofficial transfers) in 1995 was equal to 1.4 percent of Vietnam's GDP, 14.3 percent of its foreign direct investment, and 34.1 percent of official development aid Vietnam received. From 1996 to 2000, its share rose to 3.3 percent, 50.4 percent, and 70.6 percent, respectively. During the next five years, 2001–2005, its share rose further to 5 percent, 80.5 percent, and 124.7 percent, respectively. In this period, remittance played nearly as big a role as foreign investment and a bigger role than foreign aid. See Vu V. C. (2015: 46).

20. That number, however, has since increased to 1.3 million by 2017.

21. The rise, especially since the year 2000, has much to do with the changing pathway by which Vietnamese immigrate to the United States. While most who came before 2000 were refugees seeking asylum, the majority of Vietnamese who came since did so through family sponsorship—meaning they were sponsored by those who came in the first, second, and third waves.

22. "Who Are Vietnamese Americans?" Center for American Progress, April 2015, https://americanprogress.org/wp-content/uploads/2015/04/AAPI-Vietnamese-factsheet.pdf.

23. "Language Spoken at Home by Ability to Speak English for the Population 5 Years and Over," American FactFinder, February 12, 2020, https://archive.vn/20200212213140/http://factfinder.census.gov/faces/tableservices/jsf/pages/productview.xhtml?pid=ACS_10_1YR_B16001&prodType=table#; "Vietnamese in the U.S. Fact Sheet," Pew Research Center, September 8, 2017, https://www.pewsocialtrends.org/fact-sheet/asian-americans-vietnamese-in-the-u-s-fact-sheet/.

24. "Selected Population Profile in the United States," American FactFinder, February 13, 2020, https://archive.vn/20200213035751/https://factfinder.census.gov/bkmk/table/1.0/en/ACS/17_1YR/S0201//popgroup~048; See Fontenot, Semga, and Kollar (2018).
25. Gustavo Lopez, Neil G. Ruiz, and Eileen Patten, "Key Facts about Asian Americans, a Diverse and Growing Population," September 8, 2017, available at https://www.pewresearch.org/fact-tank/2017/09/08/key-facts-about-asian-americans/.
26. "Annual Remittances Data (updated as of May 2021)," *World Bank Migration and Remittances Data*, September 12, 2021, https://www.worldbank.org/en/topic/migrationremittancesdiasporaissues/brief/migration-remittances-data.
27. "Vietnam Received Around US$16.7 Billion of Remittances Last Year," *Vietnam Insider*, January 13, 2020, https://vietnaminsider.vn/vietnam-receives-around-us16-7-billion-of-remittances-last-year/.
28. Examples of notable memoirs are Trần D. and Hoàng V. (1991); Pham V. L. (2004); Lai (2015); Bui (2018); Truong Marcelino (2016; 2017; in comic form). Examples of novels include Phan A. (2013); Nguyen V. T. (2015); Vuong O. (2019). For collections of short stories and poems, for example, see Nguyen V. T. (2017); Vuong O. (2016); Phan N. H. (2019). A notable publication of oral histories is Hoang C. (2011; 2015). Notable films are *Green Dragon* (2001), *Journey from the Fall* (2007), *Bolinao 52* (2010), and *Vietnamerica* (2015).

CHAPTER 1

1. "Diễn hành xe ủng hộ Tổng Thống Trump & cảnh sát tại Nam California," *Saigon Broadcasting Television Network* [*SBTN*], October 4, 2020; "Houston chào đón đoàn hành trình từ California đến Washington DC," *SBTN*, October 7, 2020; "New Orleans & Biloxi chào đón đoàn hành trình từ California đến Washington DC," *SBTN*, October 10, 2020; "Tuần hành ủng hộ TT Trump trong khu trung tâm Thương Mại Eden," *SBTN*, October 12, 2020; "Tuần hành ủng hộ Tổng Thống Donald Trump trước Tòa Bạch Óc," *SBTN*, October 14, 2020.
2. These come from my own observations of Vietnamese American activities in the Little Saigon of Orange County, CA.
3. For use of "free-floating," see Mann (1984).
4. For Republican anticommunism as a "hegemonic ideology," see Nguyen Y. T. (2021).
5. Questions of morality are particularly notable in recent critiques of American ventures into Iraq and Afghanistan like those of Ryan and Fitzgerald (2009); M. Small (2010); Campbell (2007). For American deceit, South Vietnamese incompetence, and immorality of the war, see also Langguth (2012).
6. For a critique of how the Republic of Vietnam is treated in Vietnamese and Vietnam War studies, see Miller and Vu (2009); Tran N.-A. (2013). The latter's review of the Vietnam War scholarship points to how the Republic of Vietnam is often considered "an aberration."
7. This is most evident in Kolko (2001). See also Tran N.-A. (2013) for a critique of existing Vietnamese studies and Vietnam War literature.
8. Recent generalist histories of Vietnam that treat the Republic of Vietnam as an actual historical actor in the conflict, like those of Goscha (2016) and K. Taylor (2013), do not go into enough depth about the ideological, social, political, and institutional dimensions of the Republic to examine notions of continuity and change.
9. See "Mục Đích Xây Dựng Ấp Chiến Lược," *Chiến Sĩ* 84 (1962): 13–15; "Buổi Nói Chuyện của Ông Bộ Trưởng Nội Vụ Bùi Văn Lương về Ấp Chiến Lược," *Chiến Sĩ* 87 (1962): 11–17. The Strategic Hamlet concept was also expanded into other domains to "revolutionize" the totality of the South Vietnamese. On the formation of "Strategic Area" *Khu Chiến*

Lược to renovate governmental organs, see "Phần Thứ II: Góp Ý về việc thành lập các Khu Chiến Lược," September 5, 1963; "Khu Chiến Lược Bộ Y Tế: Khu Ước," October 12, 1963, Folder 3031, Phông Bộ Y Tế [BYT], Trung Tâm Lưu Trữ Quốc Gia II [TTLTQGII]. On "Strategic Cluster" (*Khóm Chiến Lược*) to modernize and transform urban communities, see the running series entitled "Khóm Chiến Lược," *Saigon Mới*, January 2–29, 1962.

10. On New Life Hamlet, see "Đường Lối Xây Dựng Nông Thôn Trong Năm 1967," March 29, 1967, Folder 29737, Phông Phủ Thủ Tướng Việt Nam Cộng Hòa [PTTVNCH], TTLTQGII. On Self-Defending—Self-Developing Communities, see "Đẩy Mạnh Kế Hoạch Cộng Đồng Tự Vệ-Cộng Đồng Phát Triển Địa Phương Để Kiến Tạo Hòa Bình và Thịnh Vượng," April 27, 1971, Folder 32656, PTTVNCH, TTLTQGII.

11. On the definition of *consolidation*, see Selbin (1999).

12. The conjoining of *dựng nước* and *cứu nước* manifested as early as 1958 under the First Republic. A study document of Ngô Đình Diệm's 1958 National Day Proclamation, for example, argued that the "task to save the nation and build the nation is a responsibility of all the people." "Tài Liệu Học Tập Số 7 ngày 28-10-58: Hiệu Triệu của Tổng Thống Nhân Lễ Quốc Khánh Ngày 26-10-1958," Folder 3031, BYT, TTLTQGII.

13. Ordinance 47, passed in 1956, defined being a communist or aiding communist activities as a capital crime. The infamous Law 10/59, passed under the First Republic, for example, enacted heavy penalties (including execution and forced labor) on "communists" and violent criminals. "Tòa án quân sự đặc biệt đã thành lập," *Saigon Mới*, June 1, 1959; "Chapter 5: Origins of the Insurgency in South Vietnam, 1954–1960," in Gravel (1971: 242–269).

14. "Cuộc Thi Sáng Tác Văn Nghệ do Nha Vô Tuyến Việt Nam Tổ Chức ngày 20-7-1964," June 5, 1964; "Biên Bản Phiên Họp Liên Bộ ngày 19-6-1964 vào hồi 16g tại Phủ Đặc Ủy Thanh Niên và Thể Thao v/v Chuẩn Bị Cho Kế Hoạch Phát Động Chương Trình Công Tác Xã Hội của Thanh Niên Hướng Về Ngày Quốc Hận 20-7"; "Chương Trình Lễ Quốc Hận 10 Năm Tội Ác Việt Cộng 20-7-1964," July 7, 1964, Folder 1773, Phông Bộ Công Chánh và Giao Thông, TTLTQGII.

15. See Tran N.-A. (2013) on contributions of northern émigrés to the Communist Denunciation Campaign. See also, Hoang T. (2013).

16. Apart from the infamous draconian Law 10/59 of the Diệm administration, subsequent regimes also passed laws criminalizing communism. Law 093-SK/CT, passed under Nguyễn Khánh, for example, placed heavy penalties on "individuals, parties, organizations, congregations and activities [connected to] . . . the ideology of communism or communist sympathizing neutralism." "Lần Đầu Tiên, Chính Phủ Chống Cộng miền Nam VN," *Tự Do*, February 18, 1964. Similarly, the 1965 Charter of the Directorate dictated that the primary duty of the military administration was to ensure "the retreat and extermination of the communist infiltrators." "Ước Pháp ngày 19-6-65 của Việt Nam Cộng Hoà," *Chính Luận*, June 22, 1965. The constitutions of both the First (Article 7) and Second Republic (Article 4) made explicit that any communist-related activities were federally forbidden. "Nguyên văn bản Hiến pháp Cộng Hòa VN đã được Tổng Thống sửa đổi và Quốc hội chấp thuận," *Saigon Mới*, October 26, 1956; "Hiến pháp Việt Nam Cộng Hòa," May 24, 1967, Folder 29738, PTTVNCH, TTLTQGII.

17. An editorial published in *Trắng Đen* (one of the largest news organs of early Vietnamese America) in 1976 questioned the usage of the Republican flag and the Republican anthem as symbols to represent Vietnamese exiles overseas. This editorial by Nguyễn Nhật Minh suggested the scrapping of the former Republican flag, deeming it a symbol that "the international world now disregards" because of the activities of Thiệu and his administration. Rather than using the former Republican anthem, the author suggested using Phạm Duy's iconic composition "Việt Nam, Việt Nam." This idea was never adopted by Vietnamese exiles, but it did spark debate (if not retort) by readers, as well as a response in support

of the Republican flag by the editor of *Trắng Đen*. Nguyễn Nhật Minh, "Quốc Kỳ-Quốc Ca Nào Cho Việt Kiều Lưu Vong," *Trắng Đen* 12, May 31, 1976; "Dư Âm Về Quốc Kỳ, Quốc Ca," *Trắng Đen* 19, July 7, 1976.

18. Following the First Republic, the death of Diệm was widely celebrated as the "November Revolution" by citizens in South Vietnam. Tribunals were set up by subsequent "revolutionary" military administrations, seeking to dispense justice against those who supported or aided the "corruption" and "nepotism" of the "old regime." For an extended history of the interregnum period, see Nguyen Y. T. (2021).

19. For a critique of the literature on Vietnamese America, see Nguyen Y. T. (2018).

20. My efforts to decenter American power from the analysis of specific regional conflicts in the Cold War are far from novel. As Robert Latham argues, the "U.S. is at the center" of postwar order building, "each state and society shapes the making of order to a varying degree, from local to the global" (1997: 112).

21. Ngày Quân Lực (Armed Forces Day) was annually commemorated on June 19 in South Vietnam. Historically, the date marked the transition from the civilian administration of Phan Huy Quát to the military regime of the Directorate (Ủy Ban Lãnh Đạo Quốc Gia) in 1965. The same date is commemorated annually in Vietnamese refugee communities since 1975. Other state-mandated holidays included National Day, which was originally October 26 under the First Republic to mark the founding of the Republic of Vietnam. Following 1963, National Day was on November 1 to mark the "November Revolution," which toppled the Diệm administration.

22. On the alternative name of Black April as "Ngày Quốc Hận," see Vo Dang (2008).

23. "Nhân ngày Quốc Hận 20-7: Đình chỉ ca nhạc và du hí," *Tự Do*, July 9, 1964; "Cuộc biểu tình vĩ đại nhất trong 10 năm qua: 1 triệu người biểu tình đòi bắc tiến," *Tự Do*, July 20, 1964.

24. His presentation has been heavily cited in the Vietnamese-language press (e.g., "Hội thảo: 'Nhạc Vàng,' di sản trường tồn của Việt Nam Cộng Hòa," *Voice of America* [VOA] *Tiếng Việt*, October 31, 2019).

CHAPTER 2

1. Take, for example, Ken Burns and Lynn Novick's ten-part documentary, *The Vietnam War* (New York: PBS, 2017). Though the documentary made efforts to include perspectives of Vietnamese from both sides, it still denied the nationalist genealogy of the RVN. In so doing, the documentary casts the war as conflict between only the United States and North Vietnam, ignoring the fact that the conflict was also between the communist and noncommunist Vietnamese.

2. These were the names of the northern (Bắc Bộ) and central (Trung Bộ) regions of Vietnam, respectively, during the French colonial period (1883–1945).

3. The owners and publishers of *Women's News* were Cao Thị Khanh and her husband, Nguyễn Đức Nhuận. For more on the periodical, see Marr (1981: 220–228) and Thiện (2004: 62–70). For more on the Dục Anh Society, see Nguyen-Marshall (2008: 88–91).

4. Letter from Vũ Quốc Thông, Minister of Society and Health, to the PM, September 23, 1955. The Office of the President's Office, First Republic (hereafter PTTD1), file 16,188. National Archive of Vietnam, II, Ho Chi Minh City.

5. Betty Tisdale, an American and a longtime supporter of the orphanage, was instrumental in helping Ngãi move to the United States (Dooley 1956). Chapter 14 is devoted to Vũ Thị Ngãi (Madame Ngai); see also Tisdale (2020).

6. "Betty Tisdale's Heroic Orphan Airlift," ABC News, April 30, 2010; James Eng, "'Angel of Saigon,' Viet Orphan Took Each Other to Heart," *Los Angeles Times*, August 18, 1996.

7. Lê T. S.'s (1970) Appendix is entitled "Danh Sách các tổ chức từ thiện tôn giáo."

8. The storms were Violet (September 14–15), Iris (November 2–4), and Joan (November 6–8). U.S. Weather Bureau (1965: 74–78).

9. *Bản Tin Tức* (published by the Inter-Ministerial Committee for Flood Relief of the Central Provinces) 14, no. 1–15 (1964–1965); "Cứu trợ đồng bào nạn lụt miền Trung năm 1964–5 (Tập 2: tư liệu đưa tin về công tác cứu trợ)," Prime Minister's Collection. Vietnam Archives II, Ho Chi Minh City (hereafter PPT), #29473.

10. U.S. Embassy in Saigon, "Assessment of Easter Offensive: June 24, 1972." 2122404016, Douglas Pike Collection: Unit 01—Assessment and Strategy, Vietnam Center and Sam Johnson Vietnam Archive, Texas Tech University.

11. U.S. Embassy in Saigon, 8.

12. "Dân Quảng Trị tràn ngập Huế, Đà Nẵng," *Chính Luận*, May 2, 1972, 3.

13. American Council of Voluntary Agencies for Foreign Service and Technical Assistance Clearing House, "Assistance Programs of US Non-profit Organizations," New York, March 1971, 3. 2274212005, Douglas Pike Collection: Unit 03—U.S. Economy and U.S. Mission (Saigon), Vietnam Center and Sam Johnson Vietnam Archive, Texas Tech University.

14. Người Xứ Quảng, "Nói Chuyện Cứu Trợ," *Sinh Viên Huế* 5, Dec 17, 1964, 6, 5.

15. Other voluntary development programs included the Voluntary Youth Association (founded in 1956), the National Youth Voluntary Service (1964), and the New Life Development Project (1965). The first program deployed youth to work in short-term community projects such as repairing schools and orphanages, building wells, fixing roads, dispensing basic medical care, and instructing literacy classes. The National Voluntary Service, modeled on the International Voluntary Service, required participants to commit to working and living for at least a year in host villages to carry out development work. The New Life Development Project pursued community development in several poor districts in Saigon.

16. For example, founding member Huỳnh Văn Lang received graduate training in econometrics at the University of Chicago; Đỗ Trọng Chu had an MA in international relations from Georgetown University; and Nguyễn Thái had graduated with an MA from Cornell. He later worked with the USOM government liaison office and then later the Ministry of Construction and Planning (Huỳnh V. L. 2008; Nguyễn N. N. 2014).

17. Lê Thành Cường, "Phúc trình hoạt động" [Report on Activities at the Association's General Meeting], June 5, 1955, 22, Prime Minister's Office (hereafter, PTT), file 29237.

18. Lê Thành Cường, 2–3.

19. Workers made up 27 percent. The others were unemployed (12 percent), traders (8 percent), students (10 percent), and homemakers (5 percent). The rest (7 percent) were nurses, teachers, and military personnel. Lê Thành Cường, "Phúc trình hoạt động," 2–3.

20. Bách Khoa chapters were founded in Huế, Biên Hòa, Bảo lộc (in Lâm Đồng province), Darlac (Ban Mê Thuột), Chợ Lớn, Ba Xuyên, Nha Trang, Đà Lạt, Long Khánh, Vĩnh Long, Kiến Hòa, Quảng Đức, Gia Định (Hội Văn Hoá Bình Dân 1967: 13–21).

21. For more on Lang's relationship with Nhu, see Miller (2013: 135–136, 281).

22. This was approximately 1229 USD. The 1955 exchange rate was 35 *đồng* to the dollar (Dacy 1986: 190).

23. Edgar N. Pike, "Adult Education in Vietnam," *Asia Foundation Newsletter*, September 1959, 1–3. 2322002008, Douglas Pike Collection: Unit 06—Democratic Republic of Vietnam, Vietnam Center and Sam Johnson Vietnam Archive, Texas Tech University.

24. International Rescue Committee, "Memorandum to the Foreign Operations Administration," April 23, 1955, 8. 781048026, Douglas Pike Collection: Other Manuscripts—

American Friends of Vietnam, Vietnam Center and Sam Johnson Vietnam Archive, Texas Tech University.

25. International Rescue Committee, 5.

26. International Rescue Committee, "Thirty Years of the International Rescue Committee, 1933–1963," 27–28. 1781048022, Douglas Pike Collection: Other Manuscripts—American Friends of Vietnam, Vietnam Center and Sam Johnson Vietnam Archive, Texas Tech University.

27. Thích Nhất Hạnh, "Basic Concepts of Policy and Method: Movement of Youth for Social Service," Lecture by Thich Nhất Hạnh, University of Vạn Hạnh, 1965, 19, 16–30; John Donnell, "Vietnam's Youth Associations—Social Commitment and Political Promise 1969," Report commissioned by Simulmatics Corp, 1969, 33–39. 0721005002, John Donnell Collection, Vietnam Center and Sam Johnson Vietnam Archive, Texas Tech University.

28. Thích Nhất Hạnh, as quoted in Nguyen T. V. (2006: 175–176).

29. Nhất Hạnh, "Basic Concepts of Policy and Method," 23–25.

CHAPTER 3

1. Võ Phiến's career is a good case study in these phenomena and is typical of a great many others. A literature professor at An Giang/Hòa Hảo University in Long Xuyên and Phương Nam University in Saigon before 1975, he founded the influential journal *Văn học nghệ thuật* and was a major contributor to several different newspapers in Southern California until his death in 2015. See Schafer (2016).

2. On the lack of anticommunism in education systems in the Republic of Vietnam and the lack of an overarching ideology in the Republic, see Dror (2018: 269–271).

3. See Tuan Hoang in Chapter 4 of this volume.

4. See Van Nguyen-Marshall in Chapter 2 in this volume.

5. Tuan Hoang, for example, recounts the difficulty that Nguyễn Văn Trung had with his journal *Hành Trình* during the interregnum period in 1965, when government censors deemed it too friendly to communist ideas (Hoang T. 2013: 484–485). See also Tran N.-A. (2006: 174).

6. Letter from Nguyễn Quang Trình to John Hannah, June 19, 1956, Douglas Pike Collection, American Friends of Vietnam, Virtual Vietnam Archive, accessed December 1, 2020, available at https://vva.vietnam.ttu.edu.

7. Letter from Nguyễn Quang Trình to Mr. Espinosa, Department of State, July 4, 1956, Douglas Pike Collection, American Friends of Vietnam, Virtual Vietnam Archive, accessed December 1, 2020, available at https://vva.vietnam.ttu.edu. It appears that some but not all of these requests were granted.

8. "Eight Professors from the University of Saigon to Visit the United States," press release, August 23, 1957, Douglas Pike Collection, American Friends of Vietnam, Virtual Vietnam Archive, accessed December 1, 2020, available at https://vva.vietnam.ttu.edu; letter from Robert W. Harper, program specialist for the Far East, Division of International Education, to Elinor Dubin, secretary, American Friends of Vietnam, October 17, 1957, Douglas Pike Collection, American Friends of Vietnam, Virtual Vietnam Archive, accessed December 1, 2020, available at https://vva.vietnam.ttu.edu. It appears that some but not all of these requests were granted.

9. Bách Khoa, "Thay lời phi lộ," *Bách Khoa* 1 (January 15, 1957): 1.

10. "President Ngo Dinh Diem Inaugurates Hue University," speech given at Huế University, November 12, 1957, Douglas Pike Collection, Virtual Vietnam Archive, accessed November 13, 2020, available at https://vva.vietnam.ttu.edu.

11. "German Aid to Hue University," September 10, 1960, Douglas Pike Collection, American Friends of Vietnam, Virtual Vietnam Archive, accessed November 30, 2020, available at https://vva.vietnam.ttu.edu/.

12. Also, personal communication with Nguyễn Thế Anh, November 24, 2020.

13. See also "Department of State Memorandum of Conversation: Situation in Vietnam: Dr. Erich Wulff," September 24, 1963, Virtual Vietnam Archive, accessed December 12, 2020, available at https://www.vietnam.ttu.edu/virtualarchive/.

14. The University of Huế awarded only ten degrees each from the Faculties of Letters and Science at the end of the 1962–1963 academic year. See Clevenger (1967: 17). Virtual Vietnam Archive, accessed November 30, 2020, available at https://www.vietnam.ttu.edu /virtualarchive/.

15. This was the case with the dean of the Faculty of Pedagogy at the University of Saigon, Phạm Hoàng Hộ, as discussed later in this chapter.

16. He was even famously sentenced to death by the Diệm regime for his role in advising the gangster, general, and politician Bảy Viễn. He was only saved by letters from famed French writer Albert Camus and Indian prime minister Jawaharlal Nehru (Ngo V. 2000: 226).

17. See also "Tưởng niệm cố Giáo sư Lê Văn Diệm," Le Nguyen Van Khoa Blog, March 23, 2019, accessed December 13, 2020, available at https://lnvkblog.blogspot.com/2019/03 /tuong-niem-co-giao-su-le-van-diem.html.

18. Nguyễn Thế Anh, personal communication, November 24, 2020.

19. Vietnam Feature Service, "Decade of Expansion of Higher Education in South Vietnam," 15–17, Douglas Pike Collection, Virtual Vietnam Archives, Texas Tech University, accessed December 2, 2020, available at https://vva.vietnam.ttu.edu. See also Đỗ T. H. (2012).

20. Vietnam Feature Service, "Decade of Expansion," 14; Hoshall (1971: 7).

21. Ngô Thanh Nhàn, personal communication, November 21, 2020.

22. Bac Tran, personal communication, November 22, 2020.

23. On anticommunism among first-generation Vietnamese Americans, see Dang T. V. (2005: 64–86).

CHAPTER 4

1. Portions of Chapter 4 previously appeared as "From Reeducation Camps to Little Saigons: Historicizing Vietnamese Diasporic Anticommunism," Journal of Vietnamese Studies 11, no. 2: 43–95. Copyright University of California Press. Used with permission.

2. There is no entry about anticommunism for any other group.

3. A different example is Bui L. T. (2018). While starting from a perspective critical of U.S. imperialism, this study focuses on Vietnamese American voices found in fiction, memoirs, and archival preservation.

4. A review of the critical scholarship is Le L. S. (2011a). Le offers the following observation about the general gist of the scholarship: "Is there a need to explain the anti-communist ideology? And is there a need to transcend the anti-communist ideology? For critical scholars such as Yen Le Espiritu, Nguyen Vo Thu-Huong, Linda Vo, Viet Thanh Nguyen, and Lan Duong, the answers are 'no' and 'yes,' respectively. Meanwhile, other critical scholars such as Karin Aguilar-San Juan and Roy Vu, the answer [sic] are 'yes' and 'no'" (Le L. S. 2011a: 7). See also the Introduction of this volume on critical refugee studies.

5. A different interpretation is Hoang T. (2021).

6. Not insignificantly, it is the first reference to former political prisoners in a major scholarly study of Little Saigon.

7. The book employs some primary sources in Vietnamese and offers perspectives from the refugees themselves, including musician Phạm Duy and publisher Yến Đỗ.

8. I learned this information from conversations with former political prisoners at a reunion of former prisoners of the camps Tân Lập and Vĩnh Phúc on May 11, 2014, in Westminster, California.

9. This source was cited in original as J. M. Thich (or Joseph Maria Thich). The section on Father Pierre Khang and the Catholic press during the Popular Front is drawn from Keith (2012), plus information from Hương Vĩnh (2007).

10. Ngô Văn was an active Trotskyist at the time.

11. The Vietnamese terms for *national defense* and *self-defense* teams are *vệ quốc quân* and *tự vệ*, respectively.

12. Diệm's anticommunist campaign is discussed at length by Tran N.-A. (2013).

13. Võ Đại Tôn was captured in October 1981 and spent over ten years in prison before being released back to Australia because of international pressure on Vietnam.

14. On the homeland liberation movement, see Nguyen Phuong Tran (2017) and Tran T. N. (2007). Neither work, however, considers the psychological impact caused by the abruptness of the fall of Saigon.

15. An example of second-wave memoirs is Đỗ V. P. (2008). Citations come from the edited online version available at http://michaelpdo.com/wp-content/uploads/2015/06/CTDN_PDF.pdf.

16. The leave was sponsored by his uncle, a party member. Even there, this practice was rare.

17. See Tran T. N. (2007), which examines the roles of mutual-aid associations in refugee resettlement.

CHAPTER 5

1. This chapter is based on research and writing that was a part of the author's doctoral dissertation (Gonzalez 2017).

2. The term *mutual assistance association* came into use during the period of Southeast Asian refugee resettlement in the United States to describe ethnic-based organizations that could act as service providers within the community and as liaisons between the community and government and private agencies facilitating resettlement. Though ethnic organizations and mutual-aid groups in the United States have existed since the nineteenth century and have been studied by sociologists beginning with Robert Park in the early twentieth century, they were largely informal and unincorporated into government structures until the passage of the Refugee Act of 1980. After 1980, MAAs were seen as a legitimate resource for government bodies to use in refugee resettlement.

3. *Gia Đình Việt Nam/Vietnam Family* 2, no. 1, January 1976, *Mayor Tom Bradley Administration Papers*, collection 293.

4. Letter, April Tran Hoang Ngu to Tom Bradley, September 27, 1983, *Mayor Tom Bradley Administration Papers*, collection 293.

5. "Vietnam: A Saga of Riches to Refugee," *Los Angeles Collegian*, November 20, 1981, 3, available at https://lacitycollege.contentdm.oclc.org/digital/collection/LACCNP02/id/19034/rec/2.

6. Letter, Kieu Chinh to Tom Bradley, March 2, 1981, *Mayor Tom Bradley Administration Papers*, collection 293.

7. Los Angeles County Department of Community Services, "Refugee Targeted Assistance Application/Plan," July 1983, *Mayor Tom Bradley Administration Papers*, collection 293.

8. Los Angeles County Lettergram, Office of Supervisor Edmund D. Edelman, "Request for Press Conference," March 25, 1985, *Papers of Edmund D. Edelman*.

9. Press Release, Office of Supervisor Ed Edelman, Third District, "Edelman Hosts Event to Commemorate Ten Years of Indochinese Refugee Resettlement in L.A. County," April 10, 1985, *Papers of Edmund D. Edelman*.

10. Los Angeles City Council Resolution, January 14, 1976, *Los Angeles City Council Public Record 78–182*.

11. Los Angeles City Council Resolution.

12. Los Angeles County Lettergram, Jim Miyano to Edmund D. Edelman, January 17, 1980, *Papers of Edmund D. Edelman*.

13. Motion by Supervisor Edmund D. Edelman, "Subject: Indo-China Refugee Referral Center," August 21, 1979, *Mayor Tom Bradley Administration Papers*, collection 293.

14. Interdepartmental Correspondence, Christine Ung to Tom Bradley's Office, "Subject: L.A. County Actions re Southeast Asian Refugees, Recommendations for City Actions," August 24, 1979, *Mayor Tom Bradley Administration Papers*, collection 293.

15. "LA County to Establish Refugee Referral Center," *East West Magazine*, September 5, 1979, *Mayor Tom Bradley Administration Papers*, collection 293.

16. Los Angeles County Lettergram, Jim Miyano to Edmund D. Edelman, "Subject: Coordination Meeting for Agencies Serving Indochinese Refugees," May 27, 1980, *Papers of Edmund D. Edelman*.

17. Internal Memo, Christine Ung to Anton Calleis, "Subject: Los Angeles County Indochinese Refugee Service Center: Supervisor Edelman's Request for City Participation," May 14, 1982, *Mayor Tom Bradley Administration Papers*, collection 293.

18. Letter, Los Angeles County Indochinese Advisory Board Chairman Phat Mekdara to County Supervisor Edmund D. Edelman, July 29, 1983, *Papers of Edmund D. Edelman*.

19. Letter, County of Los Angeles Department of Community Services to Quoc Hao Trong, President of the American Southern California Indochina Chinese Association, April 6, 1988, *Papers of Edmund D. Edelman*.

20. Letter, County of Los Angeles.

21. Letter, Lilia M. Reyes to Christine Ung, attached to information packet from the United States Conference of Mayors about the Office of Refugee Resettlement, August 8, 1980, *Mayor Tom Bradley Administration Papers*, collection 293.

22. Office Memorandum, Christine Ung, "Subject: Southeast Asian Refugees—D.P.S.S.," September 15, 1975, *Mayor Tom Bradley Administration Papers*, collection 293.

23. Recommendation letter, George M. Nishinaka for Daniel Dinh Phuc Le, July 17, 1975, *Mayor Tom Bradley Administration Papers*, collection 293.

24. *Gia Đình Việt Nam/Vietnam Family*.

25. Flyer and Business Card, Indochinese Refugee Social Services Program of the International Institute, April 1981, *Mayor Tom Bradley Administration Papers*, collection 293.

26. "Final Report on Refugee Leadership and Program Management Training and Technical Assistance for Mutual Assistance Associations (MAAs) in California," Indochina Resource Action Center, December 1985, *Southeast Asia Resource Action Center Records*.

27. *California State Master Plan for Refugees*, draft, volume one, June 2, 1982, State of California Health and Welfare Agency, *Mayor Tom Bradley Administration Papers*, collection 298.

28. Also referred to in organizational documents as the American Southern California Indochina Chinese Association and the Indochina Chinese Association of Southern California.

29. *County of Los Angeles Refugee Targeted Assistance Application/Plan*, Los Angeles County Department of Community Services, July 1983, *Mayor Tom Bradley Administration Papers*, collection 298.

30. Lettergram, Jim Miyano to Supervisor Edmund D. Edelman, "Subject: Thanks America Day Invitation," November 17, 1989, *Papers of Edmund D. Edelman.*

CHAPTER 6

1. World Bank, "Migration and Remittances Data 2020," accessed June 12, 2021, available at http://www.worldbank.org/en/topic/migrationremittancesdiasporaissues/brief/migration-remittances-data.

2. Among others, see City of Westminster Resolution 3750 (2003). LA Times March 11, 2003. Mai Tran and Scott Martelle. "Vietnam's Flag Raises Hackles in Little Saigon," accessed July 4, 2022, https://www.latimes.com/archives/la-xpm-2003-mar-11-me-viet11-story.html.

3. Vietnamese American NGO Network, accessed July 28, 2021, available at http://va-ngo.org.

4. "Overseas Vietnamese Contribute to Promoting Economic Development in Vietnam," *Que Huong Magazine*, October 30, 2020, accessed October 31, 2020, available at http://quehuongonline.vn/nguoi-viet-o-nuoc-ngoai/kieu-bao-gop-suc-thuc-day-phat-trien-kinh-te-viet-nam-20201030210840009.htm.

5. In this section, I partly draw on interviews collected with Vietnamese American NGO workers and volunteers in Vietnam during a study of diaspora NGOs conducted in 2008 (Truong K. C., Small, and Vuong D. 2008), ongoing observations and conversations since then, and follow-up discussions conducted in 2020 to assess the changing state of the field. To protect both the identities of individuals and organizations that may or may not be formally registered, and to avoid inadvertently overemphasizing the impact of one group over another, I am not including the names of specific participants or organizations. The maintenance of their anonymity helps to highlight the personal motivations that drive the work of such actors, unattached to any specific individual or organizational recognition or fundraising goals.

6. Asia Society, *Civil Society in Vietnam* 2012, accessed September 10, 2020, available at https://asiafoundation.org/resources/pdfs/CivilSocietyReportFINALweb.pdf.

CHAPTER 7

1. The quote is from former President Nguyễn Minh Triết. See Embassy of the Socialist Republic of Vietnam, "Pres. Nguyen Minh Triet's Historic Visit to the United States," June 22, 2007, accessed June 30, 2022, https://vietnamembassy-usa.org/relations/pres-nguyen-minh-triets-historic-visit-united-states.

2. Cited in Furuya and Collett 2009: 63.

3. Cited in Furuya and Collett 2009: 66.

4. See the work of Thuy Vo Dang (2008) and Nhi Lieu (2011), among others, for examples of how politics and culture intertwine.

5. The search parameters included "Vietnamese"/"người Vietnam" and "protest," "demonstration"/"biểu tình." Searches were undertaken using the NewsBank database, newspapers.com, nguoi-viet.com, and ocregister.com. It should be underscored that the data in Figure 7.1 represent only those events to receive media coverage in these outlets. While arguably comprehensive, this may not be exhaustive or fully inclusive of all public political/cultural activities taking place in the region over this period. The searches only go as far back as 1981, owing to gaps in full-text archival resources.

6. The duration of these events was estimated on the basis of the content of the news reports.

7. Hanoi claims long-standing sovereignty over both archipelagoes and, in line with its *Đổi Mới* policy to incorporate Vietnamese Americans into the nation, has organized tours of the region and published expatriate reminisces reflecting on "Trường Sa . . . as a sacred outpost . . . a place to meet and harmonise all the nation, where all Vietnamese hearts are always heading to" (Vietnam Union of Friendship Organizations 2019).

8. Tâm An, "Biểu tình 'Bảo vệ người Việt tị nạn' tại Little Saigon," *Người Việt Daily News*, December 16, 2018, available at https://www.nguoi-viet.com/little-saigon/bieu-tinh -bao-ve-nguoi-viet-ti-nan-tai-little-saigon/; Terry Nguyen, "Support for Trump Is Tearing Apart Vietnamese American Families," Vox.com, October 30, 2020, available at https:// www.vox.com/first-person/2020/10/30/21540263/vietnamese-american-support-trump -2020.

9. "Chamber History," VACOC, accessed December 31, 2020, https://vacoc.org/about /chamber-history/.

10. IRS Business Master Files (BMF), compiled by the NCCS, available at https://nccs -data.urban.org/data.php?ds=bmf.

11. HRV-PAC emerged in the 2012 election and, according to Federal Election Commission filings, raised $147,196 during that cycle and made $49,000 in contributions, mostly to Democratic senators and representatives. In 2014, it raised an additional $177,158 but made far fewer contributions to federal candidates. In 2016, it made only $6,000 in donations, and by 2018, the committee was terminated.

12. Sharon Simonson, "Bay Area Vietnamese Promote Uprising in Vietnam," *SiliconValleyOneWorld*, September 12, 2016, accessed December 26, 2016, available at http://www .siliconvalleyoneworld.com/2016/09/12/bay-area-vietnamese-seek-to-inspire-uprising-in -vietnam-after-huge-fish-kill/; Tuổi Trẻ Online, "Terrorist Group Responsible for Recent Rallies in Ho Chi Minh City, Police Say," June 16, 2016, accessed December 26, 2016, available at http://tuoitrenews.vn/society/34802/terrorist-group-responsible-for-recent-rallies -in-ho-chi-minh-city-police.

13. Reuters, "Vietnam Declares California-Based Group Terrorist," October 8, 2016, accessed December 28, 2020, available at http://www.reuters.com/article/us-vietnam -security-idUSKCN1271HZ; *Nhân Dân*, "Chân Tướng Các Quỹ Nhân Danh 'Dân Chủ,'" November 10, 2020. See also Ministry of Public Security, accessed January 2, 2021, http:// en.bocongan.gov.vn/terrorist/terrorist-group.html.

14. Bayard Rustin, "From Protest to Politics: The Future of the Civil Rights Movement," *Commentary*, February 1965, available at https://www.commentarymagazine.com/articles /bayard-rustin-2/from-protest-to-politics-the-future-of-the-civil-rights-movement/.

15. "An ideological movement led by the first generation, to identify, articulate, institutionalize and enforce the symbols and history of the diaspora" (Collet and Furuya 2010).

16. Cited in Collet (2008: 716).

17. Taken from a mailer distributed by Congresswoman Loretta Sanchez, May 16, 2007.

18. A search of the U.S. House Telephone Directory (https://directory.house.gov/#/) undertaken in December 2020 finds thirty-one staff with Vietnamese surnames, seventeen of whom are assigned to individual members, including Zoe Lofgren (D-San Jose) and Harley Rouda (D-Newport Beach). Rouda was defeated in 2020 by Republican Michelle Steele.

19. Michelle Krupa, "Anh 'Joseph' Cao Beats Rep. William Jefferson in 2nd Congressional District," NOLA.com, *Times-Picayune*, December 7, 2008, accessed July 1, 2022, available at https://www.nola.com/news/article_46869bac-6694-59a6-9789-785ff0ea66b1 .html.

20. In Cao's case, the recall was launched not by Vietnamese Americans but by African American ministers who took exception to Cao's "no" vote on a stimulus bill crafted by

the Obama administration. See Jonathan Tilove, "Two Ministers Leading Recall Effort against Cao Face Long Odds," *Times-Picayune*, February 19, 2009, available at https://www.nola.com/news/articlef7593167-702e-5d34-ac8b-f18546b6feee.html.

21. Vo Thy, "Backlash Continues against Garden Grove Mayor over Sister City Letter," *Voice of OC*, February 25, 2015, available at https://voiceofoc.org/2015/02/backlash-conti nues-against-garden-grove-mayor-over-sister-city-letter/.

22. "Stephanie Murphy for Congress," accessed March 6, 2021, available at https://www.stephaniemurphyfl.com/about/.

23. "Cast Forward 2022 with Stephanie Murphy," February 24, 2021, accessed March 6, 2021, available at https://www.youtube.com/watch?v=T3IlfM-HXRo&t=3s.

CHAPTER 8

1. *U.S. Census Bureau* (2018).

2. *U.S. Census Bureau* (2009). Laura Harjanto and Jeanne Batalova, "Vietnamese Immigrants in the United States," Migration Policy Institute, October 15, 2021, available at https://www.migrationpolicy.org/article/vietnamese-immigrants-united-states.

3. Mastercard Index of Women Entrepreneurs, Mastercard, 2018, accessed May 11, 2021, available at https://newsroom.mastercard.com/documents/mastercard-index-of-women -entrepreneurs-miwe-2018/.

4. Transcript of interview with Kien Tam Nguyen by Thuy Vo Dang, May 22, 2012, University of California, Irvine, Vietnamese American Oral History Project, available at http://ucispace.lib.uci.edu/handle/10575/3282.

CHAPTER 9

1. "Race and Ethnicity in the United States: 2010 Census and 2020 Census," August 12, 2021, available at https://www.census.gov/library/visualizations/interactive/race-and -ethnicity-in-the-united-state-2010-and-2020-census.html.

2. The term *Mỹ đen* in Vietnamese literally means Black Americans. White Americans are called *Mỹ trắng*, and Latinos are commonly called *Mễ*, which is a short form for Mexico or Mexicans. In Vietnamese, these descriptive terms do not carry negative connotations. Such connotations are often expressed by the articles preceding them meaning "those"; for example, *bọn* or *tụi* show lack of respect whereas *người* and *dân* are neutral. Vietnamese Americans don't say "Mỹ gốc Phi" (African Americans) or "Mỹ gốc Âu" (Caucasian/European Americans) but do say "Mỹ gốc Việt" (Vietnamese Americans). They sometimes jokingly call themselves *đầu đen* (meaning literally "black heads," referring to their black hair), *Mỹ vàng* ("yellow Americans"), or *mít* (from *Annamite*, a French word referring to Vietnamese in general, or more specifically from central Vietnam during the colonial period).

CHAPTER 10

1. This chapter adapts a version of my dissertation chapter, "Not Coming to Terms: Diaspora, Multidirectional Memory, and the Limits of Reconciliation." See Phan H.-D. (2012).

2. Nguyen T. T. and Weigl (1994); Hô and Karlin (2003); Bowen, Nguyen, and Weigl (1998); Mahony (1998); and Nguyen Q. T. (1997) all foster cultural understanding and seek reconciliation through literature. Against this backdrop, Dinh (2003) stands out for its avowed interest in the art and also for its inclusion of a greater range of voices.

3. Interview with Phan Nhiên Hạo.

4. Compare Phan's "Portraits" with Nguyễn Duy's conciliatory poem, "To the Vietnamese Living in Foreign Lands." Nguyễn Duy's poem emptied Vietnamese diaspora of its historical and political content in order to secure a conciliatory call for "Vietnamese Living in Foreign Lands" to return to a Vietnam that his poem imagined in a prewar vision of pastoral nostalgia.

5. The poem was originally published in the 2004 collection *Chế Tạo Thơ Ca 99-04* [Manufacturing Poetry 99-04] (Phan N. H. 2004). It is not included in Linh Dinh's edited and translated *Night, Fish and Charlie Parker* (Phan N. H. 2006). The translation is mine. Reprinted with permission of the author.

6. "Phác thảo cho một chân dung tự họa," in Phan N. H. (2019: 23–24). The translation is mine. Reprinted with permission of the author.

7. "Phác thảo cho một chân dung tự họa."

8. "Night's Dawn" [Rạng Đông Của Đêm], in Phan N. H. (2006: 11). Translated by Linh Dinh. Reprinted with permission of the author.

9. "As the Train Approaches" [Trong Khi Con Tàu Đi Tới], in Phan N. H. (2006: 37). Translated by Linh Dinh. Reprinted with permission of the author.

10. "Đất nước này," in Phan N. H. (2019: 55–56). The translation is mine. Reprinted with permission of the author.

11. "Radio Mùa Hè," in Phan N. H. (2019: 88–89). The translation is mine.

12. "Chế Tạo Thơ Ca," in Phan N. H. (2004: 87). The translation is mine. Reprinted with permission of the author.

CHAPTER 11

1. The other singers included Giao Linh, Thanh Tuyền, Hùng Cường, Kim Tuyến, Diễm Chi, Việt Hùng, Thu Hồng, Tuyết Hằng, Đức Hiển, Huỳnh Công Ánh, Lê Nguyên, Ngọc Thanh, and Mặt Trận's Southern California Choir [Đoàn Văn Nghệ Kháng Chiến Nam Cali]. See Việt Ánh, "11.000 Người Tham Dự Đại Hội Chào Mừng Lễ Công Bố Cương Lĩnh Chính Trị" [11,000 People Attend the Conference to Celebrate the Ceremony to Announce the Political Platform], *Báo Kháng Chiến*, no. 26 (April 1984): 15.

2. Dan Nakaso, "Dream of Return: Rally Draws 11,000 Viet Refugees," Orange County, *Los Angeles Times*, March 18, 1984, 1, accessed September 14, 2019, available at https://www.newspapers.com/image/400651670/.

3. Nakaso.

4. The meaning of the organization's name in English is the Revolutionary [*cách mạng*] Party [*đảng*] to Reform [*canh tân*] Vietnam, and thus, it is commonly referred to as the Việt Nam Reform Party, or Việt Tân, for short. The latter name has gained greater recognition in Vietnamese and international contexts, so I will refer to the organization as Việt Tân.

5. When I refer to "publicly known transnational activism campaigns," I mean strategic instances where Việt Tân carries out overt actions of resistance. Because the Vietnamese state uses repression as a tool to silence its opposition, not all activities Việt Tân organizes are publicly disclosed; the secrecy skirts state surveillance and keeps the activists safe. However, as the movement progresses toward its objective, there are times when a publicly known action becomes a tactic to directly challenge the state's authority. There is another overseas organization called *Tổ Chức Phục Hưng Việt Nam* [Việt Nam Restoration Party] with a timeline of development similar to Việt Tân's. However, since *Tổ Chức Phục Hưng Việt Nam*'s activities in the homeland are still underground, Việt Tân remains a helpful case study to examine diasporic nationalism as a strategy and tactic for activism.

6. The long-form name of Mặt Trận is *Mặt Trận Quốc Gia Thống Nhất Giải Phóng Việt Nam* [National United Front for the Liberation of Việt Nam]. References to the organiza-

tion in English have used the abbreviation NUFRONLIV, NUFLVN, or NUFLV, and the term *the Front*. Within the Vietnamese community, the organization is known as Mặt Trận, for short. To remain consistent with Vietnamese terminology, I refer to the organization as Mặt Trận.

7. For an in-depth analysis of why Việt Tân existed underground at its inception, see Bui Duyen (2020: 106–109).

8. In the early 1980s, the founders of Mặt Trận and Việt Tân planned that the movement would reach its objective within a decade. Furthermore, they weren't able to foresee the end of the Cold War. As political conditions changed during the post–Cold War period and in the new millennium, the organization's leadership decided to publicly announce the existence of Việt Tân and dissolve Mặt Trận in September 2004.

9. Quote in Vietnamese states, "Đại hội còn cho chúng ta một niềm kiêu hãnh. Kiêu hãnh vì chúng ta rất đoàn kết, rất thiết tha đến vận mệnh của dân tộc mình." See Việt Ánh, "11.000 Người," 14.

10. Phạm Văn Liễu stated in Vietnamese: "Chiến hữu Chủ Tịch đã nhắn nhủ chúng ta là chỉ có tổ quốc Việt Nam mới không xua đuổi chúng ta, chỉ có tổ quốc Việt Nam mới không ruồng rẫy con dân Việt Nam. Và Chiến Hữu Hoàng Cơ Minh đã nhắc nhở chúng ta là chưa khi nào người Việt Nam cần tới tổ quốc như ngày hôm nay." See Việt Ánh. Members in Mặt Trận and Việt Tân refer to one another as *chiến hữu* [comrade] to erase the sense of hierarchy associated with Vietnamese pronouns that indicate a person's age and gender. Members of the Vietnamese Communist Party (VCP) also refer to one another as comrade. However, they use the term *đồng chí*. In the overseas community, I have observed that people who are involved in the Vietnamese democracy movement but are not members of Việt Tân will still call one another *chiến hữu* to reflect the sense of camaraderie and allyship.

11. Mặt Trận Quốc Gia Thống Nhất Giải Phóng Việt Nam, *Mặt Trận Quốc Gia Thống Nhất Giải Phóng Việt Nam và Con Đường Cứu Nước* [National United Front for the Liberation of Việt Nam and the Road to Save the Country] (San Jose, CA: Tổng Vụ Hải Ngoại, Mặt Trận Quốc Gia Thống Nhất Giải Phóng Việt Nam, 2000), 179.

12. Mặt Trận, 181.

13. On May 5, 1995, an FBI Memorandum line item states that the statute of limitations for the investigation expires in September 1995 if no new offense can be identified in the case. See FBI, "Weekly Summary of VOECRN Investigative Activities May 1–5, 1995," Document no. 100-487539-876X4, San Francisco, May 1995. Twenty years later, a nonprofit organization focused on investigative journalism called ProPublica attempted to find new evidence that could reopen the FBI case. ProPublica partnered with the PBS show *Frontline* to broadcast a segment about the case in November 2015. The report acknowledged that the FBI and Department of Justice had to close the case because of insufficient evidence after fifteen years of investigation. See A. C. Thompson, "Terror in Little Saigon: An Old War Comes to a New Country," *ProPublica*, November 3, 2015, available at https://www.propublica.org/article/terror-in-little-saigon-vietnam-american-journalists-murdered.

14. For a fuller and more even-handed analysis, see Marr (2013: 383–441).

15. *Đại Lễ Chào Mừng Quốc Khánh Ghi Ơn Quốc Tổ* [Grand Celebration Vietnamese National Day] (Atlanta, GA: 2000), 3.

16. This Việt Tân perspective is a paraphrase from the quote "Ngày Quốc Khánh không đến từ một biến cố chính trị, trong đó có người vui kẻ buồn. Ngày Quốc Khánh cũng không là ngày chiến thắng của một phe mà sau khi tiếng súng đã im vẫn còn tiếng người nức nở. Ngày Quốc Khánh phải là ngày của thái hòa khai mở, vượt lên trên những tranh chấp của mọi thời kỳ. Ngày Quốc Khánh phải là ngày có ý nghĩa của toàn dân, từ trước tới sau." The excerpt is from a pamphlet given out at the main National Day celebration that Việt Tân organized yearly from 1987 until 2001. Within the pamphlet is a brief his-

tory of the King Hùng dynasty. It also explains why this commemoration day should be celebrated as a National Day in opposition to the one the Vietnamese state observed. See *Đại Lễ Chào Mừng*, 9.

17. Kim Tân, "Thông Qua Phương Án Xây Nhà Quốc Hội và Nghỉ Ngày Giỗ Tổ" [Approving the Plan to Construct the National Assembly Building and Declare King Hùng Commemoration a Holiday], *Việt Báo*, April 2, 2007, accessed November 20, 2019, available at https://vietbao.vn/Xa-hoi/Thong-qua-phuong-an-xay-nha-Quoc-hoi-va-nghi-ngay -gio-To/30173078/157/.

18. The excerpt in Vietnamese: "Tổ Tiên chúng ta đã chăn dắt muôn dân trong tình thương yêu bao bọc. Tổ Tiên chúng ta không xua đuổi con cháu ra biển, đi tỵ nạn." See *Đại Lễ Chào Mừng*, 9.

19. The excerpt in Vietnamese: "Chọn ngày Quốc Tổ, chúng ta còn muốn nói với những người hiện đang lầm lỡ làm công cụ cho một thiểu số lãnh đạo u tối trong đảng Cộng Sản Việt Nam nhìn ra cội nguồn tổ tông mà rời bỏ hàng ngũ hại dân hại nước trở về với đại khối dân tộc." See *Đại Lễ Chào Mừng*, 9.

20. Việt Nam Canh Tân Cách Mạng Đảng, *Trên Đường Đông Tiến* [On the Eastward Road] (San Jose, CA: Việt Nam Canh Tân Cách Mạng Đảng, 2007), 146–161.

21. "To Commemorate the Viet Nam National Day: The NRC Establishes the Art and Literature Award," *Vietnamese Resistance* 2, no. 1 (January 1987): 2.

22. "The 1987 Arts and Literature Award," *Vietnamese Resistance* 2, no. 4 (April 1987): 1.

23. Việt Nam Canh Tân Cách Mạng Đảng, *Trên Đường Đông Tiến*, 146–161.

24. "Why Is the South China Sea Contentious?" *British Broadcasting Corporation*, July 12, 2016, accessed January 13, 2020, available at https://www.bbc.com/news/world-asia -pacific-13748349; Steve Mollman, "The Line on a 70-Year-Old Map That Threatens to Set Off a War in East Asia," *Quartz*, July 7, 2016, accessed January 14, 2020, available at https:// qz.com/705223/where-exactly-did-chinas-nine-dash-line-in-the-south-china-sea-come -from/.

25. "Việt Nam Biểu Tình Đồng Loạt Chống Luật Đặc Khu" [Vietnamese Mass Protest Against the Special Economic Zone Law], *Voice of America*, January 10, 2018, accessed January 15, 2020, available at https://www.voatiengviet.com/a/bieu-tinh-dac-khu-an-ninh -mang-dong-loat/4432293.html; Quỳnh Nguyễn, "Nhìn Lại Cuộc Biểu Tình Ngày 10.6.2018" [Reviewing the Protests on June 10, 2018], *Chân Trời Mới Media*, June 17, 2018, accessed January 15, 2020, available at https://chantroimoimedia.com/2018/06/17/nhin-lai-cuoc-bieu -tinh-ngay-10-6-2018/.

26. "China Pays Close Attention to So-Called Protest in Vietnam over South China Sea," *Xinhua*, December 11, 2007, accessed December 15, 2011, available at http://news.xinhuanet .com/english/2007-12/11/content_7230702.htm. The exception to this trend was in the sum-mer of 2011, when for about eleven weeks straight, on every Sunday, people demonstrated against China after it cut the cable lines of a Vietnamese oil exploration ship. See Kerkvliet (2019: 66–73).

27. Huỳnh Lương Thiện, Phạm Phú Thiện Giao, and Việt Dzũng, "Hèn Với Giặc Ác Với Dân" [Cowardly toward the Enemy, Brutal with the People], interview by Mai Khôi, *Radio Free Asia*, July 19, 2011, accessed January 14, 2020, available at https://www.rfa.org /vietnamese/in_depth/opinio-oversea-media-ab-protes-07192011082318.html.

28. Viet Tan, "Mời Tham Dự Cuộc Thi #40nămquáđủ" [Join the #40YearsTooMany Competition], *Facebook*, April 7, 2015, accessed January 22, 2020, available at https://www .facebook.com/viettan/photos/a.10151333017390620/10153833001905620; Đoàn Hưng, "Cuộc Thi '#40NămQúaĐủ': Người Dân Việt Không Muốn Chờ Đợi Thêm Nữa" ["#40Years TooMany" Competition: Vietnamese People Do Not Want to Wait Any Longer], *Saigon Broadcasting Television Network*, April 15, 2015, accessed January 17, 2020, available at

https://www.sbtn.tv/cuoc-thi-40namquadu-nguoi-dan-viet-khong-muon-cho-doi-them
-nua/; "Vietnamese Use '40 Years Too Many' Tag to Call for End to Communism," *Aljazeera
the Stream*, April 23, 2015, accessed January 17, 2020, available at http://stream.aljazeera
.com/story/201504231341-0024710.

29. Viet Tan, "Công Bố Kết Quả Cuộc Thi #40NămQuáĐủ" [Results of the #40Years
TooMany Competition], *Facebook*, April 30, 2015, accessed January 17, 2020, available at
https://www.facebook.com/viettan/posts/10153906742135620; Đoàn Hưng, "Công Bố Kết
Quả Cuộc Thi #40NămQuáĐủ" [Results of the #40YearsTooMany Competition], *Saigon
Broadcasting Television Network*, April 30, 2015, accessed January 17, 2020, available at
https://www.sbtn.tv/cong-bo-ket-qua-cuoc-thi-%E2%80%AA%E2%80%8E40namquadu%
E2%80%AC/; BBC News Tiếng Việt, "Trong Ba Tuần Trước 30/4" [Three Weeks Before April
30], *Facebook*, May 1, 2015, accessed January 17, 2020, available at https://www.facebook
.com/BBCnewsVietnamese/photos/a.269955539683862/1026307290715346.

30. Lã Việt Dũng, Bạch Hồng Quyền, Anthony Lê, and Thúy Nga, "Phong Trào 'Tôi
Không Thích Đảng Cộng Sản Việt Nam'" [The "I Don't Like the Communist Party of Việt
Nam" Movement], interviewed by Chân Như, *Radio Free Asia*, January 14, 2015, accessed
January 4, 2020, available at https://www.rfa.org/vietnamese/news/programs/YouthForum
/i-dislike-the-communist-party-of-vn-cn-01142015103454.html.

31. The paraphrase is from a quote of Lã Việt Dũng that states: "Nếu nói xấu mà đúng
thì chính quyền phải nên lắng nghe chứ không nên đe doạ như vậy. Tôi coi đấy là một thái
độ mang tính đe doạ sự thật. Tôi nghĩ rằng vậy nếu chúng ta không thích, nhưng đấy là
thật thì liệu đấy có phải là xấu không? Và liệu như vậy chính quyền có xử lý chúng ta hay
không?" See Dũng et al.

32. Châu Văn Thi, "Thích Hay Không Thích Đảng Cộng Sản Việt Nam" [Like or Dislike the Communist Party of Việt Nam], *Dân Luận*, January 7, 2015, accessed January 23,
2020, available at https://www.danluan.org/tin-tuc/20150107/chau-van-thi-thich-hay-khong
-thich-dang-cong-san-viet-nam.

33. Patrick Winn, "A Rap Anthem Called 'F*ck Communism' Is Going Viral in Vietnam," *Public Radio International*, July 24, 2015, accessed January 27, 2020, available at https://
www.pri.org/stories/2015-07-24/rap-anthem-called-fck-communism-going-viral-vietnam.

34. Nah Sơn explained to reporter Mặc Lâm in Vietnamese, "khi qua đây học rồi thấy
nó có nhiều khác biệt với mình quá. Cách giảng dạy rất mới và đây là lần đầu tiên đi học
mà em thấy thích. Em học những vấn đề xã hội, chính trị, lịch sử . . . nó làm cho mình
nhận ra, mình ngộ ra được nhiều thứ hay lắm. Em tự tìm hiểu thêm trên Google, tự mình
đúc kết lại và thấy rõ ràng là đất nước mình đang lâm nguy và nó có quá nhiều vấn đề nên
em làm những điều này mong góp phần thay đổi đất nước." See Nah Sơn, "Nah Sơn, Một
Du Học Sinh, Rapper Bất Đồng Chính Kiến," interviewed by Mặc Lâm, *Radio Free Asia*,
January 17, 2015, accessed January 27, 2020, available at https://www.rfa.org/vietnamese
/news/programs/LiteratureAndArts/nah-son-overseas-student-dissident-rapper-ml-0117
2015095650.html.

35. "Phong Trào #ĐMCS Nối Tiếp #ToiKhongThich" [#ĐMCS Movement Connects
with #ToiKhongThich], *Dân Luận*, February 19, 2015, accessed January 27, 2020, available
at https://www.danluan.org/tin-tuc/20150219/phong-trao-dmcs-noi-tiep-toikhongthich.

36. Nguyễn Giang, "Việt Nam's Zombie Uprising," *Loa*, July 20, 2015, accessed April
14, 2019, https://www.loa.fm/our-stories/zombie.

CHAPTER 12

1. Although I use the singular form of *diaspora* here, I want to emphasize that the
Vietnamese diaspora consists of multiple diasporas, which have distinctive historical for-

mations (e.g., the precolonial-era diaspora, the colonial-era diaspora, the refugee diaspora, the socialist/post-socialist diaspora, etc.). Some of these diasporas overlap, while others exist relatively independent from one another. Nonetheless, they all share a common root stemming from territories that now encompass modern-day Vietnam and claim this entity as an original homeland. For more on the diversity of the Vietnamese diaspora, see Trần T. Đ. Đ. (2005) and Schwenkel (2017).

2. My understanding of memory and forgetting draws on French philosopher Paul Ricoeur's notion of remembering and forgetting as reciprocal processes and Viet Thanh Nguyen's notion of the dialectic of memory and amnesia.

3. James E. Young uses the concept of "memory work" to indicate the dynamic nature of memory.

4. In line with my earlier note about the multiplicity of Vietnamese diasporas, I see Vietnamese American memoryscapes as part of many memoryscapes. At the same time, Vietnamese American memoryscapes are not solely constituted by refugee experiences although it can be argued that refugee experiences dominate the landscape of remembering and forgetting.

5. Viet Stories: Vietnamese American Oral History Project, UC Irvine, accessed October 20, 2020, available at https://sites.uci.edu/vaohp. The Vietnamese American Heritage Foundation's oral histories collection has been digitized and made accessible through the Vietnamese in the Diaspora Digital Archive, a project of the Vietnamese American Heritage Foundation, accessed October 20, 2020, available at https://vietdiasporastories.omeka.net.

6. Interview with Vũ Văn Lộc by author, July 28, 2017, San Jose, CA.

7. Pulau Bidong Alumni_Tỵ Nạn Pulau Bidong Facebook Group, accessed October 20, 2020, available at https://facebook.com/groups/pulaubidong/about. This is only one of several groups dedicated to refugee experiences on Pulau Bidong. There are also similar groups created by and for other boat refugees in other camp contexts.

8. For examples of documentary films, see Duc Nguyen, *Bolinao 52* (2008), *Stateless* (2013). For examples of feature films, see Timothy Linh Bui, *Rong Xanh/Green Dragon* (2001); Ham Tran, *Journey from the Fall* (2006).

9. For example, Valverde (2012) studies the controversial installation of a nail footbath by artist Chau Huynh at the Nguoi Viet Newspaper Community Center, while Bui L. (2018) examines the F.O.B. II exhibition organized by the Vietnamese American Arts and Letters Association.

CHAPTER 13

1. According to Caodai oral and written history, the image of the Caodai Mother Goddess is based on that of a Chinese Queen Mother. As a result, whether the Caodai Mother Goddess "looks" Vietnamese or Chinese can be a matter of debate.

2. I use *worship*, *venerate*, and *honor* interchangeably in this paper. I am aware that the meanings of these words vary across different religious traditions. For example, Vietnamese Catholics worship only God and venerate or honor other religious figures, including the Virgin Mary. On the other hand, Vietnamese Caodaists worship and venerate both the (male) Supreme Being and the Mother Goddess as complementary spiritual entities.

3. There are fifty-four officially recognized ethnic groups in Vietnam.

4. Home Office, "Vietnam: Ethnic and Religious Groups," 2018, accessed June 28, 2020, available at https://assets.publishing.service.gov.uk/government/uploads/system/uploads/attachment_data/file/695864/Vietnam_-_Ethnic_and_Religious_groups_-_CPIN_v2.0_ex.pdf.

5. Caodaism has several sects. This paper focuses on the largest one, which is the Tay Ninh Caodai group.

6. Archives Nationales d'Outre-mer [French National Colonial Archives], *Province de Tayninh: Stat des Personnes Frequentantla Pagodede Caodai Pendant le Moisde Juin*, 1927, Box: Caodaism, Aix-en-Provence, France.

7. Home Office, "Vietnam: Ethnic and Religious Groups."

8. Lavang is approximately sixty kilometers north of Huế (the former capital of Vietnam) in central Vietnam.

9. U.S. Census Bureau, "American Community Survey: Vietnamese," 2016, accessed October 28, 2020, available at https://factfinder.census.gov/faces/tableservices/jsf/pages/productview.xhtml?src=bkmk.

10. "The Global Religious Landscape," Pew Forum on Research and Public Life, 2012, accessed February 2, 2022, available at https://www.pewforum.org/2012/12/18/global-religious-landscape-exec/.

11. On June 13, 1992, Vietnamese American Caodaists officially declared the establishment of the "Religious Province of California" [*Châu Đạo California*] at the Vietnamese Convention Center in Westminster City. Under the leadership of a former dignitary who was ordained by the pre-1975 Caodai Holy See, Thuong Mang Thanh, the religious province functioned as the umbrella organization and representative of all other denominational Tây Ninh Caodai religious centers in California. At the time of its establishment, member temples included one Caodai Supreme Being temple in Westminster, another one in Sacramento, and a Mother Goddess shrine and Caodai Supreme Being temple in San Jose. It was the highest and largest Caodai organization outside of Vietnam. The Religious Province of California quickly became the public face of the Caodai community, representing it at events such as neighborhood parades and city council meetings. It mediated connections and exchanges among Caodaists dispersed throughout the world, as exemplified through its regular publication of the *Qui Nguyen* magazine, maintenance of a popular website, and the distribution of CDs on community activities. The religious province also organized and hosted a number of important national and international events, including meetings among overseas Caodai dignitaries and summer youth retreats.

CHAPTER 14

1. "Pocket Diary of a Vietnamese Boat Person Refugee," James A. Schill collection of photographs and a pocket diary of Southeast Asian refugees, UCI Libraries Southeast Asian Archive.

2. "Pocket Diary," 13.

3. Archives have become both object and subject of historical inquiry. For a discussion of the various historical and present uses of the terms *archives* and *record*, see Walsham (2016: 9–48).

4. Calisphere, California Digital Library, accessed July 14, 2022, available at https://calisphere.org.

5. In 2019, I had the opportunity to host a Master of Photography Preservation Fellow, Julia Huynh, from Ryerson University in Canada. Julia processed the James Schill collection and digitized the photograph albums and diary. During Julia's residency with the Southeast Asian Archive, we discussed how to handle potentially sensitive photographs. The decision to digitize the diary aligns with the University of California's principles of making our research materials open and accessible, but ethical stewardship also involves considerations for how we will handle community requests for takedowns in the future. This is an evolving conversation, but we try to document our decisions as much as possible.

6. George Lucas, dir., *Star Wars: Episode II, Attack of the Clones*, 2008, screenplay by George Lucas and Jonathan Hales, produced by Rick McCallum (Beverly Hills, CA: 20th Century Fox Home Entertainment, Lucasfilm).

7. Norindr (1996) provides a useful critique of "Indochina" as a cultural construct, arguing that French colonialism manifests not only in physical territorial domination but also in a domination of the imaginary through cultural production and architecture.

8. Marita Sturken (1997) examines memory projects, from the Vietnam War to 9/11 memorials, and has argued that history is socially reconstructed through myth, fantasy, voyeurism, image making, and cultural amnesia.

9. Wanett Clyde, "The (Unexpected) Emotional Impact of Archiving," *WITNESS: Archiving Human Rights*, August 2015, available at https://archiving.witness.org/2015/08/the-unexpected-emotional-impact-of-archiving/.

10. Thy Phu provides an astute definition of refugee "compassion fatigue" as "an affliction that became acute in the late 1980s and remains pronounced today, denotes the exhaustion of fellow-feeling." Phu points to the mainstream media's role in the deployment of tropes that led to this public sentiment. See Nguyen V., Thy P., and Troeung (2018: 441–445).

11. Audre Lorde's 1982 speech "Learning from the 60s," delivered to Harvard University, celebrating Malcolm X, in *BlackPast*, August 12, 2012, available at https://www.blackpast.org/african-american-history/1982-audre-lorde-learning-60s/.

12. Moreover, archives creators and stewards play key roles in determining which records have historical value, who should have access to them, and how they might be made discoverable. See Cook and Schwartz (2002: 171–185).

13. Daniel (2014: 169–203) has argued that there is a need to better understand "the contextual factors that shape ethnic archiving policies and practices as well as the latter's impact on group identities and intergroup relations."

14. Jerome McDonald and Verne Harris, "How Should We Remember? Nelson Mandela's Personal Archivist Thinks Through Historical Memory," *WBEZ Worldview*, April 10, 2019, available at https://www.wbez.org/stories/how-should-we-remember-nelson-mandelas-personal-archivist-thinks-through-historical-memory/5862ac18-0926-4a28-ac68-9e304c8e46b7.

15. See Terry Nguyen, "Support for Trump Is Tearing apart Vietnamese American Families," *Vox*, October 30, 2020, available at https://www.vox.com/first-person/2020/10/30/21540263/vietnamese-american-support-trump-2020; Valerie Plesch, "Why Are Vietnamese Americans So Divided over Trump," *Aljazeera*, November 2, 2020, available at https://www.aljazeera.com/features/2020/11/2/vietnamese-american-voters; Kimmy Yam, "Who Are the Asian Americans Voting for Trump in Spite of His 'China Virus' Rhetoric?" *NBC News*, October 27, 2020, available at https://www.nbcnews.com/news/asian-america/who-are-asian-americans-still-voting-trump-spite-his-china-n1244849.

16. Bashall (Cynthia Glegge) scrapbooks, MS-SEA057, UCI Libraries Southeast Asian Archive.

References

Adorno, Theodor. 1991. "On Lyric Poetry and Society." In *Notes to Literature*, vol. 1, ed. Rolf Tiedemann, trans. Shierry Weber Nicholsen, 37–54. New York: Columbia University Press.

———. 1998. *Aesthetic Theory*. Trans. Robert Hullot-Kentor. Minneapolis: University of Minnesota Press.

Aguilar-San Juan, Karin. 2005. "Staying Vietnamese: Community and Place in Orange County and Boston." *City and Community* 4, no. 1: 37–65.

———. 2009. *Little Saigons: Staying Vietnamese in America*. Minneapolis: University of Minnesota Press.

Airriess, Christopher. 2006. "Scaling Central Place of an Ethnic-Vietnamese Commercial Enclave in New Orleans, Louisiana." In *Landscapes of the Ethnic Economy*, ed. David Kaplan and Wei Li, 17–33. Plymouth, U.K.: Rowman and Littlefield.

Aldrich, Howard E., and Roger Waldinger. 1990. "Ethnicity and Entrepreneurship." *Annual Review of Sociology* 16, no. 1: 111–135.

Alperin, Elijah, and Jeanne Batalova. 2018. *Vietnamese Immigrants in the United States*. Washington, DC: Migration Policy Institute.

Anderson, Benedict. 1991. *Imagined Communities: Reflections on the Origin and Spread of Nationalism*. London: Verso.

———. 1998. *The Spectre of Comparisons: Nationalism, Southeast Asia, and the World*. London: Verso.

Appadurai, Arjun. 1996. *Modernity at Large: Cultural Dimensions of Globalization*. Minneapolis: University of Minnesota Press.

Ashiwa, Yoshiko, and David L. Wank. 2009. *Making Religion, Making the State: The Politics of Religion in Modern China*. Palo Alto, CA: Stanford University Press.

Asia Entertainment Inc. Garden Grove, California.

Asokan, Ratik. 2021. "On Phan Nhiên Hao." In *New Left Review*, July 21, 2021. Accessed July 22, 2021. Available at https://newleftreview.org/sidecar/posts/on-phan-nhien-hao.

"Ban Giảng-Huấn, 1957–8" [Teaching Staff]. 1958. *Đại Học Văn Khoa/Annales de la faculté des lettres de Saigon* (1957–1958).

Bankston, Carl L., III, and Min Zhou. 1996. "The Ethnic Church, Ethnic Identification, and the Social Adjustment of Vietnamese Adolescents." *Review of Religious Research* 38, no. 1 (September): 18–37.

Bản Thông Tin [Bulletin]. [1971?]. Saigon: Hội Đồng Cơ Quan Từ Thiện tại Vietnam [Council of Foreign Voluntary Agencies in Vietnam].

Bảo Ninh and Frank Palmos. 1995. *The Sorrow of War: A Novel of North Vietnam*. Trans. Phan Thanh Hao. New York: Pantheon.

Bảo Thái. 2002. *Dấu Ấn Chân Tù* [Footprints of Imprisonment]. Abilene, TX: self-published.

Bảo Trân. 2005. "Lá Thư Không Bao Giờ Gởi" [Never Sent Letter]. In *Chuyện Người Vợ Tù Cải Tạo*, vol. 3.

Baumann, Martin. 2000. "Diaspora: Genealogies of Semantics and Transcultural Comparison." *Numen* 47, no. 3 (Religions in the Disenchanted World): 313–337.

Benko, Stephen. 1994. *The Virgin Goddess: Studies in the Pagan and Christian Roots of Mariology*. Leiden: Brill.

Berry, Mary Elizabeth. 1998. "Public Life in Authoritarian Japan." *Daedalus* 127, no. 3: 133–165.

Biggs, David. 2012. *Quagmire: Nation-Building and Nature in the Mekong Delta*. Seattle: University of Washington Press.

Bloemraad, Irene. 2006. *Becoming a Citizen: Incorporating Immigrants and Refugees in the United States and Canada*. Berkeley: University of California Press.

Bonilla-Silva, Eduardo. 2001. *White Supremacy and Racism in the Post-Civil Rights Era*. Boulder, CO: Lynne Rienner.

———. 2010. *Racism without Racists: Color-Blind Racism and the Persistence of Racial Inequality in the United States*. 3rd ed. New York: Rowman and Littlefield.

Borneman, John. 2003. "Why Reconciliation? A Response to Critics." *Public Culture* 15, no. 1 (Winter): 199–208.

Bourdieu, Pierre. 1986. "The Forms of Capital." In *Handbook of Theory*, ed. John Richardson, 241–258. New York: Greenwood.

Bousquet, Gisèle. 1991. *Behind the Bamboo Hedge: The Impact of Homeland Politics in the Parisian Vietnamese Community*. Ann Arbor: University of Michigan Press.

Bowen, Kevin, Nguyen Ba Chung, and Bruce Weigl. 1998. *Mountain River: Vietnamese Poetry from the Wars, 1948–1993*. Amherst: University of Massachusetts Press.

Boyles, Brenda M., and Jeehyun Lim, eds. *Looking Back on the Vietnam War: Twenty-First Century Perspectives*. New Brunswick, NJ: Rutgers University Press.

Boym, Svetlana. 2001. *The Future of Nostalgia*. New York: Basic Books.

Bradley, Mark. 2001. "Contests of Memory: Remembering and Forgetting War in the Contemporary Vietnamese Cinema." In Ho Tai, *The Country of Memory*, 196–226.

Bratton, Michael. 1989. "Review: Beyond the State: Civil Society and Associational Life in Africa." *World Politics* 41, no. 3: 407–430.

Brieger, Steven A., and Michael M. Gielnik. 2020. "Understanding the Gender Gap in Immigrant Entrepreneurship: A Multi-country Study of Immigrants' Embeddedness in Economic, Social, and Institutional Contexts." *Small Business Economics* 56, no. 3 (February): 1–25.

Bui, Diem. 1987. *In the Jaws of History*. Boston: Houghton Mifflin.

Bui, Duyen. 2020. "Organizing and Mobilizing beyond Borders: Transnational Activism in the Vietnamese Diaspora." Ph.D. diss., University of Hawaii, Mānoa.

Bui, Long T. 2018. *Returns of War: South Vietnam and the Price of Refugee Memory*. New York: New York University Press.

Bui, Thi. 2018. *The Best We Could Do*. New York: Abrams Comic Art.

Bui, Van T. 1986. *Cái Gốc Của Phước Thiện*. Tay Ninh: Tay Ninh Holy See.

Bùi, Xuân Đính. 1985. *Lệ Làng Phép Nước*. Hanoi: Pháp Lý.

Bullard, Robert D., and Beverly Wright. 2009. *Race, Place, and Environmental Justice after Hurricane Katrina: Struggles to Reclaim, Rebuild, and Revitalize New Orleans and the Gulf Coast*. Boulder, CO: Westview.

Burns, Ken, and Lynn Novick, dirs. 2017. *The Vietnam War*. PBS. September 17–28, 2017.

Burwell, Ronald, Peter Hill, and John Wicklin. 1986. "Religion and Refugee Resettlement in the United States: A Research Note." *Review of Religious Research* 27, no. 4 (June): 356–366.

Camda, Edward, and Thitiya Phaobtong. 1992. "Buddhism as a Support System for Southeast Asian Refugees." *Social Work* 37, no. 1 (January): 61–67.

Campbell, Kenneth J. 2007. *A Tale of Two Quagmires: Iraq, Vietnam, and the Hard Lessons of War*. New York: Routledge.

Cao, Văn Luận. 1972. *Bên giòng lịch sử: hồi ký 1940–1965* (On the Riverbank of History, Memoir 1940–1965). Saigon: Trí Dũng.

Caplan, Nathan, John Whitmore, and Marcella Choy. 1989. *The Boat People and Achievement in America: A Study of Family Life, Hard Work, and Cultural Values*. Ann Arbor: University of Michigan Press.

Cargill, Mary Terrell, and Jade Quang Huynh, eds. 2000. *Voices of Vietnamese Boat People: Nineteen Narratives of Escape and Survival*. Jefferson: McFarland and Company.

Carter, James. 2008. *Inventing Vietnam: The United States and State Building, 1954–1968*. New York: Cambridge University Press.

Castañeda-Liles, María Del Soccorro. 2018. *Our Lady of Everyday Life: La Virgen de Guadalupe and the Catholic Imagination of Mexican Women in America*. Oxford: Oxford Scholarship Online.

Caswell, Michelle, Harrison Cole, and Zachary Griffith. 2018. "Images, Silences, and the Archival Record: An Interview with Michelle Caswell." *disClosure: A Journal of Social Theory* 27, article 7. Available at https://doi.org/10.13023/disclosure.27.04.

Catton, Phillip. 2002. *Diem's Final Failure: Prelude to America's War in Vietnam*. Lawrence: University Press of Kansas.

Cerrato, Javier, and Eva Cifre. 2018. "Gender Inequality in Household Chores and Work-Family Conflict." *Frontiers in Psychology* 9 (August 3): 1330.

Chan Khong. 2007. *Learning True Love*. Berkeley, CA: Parallax.

Chan, Sucheng. 1991. *Asian Americans: An Interpretive History*. Boston: Twayne.

———, ed. 2006. *The Vietnamese American 1.5 Generation: Stories of War, Revolution, Flight, and New Beginnings*. Philadelphia: Temple University Press.

Chanda, Nayan. 1986. *Brother Enemy: The War after the War*. San Diego: Harcourt Brace Jovanovich.

Chánh Trung. 1989. *Những Bước Chân Tù* [Steps of the Prisoner]. San Jose: self-published.

Chapman, Jessica M. 2013. *Cauldron of Resistance: Ngo Dinh Diem, the United States, and 1950s Southern Vietnam*. Ithaca, NY: Cornell University Press.

Chapman, John. 2007. "Return to Vietnam of Exiled Zen Master Thich Nhat Hanh." In *Modernity and Re-enchantment: Religion in Post-revolutionary Vietnam*, ed. Philip Taylor, 297–341. Singapore: Institute of Southeast Asian Studies.

Chester, Eric. 1995. *Covert Network: Progressives, the International Rescue Committee and the CIA*. Armonk, NY: ME Sharpe.

Chơn Hạnh. 1970. "Đức Phật và Nietzsche" [The Buddha and Nietzsche]. *Tư Tưởng* 5 (September 1): 11–13.

Chou, Grace Ai-Ling. 2010. "Cultural Education as Containment of Communism: The Ambivalent Position of American NGOs in Hong Kong in the 1950s." *Journal of Cold War Studies* 12, no. 2: 3–29.

Chou, Rosalind, and Joe Feagin. 2008. *The Myth of the Model Minority: Asian Americans Facing Racism*. Boulder, CO: Paradigm.

Chreim, Samia, Martine Spence, David Crick, and Xiaolu Liao. 2018. "Review of Female Immigrant Entrepreneurship Research: Past Findings, Gaps and Ways Forward." *European Management Journal* 36, no. 2: 210–222.

Christnacht, Cheridan, Adam Smith, and Rebecca Chenevert. 2018. "Measuring Entrepreneurship in the American Community Survey: A Demographic and Occupational Profile of Self-Employed Workers." Working paper 2018–28, U.S. Census Bureau, Social, Economic, and Housing Statistics Division, Washington, DC.

Christopher, Renny. 1995. *The Vietnam War, the American War: Images and Representations in Euro-American and Vietnamese Exile Narratives*. Amherst: University of Massachusetts Press.

Chu, Lan. 2008. "Catholicism vs. Communism, Continued: The Catholic Church in Vietnam." *Journal of Vietnamese Studies* 3, no. 1: 151–192.

Chuyện Người Vợ Cải Tạo [Stories of Wives of Reeducation Camp Prisoners]. 2004–2005. 3 vols. Westminster: Viễn Đông.

Clevenger, J. C. 1967. *Report: Student Personnel Services in the Public Universities of the Republic of Viet-Nam*. Saigon: USAID.

Coleman, M. Cynthia. 1982. "Why Should MAA's Become Resettlement Agencies?" Presentation to the National Council on Social Welfare on Behalf of the Indochina Refugee Action Center, April, *Southeast Asia Resource Action Center Records*. MS-SEA004. Special Collections and Archives, UC Irvine Libraries, Irvine, California.

Collet, Christian. 2005. "Bloc Voting, Polarization, and the Panethnic Hypothesis: The Case of Little Saigon." *Journal of Politics* 67, no. 3: 907–933.

———. 2008. "Minority Candidates, Alternative Media, and Multiethnic America: Deracialization or Toggling?" *Perspectives on Politics* 6, no. 4: 707–728.

Collet, Christian, and Hiroko Furuya. 2009. "Contested Nation: Vietnam and the Emergence of Saigon Nationalism in the United States." In *The Transnational Politics of Asian Americans*, ed. Christian Collet and Pei-te Lien, 56–73. Philadelphia: Temple University Press.

———. 2010. "Enclave, Place, or Nation? Defining Little Saigon in the Midst of Incorporation, Transnationalism, and Long Distance Activism." *Amerasia Journal* 36, no. 3: 1–27.

Công An Thủ Đô: Những Chặng Đường Lịch Sử [Capital Police: Stages in Their History]. 1990. Hà Nội: Công An Nhân Dân.

Cook, Terry, and Joan M. Schwartz. 2002. "Archives, Records, and Power: From (Postmodern) Theory to (Archival) Performance." *Archival Science* 2:171–185.

Curtis, Erin M. 2013. "Cambodian Donut Shops and the Negotiation of Identity in Los Angeles." In *Eating Asian America: A Food Studies Reader*, ed. Robert Ji-Song Ku, Martin Manalansan IV, and Anita Mannur, 13–29. New York: New York University Press.

Dacy, Douglas. 1986. *Foreign Aid, War, and Economic Development: South Vietnam, 1955-75*. New York: Cambridge University Press.

Dang, J. B. An. 2008. "Hanoi's Catholics Continue Protests Defying Government's Ultimatum." *AsiaNews*, January 28, 2008. Accessed on August 10, 2020. Available at http://www.asianews.it/index.php?l=en&art=11365&size=.

Đặng, Lai. 2004. "Bảy Năm Tình Lận Đận" [Seven Years of a Troubled Romance]. In *Chuyện Người Vợ Cải Tạo*, vol. 1: 126–142. Westminster: Viễn Đông.

Đặng, Phong. 1999. *Việt Kiều và sự Nhập Cuộc với Kinh Tế Việt Nam*. Hanoi: Viện Kinh Tế.

———. 2000. "The Vietnamese Diaspora: Returning and Integrating into Vietnam." *Revue Européenne des Migrations Internationales* 16, no. 1: 185–203.

Dang, T. V. 2005. "The Cultural Work of Anticommunism in the San Diego Vietnamese American Community." *Amerasia Journal* 31, no. 2: 64–86.

Đặng, Văn Học. 2005. "Hồi Ký trong Tù" [Prison Memoir]. In *Không Chấp Nhận, Không Sống Chung*, 143–152. Anaheim: Tổng Hội TQLC/VN tại Hoa Kỳ.

Daniel, Dominique. 2014. "Archival Representations of Immigration and Ethnicity in North American History: From the Ethnicization of Archives to the Archivization of Ethnicity." *Archival Science* 14, no. 2: 169–203.

Đào, Thị Kim Dung. 1973. "Khảo luận về một số cô-nhi-viện hoạt động tại Đô Thành Sài Gòn." Graduating thesis, National Institute of Administration.

Đào, Văn Bình. 2000. *Ký Sự 15 Năm* [Reports from Fifteen Years]. San Jose: self-published.

Day, Kathleen, and David Holley. 1984. "Boom on Bolsa: Vietnamese Create Their Own Saigon." *Los Angeles Times*, September 30, 1984.

De Luca, Deborah, and Maurizio Ambrosini. 2019. "Female Immigrant Entrepreneurs: More Than a Family Strategy." *International Migration* 57, no. 5: 201–215.

Demmer, Amanda. 2017. "The Last Chapter of the Vietnam War: Normalization, Nongovernmental Actors, and the Politics of Human Rights, 1975–1995." Ph.D. thesis, University of New Hampshire.

DeVido, Elise. 2007. "Buddhism for this World': The Buddhist Revival in Vietnam 1920s–1951, and Its Legacy." In *Modernity and Re-enchantment: Religion in Post-revolutionary Vietnam*, ed. Philip Taylor, 250–296. Singapore: Institute of Southeast Asian Studies.

———. 2009. "The Influence of Chinese Master Taixu on Buddhism in Vietnam." *Journal of Global Buddhism* 10: 413–458. https://doi.org/10.5281/zenodo.1307112.

———. 2014. "Eminent Nuns of Hue, Vietnam." In *Eminent Buddhist Women*, ed. Karma Lekshe Tsomo, 71–81. New York: SUNY Press.

Dhaliwal, Spinder, and Peter Kangis. 2006. "Asians in the UK: Gender, Generations and Enterprise." *Equal Opportunities International* 25, no. 2: 92–108.

Dheer, Ratan J. S. 2018. "Entrepreneurship by Immigrants: A Review of Existing Literature and Directions for Future Research." *International Entrepreneurship and Management Journal* 14, no. 3: 555–614.

Dhingra, Pawan. 2012. *Life behind the Lobby: Indian American Motel Owners and the American Dream*. Stanford, CA: Stanford University Press.

Dinh, Cindy, and Bao Nguyen. 2015. "The Rise of the Vietnamese American Political Consciousness: Advocacy on Capitol Hill." *Asian American Policy Review* 25: 52–59.

Dinh, Linh. 1998. *Drunkard Boxing*. Philadelphia: Singing Horse.

———. 2000. *Fake House*. New York: Seven Stories.

———. 2002. *Three Vietnamese Poets*. Kane'ohe, HI: Tinfish.

———. 2003a. *All around What Empties Out*. Kane'ohe, HI: Tinfish.

———. 2003b. *Night, Again: Contemporary Fiction from Vietnam*. New York: Seven Stories.

———. 2005. *American Tatts*. Tucson, AZ: Chax.

———. 2006a. *Borderless Bodies*. Berkeley, CA: Factory School.

———. 2006b. *Jam Alerts*. Tucson, AZ: Chax.

———. 2007. *All around What Empties Out*. Kane'ohe, HI: Tinfish.

Đinh, Thanh Lâm. 2008. *Một Đời Xót Xa* [A Sorry Life]. Westminster, CA: Nam Việt.

Dizon, Lily. "US Ends Era of Welcome for Vietnam's Refugees." *Christian Science Monitor*, October 14, 1997. Available at https://www.csmonitor.com/1997/1014/101497.intl .intl.3.html.

Đỗ, Đức Hiếu, et al. 2004. *Từ điển văn học, bộ mới*. Hà Nội: Thế Giới.

Đỗ, Tân Hưng. 2012. "Linh Mục Thiên Phong Bửu Dưỡng (1907–1987)" [Priest Thiên Phong Bửu Dưỡng]. July 25, 2012. Available at http://motgoctroi.com/StNguoiNViec /Danhnhan/LmBuuDuong/LmDuuDuong.htm.

Đỗ, Văn Phúc. 2008. *Cuối Tầng Địa Ngục: Hồi Ký của Một Người Tù Sống Sót sau 10 Năm trong Các Trại Khổ Sai của Cộng Sản Việt Nam* [The Pit of Hell: Memoir of a Surviving Prisoner after Ten Years in Hard Labor Camps of Communist Vietnam]. N.p.: Viet land.

Dohamide. 1965. "Hồi giáo ở nước ngoài và ở Việt nam" [Islam in Foreign Countries and in Vietnam]. *Bách Khoa* 192 (January 1): 31–35.

Dooley, Thomas. 1956. *Deliver Us from Evil: The Story of Viet Nam's Flight to Freedom.* New York: Farrar, Straus, and Cudahy.

Dorais, Louis-Jacques. 2001. "Defining the Overseas Vietnamese." *Diaspora: A Journal of Transnational* Studies 10, no. 1: 3–27.

———. 2005. *From Refugees to Transmigrants: The Vietnamese in Canada.* New Brunswick, NJ: Rutgers University Press.

Dror, Olga. 2014. "Translator's Introduction." In *Mourning Headband for Huế*, by Nha Ca, xi–lxv. Bloomington: Indiana University Press.

———. 2018. *Making Two Vietnams: War and Youth Identities, 1965–1975.* New York: Cambridge University Press.

Duarte, Amalia. 1985. "'Thanks, America': Rally Commemorates Vietnam Veterans and Assistance Given to Refugees in U.S." *Los Angeles Times*, December 15.

Duiker, William. 1990. *Sacred War: Nationalism and Revolution in a Divided Vietnam.* New York: McGraw-Hill.

Dunning, Bruce. 1982. *A Systematic Study of the Social, Psychological and Economic Adaptation of Vietnamese Refugees Representing Five Entry Cohorts, 1975–1979.* Washington, DC: Bureau of Social Science Research.

———. 1989. "Vietnamese in America: The Adaptation of the 1975–1979 Arrivals." In *Refugees as Immigrants: Cambodians, Laotians, and Vietnamese in America*, ed. David W. Haines, 55–85. Totowa, NJ: Rowman and Littlefield.

Duong, Lan. 2016. "Việt Nam and the Diaspora: Absence, Presence, and the Archive." In Boyles and Lim, *Looking Back on the Vietnam War*, 64–78.

———. 2020. "Archives of Memory: Vietnamese American Films, Past and Present." *Film Quarterly* 73, no. 3 (Spring): 54–58.

Duong, Lan, and Isabelle Thuy Pelaud. 2012. "Vietnamese American Art and Community Politics: An Engaged Feminist Perspective." *Journal of Asian American Studies* 15, no. 3 (October): 241–269.

Duricy, Michael. 2008. *Black Madonnas: Our Lady of Czestochowa.* Dayton, OH: Marian.

Dutton, George. 2016. *A Vietnamese Moses: Philiphê Bình and the Geographies of Early Modern Catholicism.* Berkeley: University of California Press.

Duyên Anh. 1988. *Sài Gòn Ngày Dài Nhất* [Sài Gòn the Longest Day]. Los Alamitos, CA: Xuân Thu.

Eckstein, Susan, and Thanh-Nghi Nguyen. 2011. "The Making and Transnationalization of an Ethnic Niche: Vietnamese Manicurists." *International Migration Review* 45, no. 3: 639–674.

Elliott, Duong Van Mai. 1999. *The Sacred Willow: Four Generations in the Life of a Vietnamese Family*. New York: Oxford University Press.

Endres, Kirsten W. 2011. *Performing the Divine: Mediums, Markets and Modernity in Urban Vietnam*. Honolulu: University of Hawaii Press.

Ernst, John. 1998. *Forging a Fateful Alliance: Michigan State University and the Vietnam War*. East Lansing: Michigan State University Press.

Espiritu, Evyn Le. 2017. "'Who Was Colonel Hồ Ngọc Cẩn?': Queer and Feminist Practices for Exhibiting South Vietnamese History on the Internet." *Amerasia Journal* 42, no. 2: 2–23.

Espiritu, Yen Le. 2002. "'Viet Nam, Nuoc Toi' (Vietnam, My Country): Vietnamese Americans and Transnationalism." In *The Changing Face of Home*, ed. Peggy Levitt and Mary C. Waters, 367–398. New York: Russell Sage Foundation.

———. 2005. "Thirty Years AfterWARD: The Endings That Are Not Over." *Amerasia Journal* 31, no. 2: xiii–xxiii.

———. 2006. "Toward a Critical Refugee Study: The Vietnamese Refugee Subject in US Scholarship." *Journal of Vietnamese Studies* 1, no. 1–2: 410–433.

———. 2008. "About Ghost Stories: The Vietnam War and 'Rememoration.'" *PMLA* 123, no. 5: 1700–1702.

———. 2014. *Body Counts: The Vietnam War and Militarized Refugees*. Berkeley: University of California Press.

———. 2016. "Vietnamese Refugees and Internet Memorials: When Does War End and Who Gets to Decide?" In Boyles and Lim, *Looking Back on the Vietnam War*, 18–33.

Espiritu, Yen Le, and Lan Duong. 2018. "Feminist Refugee Epistemology: Reading Displacement in Vietnamese and Syrian Art." *Signs: Journal of Women in Culture and Society* 43, no. 3: 587–615.

Essers, Caroline, and Yvonne Benschop. 2009. "Muslim Businesswomen Doing Boundary Work: The Negotiation of Islam, Gender and Ethnicity within Entrepreneurial Contexts." *Human Relations* 62, no. 3: 403–423.

Evans, Grant. 1990. *Lao Peasants under Socialism*. New Haven, CT: Yale University Press.

Evans, Peter, Dietrich Rueschemeyer, and Theda Skocpol, eds. 1985. *Bringing the State Back In*. New York: Cambridge University Press.

Fagen, Richard. 1969. *The Transformation of Political Culture in Cuba*. Stanford, CA: Stanford University Press.

Fairlie, Robert, and Alicia Robb. 2007. "Families, Human Capital, and Small Business: Evidence from the Characteristics of Business Owners Survey." *ILR Review* 60, no. 2: 225–245.

Fernandez, Eleazar. 2003. "America from the Hearts of a Diasporized People: A Diasporized Heart." In *Realizing the America of Our Hearts: Theological Voices of Asian Americans*, ed. Fumitaka Matsuoka and Eleazar S. Fernandez, 253–273. St. Louis, MO: Chalice Press.

Fernandez-Kelly, Patricia, and Lisa Konczal. 2005. "'Murdering the Alphabet': Identity and Entrepreneurship among Second-Generation Cubans, West Indians, and Central Americans." *Ethnic and Racial Studies* 28, no. 6: 1153–1181.

Fjeldstad, Karen. 1995. "Tu Phu Cong Dong: Vietnamese Women and Spirit Possession in the San Francisco Bay Area." Ph.D. diss., University of Hawaii, Honolulu.

Fjelstad, Karen, and Nguyen Thi Hien. 2006. Introduction to *Possessed by the Spirits: Mediumship in Contemporary Vietnamese Communities*, ed. Karen Fjelstad and Hien Thi Nguyen, 7–18. Ithaca, NY: Cornell University Press.

———. 2011. *Spirits without Borders: Vietnamese Spirit Mediums in a Transnational Age.* New York: Palgrave Macmillan.

Fontenot, Kayla, Jessica Semga, and Melissa Kollar. 2018. "Income and Poverty in the United States." *United States Census Bureau*, September 12, 2018. Available at https://www.census.gov/library/publications/2018/demo/p60-263.html.

Forché, Carolyn. 2011. "Reading the Living Archives: The Witness of Literary Art; To Hell and Back, with Poetry." *Poetry* 198, no. 2: 159–174.

Fraser, Nancy, and Linda Gordon. 1994. "A Genealogy of Dependency: Tracing a Keyword of the U.S. Welfare State." *Signs* 19, no. 2: 309–336.

Frauenfelder, Mary. 2016. "Asian-Owned Businesses Nearing Two Million." *Random Samplings* (blog), July 27, 2016. Available at https://www.census.gov/newsroom/blogs/random-samplings/2016/07/asian-owned-businesses-nearing-two-million.html.

Freeman, James, ed. 1989. *Hearts of Sorrow: Vietnamese-American Lives.* Stanford, CA: Stanford University Press.

———. 1995. *Changing Identities: Vietnamese Americans, 1975–1995.* Boston: Allyn and Bacon.

Fujita-Rony, Dorothy B. 2021. *The Memorykeepers: Gendered Knowledges, Empires, and Indonesian American History.* Leiden: Brill.

Fujita-Rony, Dorothy B., and Anne Frank. 2003. "Archiving Histories: The Southeast Asian Archive at University of California, Irvine." *Amerasia Journal* 29, no. 1: 153–164.

Furuya, Hiroko, and Christian Collet. 2009. "Contested Nation: Vietnam and the Emergence of Saigon Nationalism in the United States." In *The Transnational Politics of Asian Americans*, ed. Christian Collet and Pei-te Lien, 56–76. Philadelphia: Temple University Press.

Gellner, Ernest. 1983. *Nations and Nationalism.* Hoboken, NJ: Blackwell.

Getlin, Josh. 1985. "5,000 Cheer News of Rebellion in Vietnam." *Los Angeles Times*, April 18, 1983.

Giddens, Anthony. 1987. *The Nation-State and Violence.* Vol. 2 of *A Contemporary Critique of Historical Materialism.* Berkeley: University of California Press.

———. 1990. *The Consequences of Modernity.* Stanford, CA: Stanford University Press.

Giebel, Christoph. 2001. "Museum-Shrine: Revolution and Its Tutelary Spirit in the Village of My Hoa Hung." In Ho Tai, *The Country of Memory*, 77–105.

Gold, Steve. 1994. "Chinese-Vietnamese Entrepreneurs in California." In *The New Asian Immigration in Los Angeles and Global Restructuring*, ed. Paul Ong and Steve Gold, 196–226. Philadelphia: Temple University Press.

Gonzalez, Elwing. 2017. "Creating and Contesting Refugee Identity and Space in America: Vietnamese Refugees in Los Angeles in the 1970s and 1980s." Ph.D. diss., Claremont Graduate University.

Gordon, Avery. 1997. *Ghostly Matters: Haunting and the Sociological Imagination.* Minneapolis: University of Minnesota Press.

Goscha, Christopher. 2007. "Intelligence in a Time of Decolonization: The Case of the Democratic Republic of Vietnam at War (1945–1950)." *Intelligence and National Security* 22, no. 1 (February): 100–138.

———. 2016. *Vietnam: A New History.* New York: Basic Books.

Gramsci, Antonio. 1971. *Selections from the Prison Notebooks.* Trans. and ed. Quintin Hoare and Geoffrey Nowell Smith. London: Lawrence and Winhart.

Gravel, Mike. 1971. *The Pentagon Papers: The Defense Department History of United States Decision Making on Vietnam.* Boston: Beacon.

Guillemot, François. 2010. "Autopsy of a Massacre on a Political Purge in the Early Days of the Indochina War (Nam Bo 1947)." *European Journal of East Asian Studies* 9, no. 2: 225–265.

Hà, Thúc Sinh. 1985. *Đại Học Máu* [Blood University]. San Jose: Nhân Văn.

Haines, David, ed. 1989. *Refugees as Immigrants: Cambodians, Laotians, and Vietnamese in America*. Totowa, NJ: Rowman and Littlefield.

Haines, David, Dorothy Rutherford, and Patrick Thomas. 1981. "Family and Community among Vietnamese Refugees." *International Migration Review* 15, no. 1–2: 310–319.

Halkias, Daphne, Paul Thurman, Sylva Caracatsanis, and Nicholas Harkiolakis. 2016. *Female Immigrant Entrepreneurs: The Economic and Social Impact of a Global Phenomenon*. Boca Raton, FL: CRC.

Hall, David, ed. 1997. *Lived Religion in America: Toward a History of Practice*. Princeton, NJ: Princeton University Press.

Hansen, Peter. 2009. "Bắc Di Cư: Catholic Refugees from the North of Vietnam, and Their Role in the Southern Republic, 1954–1959." *Journal of Vietnamese Studies* 4, no. 3: 173–211.

Harjanto, Laura, and Jeanne Batalova. 2021. "Vietnamese Immigrants in the United States." *Migration Policy Institute*, October 15, 2021. Available at https://www.migrationpolicy .org/article/vietnamese-immigrants-united-states.

Harrison, James. 1989. *The Endless War: Vietnam's Struggle for Independence*. New York: Columbia University Press.

Harvey, David. 2007. *A Brief History of Neoliberalism*. New York: Oxford University Press.

Haseki, Muge, Craig R. Scott, and Bernadette M. Gailliard. 2020. "Communicatively Managing Multiple, Intersecting Identities among Immigrant Women Entrepreneurs." *International Journal of Business Communication* 58, no. 2: 282–303.

Hayslip, Le Ly. 1989. *When Heaven and Earth Changed Places: A Vietnamese Woman's Journey from War to Peace*. With Jay Wurts. New York: Penguin.

Hein, Jeremy. 1997. "Ethnic Organizations and the Welfare States: The Impact of Social Welfare Programs on the Formation of Indochinese Refugee Associations." *Sociological Forum* 12, no. 2 (June): 274–298.

Herring, George. 1990. "'Peoples Quite Apart': Americans, South Vietnamese, and the War in Vietnam." *Diplomatic History* 14, no. 1: 1–23.

———. 1991. "America and Vietnam: The Unending War." *Foreign Affairs* 70, no. 5: 104–119.

———. 2002. *America's Longest War*. 4th ed. New York: McGraw Hill.

Hirsch, Marianne, and Valerie Smith. 2002. "Feminism and Cultural Memory: An Introduction." *Signs* 28, no. 1: 1–19.

Hồ, Anh Thái, and Wayne Karlin. 2003. *Love after War: Contemporary Fiction from Viet Nam*. Willimantic, CT: Curbstone.

Hoang, Carina, ed. 2011. *Boatpeople: Personal Stories from the Vietnamese Exodus, 1975–1996*. N.p.: Carina Hoang Communications.

———, ed. 2015. *Thuyền Nhân: Nước mắt Biển Đông từ sau biến cố 30/4/1975*. N.p.: Carina Hoang Communications.

Hoang, Kimberly Kay. 2015. *Dealing in Desire: Asian Ascendancy, Western Decline, and the Hidden Currencies of Global Sex Work*. Berkeley: University of California Press.

Hoang, Linh. 2006. *Creating New Spiritual Homes: Vietnamese Refugees Negotiating American and Catholic Identities*. New York: Fordham University Press.

Hoàng, Phủ Ngọc Phan. 2012. "Nhớ Về Các Vị Giáo Sư Người Đức Ở Đại Học Y Khoa Huế" [Remembering the German Professor of the Medical College in Hue]. *Sachhiem*.

net, May 5, 2012. Accessed November 1, 2020. Available at https://sachhiem.net/NDX/NDX024.php.

Hoang, Tuan. 2009. "The Early South Vietnamese Critique of Communism." In *Dynamics of the Cold War in Asia: Ideology, Identity, and Culture*, ed. Tuong Vu and Wasana Wongsurawat, 17–32. New York: Palgrave Macmillan.

———. 2013. "Ideology in Urban South Vietnam, 1950–1975." Ph.D. diss., University of Notre Dame.

———. 2016. "From Reeducation Camps to Little Saigons: Historicizing Vietnamese Diasporic Anticommunism." *Journal of Vietnamese Studies* 11, no. 2 (Spring): 43–95.

———. 2021. "South Vietnam's Flags at the Capitol Riot." *Asia Sentinel*, January 9, 2021.

Hoang, Van Dao. 2008. *Viet Nam Quoc Dan Dang: A Contemporary History of a National Struggle: 1927-1954*. Trans. Huynh Khue. Pittsburgh: Rose Dog Books.

Hobsbawn, Eric, and Terrence Ranger, eds. 1983. *The Invention of Tradition*. New York: Cambridge University Press.

Hội Đồng Cơ Quan Từ Thiện tại Vietnam. 1971. *Bản Thông Tin* [Bulletin]. Saigon: Hội Đồng Cơ Quan Từ Thiện tại Vietnam.

Hội Văn Hóa Bình Dân. 1967. *12 năm hoạt động của Hội Văn Hóa Bình Dân* [12 Years of Activities of the Popular Culture Society]. Saigon.

Holley, David. 1983. "Viet Refugees Pin Hopes on a Long Shot." *Los Angeles Times*, June 27, 1983.

Horsfall, Sara. 2000. "The Experience of Marian Apparitions and the Mary Cult." *Social Science Journal* 37, no. 3: 375–384.

Hoshall, C. Earle. 1971. *Higher Education in Vietnam, 1967-1971*. Saigon: USAID.

Hoskins, Janet. 2007. "Caodai Exile and Redemption: A New Vietnamese Religion's Struggle for Identity." In *Religion and Social Justice for Immigrants*, ed. Pierrette Hondagneu-Sotelo, 191–209. Newark, NJ: Rutgers University Press.

———. 2012a. "Can a Hierarchical Religion Survive without Its Center? Caodaism, Colonialism, and Exile." In *Hierarchy: Persistence and Transformation in Social Formations*, ed. Knut Rio and Olaf Smedal, 113–141. Oxford: Berghahn Books.

———. 2012b. "A Posthumous Return from Exile: The Legacy of an Anticolonial Religious Leader in Today's Vietnam." *Southeast Asian Studies* 1, no. 2: 213–246.

———. 2015. *The Divine Eye and the Diaspora: Vietnamese Syncretism Becomes Transpacific Caodaism*. Honolulu: University of Hawaii Press.

———. 2021. "Refugees in the Land of Awes: Vietnamese Arrivals and Departures." In *Refugees and Religion: Ethnographic Studies of Global Trajectories*, ed. Birgit Meyer and Peter van der Veer, 87–104. London: Bloomsbury Academic.

Ho Tai, Hue-Tam. 2001a. "Commemoration and Community." In Ho Tai, *The Country of Memory*, 227–230.

———, ed. 2001b. *The Country of Memory: Remaking the Past in Late Socialist Vietnam*. Berkeley: University of California Press.

———. 2001c. "Faces of Remembrance and Forgetting." In Ho Tai, *The Country of Memory*, 167–195.

Hum, Tarry. 2004. "Immigrant Global Neighborhoods in New York City." *Research in Urban Sociology* 7 (December 14): 25–55.

Hundley, Greg. 2001. "Why Women Earn Less Than Men in Self-Employment." *Journal of Labor Research* 22, no. 4: 817–829.

Huntington, Samuel. 1968. *Political Order in Changing Societies*. New Haven, CT: Yale University Press.

Hương Vĩnh. 2007. "Linh Mục Giuse Maria Nguyễn Văn Thích (1891–1978)" [Reverend Joseph Marie Nguyen Van Thich (1891–1978)]. In *Những Nẻo Đường Việt Nam* [Roads of Vietnam], ch. 23. Accessed July 24, 2022. Available at: http://www.conggiaoviet nam.net/index.php/index.php?m=module3&v=chapter&ib=20&ict=242.

Huynh, Craig Trinh-Phat. 1996. "Vietnamese-Owned Manicure Businesses in Los Angeles." In *The State of Asian Pacific America: Reframing the Immigrant Debate: A Public Policy Report*, ed. Bill Ong Hing and Ronald Lee, 195–203. Los Angeles: LEAP Asian Pacific American Public Policy Institute and UCLA Asian American Studies Center.

Huynh, Jade Quang, and Mary Terrell Cargill. 2015. *Voices of Vietnamese Boat People: Nineteen Narratives of Escape and Survival*. Jefferson, NC: MacFarland Books.

Huynh, Jennifer, and Jessica Yiu. 2015. "Breaking Blocked Transnationalism." In *The State and the Grassroots: Immigrant Transnational Organizations in Four Continents*, ed. Alejandro Portes and Patricia Fernandez-Kelly, 160–188. New York: Berghahn Books.

Huỳnh, Kim Khánh. 1982. *Vietnamese Communism*. Ithaca, NY: Cornell University Press.

Huynh, Thuan. 2000. "Center for Vietnamese Buddhism: Recreating Home." In *Religion and the New Immigrants: Continuities and Adaptations in Immigrant Congregations*, ed. Helen R. Ebaugh and Janet S. Chafetz, 45–66. New York: Altamira.

Huỳnh, Văn Lang. 2008. "Món nợ văn hóa bình dân và sứ mạng văn hóa dân tộc." Accessed July 11, 2022. Available at https://sites.google.com/site/namkyluctinhorg/tac -gia-tac-pham/e-f-g-h/huynh-van-lang/tuyen-tap-huynh-van-lang/mon-no-van-hoa -binh-dan-va-su-mang-van-hoa-dan-toc.

Irving, Doug. 2010. "Tran Concedes Congress Race to Sanchez." *Orange County Register*, November 9, 2010. Accessed July 22, 2022. Available at https://www.ocregister .com/2010/11/09/tran-concedes-congress-race-to-sanchez/.

Itzigsohn, Jose, and Matthias vom Hau. 2006. "Unfinished Imagined Communities: States, Social Movements, and Nationalism in Latin America." *Theory and Society* 35 (July 19): 193–212.

Jabeen, Fauzia, Mohd Nishat Faisal, and Marios I. Katsioloudes. 2017. "Entrepreneurial Mindset and the Role of Universities as Strategic Drivers of Entrepreneurship: Evidence from the United Arab Emirates." *Journal of Small Business and Enterprise Development* 24, no. 1: 136–157.

Jacobs, Seth. 2006. *Cold War Mandarin: Ngo Dinh Diem and the Origin of America's War with Vietnam*. Lanham, MD: Rowman and Littlefield.

Jaffe, Adrian, and Milton C. Taylor. 1961. "A Crumbling Bastion: Flattery and Lies Won't Save Vietnam." *New Republic*, June 19, 1961, 20.

Jamieson, Neil L. 1993. *Understanding Vietnam*. Berkeley: University of California Press.

Jarlson, Gary. 1981. "Vietnam War Lingers On at 2 Rallies." *Los Angeles Times*, December 21, 1981.

Joiner, Charles A. 1964. "South Vietnam's Buddhist Crisis: Organization for Charity, Dissidence, and Unity." *Asian Survey* 4, no. 7 (July): 915–928.

Jolie. 2004. "Bao Nhiêu Nước Mắt" [A Lot of Tears]. In *Chuyện Người Vợ Tù Cải Tạo*, vol. 1: 418–430. Westminster: Viễn Đông.

Jones, P. H. M. 1962. "Vietnam at School." Douglas Pike Collection, *Virtual Vietnam Archive*. Accessed November 13, 2020. Available at https://www.vietnam.ttu.edu/virtua larchive/items.php?item=2322006001.

Judt, Tony. 2006. *Postwar: A History of Europe since 1945*. New York: Penguin Books.

Karlin, Wayne, Lê Minh Khuê, and Truong Vu. 1995. *The Other Side of Heaven: Postwar Fiction*. Willimantic, CT: Curbstone.

Katz, Lawrence F., and Alan B. Krueger. 2019. "The Rise and Nature of Alternative Work Arrangements in the United States, 1995–2015." *ILR Review* 72, no. 2: 382–416.

Keith, Charles. 2012. *Catholic Vietnam: A Church from Empire to Nation*. Berkeley: University of California Press.

———. 2019. "The First Vietnamese in America." *Journal of Social Issues in Southeast Asia* 34, no. 1: 48–75.

Kelly, Gail P. 1977. *From Vietnam to America: A Chronicle of the Vietnamese Immigration to the United States*. Boulder, CO: Westview.

———. 2000. *French Colonial Education*. Ann Arbor, MI: AMS.

Kennedy, Laurel B., and Mary Rose Williams. 2001. "The Past without the Pain: The Manufacture of Nostalgia in Vietnam's Tourism Industry." In Ho Tai, *The Country of Memory*, 135–163.

Kerkvliet, Benedict. 2005. *The Power of Everyday Politics: How Vietnamese Peasants Transformed National Policy*. Ithaca, NY: Cornell University Press.

———. 2015. "Regime Critics: Democratization Advocates in Vietnam, 1990s–2014." *Critical Asian Studies* 47, no. 3: 359–387.

———. 2019. *Speaking Out in Vietnam: Public Political Criticism in a Communist Party–Ruled Nation*. Ithaca, NY: Cornell University Press.

Kerr, Sari Pekkala, and William Kerr. 2020. "Immigrant Entrepreneurship in America: Evidence from the Survey of Business Owners 2007 & 2012." *Research Policy* 49, no. 3: 103918.

Không Chấp Nhận, Không Sống Chung: Những Cây Bút Cọp Biển, Tuyển Tập 3 [Neither Acceptance nor Co-existence: Sea Tiger Writers, Selected Collection 3]. N.d. Anaheim, CA: Tổng Hội TQLC/VN Tại Hoa Kỳ [Association of South Vietnamese Marine Corps in the United States].

Kibria, Nazli. 1993. *Family Tightrope: The Changing Lives of Vietnamese Americans*. Princeton, NJ: Princeton University Press.

Kiernan, Ben. 1996. *The Pol Pot Regime: Race, Power, and Genocide in Cambodia under the Khmer Rouge, 1975–79*. New Haven, CT: Yale University Press.

Kim, Claire Jean. 1999. "The Racial Triangulation of Asian Americans." *Politics and Society* 27, no. 1: 105–138.

Kim, Elaine. 1987. "Defining Asian American Realities through Literature." *Cultural Critique* 6. The Nature and Context of Minority Discourse (Spring): 87–111.

Kokot, Waltraud, Khachig Tololyan, and Carolin Alfonso. 2004. *Diaspora, Identity and Religion: New Directions in Theory and Research*. New York: Routledge.

Kolko, Gabriel. 2001. *Anatomy of a War: Vietnam, the United States and the Modern Historical Experience*. London: Weidenfeld and Nicolson.

Kopetman, Roxana. 2013. "Vietnamese American Gays Protesting Today over Tet Parade." *Orange County Register*, February 4, 2013. Available at https://www.ocregister.com/2013/02/04/vietnamese-american-gays-protesting-today-over-tet-parade/.

Kosten, Dan. 2018. "Immigrants as Economic Contributors: They Are the New American Workforce." *National Immigration Forum*, June 5, 2018. Available at https://immigrationforum.org/article/immigrants-as-economic-contributors-they-are-the-new-american-workforce/.

Kwon, Heonik. 2008. *Ghosts of War in Vietnam*. Cambridge: Cambridge University Press.

Lai, Thanhhà. 2015. *Listen, Slowly*. New York: Harper.

Lam, Andrew. 2005. *Perfume Dreams: Reflections on the Diaspora.* Berkeley, CA: Heyday Books.

Lam, Mariam. 2008. "Circulating War Memories: The Diary of Đặng Thùy Trâm." *Journal of Vietnamese Studies* 3, no. 2: 172–179.

Lam, Tony. 2002. "Breaking Down the Walls: My Journey from a Refugee Camp to the Westminster City Council." *UCLA Asian Pacific American Law Journal* 8, no. 1: 156–165.

Landau, Ingrid. 2008. "Law and Civil Society in Cambodia and Vietnam: A Gramscian Perspective." *Journal of Contemporary Asia* 38, no. 2: 244–258.

Landsbaum, Mark. 1985. "'Freedom Fighter' Rally Draws High Praise and Protests." *Los Angeles Times*, September 23, 1985.

Langguth, A. J. 2012. *Our Vietnam: The War 1954–1975.* New York: Simon and Schuster.

Latham, Robert. 1997. *The Liberal Moment: Modernity, Security, and the Making of a Postwar International Order.* New York: Columbia University Press.

Laurent, Nicola, and Kirsten Wright. 2020. "A Trauma-Informed Approach to Managing Archives: A New Online Course." *Archives and Manuscripts* 48, no. 1: 80–87.

Le, C. N. 2007. *Asian American Assimilation: Ethnicity, Immigration, and Socioeconomic Attainment.* New York: LFB Scholarly.

———. 2009. "Better Dead Than Red: Anti-communist Politics among Vietnamese Americans." In *Anti-communist Minorities in the U.S.: Political Activism of Ethnic Refugees,* ed. Ieva Zake, 189–210. New York: Palgrave Macmillan.

Lê, Đình Thương. 2010. "Bài Phát Biểu của anh Lê Đình Thương Phó Chủ Tịch Ngoại Vụ" (Speech from Le Dinh Thuong, Vice President of the Ministry of Foreign Affairs). Accessed December 13, 2020. Available at http://ykhoahuehaingoai.com/sinhhoat/s_PhatBieuDH2010LDThuong.html.

Lê, Khắc Anh Hào. 2004. *Đoạn Trường Lưu Vong* [The Pain of Exile]. Vancouver: Hải Triều.

Le, Long Si. 2011a. "Exploring the Function of the Anti-communist Ideology in the Vietnamese American Diasporic Community." *Journal of Southeast Asian American Education and Advancement* 6, no. 1: 1–25.

———. 2011b. "Truong Van Tran Incident." In *Encyclopedia of Asian American Folklore and Folklife,* Jonathan H. X. Lee, Kathleen M. Nadeau, 3: 1215–1216. Santa Barbara: ABC-CLIO.

Lê, Nina Hòa Bình. 2020. "Radio Mùa Hè—Thơ Phan Nhiên Hạo" [Summer Radio—On Phan Nhiên Hạo's Poetry]. *Việt Báo*, January 6, 2020. Accessed 07/22/2022. https://vietbao.com/a303472/radio-mua-he-tho-phan-nhien-hao.

Lê, Thị Sâm. 1970. "Các tổ chức từ thiện tôn giáo tại Đô Thành." Graduating thesis, National Institute of Administration, Saigon.

Le, Thuy Thi Diem. 2004. *The Gangster We Are All Looking For.* New York: Alfred A. Knopf.

Le, Tieu-Khe. 2015. "'The Line between Life and Death in the High Seas Is Very Thin, Almost Invisible': Diasporic Vietnamese Remembrance." Master's thesis, University of California, Los Angeles.

Lê, Tôn Nghiêm. 1969. "Heidegger trước sự phá sản của tư tưởng Tây Phương" [Heidegger in the Face of the Bankruptcy of Western Thought]. *Tư Tưởng* (Thought) 5 (October 1): 39–97.

Le, Van-Diem. 1960. "Puritan Idealism and the Transcendental Movement." Ph.D. thesis, University of Minnesota.

Le-Van-Hao. 1961. "Feigns: Structures et problèmes d'un village français: Essai d'ethnographie." Ph.D. thesis, University of Paris.

Lê, Văn Hảo. 1966. *Hành trình vào Dân tộc học* [Journey into Ethnography]. Saigon: Nam Sơn.

Le, Viet. 2005. "The Art of War: Vietnamese American Visual Artists Dinh Q. Le, Ann Phong and Nguyen Tan Hoang." *Amerasia Journal* 31, no. 2: 21–35.

———. 2011. "Return Engagement: Contemporary Art's Traumas of Modernity and History in Diasporic Sai Gon and Phnom Penh." Ph.D. diss., University of Southern California.

Le, Xuan Khoa, and Diana D. Bui. 1985. "Southeast Asian Mutual Assistance Associations: An Approach for Community Development." In *Southeast Asian Mental Health: Treatment, Prevention, Services and Research*, ed. Tom Choken Owan, 209–224. Rockville, MD: U.S. Department of Health and Human Services.

Lee, Erika. 2015. *The Making of Asian America: A History*. New York: Simon and Schuster.

Lee, Jonathan H. X. 2015. *History of Asian Americans: Exploring Diverse Roots*. Santa Barbara: Greenwood.

Lenin, V. I. 1974. "The State and Revolution." In *Lenin: Collected Works*, vol. 25, *June–September 1917*, 406–409. Moscow: Progress.

Lewis, Robert E., Mark W. Fraser, and Peter J. Pecora. 1988. "Religiosity among Indochinese Refugees in Utah." *Journal for the Scientific Study of Religion* 27, no. 2 (June): 272–283.

Lịch Sử Quân Đội Nhân Dân Việt Nam [History of the People's Army of Vietnam]. 1977. Vol. 1. Hanoi: Quân Đội Nhân Dân.

Lieu, Nhi T. 2000. "Remember 'The Nation' through Pageantry: Femininity and the Politics of Vietnamese Womanhood in the 'Hoa Hau Ao Dai' Contest." *Frontiers: A Journal of Women Studies* 21, no. 1–2: 127–151.

———. 2011. *The American Dream in Vietnamese*. Minneapolis: University of Minnesota Press.

Light, Ivan. 2005. "The Ethnic Economy." In *The Handbook of Economic Sociology*, 2nd ed., ed. Neil Smelser and Richard Swedberg, 650–677. Princeton, NJ: Princeton University Press.

Lin Center for Community Development. Accessed October 15, 2020. Available at https://linvn.org.

Lipman, Jana. 2020. *In Camps: Vietnamese Refugees, Asylum Seekers, and Repatriates*. Berkeley: University of California Press.

Liu, William, et al. 1979. *Transition to Nowhere: Vietnamese Refugees in America*. Nashville, TN: Charter House.

Logan, John R., and Weiwei Zhang. 2013. *Separate but Equal: Asian Nationalities in the US: US2010 Project*. Providence, RI: Brown University.

Long, Mary Hoang. 2012. Interview transcript by Nina Mai Thi Long, November 13, 2012. University of California, Irvine, Vietnamese American Oral History Project. Available at http://ucispace.lib.uci.edu/handle/10575/5913.

Louie, Vivian S. 2004. *Compelled to Excel: Immigration, Education, and Opportunity among Chinese Americans*. Stanford, CA: Stanford University Press.

Luu, Trinh, and Tuong Vu, eds. 2023. *Republican Vietnam: War, Society, Diaspora*. Honolulu: University of Hawaii Press.

Lý, Chánh Trung. 1967. "Người da đen và thế giới da trắng" [Black People in a White World]. *Đất Nước* 1 (February): 117–128.

Mahony, Phillip, ed. 1998. *From Both Sides Now: The Poetry of the Vietnam War and Its Aftermath*. New York: Scribner.

Mai, Văn Tấn. 2005. "Những Biến Động ở Trại Nam Hà (1980/1981)" [Major incidents at the Nam Ha Camp in 1980 and 1981]. In *Không Chấp Nhận, Không Sống Chung*.

Malarney, Shaun Kingsley. 2001. "'The Fatherland Remembers Your Sacrifice': Commemorating War Dead in North Vietnam." In Ho Tai, *The Country of Memory*, 46–76.

Mann, Michael. 1984. "The Autonomous Power of the State: Its Origins, Mechanisms, and Results." *European Journal of Sociology* 25, no. 2: 185–213.

Marable, Manning. 1995. *Beyond Black and White: Transforming African-American Politics*. London: Verso.

Marr, David. 1971. *Vietnamese Anticolonialism 1885–1925*. Berkeley: University of California Press.

———. 1981. *Vietnamese Tradition on Trial, 1920–1945*. Berkeley: University of California Press.

———. 1997. *Vietnam 1945: The Quest for Power*. Berkeley: University of California Press.

———. 2013. *Vietnam State, War, and Revolution, 1945–1946*. Berkeley: University of California Press.

Martin, Frances. 2018. "Freed Vietnamese Have Her to Thank: Khuc Minh Tho, the FVPPA, and the Use of Grassroots Diplomacy in the Release, Immigration, and Resettlement of Vietnamese Re-education Camp Prisoners, 1977–2011." Master's thesis, Texas Tech University.

Mauss, Marcel. 1967. *The Gift: Forms and Functions of Exchange in Archaic Societies*. New York: Norton (originally published 1923 as *Essai sur le Don*).

McCormick, David H., Charles E. Luftig, and James M. Cunningham. 2020. "Economic Might, National Security, and the Future of American Statecraft." *Texas National Security Review* 3, no. 3 (Summer): 50–75. Available at https://repositories.lib.utexas.edu/handle/2152/83223.

McElhinny, Bonnie. 2001. "See No Evil, Speak No Evil: White Police Officers Talk about Race and Affirmative Action." *Journal of Linguistic Anthropology* 11, no. 1: 65–78.

McGarr, Paul. 2004. "'Quiet Americans in India': The CIA and the Politics of Intelligence in Cold War South Asia." *Diplomatic History* 38, no. 5: 1046–1047.

McHale, Shawn. 2004. *Print and Power: Confucianism, Communism, and Buddhism in the Making of Modern Vietnam*. Honolulu: University of Hawaii Press.

McKelvey, Robert. 2002. *A Gift of Barbed Wire: America's Allies Abandoned in South Vietnam*. Seattle: University of Washington Press.

McMahon, Robert J. 2002. "Contested Memory: The Vietnam War and American Society, 1975–2001." *Diplomatic History* 26, no. 2: 159–184.

Mill, John Stuart. 1999. "What Is Poetry?" In *The Broadview Anthology of Victory Poetry and Poetic Theory*, ed. Thomas Collins and Vivienne Rundle, 1212–1227. Peterborough, Ontario: Broadview.

Miller, Edward. 2013. *Misalliance: Ngo Dinh Diem, the United States, and the Fate of South Vietnam*. Cambridge, MA: Harvard University Press.

Miller, Edward, and Tuong Vu. 2009. "The Vietnam War as a Vietnamese War: Agency and Society in the Study of the Second Indochina War." *Journal of Vietnamese Studies* 4, no. 3: 1–16.

Min, Pyong Gap. 1990. "Problems of Korean Immigrant Entrepreneurs." *International Migration Review* 24, no. 3: 436–455.

———. 2008. *Ethnic Solidarity for Economic Survival: Korean Greengrocers in New York City*. New York: Russell Sage Foundation.

Mộng-Lan. 2001. *Song of the Cicadas*. Amherst: University of Massachusetts Press.

Montero, Darrel. 1979. *Vietnamese Americans: Patterns of Resettlement and Socio-economic Adaptation in the United States*. Boulder, CO: Westview.

Moon, Hwy-Chang, and Byoungho Jin. 2006. "The Diamond Approach to the Competitiveness of Korea's Apparel Industry." *Journal of Fashion Marketing and Management: An International Journal* 10, no. 2: 195–208.

Morgan, Joseph G. 1997. *The Vietnam Lobby: The American Friends of Vietnam, 1955–1975*. Chapel Hill: University of North Carolina Press.

Murphy, Stephanie. 2019. "I'm a Proud Democrat. I'm Also a Proud Capitalist," *Washington Post*, April 28, 2019.

Najam, Adil. 2006. *Portrait of a Giving Community: Philanthropy by the Pakistani-American Diaspora*. Cambridge, MA: Global Equity Institute, Harvard University.

Ninh, Thien-Huong. 2017. *Race, Gender and Religion in Vietnam*. New York: Springer.

Ngô, Trọng Anh. 1970. "Nietzsche và mật tông" [Nietzsche and Vajrayana Buddhism]. *Tư Tưởng* 5 (September 1): 29–31.

Ngo, Van. 2000. *Au Pays de la Cloche Fêlée: tribulations d'un Cochinchinois à l'époque colonial*. Paris: Insomniaque.

Ngô, Văn. 2000. *Việt Nam 1920–1945, Cách Mạng và Phản Cách Mạng Thời Đô Hộ Thuộc Địa* [Vietnam 1920–1945: Revolution and Counter-revolution during Colonial Rule]. Amarillo, TX: Chuong Re/L'Insomniaque.

Người Việt Daily News. 2014. "Biểu Tình Chống Trung Quốc ở Sài Gòn, sáng 11-05-2014" [Anti-China Protests in Saigon], May 11. Accessed June 29, 2022. Available at: https://www.nguoi-viet.com/nvtv-phong-su/nvtv-phong-su-viet-nam/bieu-tinh-chong-trung-quoc-o-sai-gon-sang-11-05-2014-2/.

Nguyen, Dinh Hoa. 1960. "Higher Education in Vietnam." *Burman*, January 10, 1960, 9. In Douglas Pike Collection, Virtual Vietnam Archive. Accessed November 13, 2020.

———. 1999. *From the City inside the Red River: A Cultural Memoir of Mid-century Vietnam*. Jefferson, NC: McFarland.

Nguyen, Duy Lap. 2020. *The Unimagined Community: Imperialism and Culture in South Vietnam*. Manchester: Manchester University Press.

Nguyen, Hai. 2011. "Post-Vietnam War: The South Vietnamese under the Policy of Reeducation." Master's thesis, Texas Tech University.

Nguyen, Hong D. 2007. "The Relationship between the State of Vietnam and the Roman Catholic Church at the Present." *Religious Studies Review* 1:14–25.

Nguyen, Hoang Anh, et al. 2020. "Vietnamese Women Entrepreneurs' Motivations, Challenges, and Success Factors." *Advances in Developing Human Resources* 22, no. 2: 215–226.

Nguyen Huu Bao. 2013. "On the Path to Freedom." In *The Vietnamese Boat People*, ed. Nguy Vu and David Maruyama. Falls Church, VA: Nguy Vu Foundation.

Nguyễn, Hữu Phước. 2019. "The Philosophies and Development of a Free Education." In *The Republic of Vietnam, 1955–1975: Vietnamese Perspectives on Nation-Building*, ed. Tuong Vu and Sean Fear, 97–99. Ithaca, NY: Cornell University Press.

Nguyễn, Huy Hùng. n.d. *Hồi Ức Tù Cải Tạo Việt Nam* [Recollections of Imprisonment in Vietnamese Reeducation Camps]. Accessed on July 10, 2022. Available at https://www.baoquocdan.org/2021/05/hoi-ky-tu-cai-tao-cua-ai-ta-nguyen-huy_0250287133.html.

Nguyễn, Huy Quí. 1973. "Nguyên nhân và sự đóng góp của các tôn giáo trong lãnh vực xã hội." Graduating thesis, National Institute of Administration, Saigon.

Nguyen, Kim. 2020. "'Without the Luxury of Historical Amnesia': The Model Postwar Immigrant Remembering the Vietnam War through Anticommunist Protests." *Journal of Communication Inquiry* 34, no. 2: 134–150.

Nguyễn, Kim Hoàn. 2005. "Những Năm Tháng Kinh Hoàng" [Horrific Times]. In *Chuyện Người Vợ Tù Cải Tạo*, vol. 3: 115–133. Westminster: Viễn Đông.

Nguyen, Le Hieu. 2010. "Flashback from Yesteryears." In *The Vietnamese Mayflowers of 1975*, ed. Chat V. Dang, Hien V. Ho, Nghia M. Vo, An T. Than, and Anne R. Capdeville, expanded ed. Scotts Valley, CA: CreateSpace.

Nguyen, Lien-Hang. 2012. *Hanoi's War: An International History of the War for Peace in Vietnam*. Chapel Hill: University of North Carolina Press.

Nguyen, Marguerite, and Catherine Fung. 2016. "Refugee Cultures: Forty Years after the Vietnam War." *MELUS: Multi-ethnic Literature of the U.S.* 41, no. 3 (Fall): 1–7.

Nguyen, Martina Thucnhi. 2016. "French Colonial State, Vietnamese Civil Society: The League of Light [Đoàn Ánh Sáng] and Housing Reform in Hà Nội, 1937–1941." *Journal of Vietnamese Studies* 11, no. 3–4: 19.

———. 2020. *On Our Own Strength: The Self-Reliant Literary Group and Cosmopolitan Nationalism in Late Colonial Vietnam*. Honolulu: University of Hawaii Press.

Nguyen, Mimi Thi. 2012. *The Gift of Freedom: War, Debt, and Other Refugee Passages*. Durham, NC: Duke University Press.

Nguyen, Minh. 2018. "Vietnamese Sorrow: A Study of Literary Discourse in Popular Music Life." Ph.D. diss., University of California, Riverside.

Nguyen, Minh, Jo Bensemann, and Stephen Kelly. 2018. "Corporate Social Responsibility (CSR) in Vietnam: A Conceptual Framework." *International Journal of Corporate Social Responsibility* 3, no. 9: 1–12.

Nguyen, Nam. 2001. "The Range of Religious Healing Options in the Boston Vietnamese Community." In *Religious Healing in Boston: First Findings*, ed. Susan Sered and Linda L. Barnes, 49–54. Cambridge, MA: Harvard Divinity School, Center for the Study of World Religions.

Nguyen, Nathalie Huynh Chau. 2009. *Memory Is Another Country: Women of the Vietnamese Diaspora*. Santa Barbara: ABC-CLIO.

Nguyễn, Ngọc Lan. 1968. "Martin Luther King: Người con da đen của Thánh Gandhi" [Martin Luther King: The Black Child of Saint Gandhi]. *Bách Khoa* 271 (April 15): 64–72.

Nguyễn, Ngọc Linh. 1961. *Niên Lịch Công Đàn*. Saigon: Công Đàn.

Nguyễn, Ngọc Minh. 2005. "Vét Đập Đô Lương, Khai Quang Lòng Hồ Sông Mực (9/1977)" [Digging the Do Luong Dam and Reclaiming the Song Muc Lake in September 1977]. In *Không Chấp Nhận, Không Sống Chung*, 499–544. Anaheim: THTQLC/VN tại Hoa Kỳ.

Nguyen, Ngoc Ngan. 1982. *The Will of Heaven: A Story of One Vietnamese and the End of His World*. New York: Dutton.

Nguyễn, Ngọc Ngạn. 2014. "Nhớ một người." *Thời Báo Online*, March 21, 2014.

Nguyen, P. A., and Dana Doan. 2015. "Giving in Vietnam: A Nascent Third Sector with Potential for Growth." In *The Palgrave Handbook of Global Philanthropy*, ed. Pamala Wiepking and Femida Handy, 473–487. London: Palgrave Macmillan.

Nguyễn, Phương. 1957. *Ánh sáng dân chủ* [Light of Democracy]. Saigon: Nguyễn Phương.

Nguyen, Phuong Thuy. 2014. "The Rivalry of the French and American Educational Missions during the Vietnam War." *Paedagogica Historica* 50, no. 1–2: 27–41.

Nguyen, Phuong Tran. 2009. "People of the Fall: Refugee Nationalism in Little Saigon, 1975–2005." Ph.D. diss., University of Southern California.

———. 2015. "Vietnamese Americans in Little Saigon, California." In *Oxford Research Encyclopedia of American History*. New York: Oxford University Press. Published online (July 2). Available at https://doi.org/10.1093/acrefore/9780199329175.013.19.

———. 2017. *Becoming Refugee American: The Politics of Rescue in Little Saigon*. Chicago: University of Illinois Press.

Nguyen Quang Thieu. 1997. *The Women Carry River Water*. Trans. Martha Collins. Amherst: University of Massachusetts Press.

Nguyễn, Thanh Liêm, Trần Hữu Thế, Nguyễn Văn Trường, Trần Ngọc Ninh, and Lê Quân Tả. 2006. *Giáo Dục ở Miền Nam Tự Do Trước 1975*. Westminster: Lê Văn Duyệt Foundation.

Nguyễn, Thanh Nga. 2001. *Đóa Hồng Gai: Hồi Ký của Một Nữ Cựu Tù Nhân Chính Trị* [The Thorn Rose: Memoir of a Female Political Prisoner]. Garden Grove, CA: self-published.

Nguyen, Thanh T., and Bruce Weigl. 1994. *Poems from Captured Documents*. Amherst: University of Massachusetts Press.

Nguyen, Thanh V. 2006. "Vietnamese Buddhist Movement for Peace and Social Transformation, 1963–66." Ph.D. diss., Saybrook Graduate School and Research, San Francisco.

Nguyễn, Trọng Văn. 1968. "Nghĩ về hiện tượng hippies" [Thinking about the Phenomenon of Hippies]. *Bách Khoa* 268 (March 1): 130.

Nguyễn, Từ Chi. 1993. "The Traditional Viet Village in Bac Bo: Its Organizational Structure and Problems." In *The Traditional Village in Vietnam*, ed. Phan Huy Lê and Nguyễn Từ Chi, 44–142. Hanoi: Thế Giới.

Nguyen, Van Canh. 1983. *Vietnam under Communism, 1975–1982*. Stanford, CA: Hoover Institution Press.

Nguyễn, Văn Dông. 2005. "Những Đấu Trí Đầu Tiên" [Initial Mental Games]. In *Không Chấp Nhận, Không Sống Chung*.

Nguyễn, Văn Thích [J. M. Thich]. 1927. *Vấn Đề Cộng Sản* [The Problem of Communism]. Quinhon: Imprimerie de Quinhon.

Nguyễn, Văn Trung. 1957. "Thay lời phi lộ" [In Lieu of a Preface]. *Bách Khoa* 1 (January 15): 1.

———. [Phan Hai]. 1958. "'Người' trong tác phẩm của Saint-Exupery" ["The Person" in the Works of Saint-Exupery]. *Bách khoa* 1 (January 15): 9–15.

———. 1965. "Chiến tranh và cách mạng" [War and Revolution]. *Hành trình* 6: 3–24.

Nguyen, Viet Thanh. 2002. *Race and Resistance: Literature and Politics in Asian America*. New York: Oxford University Press.

———. 2006. "Seeing Double: The Films of R. Hong-An Truong." *Postmodern Culture* 17, no. 1 (September). Available at https://doi:10.1353/pmc.2007.0008.

———. 2012. "Refugee Memories and Asian American Critique." *Positions* 20, no. 3: 911–942.

———. 2013. "Just Memory: War and the Ethics of Remembrance." *American Literary History* 25, no. 1: 144–163.

———. 2015. *The Sympathizer*. New York: Grove.

———. 2016. *Nothing Ever Dies: Vietnam and the Memory of War*. Cambridge, MA: Harvard University Press.

———. 2017. *The Refugees*. New York: Grove.

———. 2021. "There's a Reason the South Vietnamese Flag Flew during the Capitol Riot." *Washington Post*, January 14.

Nguyen, Vinh, Thy Phu, and Y-Dang Troeung. 2018. "Refugee Compassion and the Politics of Embodied Storytelling: A Critical Conversation." *a/b: Auto/Biography Studies* 33, no. 2: 441–445.

Nguyễn, Vỹ. 1970. *Tuấn Chàng Trai Nước Việt* [Tuan, Young Man of Vietnam]. Saigon: self-published.

Nguyen, Y Thien. 2018. "(Re)Making the South Vietnamese Past in America." *Journal of Asian American Studies* 21, no. 1: 65–103.

———. 2021. "When State Propaganda Becomes Social Knowledge: Legacies of the Southern Republic." Ph.D. diss., Northwestern University.

Nguyen-Akbar, Mytoan. 2016. "Finding the American Dream Abroad? Narratives of Return among 1.5 and Second Generation Vietnamese American Skilled Migrants in Vietnam." *Journal of Vietnamese Studies* 11, no. 2: 96–121.

Nguyen-Marshall, Van. 2007. "The Ethics of Benevolence in French Colonial Vietnam." In *The Chinese State at the Border*, ed. Diana Lary, 162–180. Vancouver: University of British Columbia Press.

———. 2008. *In Search of Moral Authority*. New York: Peter Lang.

———. 2018. "Appeasing the Spirits along the 'Highway of Horror': Civic Life in Wartime South Vietnam." *War and Society* 37, no. 3: 206–222.

Nguyễn-Võ, Thu-hương. 2005. "Forking Paths: How Shall We Mourn the Past?" *Amerasia Journal* 31, no. 2: 157–175.

Nhân Dân. 2020. "Chân Tướng Các Quỹ Nhân Danh 'Dân Chủ.'" November 10. Accessed January 1, 2021. Available at: https://nhandan.com.vn/binh-luan-phe-phan/chan-tuong-cac-quy-nhan-danh-dan-chu-623874/.

Nhất Hạnh. 1965. *Basic Concepts of Policy and Method: Movement of Youth for Social Service*. Saigon: University of Vạn Hạnh.

Ninh, Thien-Huong. 2017. *Race, Gender, and Religion in the Diaspora: The New Chosen People*. New York: Palgrave Macmillan.

Nora, Pierre. 1989. "Between Memory and History: Les Lieux de Mémoire." *Representation*, no. 26 , Special Issue: Memory and Counter-Memory (Spring): 7–24.

Norindr, Panivong. 1996. *Phantasmatic Indochina: French Colonial Ideology in Architecture, Film, and Literature*. Durham, NC: Duke University Press.

Noseworthy, William. 2015. "The Mother Goddess of Champa: Po Ina Nagar." *SUVANNABHUMI: Multi-disciplinary Journal of Southeast Asian Studies* 7, no. 1: 107–138.

Omi, Michael, and Howard Winant. 1994. *Racial Formation in the United States: From the 1960s to the 1990s*. 2nd ed. New York: Routledge.

Ong, Nhu-Ngoc, and David Meyer. 2008. "Protest and Political Incorporation: Vietnamese-American Protests in Orange County, 1975–2001." *Journal of Vietnamese Studies* 3, no. 1 (Winter): 78–107.

Orsi, Robert. 2010. *The Madonna of 115th Street: Faith and Community in Italian Harlem, 1880–1950*. New Haven, CT: Yale University Press.

Orwell, George, Ben Pimlott, and Peter H. Davison. 1989. *Nineteen Eighty-Four*. London: Penguin Books, in association with Secker and Warburg.

Park, K., 1997. *The Korean American Dream*. Ithaca: Cornell University Press.

Pearce, Susan, Elizabeth Clifford, and Reena Tandon. 2011. *Immigration and Women: Understanding the American Experience*. New York: New York University Press.

Pearce-Moses, Richard. 2005. *A Glossary of Archival and Records Terminology*. Chicago: Society of American Archivists.

Peché, Linda Ho. 2012. "I'd Pay Homage, Not Go 'All Bling': Race, Religion and Vietnamese American Youth." In *Sustaining Faith Traditions: Race, Ethnicity, and Religion among the Latino and Asian American Second Generation*, ed. Carolyn Chen and Russell Jeung, 222–240. New York: New York University Press.

———. 2013. "Searching for the Spirit(s) of Diasporic Viet Nam: Appeasing the Ancestors and Articulating Cultural Belonging." Ph.D. diss., University of Texas at Austin.

———. 2016. "Religious Spaces: Boat People Legacies and the Vietnamese American Second Generation." In *Identity and the Second Generation: How Children of Immigrants Find Their Space*, ed. Faith Nibbs and Caroline Brettell, 149–171. Nashville: Vanderbilt University Press.

Peck, Jamie. 2010. *Constructions of Neoliberal Reason*. New York: Oxford University Press.

Pedraza, Silvia. 1991. "Women and Migration: The Social Consequences of Gender." *Annual Review of Sociology* 17, no. 1: 303–325.

Pelaud, Isabelle Thuy. 2010. *This Is All I Choose to Tell: History and Hybridity in Vietnamese American Literature*. Philadelphia: Temple University Press.

Perri, David F., and Hung M. Chu. 2012. "Entrepreneurs in China and Vietnam: Motivations and Problems." *International Journal of Entrepreneurship* 16 (January): 93–112.

———. 2018. "Mastercard Index of Women Entrepreneurs 2018." *Mastercard*. Accessed on May 11, 2021. Available at https://newsroom.mastercard.com/documents/master card-index-of-women-entrepreneurs-miwe-2018.

Peycam, Phlippe. 2012. *The Birth of Vietnamese Political Journalism*. New York: Columbia University Press.

Pham, Andrew X. 2000. *Catfish and Mandala: A Two-Wheeled Voyage through the Landscape and Memory of Vietnam*. New York: Picador USA.

Phạm, Công Tắc. 1947. *Trích Thuyết Đạo* [Catechism or Religious Doctrines]. Accessed on October 1, 2020. Available at https://www.daotam.info/booksv/dpmdtkm.htm.

Pham, Duy. 2000. *Hoi Ky: Thoi Hai Ngoai*. Vol. 4. Midway City, CA: Duy Cuong.

Phạm Gia Đại. 2011. *Hồi Ký: Những Người Tù Cuối Cùng* [Memoir: The Last Prisoners]. Santa Ana, CA: Self-published.

Pham, Quang X. 2005. *A Sense of Duty: My Father, My American Journey*. New York: Ballantine Books.

Pham, Quynh Phuong, and Chris Eipper. 2009. "Mothering and Fathering the Vietnamese: Religion, Gender, and National Identity." *Journal of Vietnamese Studies* 4, no. 1 (Winter): 49–83.

Phạm, Văn Chung. 2005. "Vào Đề" [Preface]. In *Không Chấp Nhận, Không Sống Chung*, 9–11. Anaheim: THTQLC/VN tại Hoa Kỳ.

Phạm, Văn Liễu. 2004. *Trả Ta Sông Núi*. 3 vols. Houston: Văn Hoá.

Pham, Van Minh. 2001. "Socio-political Philosophy of Vietnamese Buddhism: A Case Study of the Buddhist Movement of 1963 and 1966." Master's thesis, University of Western Sydney, Sydney.

Pham, Vinh Phu. 2019. "Nation Building from Abroad: Nhạc vàng and the Legacy of Republicanism in Overseas Vietnamese Communities." Working paper presented at Studying Republican Vietnam Conference, University of Oregon, Eugene, October 14, 2019.

Pham, Vu. 2003. "Antedating and Anchoring Vietnamese America: Toward a Vietnamese American Historiography." *Amerasia Journal* 29, no. 1: 135–152.

Phan, Aimee. 2013. *The Re-education of Cherry Truong*. New York: Picador.

Phan, Hai-Dang Doan. 2012. "A Rumor of Redress: Literature, the Vietnam War, and the Politics of Reconciliation." Ph.D. diss., University of Wisconsin–Madison.

Phan, Nhiên Hạo. 1998. *Thiên Đường Chuông Giấy* [Paradise of Paper Bells]. Tân Thư.

———. 2002. "This Year I Am the Same Age as My Father." Trans. Hai-Dang Phan.

———. 2004. *Chế Tạo Thơ Ca 99-04* [Manufacturing Poetry 99-04]. San Jose: Văn.

———. 2006. *Night, Fish and Charlie Parker*. Trans. Linh Dinh. Dorset, VT: Tupelo Press.

———. 2015. "The Disjunctive Politics of Vietnamese Immigrants in America from the Transnational Perspective." *Central and Eastern European Migration Review* 4, no. 1: 81–95.

———. 2019. *Radio Mùa Hè* [Summer Radio]. San Jose: Nhan Anh.

———. 2020. "Open Secrets: An Interview with Phan Nhiên Hạo." Interview with Sarah Timmer Harvey. *Asymptote*, April 15.

Phan, Nhiên Hạo, and Hai-Dang Phan. 2020. *Paper Bells*. New York: Song Cave.

Phan, Peter. 1991. "Aspects of Vietnamese Culture and Roman Catholicism: Background Information for Educators of Vietnamese Seminarians." *Seminaries in Dialogue* 23 (Spring): 2–8.

———. 2003. *Christianity with an Asian Face: Asian American Theology in the Making*. Maryknoll, NY: Orbis Books.

———. 2005. "Mary in Vietnamese Piety and Theology: A Contemporary Perspective." *Ephemerides Mariologicae* 51, Issue 4: 457–72.

———. 2006. "Christianity in Indochina." In *World Christianities, c. 1815–c. 1914*, ed. Sheridan Gilley and Brian Stanley, 513–527. New York: Cambridge University Press.

Phan, Phát Huồn. [1965] 2004. *Việt-Nam Giáo-Sử*. Vol. 2, *1933–1950*. Saigon: Cứu Thế Tùng-Thư.

Phan, Thuận An. 2017. "Tạp chí Đại Học: Đứa con tinh thần sáng giá của Viện Đại Học Huế" [Dai Hoc: University of Hue's Prominent Intellectual Product]. *Tạp chí nghiên cứu và phát triển* 2, no. 136: 10–12.

Phi, Bao. 2011. *Sông/Sing*. Minneapolis: Coffee House.

———. 2017. *Thousand Star Hotel*. Minneapolis: Coffee House.

Phu, Thy. 2014. "Diasporic Vietnamese Family Photographs, Orphan Images, and the Art of Recollection." *TransAsia Photography Review. Photography and Diaspora* 5, no. 1 (Fall). Available at http://hdl.handle.net/2027/spo.7977573.0005.102.

Pio, Edwina, and Caroline Essers. 2014. "Professional Migrant Women Decentring Otherness: A Transnational Perspective." *British Journal of Management* 25, no. 2: 252–265.

Piperopoulos, Panos G. 2012. *Entrepreneurship, Innovation and Business Clusters*. Hampshire, U.K.: Gower.

Poggesi, Sara, Michela Mari, and Luisa De Vita. 2016. "What's New in Female Entrepreneurship Research? Answers from the Literature." *International Entrepreneurship and Management Journal* 12, no. 3: 735–764.

Popkin, Samuel. 1985. "Colonialism and the Ideological Origins of the Vietnamese Revolution: A Review Article." *Journal of Asian Studies* 44, no. 2 (February): 349–357.

Portes, Alejandro. 1987. "The Social Origins of the Cuban Enclave Economy of Miami." *Sociological Perspectives* 30, no. 4: 340–372.

Portes, Alejandro, and Ruben Rumbaut. 2001. *Legacies: The Story of the Immigrant Second Generation*. Berkeley: University of California Press.

Portes, Alejandro, and Jessica Yiu. 2013. "Entrepreneurship, Transnationalism, and Development." *Migration Studies* 1, no. 1: 75–95.

Quang Minh. 1996. *Cách Mạng Việt Nam Thời Cận Kim: Đại Việt Quốc Dân Đảng 1938–1995* [The Vietnamese Revolution in the Modern Era: The Great Vietnamese Nationalist Party, 1938–1995]. Westminster, CA: Văn Nghệ.

Race, Jeffrey. 1972. *War Comes to Long An: Revolutionary Conflict in a Vietnamese Province*. Berkeley: University of California Press.

Raijman, Rebeca, and Marta Tienda. 2000. "Immigrants' Pathways to Business Ownership: A Comparative Ethnic Perspective." *International Migration Review* 34, no. 3: 682–706.

Reed-Danahay, Deborah. 2018 "'Like a Foreigner in My Own Homeland': Writing the Dilemmas of Return in the Vietnamese American Diaspora." *Identities: Global Studies in Culture and Power* 22, no. 5: 603–618.

Reyes, Adelaida. 1999. *Songs of the Caged, Songs of the Free: Music and the Vietnamese Refugee Experience*. Philadelphia: Temple University Press.

Ricoeur, Paul. 2004. *Memory, History, and Forgetting*. Trans. Kathleen Blamey and David Pellauer. Chicago: University of Chicago Press.

Rothberg, Michael. 2006. "Between Auschwitz and Algeria: Multidirectional Memory and the Counterpublic Witness." *Critical Inquiry* 33, no. S (Autumn): 158–184.

Rutledge, Paul. 1985. *The Role of Religion in Ethnic Self-Identity*. Lanham, MD: University Press of America.

———. 1992. *The Vietnamese Experience in America*. Bloomington: Indiana University Press.

Ryan, David, and David Fitzgerald. 2009. "Iraq and Vietnam: Endless Recurrence or Stirrings Still?" *Critical Asian Studies* 41, no. 4 (November 27): 621–653.

Said, Edward. 1984. "Reflections of Exile." *Granta* 13: 159–172.

Salemink, Oscar. 2015. "Spirit Worship and Possession in Vietnam and Beyond." In *Routledge Handbook of Religions in Asia*, ed. Bryan S. Turner and Oscar Salemink, 231–246. London: Routledge.

Santa Ana Register. 1977. "Viet Refugee Rally Saturday." April 29, 1977.

Santoro, Nicolas. 2011. *Mary in Our Life: Atlas of the Names and Titles of Mary, the Mother of Jesus, and Their Place in Marian Devotion*. Bloomington, IN: iUniverse.

Schafer, John T. 2016. *Võ Phiến and the Sadness of Exile*. De Kalb: Southern Illinois University Press.

Schiller, Nina, Linda G. Basch, and Cristina Szanton Blanc. 1992. "Transnationalism: A New Analytic Framework for Understanding Migration." *Annals of the New York Academy of Sciences* 645, no. 1 (July): 1–24.

Schlund-Vials, Cathy. 2012. *War, Genocide, Justice: Cambodian Memory Work*. Minneapolis: University of Minnesota Press.

Schwenkel, Christina. 2006. "Recombinant History: Transnational Practices of Memory and Knowledge Production in Contemporary Vietnam." *Cultural Anthropology* 21, no. 1: 3–30.

———. 2017. "Vietnamese in Central Europe: An Unintended Diaspora." *Journal of Vietnamese Studies* 12, no. 1: 1–9.

Scigliano, Robert. 1960. "Political Parties in South Vietnam under the Republic." *Pacific Affairs* 33, no. 4: 327–346.

Selbin, Eric. 1999. *Modern Latin American Revolutions*. Boulder, CO: Westview.

Seyhan, Azade. 2001. *Writing outside the Nation*. Princeton, NJ: Princeton University Press.

Sheffer, Gabriel. 1996. "Whither the Study of Ethnic Diasporas? Some Theoretical, Definitional, Analytical and Comparative Considerations." In *Les Réseaux des Diasporas*, ed. George Prévélakis. Paris: L'Harmattan.

Sidel, Mark. 2007. *Vietnamese-American Diaspora Philanthropy to Vietnam*. Cambridge, MA: Philanthropic Initiative, Harvard University.

Small, Ivan V. 2019. *Currencies of Imagination: Channeling Money and Chasing Mobility in Vietnam*. Ithaca, NY: Cornell University Press.

Small, Melvin. 2010. "Bring the Boys Home Now! Antiwar Activism and Withdrawal from Vietnam—and Iraq." *Diplomatic History* 34, no. 3: 543–553.

Smart, Ninian. 1987. "The Importance of Diasporas." In *Gilgul: Essays on Transformation, Revolution, and Permanence in the History of Religions*, ed. Shaul Shaked, David Shulman, and Gedaliahu Stroumsa, 288–97. Leiden: Brill.

Smith, Andrea. 2006. "Heteropatriarchy and the Three Pillars of White Supremacy: Rethinking Women of Color Organizing. In Incite! Women of Color Against Violence." In *Color of Violence: The Incite! Anthology*, ed. Andrea Smith, 66–73. Cambridge, MA: South End.

———. 2010. "Indigeneity, Settler Colonialism, White Supremacy." *Global Dialogue* 12, no. 2: 1–13.

Smith, Rachel Greenwald. 2015. *Affect and American Literature in the Age of Neoliberalism*. New York: Cambridge University Press.

Smith, Ralph B. 1983. *An International History of the Vietnam War*. 2 vols. New York: St. Martin's.

Snow, David, and Robert Benford. 1998. "Ideology, Framing Resonance and Participant Mobilization." *International Social Movement Research* 1:197–217.

Sokefeld, Martin, ed. 2004. *Religion or Culture? Concepts of Identity in the Alevi Diaspora*. New York: Routledge.

Starr, Paul, and Alden Roberts. 1982. "Community Structure and Vietnamese Refugee Adaptation: The Significance of Context." *International Migration Review* 16, no. 3: 595.

Stein, Barry. 1979. "Occupational Adjustment of Refugees: The Vietnamese in the United States." *International Migration Review* 13, no. 1.

Stewart, Geoffrey C. 2017. *Vietnam's Lost Revolution: Ngô Đình Diệm's Failure to Build an Independent Nation, 1955–1963*. New York: Cambridge University Press.

Stur, Heather. 2020. *Saigon at War: South Vietnam and the Global Sixties*. New York: Cambridge University Press.

Sturken, Marita. 1997. *Tangled Memories: The Vietnam War, the AIDS Epidemic, and the Politics of Remembering*. Berkeley: University of California Press.

Sutter, Valerie O'Connor. 1990. *The Indochinese Refugee Dilemma*. Baton Rouge: Louisiana University Press.

Tai, Jessica. 2019. "The Power of Words: Cultural Humility as a Framework for Anti-oppressive Archival Description." In Radical Empathy in Archival Practice," ed. Elvia Arroyo-Ramirez, Jasmine Jones, Shannon O'Neil, and Holly A. Smith, special issue, *Journal of Critical Library and Information Studies* 3, no. 2. Accessed July 24, 2022. Available at: https://doi.org/10.24242/jclis.v3i2.120.

Tam, Hao Jun. 2016. "Review article of Yen Le Espiritu's *Body Counts: The Vietnam War and Militarized Refugees*." *Journal of Vietnamese Studies* 11, no. 2: 130.

Tang, Eric. 2011. "A Gulf Unites Us: The Vietnamese Americans of Black New Orleans East." *American Quarterly* 63, no. 1: 117–149.

Tariq, Memoona, and Jawad Syed. 2018. "An Intersectional Perspective on Muslim Women's Issues and Experiences in Employment." *Gender, Work and Organization* 25, no. 5: 495–513.

Taylor, Keith. 2013. *A History of the Vietnamese*. New York: Cambridge University Press.

Taylor, Nora A. 2001. "Framing the National Spirit: Viewing and Reviewing Painting under the Revolution." In Ho Tai, *The Country of Memory*, 109–134.

Taylor, Philip. 2001. *Fragments of the Present: Searching for Modernity in Vietnam's South*. Honolulu: University of Hawaii Press.

———. 2004. *Goddess on the Rise: Pilgrimage and Popular Religion in Vietnam*. Honolulu: University of Hawaii Press.

Thai, Hung Cam. 2008. *For Better or for Worse: Vietnamese International Marriages in the New Global Economy*. New Brunswick, NJ: Rutgers University Press.

Thai, Van Kiêm. 2001. "Bùi Quang Tung, 1912–2001." *BEFEO* 88: 21–23.

Thanh Thảo. 1957. *Tù Ngục và Thoát Ly: Hồi Ký Ba Năm Tám Tháng* [Prisons and Escapes: Memoir of Three Years and Eight Months]. Sài Gòn.

The Guardian. 1966. "S. Vietnam Hardly a Nation, More a Tangle of Tribes." February 7, 1966.

Thich, Minh Chau. 1969. "Searching for a Cultural Philosophy." *Van Hanh Bulletin* 1, no. 1 (July): 8–9.

Thiện, Mộc Lan. 2004. *Phụ-nữ Tân-văn Phấn Son Tô Điểm Sơn Hà*. Hồ Chí Minh: Văn Hóa Sài Gòn and Công Ty Sách Thời Đại.

Thuý Nga Inc. [dba Thuý Nga Productions]. Westminster, CA.

Tisdale, Betty. 2020. "Helping and Loving Orphan: The Betty Tisdale Story, Operation Babylift." *Adopt Vietnam*. Accessed July 22, 2020. Available at https://www.adoptviet nam.org/adoption/babylift-anlac-orphanage.htm.

Tô, Văn Cấp. 2005. "Những Chiến Hữu Thủy Quân Lục Chiến đã Chết trong Các Trại Tù Việt Cộng" [The Marine Comrades Who Died in Vietnamese Communist Prisons]. In *Không Chấp Nhận, Không Sống Chung*, 306–325. Anaheim: THTQLC/VN tại Hoa Kỳ.

Tölölyan, Khachig. 1996. "Rethinking Diaspora(s): Stateless Power in the Transnational Moment." *Diaspora: A Journal of Transnational Studies* 5, no. 1: 3–36.

Topmiller, Robert. 2002. *The Lotus Unleashed: The Buddhist Peace Movement in South Vietnam, 1964–1966*. Lexington: University Press of Kentucky.

Tran, Barbara, Monique Truong, and Khoi Truong Luu, eds. 1998. *Watermark: Vietnamese American Poetry and Prose*. Philadelphia: Temple University Press.

Tran, De, Andrew Lam, and Hai Nguyen. 1995. *Once Upon a Dream: The Vietnamese-American Experience*. Kansas City: Andrews and McMeel.

Trần, Dũ, and Hoàng Việt. 1991. *Trần Dũ—Quãng Đời Đi Qua*. Westminster: Little Saigon.

Tran, Nu-Anh. 2006. "South Vietnamese Identity, American Intervention, and the Newspaper *Chính Luận* [Political Discussion], 1965–69." *Journal of Vietnamese Studies* 1, no. 1–2: 169–209.

———. 2013. "Contested Identities: Nationalism in the Republic of Vietnam (1954–1963)." Ph.D. diss., University of California, Berkeley.

Tran, Nu-Anh, and Tuong Vu, eds. 2022. *Building a Republican Nation in Vietnam, 1920–1963*. Honolulu: University of Hawaii Press.

Tran, Quan Tue. 2012. "Remembering the Boat People Exodus: A Tale of Two Memorials." *Journal of Vietnamese Studies* 7, no. 3 (Fall): 80–121.

———. 2016a. "Anchoring Boat People's History and Memory: Refugee Identity, Community and Cultural Formations in the Vietnamese Diaspora." Ph.D. diss., Yale University.

———. 2016b. "Broken but Not Forsaken: Vietnamese Veterans and the Diaspora." In Boyle and Lim, *Looking Back on the Vietnam War*, 34–49.

Tran, Quang C. 2009. *Trung Tâm Thánh Mẫu Toàn Quốc La Vang* [The National Marian Center of Lavang]. Tổng Giáo Phận Huế [The Archdiocese of Hue]. Accessed on June 24, 2013. Available at http://tonggiaophanhue.net/home/index.php?option=com_content&view=article&id=38:phn-1-s-tich-c-m-la-vang&catid=14:duc-me-lavang&Itemid=99.

Tran Tri Vu. 1988. *Lost Years: My 1632 Days in Vietnamese Reeducation Camps*. Berkeley, CA: Institute of East Asian Studies.

Trần, Trọng Đăng Đàn. 2005. *Người Việt Nam ở nước ngoài không chỉ có "Việt kiều."* Hà Nội: Nhà Xuất Bản Chính Trị Quốc Gia.

Trần Trọng Kim. 1964. *Viêt-Nam Sử-Lược.* 7th ed. Saigon: Tân Việt.

Tran, Tuyen Ngoc. 2007. "Behind the Smoke and Mirrors: The Vietnamese in California, 1975–1994." Ph.D. diss., University of California, Berkeley.

Trần Văn Chánh. 2014. "Giáo Dục Miền Nam Việt Nam (1954–1975) Trên Con Đường Xây Dựng và Phát Triển." *Tạp Chí Nghiên Cứu và Phát Triển* 7–8 (October): 4–52.

Trần, Văn Long. 2015. "Hồi Tưởng Ngày Mất Nước Và Quãng Đời Tù Ngục Cộng Sản" [Remembrances of the Day of National Loss and the Period of Communist Imprisonment]. March. Available at http://pham-v-thanh.blogspot.com/2015/03/hoi-tuong-ngay-mat-nuoc-va-quang-oi-tu.html.

Trần, Văn Thái. 1973. *Trại Đầm Đùn* [The Đầm Đùn Prison]. Sài Gòn: Nguyễn Trãi.

Trần, Văn Thiện. 1961. *Rapport sur l'Université de Dalat.* Dalat: University of Dalat.

Trieu, Monica M. 2013. "The Role of Premigration Status in the Acculturation of Chinese–Vietnamese and Vietnamese Americans." *Sociological Inquiry* 83, no. 3: 392–420.

Trinh, Minh Ha. 1989. *Woman, Native, Other.* Bloomington: Indiana University Press.

Truitt, Allison. 2017. "Quán Thế Âm of the Transpacific." *Journal of Vietnamese Studies* 12, no. 2 (Spring): 83–107.

———. 2021. *Pure Land in the Making: Vietnamese Buddhism in the US Gulf South.* Seattle: University of Washington Press.

Truong-buu-lam. 1955. "Les debuts des relations entre la Belgique et le Japon, 1846–1866." Mémoire, Université Catholique de Louvain.

———. 1957. "Les debuts des relations entre la Belgique et le Japon, 1854–1896." Ph.D. thesis, Université Catholique de Louvain.

Truong, Kim Chuyen, Ivan Small, and Diep Vuong. 2008. "Diaspora Philanthropy in Vietnam." In *Diaspora Giving: An Agent of Change in Asia Pacific Communities?* ed. Paula Johnson, 251–283. Manila: Asia Pacific Philanthropy Consortium.

Truong, Marcelino. 2016. *Such a Lovely Little War: Saigon 1961–1963.* Trans. David Homel. Vancouver, BC: Arsenal Pulp.

———. 2017. *Saigon Calling: London 1963–75.* Trans. David Homel. Vancouver, BC: Arsenal Pulp.

Truong, Monique. 1993. "The Emergence of Voices: Vietnamese American Literature 1975–1990." *Amerasia Journal* 19, no. 3: 27.

———. 2004. *The Book of Salt.* New York: Mariner Books.

Truong, Nhu Tang. 1985. *A Vietcong Memoir.* New York: Vintage.

Trương, Thùy Dung. 2020. "The American Influences on the Higher Education of the Second Republic of Vietnam: The Case of the National Universities." Ph.D. diss., University of Hamburg.

Truong, Tran. 1999a. *The Book of Perceptions.* San Francisco: Kearney Street Workshop.

———. 1999b. *Placing the Accents.* Berkeley, CA: Apogee.

Tseng, Yen-Fen. 1994. "Chinese Ethnic Economy: San Gabriel Valley, Los Angeles County." *Journal of Urban Affairs* 16, no. 2: 169–189.

Tuan, Mia. 1999. *Forever Foreigners or Honorary Whites? The Asian Ethnic Experience Today.* New Brunswick, NJ: Rutgers University Press.

Tweed, Thomas. 1997. *Our Lady of the Exile: Diasporic Religion at a Cuban Shrine in Miami.* New York: Oxford University Press.

University of Saigon. 1967. *Prospectus.* Saigon: University of Saigon.

U.S. Census Bureau. 2018. American Community Survey, 2018/ American Community Survey 5-Year Estimates. Accessed July 7, 2022. Available at data.census.gov.

U.S. Weather Bureau. 1965. *Climatological Data: National Summary* 15:13 (1964). Asheville, NC: U.S. Department of Commerce.

Vaage, Aina B., H. Thomsen, Cecile Rousseau, Tore Wentzel-Larsen, Thong V. Ta, and Edvard Hauff. 2011. "Parental Predictors of the Mental Health of Children of Vietnamese Refugees." *Child and Adolescent Psychiatry and Mental Health* 5, no. 1: 1–11.

Valdez, Zulema. 2016. "Intersectionality, the Household Economy, and Ethnic Entrepreneurship." *Ethnic and Racial Studies* 39, no. 9: 1618–1636.

Valverde, Kieu-Linh Caroline. 2012. *Transnationalizing Viet Nam: Community, Culture, and Politics in the Diaspora*. Philadelphia: Temple University Press.

VanLandingham, Mark. 2017. *Weathering Katrina: Culture and Recovery among Vietnamese Americans*. New York: Russell Sage Foundation.

Vertovec, Steven. 1997. "Three Meanings of 'Diaspora,' Exemplified among South Asian Religions." *Diaspora: A Journal of Transnational Studies* 6, no. 3 (Winter): 277–279.

———. 2000. "Religion and Diaspora." Paper presented at the conference on "New Landscapes of Religion in the West," School of Geography and the Environment, University of Oxford, September 27–29. Accessed April 1, 2013. Available at http://www.transcomm.ox.ac.uk/working%20papers/Vertovec01.PDF.

Vietnam Asia Pacific Economic Center. 2011. *Philanthropy in Vietnam*. Accessed September 10, 2020. Available at https://asiafoundation.org/resources/pdfs/ASIAEfinal.pdf.

Vietnam Women Entrepreneurs Council. 2007. International Labor Organization Office in Vietnam, "Women's Entrepreneurship Development in Vietnam." Accessed June 12, 2021. Available at ilo.org/asia/publications/WCMS_100456/lan--en/index.htm.

Võ Đại Tôn. 1992. *Tắm Máu Đen: Bút Ký 1981–1991* [Bathing in Dark Blood: Memoir, 1981–1991]. Greenacre, NSW, Australia: self-published.

Võ, Linda Trinh. 2003. "Vietnamese American Trajectories: Dimensions of Diaspora." *Amerasia Journal* 29, no. 1: ix–xviii.

———. 2008. "Constructing a Vietnamese American Community: Economic and Political Transformation in Little Saigon, Orange County." *Amerasia Journal* 34, no. 3: 84–109.

Vo, Linda Trinh, and Mary Yu Danico. 2004. "The Formation of Post-suburban Communities: Koreatown and Little Saigon, Orange County." *International Journal of Sociology and Social Policy* 24, no. 7/8: 15–25.

Vo, Nghia M. 2004. *The Vietnamese Boat People, 1954 and 1975–1992*. Jefferson, NC: McFarland.

———. 2011. "A Pilgrim." In *The Vietnamese Mayflowers of 1975*, Chat V. Dang, Hien V. Ho, Nghia M. Vo, An T. Than, and Anne R. Capdeville, eds., expanded ed. Scotts Valley, CA: CreateSpace.

Vo Dang, Thuy. 2005. "The Cultural Work of Anticommunism in the San Diego Vietnamese American Community." *Amerasia Journal* 31, no. 2: 64–86.

———. 2008. "Anticommunism as Cultural Praxis: South Vietnam, War, and Refugee Memories in the Vietnamese American Community." Ph.D. diss., University of California, San Diego.

———. 2013. "Vietnamese American Anticommunism." In *Asian Americans: An Encyclopedia of Social, Cultural, Economic, and Political History*, ed. Xiaojian Zhao and Edward Park, 1151–1154. Santa Barbara: ABC-CLIO.

Vũ, Lục Thủy. 1997. "Tưởng niệm linh mục Cao Văn Luận" [Commemorating Father Cao Van Luan]. *Dòng Việt* 4: 23–36.

Vu, Tuong. 2007. "Vietnamese Political Studies and Debates on Vietnamese Nationalism." *Journal of Vietnamese Studies* 2, no. 2: 175–230.

———. 2014. "The Party v. the People: The Rise of Anti-China Nationalism in Contemporary Vietnam." *Journal of Vietnamese Studies* 9, no. 4: 33–66.

———. 2017. *Vietnam's Communist Revolution: The Power and Limits of Ideology.* New York: Cambridge University Press.

Vu, Tuong, and Sean Fear, eds. 2019. *The Republic of Vietnam, 1955–1975: Vietnamese Perspectives on Nation Building.* Ithaca, NY: SE Asia Publications, Cornell University Press.

Vu Van Chung. 2015. "Foreign Capital Inflows and Economic Growth: Does Foreign Capital Inflows Promote the Host Country's Economic Growth?" Tokyo: Policy Research Institute, Ministry of Finance.

Vương Mộng Long. 2012. "Viên Ngọc Nát: Hồi Ký của Thiếu Tá Vương Mộng Long" [The Crushed Pearl: Memoir of Major Vuong Mong Long]. Accessed July 10, 2022. Available at https://khoa1hocviencsqg.com/2012/07/06/vien-ngoc-nat-_-hoi-ky-vuong-mong-long-k20/.

Vuong, Ocean. 2016. *Night Sky with Exit Wound.* New York: Copper Canyon.

———. 2019. *On Earth We're Briefly Gorgeous.* New York: Penguin.

Walsham, Alexandra. 2016. Introduction to "The Social History of the Archive: Record-Keeping in Early Modern Europe." *Past and Present* 230, no. 11 (November): 9–48.

Walton, Emily. 2015. "Making Sense of Asian American Ethnic Neighborhoods: A Typology and Application to Health." *Sociological Perspectives* 58, no. 3: 490–515.

Wang, Ling-Chi. 1995. "The Structure of Dual Domination: Toward a Paradigm for the Study of the Chinese Diaspora in the United States." *Amerasia Journal* 21, no. 1–2: 149–169.

Wang, Qingfang. 2013. "Industrial Concentration of Ethnic Minority and Women-Owned Businesses: Evidence from the Survey of Business Owners in the United States." *Journal of Small Business and Entrepreneurship* 26, no. 3: 299–321.

Weber, Eugen. 1976. *Peasants into Frenchmen: The Modernization of Rural France, 1870–1914.* Stanford, CA: Stanford University Press.

Wiesner, Louis. 1988. *Victims and Survivors.* New York: Greenwood Press, 1988.

Wiktorowicz, Quintan. 2000. "Civil Society as Social Control: State Power in Jordan," *Comparative Politics* 33, no. 1 (October): 43–61.

Willbanks, James H. 2004. *Abandoning Vietnam: How America Left and South Vietnam Lost Its War.* Lawrence: University Press of Kansas.

Womack, Brantly. 2006. *China and Vietnam: The Politics of Asymmetry.* New York: Cambridge University Press, 2006.

Woodside, Alexander. 1976. *Community and Revolution in Modern Vietnam.* New York: Houghton Mifflin.

Wright, Wayne E., Linda Trinh Vo, Caroline Kieu Linh Valverde, Nhi Lieu, Rifka Hirsch, Roy Vu, Isabelle Thuy Pelaud, and Mark E. Pfeifer. 2008. "A Special Tribute to Anne Frank of the Southeast Asian Archive at the University of California, Irvine." *Journal of Southeast Asian American Education and Advancement* 3, no. 1: article 5.

X, Malcolm. 1968. "Phiếu bầu hay súng đạn" [The Ballot or the Bullet]. *Đất Nước* 7 (January): 103–140.

Yanagisako, Sylvia, and Carol Delaney, eds. 1994. *Naturalizing Power: Essays in Feminist Cultural Analysis.* New York: Routledge.

Young, James E. 1993. *The Texture of Memory: Holocaust Memorials and Meaning.* New Haven, CT: Yale University Press.

Yu, Henry. 2002. *Thinking Orientals: Migration, Contact, and Exoticism in Modern America.* New York: Oxford University Press.

Zhou, Min. 2004. "Revisiting Ethnic Entrepreneurship: Convergences, Controversies, and Conceptual Advancements." *International Migration Review* 38, no. 3: 1040–1074.

———. 2010. *Chinatown: The Socioeconomic Potential of an Urban Enclave.* Philadelphia: Temple University Press.

Zhou, Min, and Carl Bankston, III. 1998. *Growing Up Americans: How Vietnamese Children Adapt to Life in the United States.* New York: Russell Sage Foundation.

Zhu, Lei, Orhan Kara, Hung M. Chu, and Anthony Chu. 2015. "Female Entrepreneurship: Evidence from Vietnam." *Journal of Small Business and Entrepreneurship* 26, no. 3: 103.

Zinoman, Peter. 2001a. *The Colonial Bastille: A History of Imprisonment in Vietnam, 1862–1940.* Berkeley: University of California Press.

———. 2001b. "Reading Revolutionary Prison Memoirs." In Ho Tai, *The Country of Memory*, 21–45.

———. 2022. "A Republican Moment in the Study of Modern Vietnam." In *Building a Republican Nation in Vietnam, 1920–1963*, ed. Nu-Anh Tran and Tuong Vu. Honolulu: University of Hawaii Press.

Contributors

Duyen Bui is a lecturer at Hawaii Pacific University and a research fellow with the U.S.-Vietnam Research Center at the University of Oregon, Eugene. She received her Ph.D. in political science from the University of Hawaii, Mānoa. She engages in scholarship on global politics and how it intersects with social movements, contentious politics, and social justice, particularly in Southeast Asia. Her research examines the strategies and tactics of transnational activism in the Vietnamese diaspora to analyze how nonstate actors contest for political power against the state.

Christian Collet is Senior Associate Professor of Political Science at the International Christian University in Tokyo. His interests concentrate on American, Japanese, and comparative politics of the Asian Pacific with a substantive focus on public opinion and race, ethnicity, and transnationalism. He has held appointments at Vietnam National University and Doshisha University, Kyoto and lectured at the University of Tokyo. With Pei-te Lien, he coedited *The Transnational Politics of Asian Americans*, published by Temple University Press (2009).

Wynn Gadkar-Wilcox is Professor of History at Western Connecticut State University. He specializes in the intellectual history, literary history, and historiography of Vietnam from the eighteenth to the twentieth centuries and has secondary interests in cross-cultural relations, world history, religion, and philosophy. He is the author of *East Asia and the West* (with Xiaobing Li and Yi Sun) (2019) and *Allegories of the Vietnamese Past: Unification and the Production of a Modern Historical Identity* (2010), and editor of *Vietnam and the West: New Approaches* (2010).

Elwing Suong Gonzalez is a public school educator and history professor at Rio Hondo College. She received her Master's degree in History from California State University, Los Angeles and her doctorate in History from Claremont Graduate University, where she studied and wrote about Vietnamese refugee resettlement and community development in Los Angeles. She is also an artist and Los Angeles historian.

Tuan Hoang is Banche E. Seaver Professor of Humanities and Teacher Education, and Associate Professor of Great Books at Pepperdine University. His research has focused on South Vietnam and Vietnamese refugees in the United States, especially the history of Vietnamese anticommunism and the history of Vietnamese Catholics. Among his publications are "Ultramontanism, Nationalism, and the Fall of Saigon: Historicizing the Vietnamese American Catholic Experience," *American Catholic Studies* 130, no. 1 (2019); and "'Our Lady's Immaculate Heart Will Prevail': Vietnamese Marianism and Anticommunism, 1940–1975," *Journal of Vietnamese Studies* 17, nos. 2–3 (2022).

Jennifer A. Huynh is an Assistant Professor in the Department of American Studies at the University of Notre Dame. She received her doctorate in Sociology in 2016 from Princeton University and is working on a book manuscript focusing on the experiences of Vietnamese in Little Saigon, California. Her essays have appeared in the *Journal of Ethnic and Migration Studies* and *Ethnic and Racial Studies*.

Y Thien Nguyen received his Ph.D. in Sociology at Northwestern University and is currently the Teaching Fellow in South East Asian History at the University of Leeds. He previously served as the Resource Development Manager for the Vietnamese American nonprofit, Boat People S.O.S., Inc. Nguyen was born in Đà Nẵng, Việt Nam, and, as a child, immigrated with his family to the United States as refugees. He specializes on historical-comparative sociology, state formation, the Cold War, migration and collective memory. His research focuses on the political history of the Republic of Vietnam, the discursive development of Republican anticommunism, and the connectivity between Vietnamese America and Republic of Vietnam. His article "(Re)Making the South Vietnamese Past in America" is published in the *Journal of Asian American Studies*.

Nguyen Vu Hoang received his Ph.D. in Anthropology at the University of Toronto in 2017. His dissertation is focused on Vietnamese Americans and their relations with the homeland. He is currently a faculty member and vice-head of the Department of Anthropology at the University of Social Sciences and Humanities, Vietnam National University, Hanoi. Previously he was with the Institute of Cultural Studies and the Vietnam Museum of Ethnology. His chapter on urban issues and civil society in Vietnam appears in *State, Society and the Market in Contemporary Vietnam: Property, Power and Values* (Routledge, 2012).

Van Nguyen-Marshall is an Associate Professor of History at Trent University in Ontario, Canada. Her research area is modern Vietnamese history with a focus on civil society and civilian life in the Republic of Vietnam. Some of her publications include "Appeasing the Spirits along the 'Highway of Horror': Civic Life in Wartime South Vietnam," *War and Society* 35, no. 3 (2018): 206–222; "Student Activism in Time of War Youth in the Republic of Vietnam, 1960s–1970s," *Journal of Vietnamese Studies* 10, no. 2 (Spring 2015): 43–81; *In Search of Moral Authority: The Discourse on Poverty, Poor Relief, and Charity in French Colonial Vietnam* (2008).

Thien-Huong Ninh is Professor in the Sociology Department at Cosumnes River College. Her research and publications are in the areas of Religion, Race, and Gender; Immigrant Religion; Asian Religious Diasporas; and East Asian New Religious Movements. She is the author of *Race, Gender, and Religion in the Vietnamese Diaspora* (2017). One of her ongoing studies examines the global diffusion of the Vietnamese-looking Virgin Mary (Our Lady of Lavang).

Linda Ho Peché is Project Director for the Vietnamese in the Diaspora Digital Archive (ViDDA), a digital humanities project by the Vietnamese American Heritage Foundation. She is a cultural anthropologist by training, with experience in public folklore, oral history, popular religion, public history, and community outreach. Her current interests include the politics of representation in the digital humanities and working to promote engagement and collaboration between communities and academic institutions.

Hai-Dang Phan is author of the poetry collection *Reenactments* (Sarabande, 2019) and the translator of Phan Nhiên Hạo's selected volume of poems, *Paper Bells* (The Song Cave, 2020). Phan is the recipient of fellowships from the National Endowment for the Arts, Bread Loaf Writers Conference, and the American Literary Translators Association. He is Associate Professor of English at Grinnell College.

Ivan V. Small is Associate Professor of Anthropology in the Department of Comparative Cultural Studies at the University of Houston. He is author of *Currencies of Imagination: Channeling Money and Chasing Mobility in Vietnam* (2019), among others. Small has researched, published, and taught on a range of issues related to transnational migration, remittances, mobility, transportation, and emerging markets. He holds a Ph.D. in Sociocultural Anthropology and Southeast Asian Studies from Cornell University.

Quan Tue Tran is a lecturer and senior program coordinator in Ethnicity, Race, and Migration at Yale University. Her scholarship appears in the *Journal of Vietnamese Studies*; *Amerasia Journal*; the *Journal of Southeast Asian American Education and Advancement*. Her book manuscript, "Anchoring Vietnamese Boat People's Past," examines the politics of refugee memory, history, and identity in Vietnamese diaspora. Her poetry and translations appear in *Troubling Borders: An Anthology of Art and Literature by Southeast Asian Women in the Diaspora*; *Thế Kỷ 21*; and www.damau.org.

Alex-Thai Dinh Vo is a historian of modern Vietnam and East and Southeast Asia, specializing in Cold War politics and the Vietnam Wars. His works examine the social, cultural, political, and economic transformations in Vietnam, including issues such as the land reform, social-cultural control, reeducation, diaspora, and war legacies and memories. He leads the Vietnam War Oral History Project and is currently an Assistant Research Professor at the Vietnam Center & Archive, Texas Tech University. Formerly he served as a historian with the Defense POW/MIA Agency and a research scholar with the U.S.-Vietnam Research Center at the University of Oregon. He holds a Ph.D. in History from Cornell University.

Thuy Vo Dang is Assistant Professor of Information Studies at the University of California, Los Angeles. From 2003 to 2022, she served as Curator for the Southeast Asian Archive in the University of California, Irvine Libraries. She holds a Ph.D. in Ethnic Studies from the University of California, San Diego, and was the inaugural Project Director for Viet Stories: The Vietnamese American Oral History Project. She is the coauthor of two books: *A People's Guide to Orange County* (2022) and *Vietnamese in Orange County* (2015).

Tuong Vu is Professor and Department Head, Department of Political Science, University of Oregon, and Director of the U.S.-Vietnam Research Center. His research has focused on the comparative politics of state formation and revolutions in Southeast Asia and, more recently, on Vietnam's modern history and politics. He is the author or co-editor of many books, including (with Trinh Luu) *Republican Vietnam, 1963–1975: War, Society, Diaspora* (Hawaii 2023); (with Nu-Anh Tran) *Building a Republican Nation in Vietnam, 1920–1963* (Hawaii, 2022); (with Sean Fear) *The Republic of Vietnam, 1955–1975: Vietnamese Perspectives on Nation Building* (Cornell, 2019); and *Vietnam's Communist Revolution: The Power and Limits of Ideology* (Cambridge, 2017), among others.

Index